HISTORY OF
THE UNITED STATES
TO 1865

D1236401

HISTORY OF
THE UNITED STATES
TO 1865

James P. Shenton, *Ph.D.*

Associate Professor of History
Columbia University

A COLLEGE COURSE GUIDE

DOUBLEDAY & COMPANY, INC., GARDEN CITY, NEW YORK

To my mother

To my mother

Preface

"History," wrote Thomas Jefferson, "by apprising [men] of the past, will enable them to judge of the future." Though there are many reasons for studying history, perhaps as many as there are students of the subject, the idea that from scrutiny of the past we may better understand, predict, and shape the future has long been recognized as of prime importance.

What is history—an accumulation of chronological facts about a nation? It is that, of course. But "facts" alone do not tell the whole story. More important, more significant, and more interesting are the theories, the problems, the reasons *behind* the facts. History, then, answers not only *what?*, *where?*, *when?*, and *who?*, but also *why?*, and *how?*

This book is designed to explain American history to 1865 in all dimensions. Beginning with the discovery of the New World, it examines the complex influences that shaped our nation from the very outset. The names, dates, places, and battles are discussed in detail. And these "facts" are enriched for the reader, and made more meaningful to him, by thorough and thoughtful examination of such important matters as: the forming and changing of a "national temperament"; the effect of geography upon economics, and the effect of economics upon politics; the importance of the personalities and psychological makeups of the men who influenced our country's destiny; the effect upon America of various cultural and social traditions; the spiritual revolutions affecting man's relations with his fellow man, with his nation, and with his God; the results in America of occurrences in other nations; and the complexities, the ambivalences, the needs, and the ideals that brought a heterogeneous group of men together in 1776—and that drove them apart in 1861.

This text is broad and inclusive in its coverage so as to meet the varying needs of individuals in their study of American history. Intended to provide the fundamentals of a general introductory college course in American history, suitable both for study and for review, the text aims to be clear and understandable in plan and detail. A reader who wishes to use it for home study may well do so.

The book is divided into four parts: The Colonial Experience, The Revolutionary Experience, The Early Republic, and The Sectional Republic. A number of maps are included which graphically depict various significant changes in the geographical development of America, as well as important military campaigns of the American Revolution and the Civil War. The tables of information concerning the Presidents at the back of the book are designed for helpful and efficient use as a reference tool.

It has been the author's intention throughout to make his account of American history interesting and informative. It is his hope that this book will serve to acquaint the reader with the grandeur, vitality, validity, and significance of our country's past, and to inspire in him a desire to use his knowledge of that past in his efforts for the continuing progress of our country as it moves through the present into the future.

The author wishes to acknowledge indebtedness to Henry Ebel of Columbia University for his cheerful criticism and tart excisions; and to Donald J. Davidson, Lewy Olfson, and Lawrence W. Lamm of Copeland & Lamm, Inc., for their careful editorial work.

J. P. S.

Contents

PART TWO

The Revolutionary Experience

PART THREE

The Early Republic

PART FOUR

The Sectional Republic

List of Maps

List of Maps

HISTORY OF
THE UNITED STATES
TO 1865

Part One

THE COLONIAL EXPERIENCE

Chapter 1

Europe Discovers the New World

By accident, on October 12, 1492, Christopher Columbus discovered America. His purpose in undertaking his famous expedition was to prove that by sailing west one could reach India and the Far East, those fabled lands so excitingly described by overland travelers. Instead, his voyage brought him to the shores of a new world. We cannot know for certain whether Columbus ever suspected—either on this trip or on any of his three later journeys to the Caribbean (1493, 1498, and 1502–4)—that he had discovered two new continents, vast in extent and with untapped resources beyond his most extravagant dreams of riches.

Other men of Columbus' day had deduced that the world was probably round; some had even made fairly accurate estimates of its size. But Columbus and his contemporaries did not know that, centuries before, voyagers from the north of Europe had reached a new western continent. Therefore it was with no certain idea of what he would find beyond the uncharted waters of the Atlantic Ocean that Columbus set sail. But he was goaded on by a vision; and though he knew of the dangers and uncertainties that lay before him, he confronted them with courage—a unique courage that many considered foolish.

Courage was not new to Columbus. He had been courageous in his attempts to find a patron, courageous in his long experience with frustration. As early as 1484 his scheme for sailing west was rejected by the King of Portugal, who refused him aid. Hoping subsequently to interest the Spaniards, he found himself opposed by learned men, rich men, and powerful men, all of whom challenged his idea that the world was round. It was contrary to common sense and logic, they claimed; and graver still, it was contrary to the teachings of the Bible. But the Genoese sea captain would not, could not relinquish his dream. Eventually, his courage prevailed. Ferdinand and Isabella, rulers of Spain, were envious of Portugal's wealth. Freed at last from the struggle to conquer the Moors, a struggle which had been making extensive demands on the Royal Treasury, they agreed to finance the expedition. On August 3, 1492, Columbus sailed out of the harbor of Palos, Spain, in command of a small fleet—the *Nina,* the *Pinta,* and the *Santa Maria,* ships barely 75 feet long. The westward voyage was begun, and Columbus had become the first of the adventurous navigators whose explorations would, during the next four centuries, result in the permanent settlement of the Western Hemisphere.

THE AGE OF DISCOVERY

The Earliest Adventurers. Fragmentary evidence exists to prove that other Europeans had stumbled upon the New World long before Columbus. In the sixth and seventh centuries, Irish explorers reached Iceland and established permanent settlements on that rugged island. There exists no evidence that the Irish went farther west. It remained for the Scandinavians in the ninth century to follow the Irish to Iceland, forcing them to surrender the island. In the following century, the Scandinavians established outposts on the west coast of Greenland. In the year 1000, Leif Ericson sailed from Greenland to explore land which had been sighted farther west by Bjarni Herjulfson. The land he discovered was called Vineland, and was probably located somewhere between Cape Cod and Baffin Island. A decade or so later, a small settlement of Vikings was established in the area, only to be abandoned the following year as the result of the unfriendly behavior of neighboring Indians. After their departure from America, the Norsemen wove memories of that barbaric, unexplored land into their myths, legends, and sagas.

In Search of the Orient. By the thirteenth century, a lively and profitable trade had grown up between the Mediterranean Basin and the Far East. Italian traders, especially those from Genoa and Venice, established close ties with the Byzantine Empire, and imported from it fine silks and other luxury items. As western Europe increased its demands for Oriental goods, the energetic Italians, in the fortunate position of middlemen, pushed into southern Russia and northern Africa in search of new profits. In 1475 a remarkable Venetian, Marco Polo, accompanied by his father and uncle, traversed the seemingly endless expanses of Central Asia and reached the exotic court of the Chinese emperor, Kublai Khan. Polo's chronicle of his adventures, written while he was a Genoese prisoner, noted that the Chinese empire bordered upon a great eastern sea, a fact substantiated by other travelers to the Celestial Empire. This information encouraged the thought that the Orient could be reached from western Europe by an all-water route.

Portugal Leads the Way. Technological advances in seafaring ultimately enabled hardy explorers, especially those of Portugal, to test the hypothesis that there existed an ocean route from western Europe to the Orient. The invention of the compass, the astrolabe, and the cross-staff gave the ocean voyager a satisfactory means for determining his direction of travel and approximate location, while the appearance of reliable maps, covering at least the more familiar coastlines, provided additional safety in ocean travel. The advances in shipbuilding also culminated at this time in the Portuguese caravel, a swift, maneuverable ocean vessel that was able to sail all but the shallowest coastal waters. Portuguese experiments with the carrack, the usual Mediterranean merchant ship, led to the construction of the huge three-decker East India carracks.

On the remote promontory of Cape St. Vincent, at the southwestern corner of Portugal, Prince Henry the Navigator laid the plans that were to lead Europeans across the seas to the legendary riches of the Orient and the then-unimagined continents of the Western Hemisphere. This recluse prince sponsored a maritime school where the most advanced techniques of seamanship were taught. There the most skilled navigators of Europe gathered. Under his sponsorship, Portuguese seamen pushed south along the west African coast, charting more than six hundred miles of the Dark Continent's shoreline. When Henry died in 1460, Portugal had irretrievably committed herself both to the search for a sea route to India and to the conversion of the natives of Africa to Christianity. In 1487, Bartholomeu Dias rounded the Cape of Good Hope, putting the Portuguese almost on the threshold of India. Eleven years later Vasco da Gama sailed into Calicut, returning to Lisbon the following year with a cargo of spices, silks, and jewels. By smashing with their naval power the dominance of Moslem merchants in the Indian Ocean, the energetic Portuguese seized for Lisbon the distinction of being the leader of the Oriental trade. But for a kingdom of less than two million the task of keeping a monopoly of the trade proved impossible, and Ferdinand Magellan, though a Portuguese navigator, was to accomplish his circumnavigation of the globe (1521) in the service of a Spanish monarch. Portugal had blazed the way for others to follow, but ultimately she had only the tenuous papal grant of 1493 (the Convention of Tordesillas) on which to base her claim to the southern route to India and her title to Brazil.

The Emergence of Spain. As the glory of Portugal faded, Spain entered her golden age. During the sixteenth century, her power seemed beyond challenge. Aggressive *conquistadores* carried Spanish dominion as far west as California and as far south as Cape Horn. Hernando Cortes, in an astonishing campaign, led 550 men from Cuba who succeeded, by 1521, in conquering the vast wealth of the Aztec empire in Mexico. In 1535, Francisco Pizarro conquered the even wealthier Inca empire in Peru. The determined Spanish search for wealth resulted in the brutal enslavement and near-extermination of the Caribbean Indians. To meet the insatiable demands for labor with which to exploit the wealth of the New World, the Spaniards introduced into the Caribbean both Negro slaves and the system of *encomiendas,* a landholding arrangement which permitted the Spaniards to force millions of Indians into serfdom.

Complementing the Spanish search for wealth was their equally determined, if not always consistently pursued, effort to convert the Indian to Catholicism. With anguished eloquence the Spanish monk Bartolomé de las Casas protested the brutalization of the Indian. But the curious mixture of sword and salvation became the hallmark of the Spanish conquest. It propelled Juan Ponce de León to search for the fountain of youth (and so to discover Florida) in 1513; Vasco Núñez de Balboa to discover the Pacific Ocean in 1517; and Francisco Vásquez de Coronado to look for the Seven Cities of Cibola (1540) and in the process to explore the American Southwest. By 1541, Hernando de Soto, pursuing dreams of wealth, had discovered the Mississippi River. Spanish explorers ranged from the Carolinas to Patagonia during the sixteenth century. Stirred by the passions of greed and faith, Spanish *conquistadores* and missionaries succeeded in conquering an empire whose extent staggered the European imagination. Stirred by envy and torn between fear and ambition, the neighbors of Spain began to challenge her imperial might. This challenge was to occur against the background of a western Europe in flux, overthrowing its medieval heritage and creating the modern world.

THE CONTINENTAL BACKGROUND

The Renaissance. As the great Swiss historian Jakob Burckhardt observed, the Renaissance "first gave the highest development to individuality, and then led the individual to the most zealous and thorough study of himself in all forms and under all conditions." It was this search that led to the Renaissance concern with new techniques in the arts and sciences, and manifested the willingness of men to experiment with new modes of behavior and to question the value of old institutions. The result was an intellectual environment that allowed Europeans to see in the New World a place where original social and political experiments could be launched. As the spirit of the Renaissance flourished, it spread from Italy northward across Europe to the low-lying flatlands of the North Sea plain. There, in the flourishing commercial towns of the Lowlands, the new bourgeoisie became patrons of the arts. In these northern areas individual thinkers and artists tried to reflect the still-potent religious beliefs of the day, as well as the rapidly growing interest in commerce and industry.

Whatever dismay may have been provoked by ecclesiastical lapses from grace or by the princely displays of the Renaissance, intellectual activity flourished. Enraptured by the apparently endless possibilities of human creativity, the humanists called for the release of man from inhibitions upon his artistic powers. Though preoccupied with religious subjects, the Renaissance artist, thoroughly versed in human anatomy, depicted God and His saints not in the hieratic manner associated with Byzantine art but in human guise. It might be said, indeed, that the Renaissance re-created God in man's image. Traditional restraints on human endeavor crumbled; visions of limitless human achievement agitated the human imagination. The European re-examined his traditional beliefs at home and probed with insatiable curiosity the four corners of the globe. Change was in the air; it was destined to have a profound influence wherever the western European chose to settle.

The Reformation. The religious upheavals that shook Europe during the sixteenth and seventeenth centuries were both to affect vitally established European economic policy and to create a political turmoil that would radically change the European power balance. Yet, when the Reformation first began, its conscious intention was not to fragment the Church into numberless sects but to restore the universal church of Christ to its original purity. The reformers were rebelling, among other things, against the increasing preoccupation of the papal authority with secular matters. In Italy, the Church had often presented to outsiders the face of an institution committed to the flesh. A startled Luther viewed with dismay the lavish display of the papal court, its preoccupation with secular art, and its seeming disinterest in theology. The men who joined in the reforms initiated by Luther did so because religion seemed to them of overriding importance in the world order, and no personal sacrifice seemed too great if it helped to achieve the purification of Christian doctrine. The intensity of their belief soon added a new dimension to colonization of the New World—for many Christians, colonization offered an opportunity to escape the forces of Antichrist in Europe and to revitalize the Christian religion in the New World.

The Reformation was born in Luther's assertion that faith alone justified human salvation. When he added that priestly absolution in the sacrament of penance could not free a sinner from his sin, but that faith and inner grace alone could work salvation, the Papacy accepted this as a direct challenge to its own special mission. If Luther was right then the priesthood served no essential purpose in the relationship between man and God. Any doubt that this was in fact Luther's belief ended when he asserted that every believer had the right to interpret the Bible as his conscience dictated.

Luther unwittingly gave the signal for revolution when he declared the doctrine of the priesthood of the believers. In time, already caught in a struggle between the Hapsburg Holy Roman Emperors and the minor German princes, he would express horror when this leveling doctrine was used by the Anabaptists to justify a social revolution; but such usage was typical rather than perverse. In challenging papal authority Luther had sounded an alarm bell that heralded the increasing willingness of men to question and to oppose authority, whether such authority was ecclesiastical or political. But he also taught a doctrine of submissiveness to the state that profoundly affected English history. When Henry VIII forced a union of church and state, with the monarch as the supreme embodiment of that union, religious dissent became tantamount to treason. In England, particularly, dissent nurtured the seeds of revolution.

It remained for Calvin, in his severely logical *Institutes of the Christian Religion,* to provide a theology that transcended the secular state. Emphasizing the doctrine of predestination, which was founded in the omnipotence and omniscience of God, Calvin viewed the world as irrevocably divided between the elect and the damned. It was the duty of the "elect" to demonstrate their election by living a saintly life, no matter what the temptation. Though few in number, this group had the sublime knowledge that it was a divine aristocracy, permitted by a just God to know and manifest its chosen condition. Calvinism attracted the confident—some thought arrogant—spirits, who resolutely and aggressively demanded recognition of their holy state.

Such persons were not apt to give homage to monarchs or bishops, all of whom they believed damned. Far from accepting the subordination of the church to the state, Calvinists insisted it was the responsibility of the elect to create a state in which man's duty to God would have precedence. Religion was to them of overriding importance. As the visible elect, they rejected the idea of a church governed by bishops; instead, they insisted that the governance of the churches should be in the hands of presbyteries, courts of elected ministers, and devout elders. Though far from democratic—they rejected the idea that the damned should help order the human condition—they nevertheless raised a formidable challenge to the omnipotence of the state. Under the Calvinist scheme the wielders of secular power were answerable for their moral conduct. Within the presbyteries the elect, at least, received a formidable training in self-government. But the Calvinist doctrine of the "calling," which made labor a religious act, propelled the Calvinists into aggressive economic activity. They justified this activity by quoting from the Bible: "Seest thou a man diligent in his *business*? He shall stand before kings." In the burgeoning mercantilist economies of western Europe the Calvinist flourished, convinced that by the success of his economic pursuits he proved his election. Where Luther had preached against the sinfulness of usury, the Calvinist saw in profit the mark of divine favor. A New World colony founded by Calvinists would almost invariably display a marked inclination toward capitalist endeavor.

The Protestants, Lutheran and Calvinist, accomplished a revolution. They undermined established secular authority and bequeathed to the world the idea that the human conscience could never surrender its autonomy.

The Nation-State. Perhaps no single development of the fifteenth and sixteenth centuries had a greater effect on the course of western European history than the emergence of nation-states. The institution of monarchy was the means used to cement the newfound political unity of France, England, and Spain. Under the feudal system, the kings were circumscribed by the bulk of common law upon which the feudal nobility based their inherited rights. A realignment of class interests was required if the king were to gain dominance. By tradition, the king held the rank of first noble—whether he was first among equals or superior in rank was a moot point. In theory, his interests were those of the nobility; in fact, the nobility comprised his chief antagonists. Where the king wished to be supreme, the nobility were intent on subordinating him to themselves. From this struggle emerged the new monarchs.

Intent upon gaining absolute power, the king became aware of a mercantile class with a vested interest in the creation of a stable social order which would insure the safety of its property. Resentful of interference in their affairs by demanding marauding lords, sickened by the petty feuding of the nobility (in which feuds they often became innocent victims), the merchants entered into a natural alliance with the king. For security they were prepared to support the royal struggle for power. By paying taxes into the royal exchequer they empowered the king to raise armies with which to suppress his noble rivals. Suppression alone, however, was but a prelude to the second struggle—the destruction of the mass of feudal law. Although implicit in the rise of the new monarchs, the royal desire to establish its absolute control could only be fully achieved by the construction of a governing apparatus with effective central powers. From the diversity of feudalism the king sought to consolidate a nation obedient to his will.

It was these new monarchies that carried out the initial European exploitation of the New World. The mercantilist idea of national development through royal and mercantile cooperation expanded quickly to include utilization of the New World. But the merchant-adventurer soon realized that this cooperation often involved great risk on his own part without a commensurate gamble by the king. If the merchant had been powerless to defend himself against the nobility, he was hardly better able to do so against the consolidated royal power. In time, the cooperation of mercantile interests and royal aspirants would be revealed for what it was, a marriage of convenience; and like such marriages, it would prove to be open to sudden partings.

Mercantilism. Perhaps the most compelling motive leading to continued migration to the New World has been the desire for economic security and gain on the part of settler and sponsor alike. This desire manifested itself in the origins of the earliest settlements, when the colonizing power saw in empire an opportunity to secure a self-sufficient economy that would have as its natural corollary the strengthening of the nation-state. To achieve these goals it was believed necessary to gain a favorable balance of trade, one in which a nation's exports exceeded in value its imports, and compelled other nations to pay the balance in the world's limited bullion. The possession of a monopoly in an item of commerce took on enormous significance, since it seemed to guarantee maximum profit. The additional assumption that the amount of wealth in the world was limited gave a fillip to the race for control of the world's resources. Success meant the difference between national survival and failure. This system became known as *mercantilism*.

As the new nation-state struggled to survive, it came to view its economy as an instrument of state policy. In the sixteenth century, efforts were increasingly made to uproot the old medieval guilds, since it was felt that their local orientation endangered the centralizing policies of the new monarchs. Government assumed a positive role in subsidizing new industry and in protecting old industries from foreign competition. Systems of national tariffs were developed and superimposed on the old medieval system of provincial and municipal tariffs. Though mercantilists in nations throughout Europe would have preferred to abolish these internal tariffs, only the English were successful. Mercantilism actively fostered alliances between government and the private entrepreneur. These found expression in the formation of great companies which attracted private capital to the support of governmental enterprises. Normally, the charters of these companies granted them monopoly privileges in the conduct of trade with a particular part of the world. The private participants believed they were assured of substantial profits, while the state hoped for an expanded treasury from the influx of gold and silver. A combination of public and private initiative lay at the foundation of empire building from the sixteenth to the late eighteenth century.

THE STRUGGLE FOR EMPIRE

The Spaniards. No nation, as previously shown, was more successful as a colonizer in the sixteenth century than Spain. But its success was ephemeral, for within the polity of Spain there existed fundamental weaknesses. These deficiencies would deny Spain the strength needed in the long struggle for empire. The Spanish kingdom was actually a union of Castile and Aragon resulting from the marriage, in 1469, of Ferdinand of Aragon and Isabella of Castile. Spain, as a result, lacked the cohesiveness of common national institutions. The two sections had only the shared experience of centuries of Moorish occupation, and of the unceasing hostility of the Roman Catholic Church to the Moors, to

ENGLISH, SPANISH, AND FRENCH TERRITORIAL
CLAIMS IN NORTH AMERICA IN 1664

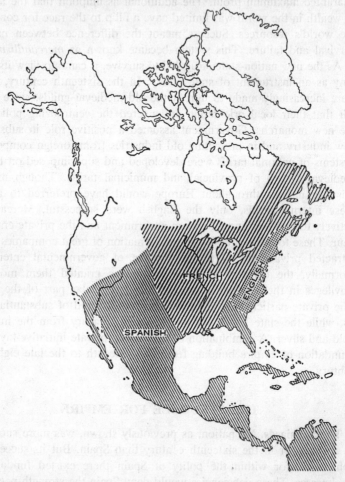

unite them. To maintain the faith intact during the period of Moorish occupation, the Church evolved a church court, the Inquisition, which eventually extended its authority into all corners of the kingdom. The final conquest of the Moors in 1492 at Granada completed the outline of Spain; it did not provide the unifying cement. Unlike their European counterparts, who used the merchant classes in their struggles, the Spanish monarchs seized upon Catholicism as their weapon for uniting Spain. The Sephardic Jews, long resident in Spain, were expelled in 1492 in an attempt to make the faith even more secure. The centuries-old struggle to keep the faith against the allures of the Moor now became a struggle against the Marranos (Jews who had converted to Catholicism) and the Moriscos (Moors who had likewise converted). Spain's national identity was forged with the steel of intolerance: to be Spanish was to be Catholic, and the Spanish king was "His Most Catholic Majesty." Unfortunately for the future of Spain, the refusal to foster the aspirations of an expanding middle class deprived the Spanish monarchy of the ambition and energy that might have enabled it to win the sixteenth-century struggle for empire.

Ruled by a central government with all-pervasive powers, Spain operated under a rigidly defined class and caste system. The authority of the Spanish king was absolute. Royal authority in the colonies was enforced through the Council of the Indies, which was permitted to make laws without consulting the Spanish or native inhabitants, to appoint all governing officials, to serve as a final court of justice, and to regulate colonial economic life. A branch of the council called the Casa de Contratación rigidly supervised Spanish trade as a royal monopoly, denying access to American ports to all but those Spanish merchants authorized by the Casa. No effort was made to conceal the purpose of the royal trade monopoly—it was to insure the Crown an abundance of precious bullion. This Spanish preoccupation with bullionism resulted in her failure to develop home industry; rather, she looked to northern Europe to supply her with her manufactured needs. It is now evident that Spain, in serving to funnel a vast quantity of new wealth into western Europe, stimulated an infant capitalism that later helped to undermine Spanish hegemony in the New World.

Paralleling monarchical centralism were the activities of the Inquisition. With fierce energy the Inquisitor stamped out heresy wherever found. To keep Spanish Catholicism pure, a rigid and arid censorship repressed the intellectual life of both the Iberian and colonial Spaniard. No nook or cranny of Spanish life escaped the authority of the Crown and the Church. Before the end of the sixteenth century, Philip II had brought priestly asceticism to the monarchy. From the bleak monastery of San Lorenzo de Escorial, Philip launched the Spanish Armada on its mission to subdue the arch-heretic, Elizabeth of England. With the defeat of the Armada in 1588, the power of Spain gradually but steadily declined; and the steady accession of England to world dominance began.

The Beginnings of New France. Britain was not alone in her challenge to Spain. France, struggling to resolve the civil wars that divided her, had neglected empire building before the seventeenth century. Between 1461 and 1483 Louis XI built up a royal army with which he ruthlessly suppressed brigands and recalcitrant nobles. Able to rule, as a result, without the Estates-General, he energetically suppressed feudal rights, forced towns to relinquish their ancient charters, and compelled the nobles to accept his pre-eminence. Francis I of France, who succeeded to the throne in 1515, agreed to divide control of the Gallican Church with the Papacy. In return for a secure income from the French hierarchy, Pope Leo X surrendered appointment of the hierarchy to the French King. A series of struggles between the monarchs, the noblemen, and the Catholic hierarchy ensued.

The accession of Henry IV to the French throne in 1589, and the issuance in 1598 of the Edict of Nantes, which assured the Huguenots religious toleration and political safety, eased religious conflicts. As civil controversy declined, Henry IV set out to revitalize French claims to the New World north of the fortieth parallel. The explorations of Verrazano (an Italian sailing for France in 1524), de Gonneville, and the three voyages of Jacques Cartier (1534, 1536, 1541) provided the basis for a royal grant in 1603 to Pierre du Guast, comte de Monts, a Huguenot nobleman, of that part of the North American continent between the latitudes 40° and 46°. This generous grant of land in an area claimed by England became the source of the more than a century-and-a-half struggle between the English and the French for control of the North American continent.

Almost from the start the French occupied themselves with exploiting the fur trade. Beginning in 1609, under the guidance of Samuel de Champlain, a complex system of alliances between the French king and the Algonquin-Huron Indians was constructed. However, Champlain earned for France the undying enmity of the Iroquois Confederation by helping to drive them from the St. Lawrence Valley. The Iroquois, allying themselves first with the Dutch traders in northern New York and later with the English, presented an impenetrable barrier to French expansion southward. Champlain had also explored (or sent other Frenchmen to explore) much of the upper Mississippi Valley. At Quebec, Champlain and de Monts established a colony which conducted the fur trade. French settlers, known as *habitants,* farmed the banks of the

St. Lawrence River for large landholders who developed a near-feudal system.

As with the Spaniards, French Catholic missionaries, especially Jesuits, actively propagated their faith among the Indian tribes and aided in the exploration of New France. In 1673, Père Jacques Marquette, a Jesuit, and his companion, Louis Joliet, explored the upper Mississippi River.

Extension of royal supervision became the characteristic policy of the French after Louis XIV assumed personal direction of French affairs in 1661. Canada was ruled by an *intendant* directly responsible to the king, and vested with the full power of his royal master. Jean Talon, the first *intendant*, made swift use of his authority by attacking and defeating the Iroquois in 1666. Employing accepted mercantilist principles, Talon reorganized the fur trade with the intention of maximizing profits for France. A successor, Louis, Count de Frontenac, using the talents of the brilliant Robert Cavelier, sieur de La Salle, erected a series of forts as far west as the Illinois River. In 1684 La Salle himself launched an attack upon Spanish holdings at the mouth of the Mississippi River, but this effort failed when La Salle was murdered by members of his expedition.

When, in 1689, Louis XIV questioned the legitimacy of William of Orange's accession to the English throne, the first of four wars between France and England erupted. Known in America as King William's War, it was but a minor skirmish in the larger struggle of Louis XIV to establish French dominance over western Europe. Unable to best the combined fleets of England and the Netherlands, France finally accepted the Peace of Ryswick (1697), which left unresolved the issues that had provoked the war. In the New World, English efforts to conquer Quebec failed.

The tendency toward an increasing concentration of power within the French monarchy, amply evident after the accession of Louis XIV to the throne, fostered a crucial weakness. What the king willed was done; what he ignored was left undone. An all-pervasive power, extended into the New World, eventually proved stultifying.

The Dutch. The Spanish Hapsburgs had inherited the Netherlands through a wisely arranged marriage. But the antagonisms between the Netherlands and Spain intensified as religious controversy accentuated the obvious differences between the two countries. The bleak Calvinism of Holland, supplemented by its love of personal liberty, proved a vigorous match for the severities of the Spanish Inquisition and the feared Spanish infantry. The repulse of the Armada intensified the Dutch revolts which terminated, in 1648, in the establishment of Dutch independence. The Dutch Republic, ruled by a States-General and a hereditary *staathalter,* the eldest male of the House of Orange, then launched a vigorous campaign to create an empire of its own.

The Dutch East India Company was organized as early as 1602 to guide Dutch expansion abroad, and within a short time it had practically expelled the Portuguese from the East Indies and gained a near-monopoly in the distribution of spices in Europe. In 1621 the West India Company was formed to supervise Dutch exploitation of New World wealth. In 1609 Henry Hudson, searching for the Northwest Passage, established the Dutch claim to the majestic harbor and river valley that would become New York, but it was not until 1624 that the West India Company exploited this claim with the establishment of New Amsterdam at this vital point as a trading post. The energetic Company traders, who had already built a merchant fleet of more than 10,000 ships, gave to the Dutch settlement here and northward in the Hudson Valley one of its essential characteristics—the pursuit of profit. Equally important, the extension of toleration in 1632 to the Arminians, a radical Protestant sect, inaugurated the policy of religious tolerance that soon made New Amsterdam a polyglot port.

The Dutch temporarily extended their influence in 1655, when they expelled the Swedes from a colony they had established in 1639, under the Swedish flag, in the lower Delaware Valley. But the Dutch had failed in several respects, and what had at first seemed a flourishing colony was actually entering a sustained decline. A lack of political rights for colonists had highlighted the autocratic regime of the West India Company from the beginning. Though Peter Stuyvesant is probably best remembered as a colorful, peg-legged governor, he was—as were his predecessors—a petty tyrant. In addition, the Dutch, fearful of the growing power of the English settlements north and south of their holdings, encouraged settlement in the New Amsterdam area by offering vast grants of land to anyone who brought fifty families to the New Netherlands at his own expense. These patroons exercised (even into the nineteenth century) a near-feudal power over their tenants. When the West India Company went bankrupt in its unsuccessful attempt to invade Brazil, the Dutch North American colonies fell easily to the aggressively expanding English and their New England colonies.

The English. Each of the colonizing powers in the New World, whether Portugal, Spain, France, or the Netherlands, soon had to contend with England's ambitions. England, which first challenged rival claims in the New World and eventually seized nearly the whole of the North American continent, owed its ability to do so to its peculiar institutional development, specifically the establishment of a government in which the doctrine of parliamentary supremacy was accepted. Although English colonizers shared the same aims in colonization as did the other empire builders, they possessed a flexibility in meeting novel experiences that made it possible for them to adjust more readily to the experience of the frontier. But ultimate English success did not prevent other European colonizers from leaving their strong imprints upon the vast region which was to become the United States.

In England, the same social forces were at work as in the other emergent nations of Europe. The War of the Roses decimated the nobility as they divided and fought for the conflicting claims of Lancaster and York. When the war finally ended in 1485, Henry VII, who resolved the conflicting claims of both factions in his birth and marriage, secured national control by denying to the surviving nobles, or to newly created nobles, the right to maintain private armies. The Star Chamber dispensed ruthless justice under the king's authority. Henry was both calculating and cautious, seeking to preserve his country from further war and to secure his hold upon the throne. His legendary miserliness also added to the throne the strength of independent means.

When Henry VIII succeeded his father in 1509, he inherited a stable throne. Tearing a leaf from his father's book—Henry VII had married Elizabeth of York to terminate the hostilities that had riven England—Henry VIII married his brother Arthur's widow, Catherine of Aragon, daughter of Ferdinand and Isabella, for which marriage he had received a papal dispensation. The king candidly admitted that his queen was a link in his proposed chain "to bridle French ambition." It was a marriage which had explosive consequences. Henry was determined to have a son, and when, after eighteen years of marriage, it appeared that Catherine would have no more children (she had given birth to only one child who survived infancy—Mary), the king determined to divorce her, claiming that the original papal dispensation had been invalid. Although Henry had earned from the Pope the title "Defender of the Faith," he could not earn the necessary papal decision to annul his marriage to Catherine. (The Pope could scarcely offend Catherine, whose nephew was the Holy Roman Emperor, Charles V.) Instead of acquiescing, Henry severed his relations with Rome and created the curious English brand of Protestantism, the Anglican Church—which some have described as the Roman Church without a Pope. With himself at the head of the new church, Henry divorced Catherine and married Anne Boleyn. Within three years, however, having given birth only to a princess—Elizabeth—Anne was arrested on trumped-up charges and sent to the headsman's block, leaving the path clear for another royal marriage. Henry VIII married, in all, six wives, and added a lusty patina to kingship.

Both of the Henrys Tudor worked through Parliament in the belief that the royal will, combined with that of the chosen spokesmen of the people, secured for the monarchy an unchallengeable position. The Act of Supremacy, passed in 1534, gave the king supreme ecclesiastical power, and obliged all his subjects to swear an oath accepting the supremacy of the king and rejecting that of the Pope. Henry, eager to replenish the royal coffers, then seized the vast monastic lands of England for use as rewards to the faithful retainers of the monarchy. When he died in 1547, he bequeathed to his young son Edward VI a monarchy greatly expanded in its power. During the six years of the boy king's reign Protestant influence was extended in the developing Anglican Church. Though Henry VIII had not intended to reform the Church, he established a critical precedent the moment he usurped papal power: if papal power were in error, then it was reasonable to assume that other religious practices were also open to question. Whatever his original intention may have been, his divorce opened thirteen decades of civil strife.

Mary Tudor, a true daughter of Catherine of Aragon—bitter, implacable, and possessed by the Spanish obsession to defend the true faith—worked to restore Catholicism to England when she succeeded Edward VI to the throne. Her marriage to her distant cousin, Philip II of Spain, sharpened the classic English suspicion of Iberian intentions, especially insofar as it gave her Spanish husband the title of King of England. She gained her infamous nickname of "Bloody Mary" by mass executions of suspected heretics. Historians have noted that scarcely three hundred persons perished in this fashion; but unfortunately for Mary's reputation, the English viewed these events with undisguised horror. Unwittingly, Mary had embedded a deep-rooted suspicion of Roman Catholicism in English Protestantism, one that time and distance did not quell.

The coronation of Elizabeth I completed the succession of the "Tudor bastards" to the throne—Henry VIII had pronounced both his daughters, Mary and Elizabeth, illegitimate. Harassed by the perpetual danger inherent in being a Tudor heir, Elizabeth had developed in her journey to the throne a character that was most remarkable in its capacity for dissembling. She had learned to hold her tongue, to bide her time, and to avoid trouble, sensibly assuming that trouble left alone is trouble that disappears. In another sense, Elizabeth chose simply to muddle through. Under her the Anglican Church drifted in a Lutheran direction, though it is just as likely that she would have permitted Anglicanism to drift back toward Rome had English opinion so wished.

Between Elizabeth and her subjects there existed a rapport that grew ever greater with time. "I have placed my chiefest strength and safeguard in the loyal hearts and good will of my subjects," she asserted. Deeply concerned with the problem of conserving the royal finances, she nevertheless subsidized the eventually profitable depredations of Francis Drake and John Hawkins upon the Spanish treasure fleets. Grudgingly, she parted with the subsidies used to finance the Protestant armies on the Continent who were opposing the Spanish Hapsburgs and the House of Valois. She pursued with great diligence the policy of binding the interest of Parliament to that of the Crown, though by the end of her reign a well-defined Puritan opposition had developed. Yet even this opposition was still loyal to its queen; they might be "doctrinaire and fanatical," she *"politique,"* but between them there existed a mutual loyalty that excluded any thought of divorce. In Elizabeth the Tudor dynasty was fused with an emergent English nationalism, and during her lifetime the inherent conflict between monarch and Parliament remained subdued. But with her death the Tudor dynasty came to an end.

James I, previously James VI of Scotland, son of the tragic Mary Stuart, Queen of Scots, came as a foreigner to the English throne. Where Elizabeth had carefully avoided the shoals of parliamentary dispute, James inaugurated a ferocious rivalry between monarch and Commons. Though diffused in its original form, the struggle increasingly focussed on those aspects of taxation which were under direct royal control. Projects for the union of England and Scotland readily stirred national feelings, no matter how strongly the king desired the union; but the growing suspicion among Puritans that the Stuarts contemplated a return to Rome aroused them to increasingly vigorous parliamentary opposition. When Charles I actively aided Archbishop William Laud in his efforts to impose high Anglican doctrine, the Puritans were compelled to resort to drastic remedies—migration and revolution. Between the conservative and radical Protestants the gulf widened. In spite of the Elizabethan example of conservative moderation in matters of religion, the Stuarts attempted to actively stem the tide of Protestant revisionism, and failed because they did not assess accurately the force of Puritan resentment.

The Stuarts also inherited the aggressive Tudor policy of securing wealth for England. The Tudor willingness to rest content with lunges at the Spanish treasure fleets, a tacit recognition of the formidable power of the Spanish, dissolved after the repulse of the Armada. Though Spanish power still commanded respect, it had lost its reputation for invincibility. The English thought increasingly of establishing colonies on the eastern shores of the North American continent. Sir Humphrey Gilbert flirted with the idea of setting up North American plantations as early as the 1570s. A Bristol clergyman, Richard Hakluyt, set forth the case for English colonization in his classic *A Particular Discourse concerning Western Discoveries,* a manuscript copy of which reached Queen Elizabeth. In 1585, Sir Walter Raleigh, under a patent from the queen, established two colonies on Roanoke Island. One group of colonists returned to England within a year; when ships returned to the colony in 1590 its remaining members had disappeared, their fate uncertain to this day. But the interest in colonization had been firmly established; the question was no longer whether, but when, the English would finally begin full efforts at settlement of the New World. The decision of James I to end the war with Spain shortly after his accession in 1603 permitted the full energy of the British nation to turn to colonization. In 1607, English colonial settlement began in earnest.

Chapter 2

The Colonial Settlement

The desire for profit motivated the founding of the first successful English colony. Two companies were organized in 1606 to establish colonies in Virginia. The London Company received a patent to settle a colony in southern Virginia; the Plymouth Company was designated to colonize northern Virginia; the Crown asserted its interest in the colonial settlement through the supervisory agency of a thirteen-man council. The first permanent colony was established in 1607 when a small group of colonists was settled at Jamestown, Virginia. Almost immediately, two major obstacles to progress emerged: the Virginia Company, operating on a joint-stock plan, insisted upon quick profits; and the English government sent to the colony as settlers primarily those who were either the dregs of London life or the younger sons of the gentry, left by primogeniture to earn their own fortunes. Neither group adjusted readily to the grueling work required in the new environment. Afflicted with food shortages, disease, and the depredations of hostile Indians, the Virginia colony barely survived its first years; only the arrival of six hundred additional settlers from England in 1609 prevented its immediate failure. By June 1610 the desperate colonists had for the second time decided to abandon Jamestown; once more, however, the fortuitous arrival of new settlers and supplies, under Lord De La Warr, saved Jamestown. At last, with a vigorous reorganization, resettlement on healthier sites, and the inauguration of stern disciplinary measures toward nonworkers, the colony began to improve. It was the introduction of tobacco culture in 1615, however, that finally supplied the settlers with a product that brought substantial (if erratic) profits and eventual prosperity.

PRINCIPAL EARLY SETTLEMENTS ALONG THE ATLANTIC COAST

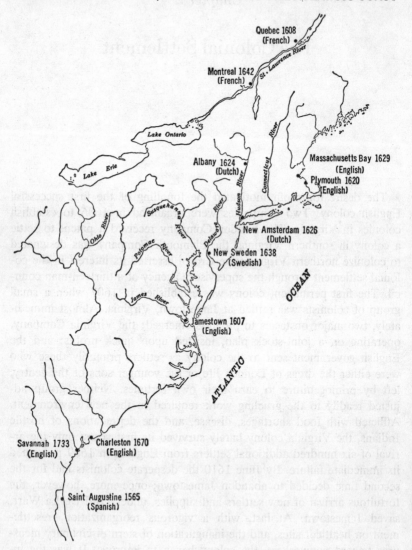

THE SOUTHERN COLONIES

Almost from their establishment, the Southern Colonies were occupied with the growth of staple crops that had a large export market. The resulting profits of agriculture gave to British settlement a stability unique in the New World. Unlike the Spaniards, who found a large native population that could be forced into serfdom, the English had to rely on the efforts of English immigrants from the outset. The result was the extension into the New World of a social order similar to that found in England. The passing of time was to change and modify it, but it would never wholly eliminate traces of its English origin. By as late as 1776, however, the distinct and separate traditions, institutions, and personalities that we now regard as southern had not yet emerged. The Southern Colonies in the seventeenth and eighteenth centuries revealed a heterogeneous character that makes generalizations hazardous. There were five separate and surprisingly diversified colonies, each of which had its own unique flavor. Though they all maintained the Anglican Church as the established church, their commitment to it was more nominal than real. The existence of Negro slavery in each colony resulted in a wide divergence of opinion. South Carolina and Georgia, both of which reaped wide profits from their rice and indigo crops, stubbornly defended the institution, but Virginia and Maryland, confronted with declining tobacco profits, increasingly viewed slavery as a profitless burden. By the mid-eighteenth century, Virginia contemplated termination of the institution if its slaves could be expatriated. The substance of political unity was present in the common English inheritance; later, and to a limited extent, Virginia would provide the tone that has come to be known as distinctly southern.

Virginia. The Old Dominion, as already noted, was the site of the first successful English settlement. Drawing her existence from a charter grant by the king, Virginia was an amalgam of government subsidy and private enterprise. Two disastrous years had convinced the company's leaders that profit existed not in hidden gold but in the cultivation of the soil. In 1609, a royal councilor and a director of the original company, Sir Edwin Sandys, received a new charter which extended the Virginia Company's boundaries to include the Chesapeake area and which tightened the company's control over the colony's government. Within a short time, Sir Thomas Smith, the company's manager, had launched a campaign "to plant an English nation" in the New World.

By 1611 it was clear that the Jamestown settlement would survive, and in the following year the charter was revised for the final time. Bermuda was placed under the company's jurisdiction, and the Royal Council in Virginia under its full control. Until 1624, the company effectively controlled Virginia. The collective approach which had characterized the original agriculture of the colony and which had deprived colonists of the incentive needed to make Virginia prosper was abandoned in 1613 when Sir Thomas Dale, the colonial governor, rented three acres of land to each colonist. All income above and beyond the rent, which was paid in produce, remained in the hands of the individual farmers.

In 1618 the company offered fifty acres in Virginia to anyone buying one of its shares. The offer served to lure land-hungry Europeans to the New World. The development of an extensive land-holding population in the colony had an unforeseen consequence: the immigrants vigorously protested the harsh policies of the company representatives. To pacify them, Sandys, in 1618, extended a Charter of Grants and Liberties which made government contingent upon the popular will. Sir George Yeardley, the new governor, implemented this decision by calling for a democratically elected House of Burgesses. When this legislature met in Jamestown in July 1619, its twenty-two members inaugurated self-government in the colonies. The further introduction, in 1621, of the proviso that no company directive would be carried out without the prior approval of the Burgesses, extended the principle of self-government. A lively awareness of individual rights was being fostered in Virginia. It would no longer be a simple matter for any individual, no matter how great, to substitute his individual decisions for the collective will.

As Virginia obtained a substantial measure of self-government, the Virginia Company began to disintegrate. The failure to secure a permanent monopoly contract for the import of tobacco into England proved fatal to it. As tobacco became more profitable, the king and his officials chose to exact an increasingly large share of the profits from it for the royal treasury. Mercantilist policy dominated the planting of the new crop. A heavy import tax was imposed on tobacco in England at the same time that the Virginians were forbidden to export it to any other country. Finally, when an outbreak of Indian warfare in 1622 caused the deaths of many colonists and the destruction of much property, the Crown became convinced of administrative mismanagement, and, overriding Parliamentary objections, dissolved the company. Thus, in 1624, Virginia became the first royal colony.

The colony that emerged had not only a rudimentary legislature but also an established church—the Anglican Church. Though in theory funds from tax moneys were set aside to support the Anglican establishment, the clergy had to struggle almost constantly to obtain payment. Often they had to settle for token remuneration. Nor was religious conformity maintained in the colony. Substantial evidence exists that the Anglican Church in Virginia soon deteriorated into a social center where more gossip than prayer was offered. More important, Virginia developed a tradition of unofficial tolerance within which liberal religious views flourished.

Maryland. Unlike Virginia, Maryland was founded, at least in theory, to provide a place where English Catholics could obtain toleration. Created from a grant of 10,000,000 acres made by Charles I to George Calvert, first Lord Baltimore, Maryland was the near-feudal domain of its proprietors. But they were obliged to consult with their freemen about legislation and to follow customary English common-law practice.

From the very start, the Calverts, a noble Catholic family, had no illusion about their ability to populate the colony with Catholics alone. They therefore invited Protestants to join them in settlement. In 1649, the Assembly passed an Act of Toleration, granting religious freedom to all sects that accepted the Trinity. But toleration was abruptly ended in 1654 when the Puritan Party gained control of the Assembly, and revoked the Act of Toleration. Though the Calverts had pretensions to absolute power, their assembly of freemen strenuously opposed them and insisted that it alone had the right to introduce laws. After a brief loss of proprietary prerogatives, Baltimore made a direct personal appeal to Cromwell in 1657 and regained control, and in 1658 restored the original Toleration Act.

An irritating factor which did much to upset Maryland's tranquillity was the recurring controversy between the proprietor and the colony's inhabitants over quitrents, the small annual payments made to him as evidence of his proprietary rights. Few settlers felt they owed payment to anyone. In the eighteenth century this issue frequently exacerbated affairs, not only in Maryland, but in the colonies of New York, New Jersey, and North Carolina.

The Carolinas and Georgia. The decision of 1624 to make Virginia a royal colony meant that its ungranted lands were now the king's, to do with as he saw fit. Charles I attempted unsuccessfully to stimulate settlement of the Carolinas. Settlement in the area of Albemarle Sound by discontented Virginians started around 1663, when Charles II granted to a number of West Indian sugar planters and members of his official entourage a charter for the region between latitude 31° and 36° "to stretch as far as the south seas"—a generous grant indeed. This charter, like that of Maryland, also enjoined the proprietors to enact laws only with the approval of the freemen or their delegates, and to take care that colonial law conformed to English precedent. Once again the seeds of self-government were sown by royal intervention.

At first, government was guided by the liberal "Declaration and Proposals to All that will Plant in Carolina" which vested considerable power in an elected assembly. But political confusion quickly dominated the Carolina settlement, since the eight proprietors, who operated through a proprietary board which met irregularly, often had no idea of what they wished to achieve with their colony. The result was a government that demoralized the governed.

In 1669, John Locke, at the behest of Lord Ashley, one of the proprietors, composed the Fundamental Constitutions of Carolina, a document that proposed the establishment of a near-feudal government. It explicitly stated that its purpose was to "avoid erecting a numerous Democracy." Though some of the provisions of the 120 paragraphs were effectuated—such as the provision for the Palatine Court, with its odd confusion of landgraves, caciques, and popular representatives—the cumbersome document was never fully implemented. Despite four revisions, and after thirty years of partial use, the document was finally abandoned.

The rapid growth of population in the region of Albemarle Sound persuaded the proprietors in 1691 to divide the territory into two parts, North and South Carolina.

Perpetual tumult, a lively indifference to authority, and an isolated condition of life made North Carolina one of the most rambunctious of the colonies. As early as 1677–78 an armed uprising, Culpeper's Rebellion, rocked the colony as the proprietary and antiproprietary factions struggled for power in North Carolina. The laxity of authority served to attract to the colony discontented Virginians who saw there an opportunity for making their own freedom.

South Carolina proved an entirely different experiment. Its proprietors worked to guarantee orderly settlement and development of the colony's resources. Its magnificent harbor at Charleston, close to the West Indian possessions of Great Britain, and the adaptability of the colony's soil to the growing of rice and indigo, seemed to promise considerable profit.

Where North Carolina had ignored Locke's constitution, South Carolina's proprietors attempted to establish it in fact as well as in theory. Conflict erupted between the elected "Parliament" and the proprietary governor. Only after an unfortunate experiment in arbitrary decision by the governor did the proprietors agree to restore an independent assembly.

Despite political conflict, South Carolina flourished. The proprietors invested more than £10,000 by 1675 and, though discontented with their returns, they persisted. Soon a flourishing rice and indigo agriculture, using first Indian and then Negro slavery, brought sizable profits. By 1708, the city of Charleston was a cosmopolitan port of more than 3,000 inhabitants. The influx of French Huguenots after the revocation of the Edict of Nantes gave to the colony a heterogeneous character and an energetic commercial class. Strongly influenced by West Indian plantation precedents, which were based on a staple (and therefore profit-making) rather than a subsistence agriculture, South Carolina introduced a harsh slave code and extensive plantations, and elements that were later to become associated with the South were already in evidence in South Carolina: slave gangs, plantations, and an expanding staple agriculture. This expansion inevitably brought English settlement into conflict with both Spanish claims in Florida and French claims in the lower Mississippi Valley. As settlers pushed into the interior of Carolina they helped to protect the developing agriculture of the Charleston region from marauding Indians and from England's Latin rivals.

The settlement of Georgia, begun in 1732, stemmed from the desire to form a buffer colony between Florida and South Carolina. The aspiration of James Oglethorpe, a sensitive idealist, to found a refuge for the unfortunate classes of England (especially debtors) provided an additional reason for the formation of the new colony. The charter for Georgia, issued to Oglethorpe and twenty other trustees, denied them proprietary rights, and provided for the reversion of the colony to the Crown after twenty-one years. Though religious toleration was established for all but Catholics, the charter, unlike those of the other southern colonies, made no provision for representative government. Until 1751, when a popularly elected assembly met, the colony was regulated by a "Common Council" chosen by the trustees. It is worth noting, however, that a representative assembly had been organized just before the colony came under royal control. From the outset, Georgia's agriculture resembled that of South Carolina: rice, indigo, and food crops were raised by slaves, who in 1760 constituted one-third of the population of 9,000.

"The South," therefore, really consisted of five distinct and diversified colonies before the Revolution. Eventually, however, time and proximity imposed upon them common characteristics. But it is worth noting that every English colony had slaves before 1776; slavery was a colonial —not a "Southern"—institution.

THE MIDDLE COLONIES

Between the clearly English colonies that stretched from Chesapeake Bay to Spanish Florida and those collectively called New England were the heterogeneous colonies destined to become the Middle Atlantic states. Here, as a consequence of English and Dutch rivalry, a polyglot society developed. The English based their claim to the Hudson and Delaware Valleys on the explorations of John Cabot in 1497–98, while the Dutch maintained the importance of the voyages of Henry Hudson in 1609 and those of Adriaen Block and Cornelius May in 1612–14. Hudson, in particular, had established good relations with the Iroquois and had encouraged the Dutch to establish a trading post in 1614 at Fort Orange, on the site of present-day Albany. Capitalizing on the desire of the Indians for firearms and "firewater," the Dutch quickly developed a flourishing fur trade with the Iroquois.

New Amsterdam and the Dutch. The West India Company, chartered by the Dutch States-General in 1621, received exclusive trade rights and political jurisdiction over the Hudson region. Although the company denied to the English that it had any intention of settling families there, it in fact fostered settlement by providing free transportation to colonists, granting them a subsidy of food and supplies during their first two years of residence, and providing them with indentured servants who were bound to work as directed by the company. Colonization flourished after the establishment, under Peter Minuit, of the town of New Amsterdam (1626).

Unlike the English colonies, New Amsterdam had no representative assembly. The governor, though nominally the representative of the company, was commissioned by the States-General. When English settlers on Long Island complained against the arbitrary rule of the governor and his five-man council, Governor William Kieft rejected their protests with the assertion: "In this country I am my own master and may do as I please. . . ." When the protesters then appealed for relief to the States-General, Kieft was recalled, only to be replaced by the equally arbitrary Peter Stuyvesant.

Stuyvesant, whose peg leg made him one of the more colorful figures of colonial history, did not hesitate to threaten hanging for anyone who protested his policies. When he yielded in 1647 to the popular clamor for consultation on taxation, he permitted the election of eighteen men from whom he chose an advisory board of nine. Far from eliminating public discontent, this led Stuyvesant into a feud with his advisers, and eventually into the arrest and imprisonment of Donck, the leading spokesman of the nine-man board. Appeals by the board to the States-General for relief proved futile. After the outbreak of war between England and the Netherlands in 1652, the settlers, especially the English, took sharp issue with the arbitrary nature of Dutch rule. Stuyvesant, ever aggressive, replied bluntly: "We derive our authority from God and the Company, not from a few ignorant subjects."

The restoration of peace between the English and Dutch in 1654 temporarily secured the power of Stuyvesant. But hostility to his rule and to the company was rampant, and became even more intense when he attempted both to force the Dutch Reformed faith upon everyone in New Amsterdam and to enforce the company's trade monopoly as well.

Further antagonisms were aroused by efforts to develop a patroon system of landholding. To encourage migration the company, in 1629, had offered a grant of land to anyone who, within four years, could settle more than fifty persons over fifteen years of age in the colony. The grant would extend for sixteen miles along a navigable river, and the patroon, as he was called, would have near-feudal rights over his tenants, who were bound to him for ten years. Efforts to obtain tenants proved difficult, since few settlers were prepared to accept the pretensions of patroons when large amounts of good land were available elsewhere. The would-be patroons resented the failure of the company to help them obtain docile tenants. Only one patroon, Kiliaen Van Rensselaer, succeeded in meeting the requirements, and by 1646 the company abandoned the patroon grants. Farmers were alienated by the company's insistence that it receive possession of every other calf born and first option on all crops of free farmers. Moreover, the heterogeneous nature of the population left many of the inhabitants indifferent to the fate of the Dutch colony. They accepted English conquest in 1664 phlegmatically.

New York and the English. In the end, the protests of English settlers on Long Island against "their cruel and rapacious neighbors" which were used to justify English intervention settled the Dutch fate in the New World. Charles II granted New Netherlands and the adjacent lands to his brother, the Duke of York. When the British fleet arrived off New Amsterdam, in August 1664, the inhabitants of New Netherlands, despite the bellicose declarations of Stuyvesant, surrendered after only minor skirmishing. The English had the good sense to grant their new subjects, in addition to the traditional privileges of English subjects, the right to religious freedom and to the maintenance of traditional Dutch social and cultural customs and practice. Later, the right to elect local officials without a religious test for voters and the right to jury trial were established. It was not until October 17, 1683, however, that the Duke of York permitted the establishment of an eighteen-member assembly elected by freeholders. This was done to encourage the New Yorkers' acceptance of Thomas Dongan, a Catholic, as their governor, whose negotiation of a treaty—the Dongan Treaty (July 1664)—with the Iroquois, under which the Indians agreed to accept the new status of subjects of the English king, had laid the foundation of an alliance that would check French expansion southward.

New Jersey. One important result of the conquest of New Netherlands was the assignment of a proprietary grant for New Jersey by the Duke of York to Sir George Carteret and Lord John Berkeley (June 1664). Though not originally granted political authority, the two proprietors assumed it, and, in February 1665, issued the Concessions and Agreement, a document which authorized the annual election of an assembly that could pass legislation subject to proprietary review. Large land grants and religious toleration attracted considerable numbers of Puritans to New Jersey, with the usual consequence: eventual restriction of the franchise, and of office-holding, to Puritans.

These concessions to the Puritans did not keep the proprietors and settlers from engaging in lively disputes. Governor Carteret took exception to the severely puritanical laws passed by the first assembly in 1668. When the proprietors tried to collect quitrents in 1670, rioting rocked the colony. Berkeley, discouraged, sold his share of the colony to a Quaker in 1674. The colony was then divided into East and West Jersey, with the former remaining under Carteret's control and the latter passing to its new owner. East Jersey remained in turmoil until, in 1682, Carteret sold his rights to twelve Quakers. These worthies brought in twelve more Quakers with whom they formed an unwieldy twenty-four-man proprietorship. Their effort to collect quitrents from the prosperous East Jersey farmers, who showed no greater enthusiasm for the payment of fees than they had when Berkeley and Carteret tried to collect them, provoked new riots. Such disputes between agents of the proprietors and the New Jersey residents over the matter of quitrents persisted until well into the eighteenth century.

Pennsylvania. George Fox, an English Quaker, had undergone an intensely personal religious experience resulting in his conviction that religion is a matter between the individual and God. He dismissed the need for ritual and priests, and considered compulsory religious obedience, whether exacted by church or state, contrary to the just demands of individual conscience. Fox began to preach in 1649, and soon his sermons attracted larger and larger crowds. In time, thousands joined his Society and became Friends, also known as Quakers. Their doctrine of the pre-eminence of the spirit, and their open defiance of official and religious edicts, brought sharp persecution upon them. When Charles II forbade Quaker meetings and ordered punishment for any who refused to take the oath of allegiance to the Crown, some thirteen thousand Quakers chose imprisonment rather than submission.

As early as 1653 Quakers began to migrate to the New World, but it was the passage of the Conventicle Acts of 1664 and 1670, which made worship outside the Anglican faith a criminal act, that hastened the departure from England of many Quakers. In the New World they met with severe repression, particularly in Massachusetts where four Quakers, one a woman, were hanged for defying an expulsion order. George Fox, disturbed by the savagery of such persecution of his followers, visited the colonies in 1672 to find a location suitable for a separate Quaker colony.

Fox's search proved fruitless until he was joined in America by William Penn. This eminent young man, the son of an admiral who was a close personal friend of Charles II and the Duke of York, had ready access to the highest circles at court. His conversion to Quakerism while a student at Oxford outlasted his father's urgent efforts to make him sever the connection. Penn was briefly imprisoned under the Conventicle Act, but his family connections protected him from the more extreme forms of persecution directed against Quakers. With the death of his father in 1670, he achieved financial security; in addition to an extensive estate, he inherited a £16,000 claim against the Crown, which Penn eventually offered to settle in return for a proprietary grant in the territory between New York and Maryland. In spite of grave reservations about the advisability of doing so, Charles II granted young Penn a charter in 1681 including a proviso that the new colony be called Pennsylvania in memory of Penn's father.

The charter conformed to the developing royal policy of regularizing relations between the colonies and the mother country, and in particular of extending royal control over, and enforcement of, mercantilist policies. Within these confines Penn launched a "holy experiment" that emphasized self-government without reference to race or creed. To the Indians he accorded a respectful understanding. His Frame of Government stated: "Any government is free to the people under it where the laws rule, and the people are a party to those laws. . . ." An assembly of two hundred, popularly elected, was authorized to pass upon legislation initiated by the council. This council comprised seventy-two men, twenty-four of whom were elected each year by freemen to serve a three-year term. Thus, in any given year, forty-eight of the popularly elected councilors retained their positions.

The "holy experiment" faltered almost immediately under a steady barrage of proposals for changes in the structure of government. Finally, a code of law called the "Great Law" reduced the assembly membership to seventy-two representatives, one-quarter of whom were councilors. Frequent changes in this basic law caused considerable resentment against the proprietor until Penn, in 1701, issued a "Charter of Privileges" which provided for a unicameral legislature and confirmed the existing extensive toleration. This charter remained the fundamental law of Pennsylvania until 1776.

A liberal land policy, religious toleration, and careful planning brought a near-flood of immigrants to Pennsylvania. Philadelphia, which Penn had laid out with taste and careful planning, became a thriving, well-to-do community. The Quakers proved particularly adept at commerce, and the influx of English, Welsh, and Germans, who settled in the middle and western sections, gave to the colony a stable base of hard-working farmers. Pennsylvania seemed destined to flower as the garden of the New World.

New Sweden (Delaware). Along the lower reaches of the Delaware Valley lay the colony that was one day to be named Delaware, after Lord De La Warr, who is thought to have explored the bay area for the English in 1610, a year after Henry Hudson's explorations for the Dutch. As early as 1638, Peter Minuit, who had aided in the founding of New Amsterdam, led a group of settlers sponsored by the New Sweden Company to form a colony at the site of present-day Wilmington,

Delaware. New Sweden, as the settlement was called, languished in spite of the efforts of the Swedish government to keep it alive. By 1653 the population consisted of fewer than 250, mainly Dutch and Finns who lived rustic, simple lives. (It was the Finns who introduced the once omnipresent log cabin into America.) In 1654, a dispute between New Netherlands and New Sweden erupted over the occupation of Fort Casimir by the Dutch. The Dutch were expelled from the fort, but the incident increased the tension between the two colonies—whose relations, at best, had been strained—and in 1655 Stuyvesant turned upon his weaker neighbor and took possession. Dutch rule of the colony, however, was short-lived. After the fall of New Netherlands, the Duke of York obtained New Sweden as part of the grant of 1664. Left to itself, the heterogeneous population developed a liberal government and a liberal religious policy, and considered themselves a self-sufficient community. Much to their dismay, they were included in the Duke of York's grant to William Penn in 1682. Feeling was so bitter and competitive between the residents of Pennsylvania and Delaware that Penn, in 1691, appointed a special deputy governor for the "lower counties." Under the "Charter of Privileges" the Delawarians restored their own legislature, but the Governor of Pennsylvania was their governor also, and Delaware remained in the shadow of its great northern neighbor, subject to the jurisdiction of the Penn family. Only prolonged and stubborn opposition prevented its complete absorption into the larger domain of Pennsylvania.

The Gift of Tolerance. The Middle Atlantic colonies were the most heterogeneous of England's colonies. It was here that England's colonial policy revealed unusual wisdom. Far from attempting to impose a common character upon these colonies, the English pragmatically accommodated themselves to circumstances. Effective political control was most readily secured by respecting the customs and practices already established. The varieties of ethnic strains and religious sects found in the area prevented any one group from dominating the rest; and the extensive toleration guaranteed sectarian security for all. In some ways, such forced accommodation to variety foreshadowed the America to come. Here were sown the seeds of a pluralistic democracy.

NEW ENGLAND

One might have suspected that the stern and forbidding coast of New England, storm-tossed, plagued with harsh winters and a stony soil, would have dissuaded the settlers. Only a stern breed of man would have ignored the obvious disadvantages and staked a claim upon these shores. Indeed, it was a harassed and dedicated people who chose to make New England their new home. Settlement of this region was a direct consequence of the bitter and growing controversy between monarch and Parliament which centered on religion, but involved as well the larger question of whether king or Parliament would possess supreme power.

Puritans and Pilgrims. The fusion of church and state in England, symbolized by Henry VIII's assumption of supreme power in the Anglican Church, made it certain that any subsequent effort to extend Protestantism would be viewed by the king as a challenge to his authority. The demands of radical Protestants for the abolition of bishops and the establishment of control by presbyters, congregations, or synods, provoked James I into the utterance: "No Bishop, No King." James saw that if the authority of the church were made subject to the governance of its members, then the same control could be extended in time to the authority of the state. In spite of severe laws passed to dissuade them from challenging Anglican practice, the dissenters insisted that their intention was to "purify" the church, not to destroy it. Indeed, the critical point is precisely that the Puritans were not struggling for toleration; they were struggling for control both of the Anglican Church and of a king who was suspected of desiring to increase his political power.

The Pilgrims were even more radical. These dissenters risked their very lives, when they insisted on total separation of church and state. As separatists they were committed to the destruction of the Church of England as it was then organized. Such a commitment challenged the religious authority of the monarch, for the separatists believed in the creation of independent congregations, each autonomous and self-governing. James I viewed these dissenters with outraged indignation, and he ordered rigid enforcement of the Act of 1593 which made separatist meetings illegal and punishable by prison terms.

Plymouth. In 1608, the Scrooby congregation under the leadership of William Brewster fled to Holland. Though accorded toleration there, the Pilgrims grew discontented in their Dutch environment, isolated as they were from their traditional way of life, and especially fearful that their children would lose their English identity. The intensity of their sense of national identity culminated in their decision in 1617 to try to find a way to establish a community under English auspices in distant America.

Through Brewster's personal friendship with Edwin Sandys, one of the sponsors of the London Company, the Pilgrims were able to obtain a patent to migrate to Virginia. On September 16, 1620, the *Mayflower,* a 180-ton vessel, sailed from Plymouth, England, with 101 passengers aboard, only thirty-five of whom were from the Dutch community. As George Williston noted, less than half of the passengers were "saints"; the remainder, including Miles Standish, were "strangers." After a gruelling trip, the Pilgrims cast anchor on November 21, 1620, off the tip of Cape Cod, far from their Virginia destination, and safe from any interventions in the religious experiments they were to make.

On the day they made landfall the Pilgrims, led by William Bradford, joined with responsible "strangers" to compose the Mayflower Compact, through which they hoped to establish a stable government. Inasmuch as many of their passengers were unreliable men who did not regard themselves as bound by the patent granted to the Pilgrims, Bradford felt it was imperative to attempt to establish some sort of government even before the band of travelers reached shore. After moving across the bay to Plymouth Harbor the Pilgrims disembarked, and on December 25, 1620 (a day the Pilgrims treated as ordinary, since the celebration of Christmas was regarded by them as a pagan festival), they set to work establishing the community of Plymouth.

Barely fifty people survived that first winter, and these were threatened with Indian war in the spring of 1621. Only the aggressive response of Governor Bradford deterred the Narragansett Indians. A brief experiment with communal use of the land was abandoned after a near-famine in 1623, and each family was granted an acre of land on which to grow grain. By 1627 the Pilgrims felt economically strong enough to buy out the merchant adventurers who had financed their original migration; moreover, they had made friends among the Indians—notably Samoset, Squanto, and Massasoit—who taught them many things that helped in their fight for survival. The Pilgrims had demonstrated that it was possible to survive and flourish in inhospitable New England. The experiment was an evident success.

In 1630 the Pilgrim settlement of New England, originally unauthorized, obtained a patent from the Council of New England defining its territories; but the patent never received royal sanction. For its government a General Court with legislative powers was set up, consisting of the signers of the Mayflower Compact. The governor and his seven councilors were chosen annually by vote of the freemen, and newcomers were quickly accorded freeman status. The Fundamentals of Plymouth, adopted in 1637, provided a regular code of law, which, among other things, confirmed the General Court as a legislative assembly. (This was made necessary by the expansion of the colony.) All law required the approval of the General Court. A rude democracy existed; but ironically, as the colony grew older its treatment of suffrage rights grew more conservative. In 1660, a property qualification was required; in 1668, membership in the Pilgrim Church was made mandatory for voters.

The expansion of the Plymouth Colony brought rapid growth of local representative government. Town meetings flourished, enabling voters to follow local problems at close hand and to participate actively in their solution. Though soon overshadowed by the Massachusetts Bay Colony, its larger neighbor to the north, Plymouth remained independent until 1691, when it was united with Massachusetts. Perhaps the explanation for Plymouth's survival is that in spite of the vastly larger number of Puritans, both Puritan and Pilgrim followed the congregationalist principle—the principle which stated that ultimate authority within the church was vested in the congregation itself, a condition which was believed to have existed in the original church of Christ—in the management of their respective churches. As one Pilgrim divine explained it, "the Primitive Churches [those practicing the congregationalist idea] were and are their [Puritan] and our [Pilgrim] mutuall patternes and examples." Because of this basic similarity of religious opinion, Pilgrim and Puritan were complements rather than rivals.

The Massachusetts Bay Colony. The Puritans of England, as stated earlier, were not separatists. They meant to purify the Church of England. They especially emphasized the proposition that God had defined the essence of the church's constitution and that every man, even one of royal blood, was bound by God's law. Ecclesiastical authority depended, therefore, "not upon the authority of Princes, but upon the ordinaunce of God." Of the many ordinances of God, two were of crucial import in the understanding of Puritanism. The first was the Covenant whereby God made His will comprehensible to man; the second was the decree of God whereby all mankind was irrevocably divided between the damned on the one hand and the saved (or "elect") on the other. The distinguishing characteristics of the elect were that they alone possessed faith, and that they alone could administer God's visible world in an orderly manner. Though God alone knew His chosen children, the Puritan conceded that if the church rigorously examined its candidates and painstakingly supervised its membership, it could be reasonably certain that its members constituted the visible elect. In theory each congregation was self-governing since the proved elect would manifest God's will in their decisions. From the Bible came the pattern God had decreed for His true believers. "Unto all the power, learning, deceit, rage, of the False Church," the Puritan declared, "we oppose that little Book of God's Word, which . . . as a heavy millstone shall press her and all her children . . . down to hell." One need hardly point out that such doctrine was dangerous to the established church, to royal authority, and to any religious sect that dissented from Puritan practice. For at the heart of Puritanism was the harsh intolerance generated by the Puritans' conviction that they—and they alone—constituted a divine elite.

Under the Stuarts the Puritans were soon deeply embroiled with their royal masters over the scope of royal authority in religious matters. By the 1620s numerous Puritans actively considered emigration. In 1628, the Council for New England issued a patent to the newly formed New England Company. In the same year John Endecott and sixty other men set out to establish a trading post in northern New England. At Endecott's behest a new charter, issued in March 1629, organized the Massachusetts Bay Company. The charter provided members of the company with the rank of freeman, and guaranteed them the right to participate in government. Executive administration was provided by a governor, deputy-governor, and eighteen assistants. The members of the executive branch, together with the freemen of the company, constituted a General Court. As crucial to the future development of the colony as the inclusion in the charter of these provisions was the omission of two items: the charter failed to specify that either the charter or the company was to remain in London.

A second group of two hundred settlers came to the Massachusetts Bay colony in May 1629, with Puritan merchants as their leaders. This migration occurred shortly after Charles I decided to curb the Puritans in politics and religion. The conjunction of economic depression in the woolen industry, in which many Puritans were employed, and the revocation by the king of many patronage posts held by the Puritans, made their economic plight desperate. "All other Churches of Europe are brought to desolation," John Winthrop mourned, "and our sins for which the Lord begins already to frown upon us and to cut us short, do threaten evil time to be coming upon us." From this despair came the decision to launch a great migration that would carry the Puritans into the wilderness to found a land where God's word would rule. The New World was to become the haven and the abode of God's chosen.

Unlike the poverty-stricken enterprise of the Pilgrims, this mission attracted the attention of a number of wealthy Puritans. John Winthrop proved to be the chief agitator for the project. He was joined by John Cotton, Fellow of Emmanuel College, Cambridge, and Thomas Dudley, a member of the landed gentry. Soon, twelve prominent Puritans pledged to move themselves and their families to New England on March 1, 1630, if they were able to take with them a charter authorizing a colony in the New World. The Puritans shrewdly took advantage of the fact that the charter for Massachusetts Bay contained no provision requiring the charter document itself to be kept in England, nor requiring that the chartering company maintain its headquarters there. In August 1629, after secret negotiations, the Massachusetts Bay Company was sold to a group of Puritan stockholders. The subsequent election of Winthrop as governor and Dudley as deputy-governor placed the company under the jurisdiction of the men pledged to migrate.

Early in March 1630, Winthrop led the first contingent to the New World. With him he carried the charter that provided the legal basis for the extensive settlement which followed. By the year's end, seventeen vessels had carried some two thousand migrants to the new colony. Although a severe winter caused heavy mortality and some slowing of migration, the inflow of settlers swelled to a flood from 1633 onward. By 1643 some 20,000 people had made the long journey at a total cost of £200,000. No more than a quarter of these were Puritans; but political power was concentrated in the hands of that quarter. The king tried vigorously to assert his authority over the New Englanders; but the undisputable legality of their actions frustrated his efforts at dominance. When civil war erupted between king and Parliament, the Puritans were fortuitously provided with a respite from the king's antagonism, and during the twenty years of conflict in England which followed (1640–60), the colony at Massachusetts Bay pursued a lively independence.

Under pressure from the colonists, Winthrop and his fellows permitted the development of a qualified representative government. In May 1631, the General Court at Boston opened the franchise to church members, thereby restricting political power to Puritans. These voters were permitted to choose, for lifetime terms, assistants, in whom the executive powers were invested, thereby explicitly contradicting the original charter's requirement for annual elections. The assistants were drawn from the General Court and the governor, in turn, was drawn from and elected by the assistants. The critical power to make and enforce laws was vested in the governor and this group.

The creation of agricultural villages strengthened oligarchical control. In such communities the local minister supervised the inhabitants—and their town meetings. Although care was taken to grant each new settlement considerable autonomy, migrations into the interior were strictly supervised. Moreover, since only the freemen were given the power to vote, Puritanism was able to dominate both church and state during the seventeenth century. But though the Puritan oligarchy was able to protect itself well from serious infringements upon its power by those within the colony, it was to prove less successful in forestalling indefinitely the intervention and interference of the Crown.

THE EXPANSION OF NEW ENGLAND

Efforts to maintain religious orthodoxy in the New England colonies also proved difficult. The presence of large numbers of "strangers" made it almost inevitable that the Puritans—not inclined toward liberalism—would make strong efforts to restrict the behavior of the non-Puritans. When Thomas Morton erected a Maypole at "Merry Mount," he outraged the Pilgrims, who claimed he had invited his friends to join some Indian squaws "for their conforts, dancing and shriking togither, and worse practises." The latter were not specified, but one of them may have been Morton's practice of paying the Indians more for furs than the other Plymouth traders paid. Morton was expelled from the colony, and his fate became that of most other dissenters as well. Fourteen persons were expelled from Massachusetts in 1630 alone.

In some instances the object of expulsion was, by our standards, clearly superior to those who judged him. Such was the case of Roger Williams, the greatest of those dissenters who advocated religious liberty. From the moment of his arrival in Massachusetts in 1631 he proved a problem; though a Puritan, he insisted on complete and absolute separation of church and state. After a brief stay in Plymouth, Williams had convinced his Pilgrim hosts that he was "a man godly and zealous, having many precious parts, but very unsettled in judgemente." When Salem called him to its pulpit Plymouth sent him forth, but took care to notify his new parishioners of his peculiarities.

The parishioners of Salem soon regretted that they had not taken heed of Plymouth's warning. Williams rejected the idea of an established church, supporting instead the primacy of individual conscience. He argued for complete religious toleration, and directed vitriolic attacks against the Puritan oligarchs. Swiftly, a movement developed to expel him. It gained strength when he openly questioned whether the charter granted the Puritans the authority they claimed. Since the king was making repeated demands for the return of the charter so that he might re-examine it, Winthrop and his colleagues feared that news of Williams' agitation might lead to a royal revocation. He was censured by the General Court, and, when that discipline proved insufficient to silence him, he was removed from his pulpit. That Williams would eventually be expelled from the colony seemed a certainty.

The existence of such intolerance in Massachusetts Bay made it inevitable that dissenting colonists would move elsewhere to escape the wrath of the Puritans. As a result, the settlement of New England was extended. The order of expulsion that lay upon Williams—though it was not to take effect for several months—did not discourage his outspoken behavior. Indeed, he was more vocal than ever in his attacks upon the leaders of the Puritan community. Pressure finally built up for his immediate return to England, however; and as he faced the prospect of a trial for treason there, he chose the better part of valor and fled from Massachusetts, accompanied by five friends. Helped by the friendly Narragansett Indians, Williams and his little band of followers survived the rigors of their homeless existence. Subsequently he purchased a tract of land from the Narragansetts—the site on which Providence now stands—and there Williams established a colony that was to serve as a refuge for the oppressed dissidents of the New World.

Rhode Island. The haven offered by Williams attracted settlers from the very beginning. As time passed, more and more people who had been persecuted elsewhere were drawn to his community, and Rhode Island expanded.

In March 1640, Providence and its neighboring towns, lacking a royal charter and threatened with destruction by Massachusetts, formed a defensive union based upon a democratic government. In 1644, application was made to Parliament for a confirmation of their land title, and in March of that year a royal grant established Providence Plantations and provided for the establishment of a government with popular election of officials and the passage of laws in conformance with English practice.

Disputes soon developed between Massachusetts and Providence over the toleration of Quakers. Though Williams viewed the Society of Friends skeptically, he insisted that toleration be extended to them. In

Providence, he proudly contended, a man's conscience was his own. When Charles II granted a royal charter in 1663, it contained the proviso that no one should be "molested, punished, disquieted, or called in question, for any differences of opinion in matters of religion." Since it soon became the home of a variety of dissidents, orthodox New Englanders referred to it as "Rogue's Island," a play on words based on "Rhode Island," the Royal Charter's official designation of the colony.

As had been the case with Providence, the refusal of a stubborn individualist to submit to authority brought about the founding of another new colony in the Rhode Island area. Anne Hutchinson, whom the Puritan leaders had charged with the possession of "a vary voluble tongue," called for a theology based upon the "inner light." Her belief in divine revelation proved too mystical for church authority. Moreover, her contention that she received enlightenment directly from above put her in an impregnable position in any theological debate. A direct contradiction of the traditional view of the Bible as irrefutable, Mistress Hutchinson's argument for the validity of continuous divine revelation was tantamount to a demand for continual amendment of Holy Writ.

The radicalism of their views notwithstanding, proponents of the inner light won a surprising victory in 1636 in the election of Henry Vane, who had run against the dyed-in-the-wool Puritan, Winthrop, to the post of Governor of Massachusetts. For the next year orthodox leadership fought grimly to regain control of the colony, using a variety of tactics ranging from ridicule to political intrigue. In the next election—held at Newtown, one of the oldest strongholds of orthodoxy—Winthrop was re-elected. Anne Hutchinson was summarily ordered to leave Massachusetts, and she fled with her followers to Rhode Island, where she founded the colony at Portsmouth. In 1640, Portsmouth and Providence agreed to unite, forming the Providence Plantations. The efforts of such religious pioneers as Roger Williams and Anne Hutchinson had brought toleration to at least a corner of New England.

Connecticut. The Puritan and Pilgrim recognition of the strategic importance of the Connecticut Valley as a pathway for marauding Indians persuaded them to establish permanent settlements in Connecticut. In addition, the superior fertility of the valley made it agriculturally attractive. The value of the valley had become singularly apparent when in 1633 the Dutch established a post at the site of modern Hartford. In 1635, John Winthrop, Jr. settled with a small group of Puritans at Saybrook, Connecticut. The Massachusetts Bay Colony aggressively pressed its claim on the territory by sending Thomas Hooker to settle another Puritan community in the valley.

Hooker, who had his own private differences with Puritan practice, was granted the settlement at his own behest. Though fully and firmly committed to the theology of Puritanism, he took sharp issue with its political practices. He believed that "the foundation of authority is laide in the consent of the governed." Rather than provoke disquieting debate, Hooker emphasized the economic motive for his move, especially the agricultural promise of the valley. He also pointed to the danger from others who might seek to possess its fertile richness. The Puritan authorities, uneasy at the large-scale emigration Hooker's move might inaugurate, reluctantly granted permission. In May 1636 Hooker and his flock of one hundred moved to Hartford.

Massachusetts struggled to maintain control over the "river towns" that grew up along the Connecticut River, but soon lost the battle. On May 1, 1637, the Connecticut towns organized their own General Court. The independent existence of Connecticut was formalized with the passage in 1639 of the Fundamental Orders. The form of government thus established resembled the Massachusetts government, but there was a major difference: no religious test for voting was to be imposed. Furthermore, the governor, though he had to be a church member, was chosen by a comprehensive franchise, and was limited to one term in office.

As often happened in the colonies, Connecticut, in growing older, became less liberal. In 1657 and 1662 the establishment of property qualifications for voting caused the disenfranchisement of the poorer classes. Also, the governor gained the right to succeed himself. These restrictions stemmed from economic rather than religious considerations. The wealthier inhabitants of the valley sought to make themselves secure from the potential excesses of their lesser brethren.

The fears of orthodox Puritans that Boston was lapsing from traditional Congregationalism led to the establishment of another colony in 1638. New Haven, founded by a wealthy merchant, Theophilus Eaton, and a Dissenter minister, John Davenport, was governed wholly by the teachings of Scripture. The Old Testament was applied literally, and Mosaic Law rather than English common law prevailed. Since jury trial was nowhere mentioned in the Bible, none was provided. All civil and ecclesiastical powers were tightly vested in a twelve-man council which governed both church and state. But the subsequent expansion of settlement about New Haven brought the organization of a General Court in

1643. After the restoration of Charles II in 1660, New Haven's future grew bleak. Suspected of hostility to the king, of having aided the assassins of Charles I, and of harboring the desire to gain total independence, it was incorporated into Connecticut by the Charter of 1662. After two years of stubborn resistance to incorporation, New Haven finally submitted.

New Hampshire and Maine. One of the by-products of the Anne Hutchinson controversy was the founding in New Hampshire of Exeter in 1638 by John Wheelwright, a minister, and a handful of subscribers to inner light doctrine. This settlement was followed shortly afterward by an orthodox Puritan settlement at Hampton. Unlike the other New England colonies, the New Hampshire settlements contained a sizable number of Anglicans. Confusion as to exact status characterized the new colonies. The charter grant to Ferdinando Gorges and John Mason by the Council for New England had included Maine and New Hampshire. In 1629 the two proprietors had divided the territory, with Mason gaining most of present-day New Hampshire. Massachusetts, to the dismay of Mason's heirs, asserted its claim to New Hampshire in 1641. The Puritans held to their claim until 1677, but in that year the English Court of King's Bench declared that Massachusetts was not entitled to New Hampshire. In 1679, England made it the first of the royal colonies in New England.

Maine had an equally confused early history. Gorges tried to give substance to his proprietary grant by establishing a number of settlements between 1640 and 1650. A General Court was organized to govern the region in 1649 and extended toleration to those who practiced their beliefs "in a Christian way." Although the Privy Council ruled that Massachusetts' claim to Maine was invalid, the Puritan oligarchs secured control in fact by secretly buying out the Gorges claim. Puritan control was officially confirmed by William and Mary in the Massachusetts charter of 1691.

The New England Confederation. As the New Englanders dispersed through the countryside, they were forced to experiment in interdependence. Threatened on all sides—by the French, the Dutch, and the omnipresent Indians—they discussed the possibility of a loose union to secure themselves from attack. The coming of civil war in England in the early 1640s exposed the colonies to attack, but at the same time removed any threat of immediate British retaliation to prevent union. In May 1643, Plymouth, Connecticut, New Haven, and Massachusetts formed a defensive alliance "for mutuall help and strength in all our future concern-ments." Religious orthodoxy was the binding link; Rhode Island was excluded because of its religious liberality, and New Hampshire for its democratic inclinations.

The Confederation lasted, at least in theory, from 1643 to 1691. It pursued a near-independent course in the conduct of foreign affairs prior to 1660. In 1645 its members, seeking to expand their land holdings, defeated the same Narragansett Indians who had provided yeoman assistance in the defeat of the Pequot Indians eight years before. The Dutch were excluded from the Connecticut Valley by treaty in 1650. The Confederation also tightened Puritan control by passing tithe laws, restricting church membership, and passing anti-Quaker laws. But Massachusetts expressed increasing discontent with a union that gave all members political equality while obliging the Bay Colony to provide the bulk of fiscal and manpower resources. With the restoration of Charles II in 1660 increasing hostility toward the Confederation was manifested by the London government. The Confederation endured only as a pale shadow of its original self, but continued to suggest the advantages of colonial cooperation and to serve as proof that the experiences which bound New England colonies together were stronger than those which divided them. The South as a distinct and unique region might not yet exist; New England did.

Chapter 3

The Cultural Inheritance

Perhaps no historical problem is more difficult to resolve than attempting to determine the sources and foundations of national character. The first American settlers, primarily emigrants from Great Britain and western Europe, brought with them habits of mind, customs and mores, traditions and prejudices which inevitably were to become a part of the American character. The environment in which these settlers found themselves, however, compelled substantial modification of their European heritage. The task of subduing the raw American wilderness frequently became an all-absorbing occupation, so that many Americans looked back to Europe for their intellectual development. That the distinctive American character which emerged was an amalgam of old and new ideas is clear; that European thoughts were reshaped by American experiences cannot be doubted. But just how much of the new national character was molded by heritage and how much by environment can probably never be precisely determined.

THE ENGLISH HERITAGE

The Englishmen who crossed the wide Atlantic in the seventeenth and eighteenth centuries did not immediately discard their identity as Englishmen. They carried with them the language of Chaucer and Shakespeare, of Donne and the King James Bible. The colonists frequently shared the intense religious vision and poetic imagery of their contemporaries, Milton and John Bunyan, and the aspirations of the political theories of John Locke and James Harrington. The Puritan Revolution which shook British life to its foundations between 1640 and 1660, and the Glorious Revolution of 1689 which confirmed the results of the Puritan Revolution, established for the colonial the limits of political authority and the scope of individual rights. The early Americans firmly subscribed to the centuries-old common law, with its deep-rooted emphasis on precedent. Only when the new environment dictated modification of old customs, would the new settlers tamper with the established laws and social precedents; and even when circumstance made change imperative, such changes were introduced reluctantly. John Winthrop noted that in orthodox New England care was taken that English laws and Puritan beliefs "were digested" gradually and circumspectly, "with divers alterations and additions."

The colonial Englishman, when he spoke of himself, might have echoed John Adams in saying that he was the descendant of Englishmen who had left England in an earlier and purer time. Deep in the colonial consciousness was the conviction that the ancient English liberties had been purified in the New World. Gradually, these "Englishmen abroad" came to think of themselves as Americans. For them, the English tradition began to accommodate itself to the untamed wilderness. Hector St. John de Crèvecoeur, the French writer, described the "new man" that had emerged in America by the end of the eighteenth century as one who acted "upon new principles." He might more accurately have noted that these "new principles" were, in fact, the old English liberal ideas, drawn from the seventeenth-century revolutionary upheavals, distilled by the American wilderness, refined by the American experience, and followed by the colonial settler to their logical conclusions.

THE FOUR AMERICAS

"Whether we remain in one confederacy," Thomas Jefferson wrote in 1804, "or form into Atlantic and Mississippi confederations, I believe not very important to the happiness of either part." The idea of a single American identity, politically united, was one that the colonial barely perceived. Even so vigorous a patriot as John Adams could, some six months after the battles at Lexington and Concord (April 19, 1775), describe New England as having "the advantage of every other colony in America." Provincial loyalties and interests, as the men who drew up the Constitution were to discover, overrode appeals for loyalty to a larger political identity. Only a compromise which permitted the retention of the rights and identity of each old colony made union possible. There existed, however, evidence that four separately identifiable sections were being formed during the colonial period, those of the South, the Middle Colonies, New England, and the Frontier, each possessing distinctive and unique characteristics. Diversity rather than uniformity was the hallmark of American civilization in its formative years.

SOUTHERN SOCIETY

At first, generalizations would hardly seem to apply to Southern society in the seventeenth and eighteenth centuries. A traveler progressing across the vast reaches of the colonial South would have been struck by the variation in dwellings, ranging as they did from great manor houses to frontier lean-tos. A superficial glance would have impressed the observer with the relaxed, democratic attitudes that seemed to characterize Southerners. But closer scrutiny would have revealed a severely stratified society.

The Gentry Tradition. Though few Southerners were descended from the English gentry, the gentry ideal prevailed as the ultimate symbol of success in the South. Coming as they did from the English yeomanry, and from even lower strata of English society, the Virginians, according to Carl E. Bridenbaugh, "sought with determination to preserve in Virginia what they fancied and recalled of the life of the English countryside." It hardly matters that their vision of English country life scarcely conformed to reality; the point is that the early Virginian did not repudiate his past, but drew from it his new aspirations.

The Slave. At the mudsill of Southern society were the Negro slaves, who were doomed to a lifetime of forced labor. Originally, their social habits had reflected their tribal origins and African past, but they had come to emulate in dress and language their masters and mistresses. In spite of inferior status, the slave had a subtle influence upon the daily lives of his white masters, for the social mores and legal codes of the South were evolved from concern with the fact of slavery. The number of slaves alone assured that they would be a major factor in Southern life. On the eve of the Revolution no less than 170,000 slaves dwelled in the regions adjacent to Chesapeake Bay, a total slightly less than half the area's population. In South Carolina and Georgia the proportion was even higher, 74 per cent of the population being slaves. Ever fearful of insurrection, the white minority imposed harsh restrictions on the Negro, giving the area around Charleston a military character. It was the presence of the black man, more than any other single factor, that gave the South its particular identity.

The Poor Whites. Slavery had a dismal, debilitating impact on the poorer whites. These whites bitterly resented the Negro whom they viewed as a competitor. As the slave assumed the tasks of house servant, plantation artisan, and field hand, the only activity left to the whites was farming. The poverty which characterized the lives of many whites often made his lot scarcely better than that of the Negro. His sole distinguishing feature, color, became a matter of considerable concern for the poor white. He refused to perform tasks similar to those done by slaves lest he be identified with them in their pitiable state. The oft-noted uncouthness, ignorance, and laziness charged to these whites was a further consequence of an economic system that had small use for them.

Hard as the poor, free white found his lot as the result of the practice of slavery, life was grimmer still for the white indentured servant. Because Negro slaves served their masters until death, the Southern plantation owner saw few advantages in securing the services of indentured servants. On the few occasions when the use of indentured servants might prove attractive, the Southern master would draw his laborers from among convicts whose terms of indentureships were generally for life—putting them, in effect, in the same class as slaves. And as the availability of land decreased during the eighteenth century, those servants whose terms of indenture expired found no opportunities available. They could expect nothing more than poverty. And for both classes of poor southern whites—the free and the indentured—there existed the fearful threat that they, too, might become slaves some day.

The Southern Farmer. A large number of whites, working alone or with small gangs of slaves, drew from a bountiful country a full, though rude, comfort. Some were content with a subsistence level of life; others grew a substantial surplus of tobacco or of wheat which earned them enough profit to work their way into the upper echelons of Southern society. The more fortunate colonial farmers built brick dwellings, farmed several hundred fertile acres with twenty or more slaves, and approximated the life of the lesser English gentry. Those who attained material success but lacked the accompanying social grace usually identified with the gentry tradition composed for one observer a "semi-barbarian population," utterly without taste or restraint, and imposing much savage turbulence upon Southern society. Though some of the violence was directed against defenseless slaves, more was being unleashed against other members of white society. Eye-gouging and other brutalities characterized the rough and tumble fights in which the lower orders indulged.

The Southern Aristocrat. Presiding over this stratified society were the "First Families" of the Chesapeake. When one spoke of the Lees, Randolphs, Carters, Fitzhughs, Carrolls, Galloways, Byrds, and Dulanys, one spoke of the nearest approximation of nobility America possessed. Living in great manor houses, surrounded by thousands of acres, and served by numerous slaves, they gave to the Southern colonies an aristocratic tone that was completely lacking in the more democratic colonies of the North. Essentially an aristocracy of wealth, they respected the form rather than the substance of education; graduation from college—any college—was considered sufficient qualification for social acceptance. Possessing ample leisure, they often surrounded themselves with great libraries, from which some of them read copiously and well. Accustomed to wielding power, they expected social deference as their natural due.

Although power and wealth were founded originally on the ownership of vast acreage and numerous slaves, by the eighteenth century the Southern aristocrat had diversified his economic activities. Tobacco had been the first source of wealth. Subsequently, flour-milling, lumbering, naval stores, shipbuilding, and trade were added. Speculation in land was a natural addition to Southerners' money-making pursuits, since their monopoly of political offices allowed them to obtain new lands easily. But a critical weakness endangered the serene, self-confident world of the Chesapeake aristocrats: they lived beyond their means, piling up debts that ultimately they would be unable to redeem.

The Decay of the Tidewater Settlements. Poor farming habits, reinforced by the extensive availability of land, caused waste of much of the land that was immediately accessible to water transportation. Tobacco, the chief crop, exhausted the soil within five to seven years. The major centers of agriculture in Virginia, Maryland, and North Carolina steadily moved inland, penetrating the Piedmont region beyond the fall line of the rivers of the Chesapeake hinterland.

The search for fresh land compelled the Southern aristocrats and more successful farmers to engage in hazardous land speculations. The fluctuation of staple prices also made it difficult for Southerners to predict with certainty their margin of profit. Only by obtaining credit from their factors (agents in Britain who supervised the sale of their produce and placed orders for manufactured goods), were the more prosperous Southerners able to buy land and maintain their scale of living. Desperate measures were frequently employed to escape bankruptcy. In one case, John Robinson, Speaker of the House of Burgesses, loaned hard-pressed planters £100,000 from currency that had been withdrawn from circulation. Such measures provided only temporary relief as the First Families of the Chesapeake, united by blood and a mutually shared genteel vision, sank deeper in debt to British merchants and factors. By 1775, much of the Tidewater region had reverted to its original state of wilderness, and the debt-burdened aristocrats looked to revolution as a dramatic, saving stroke that would make it possible for them to repudiate their obligations.

Virginia and South Carolina. Farther south, in South Carolina, and later in Georgia, the stratified society which emerged differed from that of Virginia. Here, the wealth of the aristocracy was real, and based on substantial capital accumulation. As capital poured into Carolina, great plantation houses were built, just as in Virginia; but fear of the huge gangs of slaves and the mysterious diseases that plagued the Carolina lowlands persuaded the successful Carolinian to settle in Charleston. The resulting urban orientation of the Carolina aristocracy contrasted sharply with the profoundly rural tone of Virginia's gentry. More than one visitor to Charleston commented on the lack of frugality and the ostentation which characterized the Charleston aristocrat. In great town houses—some three hundred were built between 1768 and 1772 and furnished in the London style—the rounds of entertainment never ceased. Dress of the most fashionable sort and lavish personal adornment preoccupied the Carolinian. Social clubs, Masonic lodges, military troops, and riding to the hounds created an air of constant excitement in the city. Crèvecoeur, after a visit, concluded that the Charlestonian seemed irresistibly drawn "to dissipation and pleasure."

Anglicanism and Education. The convivial atmosphere of Southern life was omnipresent; it extended even to the church. In both Virginia and Carolina, religion was a social experience. Men and women went to church to see and be seen, and to catch up on the week's gossip. The absence of religious fervor in much of the South was traceable to the Anglican Church being the established church throughout the region. It was a church that had been built not by individual fervor, but by government edict. Nevertheless, the Anglican Church provided a cultural and religious link between the South and England. The religious tie was reinforced by the absence of an American bishop. The Bishop of London had jurisdiction over the South, and since Anglican priests had to be ordained by a bishop, it meant that they were either British by birth or colonials who had spent some time in Great Britain. In addition, the

Anglican missionary society, the Society for the Propagation of the Gospel in Foreign Parts, provided money to support church work and prepared teachers to staff Anglican schools. The Anglican priest consistently reminded his congregation of the "religious obligations and important motives of dutiful respect and submission to the established authority, together with proper confidence in the great wisdom of the government of our parent country." When revolution came, the Anglican clergy solidly supported the British cause.

Though the Southern aristocracy—especially in South Carolina—expressed *noblesse oblige* by liberal donations to orphanages, academies, libraries, and hospitals, in neither Virginia nor South Carolina was there much interest in original creative endeavor. Southerners were secure in their knowledge that, as Englishmen, they shared the vast cultural heritage of Great Britain. For the well-born there existed private educational facilities, but for most Southerners only the barest education was obtained. For the few who were interested in higher education, William and Mary College, founded in 1693 at Williamsburg, Virginia, or one of the Northern colleges usually was chosen. Occasionally a Southern scion would be enrolled at Cambridge or Oxford.

The Southern Genius. Perhaps the most striking characteristic of Southern society was the extent to which a handful of whites was able to impress its vision upon the whole society. The Carolinian gentry numbered barely two thousand, and that of the Chesapeake region a few thousand more; yet these men commanded and directed the energies of the entire society around them. In Virginia, this capacity for and experience with leadership found its fullest expression in political genius, a genius that would imprint itself unmistakably upon the republic that was to come.

THE MIDDLE COLONIES

The American Way. The colonies of New York, New Jersey, Delaware, and Pennsylvania, unlike the Southern and New England colonies, drew their populations from diverse sources. English, Scottish and Scots-Irish, Welsh, Dutch, German, Swedish, Finnish, French, and Spanish-Jewish families settled in the region. The absence of a homogeneous society, particularly the failure of any one ethnic group to establish dominance over the other minorities, gave the Middle Colonies a diverse character. By necessity settlers there were more tolerant of differences in custom and outlook, making easy generalizations about the region difficult. Great Britain encouraged this diversity by permitting the Dutch in New York and New Jersey to retain their language, religion, and customs. Within this region, many of the characteristics one associates with modern America were present: a multiplicity of languages, customs, traditions, and religions, all kept in balance by an even-tempered tolerance.

The Growth of a Pluralistic Society. Diversity of opinion and tradition compelled the Middle Colonies to seek a middle way. They accepted the idea that a society in which each man was permitted to retain his past heritage and allowed to contribute his unique talent would ultimately benefit by extracting from each his best contribution. Today, modern sociologists describe such a society as "pluralistic." Such a society precludes emphasis upon extreme values or exclusive authority. It accepts the proposition that each national group or religious sect is of distinct value. In such a society the golden mean will command the highest respect. Its citizens will rarely be zealots, but will often lapse into the assumption that all values carry equal weight. The prime danger for such a society is that it may lose all perspective and accept the idea that what is, is right. Its prime strengths are that it provides ample room for difference of opinion; it is receptive to new ideas; and it tends to judge the implications of an idea or the achievement of a man not by abstract principles but by demonstrable results.

Religious Tolerance. James Madison, arguing before the Virginia convention called to ratify the Constitution, observed that religious freedom "arises from that multiplicity of sects, which pervades America, and which is the best and only security for religious liberty in any society." Religious toleration was hardly perfect. Pennsylvania, probably the most tolerant colony, offered religious equality only to all Christians; the other Middle Colonies offered refuge to German Pietists, Scotch Presbyterians, Methodists, Baptists, Quakers, and Catholics. British official policy, which encouraged widespread toleration, was partly conditioned by the desire to extend Anglican influence, for in New England, where the Congregational Church was the established authority, Anglicanism needed official support to obtain a foothold. Perhaps of greatest significance in the increase of tolerance was the steady decline in the late seventeenth century and the eighteenth century of militant Protestantism. The process was most advanced in the Middle Colonies where tolerance bred not only many sects but also religious indifference. As opposition to Britain grew in the Middle Colonies and the South, where the British had either established or attempted to establish the Anglican Church, the conviction developed that "there is not a shadow of right in the general government to intermeddle with religion."

The Enlightenment. In Great Britain and western Europe during the seventeenth and eighteenth centuries, a revolution in science profoundly affected all shades of thought. Two men, the Englishman Francis Bacon (1561–1626) and the Frenchman René Descartes (1596–1650), had questioned how man, drawing upon extant scientific texts, could have a dependable knowledge of nature. They repudiated the previous heavy reliance upon the texts of Aristotle and other thinkers of antiquity. Challenging the medieval habit of establishing as an *a priori* fact the truth of a given proposition which was then deductively demonstrated to be true, they contended that truth was the end product of a long effort at investigation, experiment, and analysis. From such effort, it was assumed, man could reduce natural phenomena to formulas and equations, permitting him, in the words of Descartes, to achieve "a practical philosophy by which, understanding the forces and action of fire, water, air, the stars and heavens and all other bodies that surround us, as distinctly as we understand the mechanical arts of our craftsmen, we can use these forces in the same way for all purposes for which they are appropriate, and so make ourselves the masters and possessors of nature."

Isaac Newton and His Law. The supreme achievement of the new science was the discovery by the Englishman Isaac Newton (1642–1727) of the Law of Universal Gravitation. Newton set forth his findings in *Mathematical Principles of Natural Philosophy*. In this book, he demonstrated that all measurable motion fit a single mathematical formula. Matter moved as if every particle attracted every other particle with a force proportional to the product of the two masses, and inversely proportional to the square of the distance between them. The results of Newton's findings were put to immediate use. Shipping and naval operations were affected by the discovery of how tides resulted from the gravitational interplay of sun, moon, and earth. New instruments such as the chronometer, which allowed precise calculation of the longitude of a ship at sea, were invented and developed, and cartographers were enabled to draw more accurate maps. In the field of mathematics, knowledge of curves and trajectories was extended. Science had been revealed not only as setting forth abstract laws but also as having practical and beneficial applications.

The American Enlightenment. Though separated by the wide Atlantic from Great Britain and western Europe, the English colonies were kept fully abreast of the growing literature of the New Science. The improvements in ocean transportation alone were bound to command the respect of a people dependent on overseas commerce. The New Science also appealed to the American preference for learning from experience; learning to live in a wilderness had made many of the habits of mind, which had been suitable for living in a settled Europe, no longer tenable. Appeals to *a priori* solutions simply did not fit into the realities of the colonial experience. Experimentation, a willingness to accept evident results rather than abstract theories, and a feeling that the ordinary man wrestling with a practical problem came closest to the true scientific temper characterized American scientific thought. But because colonial achievements were in the realm of applied rather than theoretical science, many Europeans agreed with the Abbé Raynal when he observed much to the chagrin of the colonials, "America has not yet produced one good poet, one able mathematician, one man of genius in a single art or a single science."

Empiricism. Observation of natural phenomena was the key to understanding; similarly, the colonial assumed, observation of social behavior would instruct him on how to meet the problems of everyday existence. The consensus of every man, rather than the dictum of an intellectual elite, was most apt to establish the answer to a given question. The self-taught man commanded the highest respect from his fellow Americans, whereas the narrow scholar, intent upon achieving thorough command of a single field, was viewed with condescension. One such "self-made" man was David Rittenhouse (1732–96), who gained the awed respect of Jefferson. His astronomical research, his knowledge of munitions, metals, and mathematics—all self-taught—were sufficient to convince the Virginian that he was first in genius among the world's astronomers. But Rittenhouse's primary achievement in astronomy was drawing the boundaries between such colonies as Maryland, Delaware, and Pennsylvania, a boundary better known as the Mason and Dixon Line. The self-made record of a Rittenhouse approximated the self-made achievement of most Americans. Each had carved a home for himself from the wilderness, or had at least observed fellow Americans doing as much. Tangible evidence that the condition of life had been steadily improving was ample; it is therefore not surprising that the colonial concluded that ingenuity could subdue any obstacle. Thus Americans occupied themselves with inventing stoves, plows, and other mechanical devices with which to master their rugged environment. From observation of the American experience, the colonial drew the obvious conclusion: America possessed a unique place in the scheme of nations.

Benjamin Franklin. The emphasis upon the validity of observation was particularly strong in the Middle Colonies. The existence of numerous urban centers such as Philadelphia, New York, Newark, Lancaster, and Perth Amboy made it possible to organize societies like the American Philosophical Society. Colonial intellectuals found the absence of strong prejudices in the region also conducive to empirical inquiry. No man embodied the commitment to empiricism more completely than Benjamin Franklin. A Bostonian, born into a family of small means, Franklin went abroad to Philadelphia while still a youth. His life serves as consummate proof that self-schooled intellects could be as productive as those trained at a university.

A list of his accomplishments would form a catalogue of the pursuits open to the practical man: printer, postmaster, almanac maker, essayist, chemist, orator, tinker, inventor, professor of housewifery, ambassador, maxim monger, wit, herb-doctor—in short, he was a veritable Jack-of-all-trades. The practical and the obvious appealed to his nature. Made tolerant by his own religious indifference, Franklin practiced a philosophy of the useful and the comfortable which he believed would better the lot of the common man. His commitment to this philosophy is reflected in the practicality of his inventions; he improved such accepted conveniences as chimneys, stoves, and carriage wheels, and he devised new aids such as bifocals and the lightning rod. His observations of electricity, demography, and navigation resulted in original discoveries in each field. And fearful lest he confine himself to an ivory tower, he participated in both civic and political activity. He organized fire departments, a library, the post office, and an insurance company.

Middle Colonial Education. The respect for the self-educated man was not only a commentary on the American mind but also on the quality of higher education. Most students preparing for college devoted intensive study to the classics, learning Latin and sometimes Greek and Hebrew by rote. As Franklin realized, education in America had little relevance to the special conditions of American society. A student at college was taught the same curriculum his father had studied. In the one hundred and thirty-three years that elapsed between the founding of Harvard (1636) and Dartmouth (1769), no major changes occurred in the courses of instruction, which were derived from those offered at the two British universities and the western European institutions of higher education. The student spent his first two years studying the medieval *trivium:* Latin grammar, rhetoric, and logic. The last two years were devoted to mathematics, metaphysics, ethics, and natural philosophy. Under the latter heading, students were instructed in a smattering of physics, astronomy, and chemistry. The orthodoxy of colonial education was such that Benjamin Franklin, who wished to shift the emphasis of higher education toward a more practical program, failed to alter to any considerable degree the program of the College of Philadelphia (now the University of Pennsylvania—1740). A student attending the Middle Atlantic colleges of Philadelphia, the College of New Jersey (now Princeton—1746), King's College (now Columbia—1754), or Queen's College (now Rutgers—1766) studied identical subjects. Most of these schools offered a senior course in theology which sought to provide the student with a broad basis of religious knowledge free from sectarian bias. Higher education reinforced accepted knowledge, avoided experimentation, and permitted educated Americans to communicate freely and easily with their European counterparts.

The New American. In most colonies, the colonist thought of himself as a Virginian, Carolinian, or New Englander, but in the Middle Colonies, the polyglot population had submerged its diversity by accepting a new identity, that of the American. When, in 1754, Franklin attempted to persuade the colonials at Albany to enter into a union, arguing "United we stand; divided we fall," he displayed his acute awareness of his American identity. Recognizing somewhat earlier than most that the phenomenal growth of America made it unlikely that the colonials would much longer accept a position subordinate to the mother country, Franklin pressed for the creation of an American nation. He denied that the British ought to fear such a development, contending that an expanding American population added to the wealth of the British Empire and that the observable wealth of America outmoded accepted mercantilist policies. Rather than dwell on the limits of the world's resources, he insisted that the untouched riches of America warranted energetic exploitation. It was British efforts to impede the independent economic growth of America, more than any other factor, that was to lead Franklin and like-minded men to urge independence.

In middle America, a practical, tolerant people, little given to speculation, and surrounded by a diversity of beliefs and nationalities, allowed experience to determine what should survive and what should perish. Far from being intimidated by diversity, they accepted it; and, contrary to all European experience, they flourished.

NEW ENGLAND

New England had begun as a holy experiment in which a state governed by God's ordinances would be built. "Our fathers were Englishmen which came over this great ocean, and were ready to perish in this wilderness," the Pilgrim father William Bradford had sung, "but they cried unto the Lord, and he heard their voyce, and looked on their adversitie."

A society dedicated to God did not mean that a society of equals was to be created. As John Winthrop carefully warned, "In all times some must be rich, some poor, some highe and eminent in power and dignitie; others mean and in subjeccion." At the heart of both the Pilgrim and Puritan belief was the certainty that they had been chosen by God to build a state in which the work of God would be pre-eminent. Their state would serve as a beacon, lighting the way to men fallen away from God and His spirit.

The Puritan Oligarchy. The Puritans had early accepted the investment of authority in the "visible saints," those few members of the congregation who had demonstrated to the satisfaction of other members that God had chosen them as His own. In the early history of the Puritans, the men chosen to serve as elders, as the "visible saints" were called, had been those whose way of life placed them beyond reproach. Usually, they combined devoutness with a strength of character which made them the logical candidates for wielding the authority of the congregation. The number of elders varied from congregation to congregation, but their number rarely exceeded ten. As early as 1635, the Massachusetts General Court, the name given the colonial legislature, voted to give the various towns a considerable measure of autonomy. It permitted freemen "to choose their own particular officers, as constables, surveyors of highways and the like." Care was taken, however, to restrict office holding to church members, thereby insuring that secular authority would support ecclesiastical authority. The elect, full members of the Church, were bound together by a belief in the convenant between God and man, and that between man and man. In the first instance, they accepted the idea derived from the Bible that God had covenanted with His chosen few to reveal His purpose and to make known to them their election. In the second instance, the elect pledged that in "this particular company and society of saints, we promise . . . that we will cleave one unto another in brotherly love and seek the best spiritual good each of other, by frequent exhortation, seasonable admonition and constant watchfulness according to the rules of the Gospel."

Upon entering into a covenant, the congregation was designated as organized and its membership elected a minister. Those individuals who could not in good conscience join the congregation, as well as those whom the congregation refused to admit into membership, were obliged, nevertheless, to support and to attend church services. The first church members had freely chosen Congregational beliefs, and the intensity of their religious convictions had been strong enough to propel them across the ocean into an unknown land. Their devotion, however, was not sustained by the next generation. This proved crucial since the survival of a congregation required a constant renewal of the covenant as new members chose to enter into it, and the second and third generations lacked the emotional involvement needed to insure continued vitality in Puritanism. Probably as many as half of the population of New England were originally not members of the Congregational Church; the number of members decreased during the seventeenth century, until only two out of five New Englanders belonged to the church. The number of "strangers" (as nonmembers were called) had increased as the original intensity of Puritan belief declined. By 1660, the Congregational Church faced the genuine danger of disintegration from a lack of new members.

The Half-Way Covenant. To meet this danger, the Congregational Churches in 1662 convoked a synod at Boston to admit the children of the elect into the covenant, and consequently into membership in the congregation. This arrangement was called the "half-way covenant" since it admitted the children of the elect to church membership but denied them the right to partake of the sacrament of communion. Not only did this compromise insure survival of the church, but it also perpetuated the social, political, and economic benefits church membership conferred. Religion had created a privileged class which did not intend to allow its children to lose their advantages.

Benefits of Membership in the Oligarchy. Membership in the oligarchy was the means not only to religious power but also to secular authority. Since most of the land in Massachusetts was distributed at the discretion of the General Court, and election to the Court required that one be a member of the church, church members were guaranteed favorable disposition of land. This became increasingly true as the General Court appointed "town proprietors" to supervise the settlement of new townships, to distribute property, and to insure the creation of a common field in which everyone would be permitted to graze their livestock. The proprietors usually retained water rights, which they assigned to millers. In time, two distinct classes came to exist in almost every New England town: proprietors and nonproprietors. The former controlled land distribution while the latter increasingly dominated the town meeting. In the ensuing struggle over the "undivided lands," the nonproprietors finally forced the proprietors to surrender the lands to the selectmen, who were elected at town meetings to conduct discussion and voting, but generally only members of the church were elected as selectmen. Though the religious character of the Puritan settlements was still amply evident, time had brought a visible lessening of religious fervor.

King Philip's War. At the time Puritanism was struggling to retain its original integrity, New England was the victim of a series of severe afflictions. Most immediate in its devastation was King Philip's War, which raged from 1675 to 1678. Constant encroachments upon Indian lands, the frequent cheating of Indians by Puritan traders, and the contempt with which whites treated the red men finally provoked the Wampanoag chief, Philip, to organize an uprising of the various tribes so that an end might be put to continued Puritan aggression. In June 1675 Philip began a series of attacks on towns in western New England; and, in September, the New England Confederation declared war on the rampaging Indians. The following year the back of Indian resistance was broken with the killing of Philip, but sporadic fighting continued until April 1678, when a peace treaty was concluded at Casco, Maine. The cost of the war had been grim: more than one-sixteenth of New England's population had perished and twenty towns in Rhode Island and Massachusetts had been razed. Every branch of trade had suffered severe losses, and military expenditures had exceeded £100,000. "Ruine upon Ruine, Destruction upon Destruction," mourned one minister, "until one stone were not left upon another." Increase Mather, blunt spokesman for orthodox Puritanism, maintained that the war had been God's punishment for New England's lapse from its holy mission.

Revocation of the Massachusetts Bay Charter. Further catastrophe overtook the Puritans when, in 1684, Charles II revoked the charter which had established Puritan control of the Massachusetts colony. During the previous decade, Puritan authorities had fought to retain their charter against demands both in London and in New England for the termination of oligarchical authority. Charles II had embarked upon a program of colonial reform with the intention of extending royal governments, consolidating the colonies along regional lines, and extending the power of the governors at the expense of the colonial legislatures.

Although not explicitly stated, the Crown also intended to curb the obstreperous and aggressive Congregationalists. The "strangers" of the colony aided the Stuart program of centralization by petitioning for charter revocation, aware that such an action would undermine the oligarchy's domination. The Puritan leaders complained, "It is the hard condition of magistrates and ministers that they must bear all the murmurings of discontented people and be loaded with all the obloquies and injurious reproaches that can be."

The Dominion of New England. The first action taken after the charter revocation was the unification of New Hampshire and Maine with the Massachusetts Bay Colony in 1685. This was a step toward consolidating all of New England, and, eventually, creating a union of all the North American colonies. Through consolidation the British expected to achieve both more effective and more economical government. Increased development of colonial resources and the implementation of mercantilist policies were also expected to follow unification. The ever-present threat of Indian and French aggression made defense expenses heavy and the British government wished to reduce the cost. The death of Charles II in 1685 temporarily halted plans for consolidation, but the following year James II renewed the program.

With the arrival at Boston, in December 1686, of Sir Edmund Andros, appointed Governor-General of the Dominion of New England, Plymouth was forced into union with its northern neighbors. During the following year, Rhode Island, Connecticut, New York, and New Jersey also found themselves compelled to enter the union. The new dominion of New England vested nearly all power in the governor. Andros had the power to impose taxes, supervise the courts, determine the legality of existing land grants, enforce quitrents, and protect liberty of conscience, (the last-named power plunging the Puritans into aching despair). Andros also directed the defense program of the region with British troops sent to support the proposed reforms. Though the colonies had developed a lively tradition of self-government, no provision was made for a new assembly. Within a short time, Andros ordered the payment of old and new taxes, challenged the legitimacy of New England land titles, enforced trade laws, curbed town meetings, and attempted to establish the Anglican Church throughout the Dominion. "It would take a long summer's day to relate the miseries which were come in," complained Cotton Mather, "upon poor New England by reason of the arbitrary government then imposed on them." Pathetic appeals for restoration of New England's traditional rights were made by Increase Mather, who appeared before James II, but all seemed hopeless, until the Glorious Revolution (1689) swept James into exile.

The Charter of 1691. New England responded to the news of the Glorious Revolution with swift action. Andros and his supporters were arrested and jailed on April 18, 1689. Two days later, an effort to restore the old charter government was begun; but the new monarchs, William and Mary, showed no disposition to allow Massachusetts to return to its semi-independent status. In October 1691 a charter substantially reducing the power of the old oligarchy was promulgated. The governor now obtained his authority from the Crown, but his council was chosen by an elected lower house. Puritan power was trimmed by the decision to make property rather than religion the qualification for the right to vote. This resulted in a substantially larger electorate, since many non-Puritans could meet the property qualification of an annual income of £40 or ownership of property valued at £100. The charter also confirmed the union of Massachusetts Bay, Plymouth, and Maine, though the other participants in the Dominion of New England were allowed to revert to their former status. But for Massachusetts the changes were extensive and lasting; the Puritan oligarchs had lost their struggle.

The Merchant and the Minister. By the end of the seventeenth century the rapid expansion of New England trade had made the region an effective competitor in the West Indian and Mediterranean trade with the mother country. One of the purposes behind the formation of the Dominion of New England had been to restrict this competition. The wealth of New England could be seen in the importation of Barbados cotton and sugar, Spanish fruits, oils, and wine, and English manufactures. As the taste for comfort and luxury grew, the Puritan oligarchs expressed dismay at the subordination of religious interests to secular ones. With the growth of trade, a challenge to the domination of the ministers— covert at first but later open—developed within the merchant class. The growing challenge of this sophisticated mercantile class, indifferent to ancient beliefs, drove the ministers to ever more desperate attempts to revitalize clerical influence. Their attempts led to a catastrophic event— the Salem trials for witchcraft.

The Salem Witchcraft Trials. To understand the hysteria that seized Salem and neighboring regions in 1692, one must realize that a deep and firm belief in witches was held almost universally in the seventeenth century. The Puritans, creatures of their time, shared the fears of the supernatural that existed throughout the western world. Every colony had laws against the practice of witchcraft and could cite in support of them the injunction in Exodus: "Thou shalt not suffer a witch to live." The wave of trials that had already swept New England between 1647 and 1663 had condemned to death no fewer than fourteen persons found guilty of practicing the black art.

In 1684, the publication of Increase Mather's *An Essay for Recording of Illustrious Providences* revived interest in witches and their evil craft. His son, Cotton Mather, produced a case study entitled *The Wonders of the Invisible World,* which described a young girl possessed by the devil. The ministers, oppressed by many afflictions, did not hesitate to add to their list of injuries the prevalence of witches. The mind of the Puritan had always been susceptible to a vivid portrait of hell, and whole generations of Puritan children had been brought up on Michael Wigglesworth's fire-and-brimstone poem, *The Day of Doom.* They had learned that the growing indifference to the ways of heaven was Satan's method of luring the unsuspecting to eternal damnation. His agents were those who doubted or scorned the pre-eminent authority of the minister.

Cotton Mather added to the turmoil resulting from the Salem revelations by taking suspected witches into his home for examination. He released his findings to the public domain by publishing *Memorable Providences Relating to Witchcrafts and Possessions.* That a witch hunt erupted is hardly surprising. It reached its climax at Salem, Massachusetts, where two young girls charged that they had been bewitched. Before long, eccentrics, aged women, avowed doubters, and innocents who just happened to strike the fancy of a beset imagination crowded local jails. The Mathers led the clergy in demanding swift trials with uncompromising justice. The attacks struck into the homes of high and low alike; respected widows, merchants, and ministers were accused, and even the governor's wife was suspected. After twenty victims had been executed, most by hanging but one by being pressed to death, a reaction set in as the comprehensive scope of the charges caused community leaders to doubt their validity. The Salem proceedings had taken on the trappings of a ministerial inquisition, and suspicions grew that the accusations stemmed mainly from an ecclesiastical desire to arrest the expanding secularism in New England. With the subsequent withdrawal of support by community leaders, the Salem trials abruptly came to an end. The special judge, Samuel Sewall, was afterward to confess his error and express regret for his part in the Salem disturbances. More than one merchant bluntly questioned the responsibility and intelligence of his minister in the matter. The influence of the parsons in New England had entered into a decline that would not end until they agreed that their function was to minister to man's spiritual wants, and not to govern his society.

New England Education. To make Puritanism feasible required a literate congregation; otherwise the detailed individual study of the Bible, required by church doctrine, would not be possible. Of equal importance was the maintenance of an educated ministry, well-versed in the nuances of theology. As early as 1642, and again in 1647, Massachusetts passed school laws that implied the principle of an elementary education for all, and made local authority responsible for supplying education. Connecticut and the other New England colonies followed Massachusetts' lead, but the principle of universal education was imperfectly administered. What elementary education was given emphasized the "three R's" and the basic tenets of religion. Secondary education emphasized the classics. "Dreading to leave an illiterate ministry to the Churches," the Puritans established Harvard College in 1636. For almost forty years, New England educators performed their prescribed function; but the decline in religious fervor brought the educational system to a crisis, which the Synod of 1674 assigned to "the proneness of most men to seek their own ends rather than Christ's."

In 1699, a number of influential Bostonians founded the Brattle Street Church. They supported the half-way covenant, rejected public confession as a prerequisite for church membership, and granted noncommunicants a share in the church government. When the liberal element of this group gained control of Harvard with the election of John Leverett to the college presidency, the conservatives set up Yale (1701) to guarantee the continuation of a conservative clergy. As the Congregational Church divided into liberal and conservative wings, each group struggled to secure its own survival, and New England's educational system expanded.

The Yankee Genius. Dwelling in a harsh land, from which he was unable to draw a suitable existence, the New Englander had revealed considerable adaptability and ingenuity. He had turned to trade, commerce, manufacturing, and fishing, revealing a business sense that enabled him to compete successfully with Britain. His thrift and craftsmanship became legendary. His religion had given him a self-confidence that made it difficult for him to bow to a higher authority, and though he granted the need for authority, he assumed that authority was bound by law, and that if it were to step beyond the bounds of legality the governed were released from their obligation to obey. Stubborn, self-righteous, and self-reliant, the New Englander had developed a vigorous theory of personal liberty which boded ill for any authority which attempted to infringe upon his rights as he saw them.

THE WILDERNESS

Within a short distance of each colonial settlement lay a tract of unexplored wilderness. For many Americans these areas of rugged, uninhabited forest were an irresistible attraction. Tempted by the potential wealth and fertility of these lands, seeing in them a haven from religious, social, and political persecutions, many colonials began to migrate into the frontier regions, there repeating the process that the very first settlers had gone through; hewing out homesites and helping them to flourish into established, successful communities. The pace of westward movement was slow, new settlements rarely growing up more than two hundred miles inland from the sea. Large areas along the coast itself remained untouched by the frontiersman, who, in his migration, followed the geographical line of least resistance, and moved into the interior along the valleys, north and south, that paralleled the Appalachian Mountains.

The migration into the interior created constant reorganizations and dislocations of colonial government as the citizens of the newer settlements demanded political representation. But though the steady movement of his adventurous neighbor may have been an annoyance to the urban New Englander, the colonies as a whole were to reap many benefits from this broadening of geographical boundaries.

The Back Parts. By the time of the Revolution, settlement had extended to the foothills of the Great Smoky Mountains of the Carolinas, the Alleghenies of central Pennsylvania, and the Berkshires of western Massachusetts. Where only Indians and deer had dwelt in 1730, well over a half million people had settled by 1775. The population—especially in the South and Middle frontier—was polyglot in composition, immigrant Germans from the Palatinate and Scots-Irish comprising the largest ethnic groups. The Germans showed themselves to be unusually proficient agriculturalists, but the Scots-Irish of Pennsylvania proved to be a contentious population that seemed bent upon disturbing the peace. They seemed to believe that "unless we bang the Indians stoutly, and make them fear us, they will never love us, nor keep the peace long with us." The Proclamation Line of 1763 was designed, in part, to put an end to these depredations.

There is a tendency to assume that the frontier provided a natural leveler, one which brought into being an equalitarian society. Though one of the natural consequences of the frontier environment was the lowering of social and civic standards, and though established authority tended to become more tenuous as one moved into the more newly settled regions, the new settlers retained the sharp class distinctions characteristic of older settlements, and eagerly sought to emulate the patterns of success they had known previously. For those who had recently arrived from Europe, there was a repetition of the agricultural and social habits that had been characteristic of their homelands. If anything, the frontier tended not to emancipate men from older traditions, but rather to accentuate these older traits.

THE GREAT AWAKENING OF THE WESTERN WORLD

The decline of Puritan belief in the last decades of the seventeenth century reflected the general tapering-off of militant Protestantism throughout the western world. The religious wars of the sixteenth century had terminated in a series of compromises.

The Effect in France. In France, Henry IV had issued the Edict of Nantes (1598), according French Protestants equality with Catholics and allowing them to maintain one hundred fortified towns garrisoned by Protestants under Protestant leadership. In 1685, Louis XIV, intent upon consolidating monarchical power, had revoked the Edict.

The Effect in Germany. From 1555, following the Peace of Augsburg, the government of each German state had been allowed to prescribe the religion of its subjects. The continued gains of the Lutherans and the growth of Calvinism, however, culminated in a savage German civil war, the Thirty Years' War (1618–48). Before it had ended, most of the major powers of Europe had entered the dispute, and the Germans, victims of both religious intolerance and foreign occupation, wanted only peace. At the Peace of Westphalia (1648) the principle of *cuius regio eius religio* (the religion of the ruler is that of the ruled) was reaffirmed, settling the boundary lines of Protestant and Catholic control. With as much as a third of its population decimated, Germany had not only ceased to be a major factor in European power politics, but also a major source of emigrants to the New World.

The Effect in England. In the aftermath of the Puritan Revolution, Britain witnessed a precipitous decline in religious sentiment. Parliament passed the Toleration Act of 1689, which allowed Protestant Dissenters religious freedom, but excluded them from public life. The latter restriction was neatly circumvented by Dissenters accepting nominal membership in the Anglican Church.

The New Religious Sects. Beginning in the last decade of the seventeenth century, numerous evangelical sects sprang up in western Germany. Emphasizing a literal adherence to the teachings of the Bible, these sects hoped to obtain toleration from political authority. They professed indifference to political matters, leaving it to God to judge temporal rulers. The revocation of the Edict of Nantes left the French Huguenots a choice between conversion to Catholicism or flight, and many chose the latter. In Britain, John Wesley launched his Methodist Episcopal movement, which was designed to revitalize the Anglican Church. Thus, between 1690 and 1730, Europe was swept by a series of religious movements, all of which promised to revitalize Protestant Christianity. America, the western frontier of Europe, did not remain immune to the religious turmoil that enveloped Europe.

The Fragmentation of New England Congregationalism. The half-way covenant had been but one of the modifications of original Puritan doctrine. Another major change, innovated by Solomon Stoddard of Northampton, extended the covenant to anyone who would accept it. In five "harvests"—1679, 1683, 1696, 1712, and 1718—he led into the church and to the Lord's Supper anyone willing to follow. The orthodox ministers, led by the Mathers, expressed horror at the democratization of the covenant, but Stoddard's successful method of bringing new members into the fold was soon imitated throughout the frontier areas of New England. A schism divided the Puritan establishment as some congregations disputed the legitimacy of Stoddard's practice.

As has been noted, the intensity of the disputes racking Puritanism had manifested itself in the founding of Yale when the growing sectarianism and liberalism of Harvard had so disturbed the orthodox that they felt it imperative to erect their own college at New Haven. Since the bulk of higher education, and most secondary education, was church oriented, sectarian disputes over education were bound to arise. Beyond New England, religion had lost its deepest significance; men belonged to a church in response to social custom rather than because of the needs of their souls. Religion had become largely preoccupied with the form, rather than the substance, of belief.

George Whitefield and the New Faith. It was not until 1739, with the arrival in America of George Whitefield, a passionate English evangelist and friend of Wesley, that America was fully exposed to the Great Awakening. Whitefield's revivalist sermons received a friendly reception throughout the colonies, his sermons drawing an audience of thirty thousand on Boston Common. Spectators stood rapt in fields, towns, and groves as the English evangelist poured out emotional tirades that made "hell so vivid that one could locate it on an atlas." Men were ready for an overwhelming emotional experience that permitted them to fall into trances, during which they beheld heaven and hell. At church services the people wailed, rolled on the ground, and bellowed jubilant hymns. The minister no longer simply led; he exhorted his flock to salvation. Even staid Calvinist doctrine succumbed to the new spirit.

Jonathan Edwards' Efforts to Revitalize Puritanism. Jonathan Edwards, the grandson of Solomon Stoddard and the inheritor of his pulpit at Northampton, brought to it (along with his own intense religious fervor) a vision of an omnipotent God who had predestined man to an eternal fate, a fate justifiable by the concept of original sin. Edwards sensed the feelings behind the American predilection for revivalism, and between 1733 and 1735, he led a series of revival meetings at Northampton which emphasized the awesome and fierce majesty of the Calvinist God. The response of his parishioners was intense, suggesting that the isolation of their daily lives led to a craving for participation in social events. The revival meeting, with its emotional crisis and cathartic soul-purging, provided not only social activity but social approval, a sensation extremely valuable to people who had been stifled by the loneliness of life on the frontier.

In a curious way, Edwards democratized salvation. He rejected the idea that good works, reputation, or individual effort could assure salvation. He insisted instead that an omnipotent and inscrutable God alone knew the fate of each man. He confronted his congregation with the thought that whether their earthly estate were high or low, in the hands of God all men were equal. Edwards viewed it as his duty to lead men to accept a freely given salvation, and to denounce with savagery all that diverted his congregation from contemplation of Divine Will. Though most of his sermons dealt with God's mercy, the most memorable ones were those that dealt with the horrors of eternal damnation. Unless God's wrath were placated, he threatened his congregation, "your bodies, which shall have been burning and roasting all this while in these glowing flames, yet shall not have been consumed . . . will remain to roast through an eternity yet, which will not have been at all shortened by what shall have been past." In his most famous sermon, *Sinners in the Hands of an Angry God,* he achieved an apogee of pure terror. God's anger was made acute by the decline of true belief, by a crass preoccupation with wealth, and by the deterioration of traditional authority. Edwards bluntly accused the rich and powerful "River Gods"—the epithet applied to wealthy Connecticut Valley merchants—of a mean concern with private interest; they were, he charged, ready "to defile their hands to gain a few pounds, . . . to hip and bite others, grind the faces of the poor, . . . [and] take advantage of their authority or commission to line their own pockets with what is fraudulently taken or withheld from others." The struggle between minister and merchant had finally burst into the open.

Where once Puritanism had gloried in being a silent democracy served by a speaking aristocracy, Edwards ordered the democracy to be silent no more. In so doing, he unknowingly shattered the traditional power arrangement within Congregationalism; by calling upon the congregation to speak its mind, he made the minister its spokesman, but also its servant. Both Harvard and Yale renounced him; the commercial masters of the Connecticut Valley drove him from the Northampton pulpit. He retired to preach to the Indians. In 1754 he was called to the presidency of Princeton, but he died before he could be installed in office.

The Evangelical Sects. The enormous appeal of the Great Awakening was most noticeable in frontier communities. By rejecting the dry, dusty, theological hair-splitting of the past, the Great Awakening offered the frontiersman an emotionally satisfying religious experience. It established the individual's interpretation of the Bible as the ultimate religious authority. By depicting God as a power governed by love and compassion, it made the harsh realities of frontier life more bearable, for it seemed to promise eternal bliss after the brief interlude of earthly pain. Beginning in the 1720s, the Dutch Reformed Church, under the guidance of Theodore Frelinghuysen, had modified its Calvinist theology. Frelinghuysen had urged that an itinerant clergy, trained at "log-cabin colleges," and versed in emotional preaching, be established to bring the message of God to the hinterlands. A similar effort was made in Presbyterianism by William Tennent and his sons. And in the wake of George Whitefield, the first influx of members into the Methodist and Baptist sects began.

The Effects of the Great Awakening. The Great Awakening divided American Protestantism into conservative and liberal factions. Those who clung to orthodoxy were known as "Old Lights," while those who agitated for a universal priesthood of believers were known as "New Lights." Congregationalism split among those who followed and those who opposed Edwards. In other sects, particularly the Presbyterian, schisms occurred as factions agitated for more evangelical preachments. In addition, throughout the colonies there was an upsurge of church membership and a shift of church members. The greatest beneficiary was the Baptist sect, whose democratic organization and emotional doctrines proved congenial to revivalism, while the Anglican and Congregational professions decreased in influence.

The lay element assumed greater authority in the management of church affairs, and the trained ministry was joined by a rough-hewn, self-trained clergy versed in the words of the Bible but ignorant of the nuances of theology. Everywhere the effect was to undermine the long-established churches. The decline in religious authority coincided with a new questioning of all forms of political authority. A leveling mood gripped the colonies as men began to consider that the logical complements of religious liberty were political and economic liberties. Increasingly, protests against social injustices (such as slavery and the maltreatment of orphans) stirred moral consciences. Since the Great Awakening was an intercolonial experience, it was another force acting to reduce provincialism. Numerous colleges were founded to provide the various sects with a trained ministry: Brown (Baptist—1764), Dartmouth (Congregational—1769), Princeton (Presbyterian—1746), and Rutgers (Dutch Reformed—1766). Everywhere Americans felt a quickening sense of their own dignity as they worked out their destiny on the new frontier. Slowly, on the edge of a wilderness, they forged a nationality which was new and vital, yet which retained its larger identity as part of western European culture.

Chapter 4

The Mercantilist Tradition

By the seventeenth century the economic philosophy now known as mercantilism had gained considerable prestige and support in England. Simple emphasis upon bullionism no longer seemed reasonable as an economic way of life. The mercantilists' definition of wealth, which had originally encompassed only gold and silver, now was extended to include all commercial activity. This extension explains the mercantilist view of empire building: each colony's function was to provide the mother country with raw materials, and each was to serve as a market where manufactured products would be consumed. "Our . . . plantations . . . in New England, Virginia, Greenland, the Summer Islands and the Newfoundland," noted the great mercantilist theoretician Thomas Mun (1571–1641), "afford . . . much wealth and employments to maintain a great number of poor, and to increase our decaying trade." The English Parliament actively legislated to protect that trade.

THE BRITISH ACTS OF TRADE
AFFECTING THE COLONIES

Parliament had originally placed strict limits upon the conduct of colonial trade when chartering the joint-stock companies designated to establish colonies, but it had neglected comprehensive trade regulations until 1651. The Navigation Acts of 1650 and 1651 compelled the colonists to trade only with England. But the acts carried a reciprocal advantage: though the English received a closed market in the colonies, the colonials were guaranteed a market in England.

The Navigation Act of 1651. The Navigation Act of 1651 was preceded by the appointment of a parliamentary commission. Its purpose was to discover more satisfactory ways of regulating the colonial trade so as to free the English nation from external dependence. In 1650 Parliament had made an effort to exclude foreign vessels from participating in the colonial trade. (This effort at regulating the carrying trade was not an innovation on the part of Parliament, but was already part of an established tradition; such legislation had been passed as early as the reign of Richard II.)

The Act of 1651 aimed to define the role of English shipping in the conduct of both the import and export trade. It was also candidly admitted that the Act was intended to increase and encourage the national shipping. The law allowed only English and colonial ships to conduct the national trade, the sole exception being in the case of transportation of imported goods; these could be transported by the producer. A serious defect in the act—a defect which was to be present in navigation acts for more than a century—was the absence of provision for an effective regulatory agency. Since nothing existed to prevent trading with alien ships, the natural tendency to evade the intent of the acts led to extensive smuggling. The Act also provoked a war with the Dutch in 1652, since the ambitious Lowlanders did not intend to surrender peacefully their right of participation in the colonial trade.

War did not deter the English merchants from proposing further extensions of the navigation regulations. As early as 1656 the London merchants seriously considered whether a more extensive regulation of trade was not in order. Charles II, restored to the throne in 1660, did not reverse the mercantilist policies established during Cromwell's Commonwealth. In fact, the Stuart family's extensive investments in the fur and slave trades added court influence to the increasingly strong demands of English merchants for an extension of trade regulation.

The Enumerated Commodities Act of 1660. The Act of 1651, along with all other acts passed during the Commonwealth, was declared invalid by Charles II. Almost immediately, a parliamentary committee chaired by George Downing prepared replacement legislation. The resulting Navigation Act of 1660 paralleled the intent of its 1651 predecessor in regulating the carrying trade. However, it added an enumerated list of articles including sugar, cotton, tobacco, wool, and indigo, which could be consumed only within the empire. It was hoped that this would increase the self-sufficiency of the empire by reducing England's dependence on foreign resources. In 1662 an Act of Frauds, passed to clarify some obscure points in the 1660 Act, permitted English-owned, foreign-built ships to participate in the carrying trade, and also provided for participation in English trade by colonial shipping.

The Staple Act of 1663. The logic of mercantilism led to increasingly rigid regulation of colonial trade. The 1660 Navigation Act secured for the English merchant a monopoly in the articles listed, and each monopoly fostered another. Soon, the remaining right of the colonials to import directly from countries other than Britain, and their right to export non-enumerated articles to countries outside the empire stirred another protest among English merchants. As a result, the Staple Act of 1663 was passed. This act required that all goods destined for the colonies be shipped through English ports. Those who benefited most from this act were the English middlemen. Though the English duty on colonial imports was rebated, thereby enabling the colonial consumer to purchase goods more cheaply than could his English cousins, fees charged for processing imports added considerably to the colonial cost of these items. Though the enumerated clause gave the colonies a guaranteed market in England, it compelled them to make heavy payments to English agents. Finally, by requiring the colonials to use English ships, the law deprived them of the advantages offered by the lower rates of the Dutch shipping companies.

The Plantation Duty Act of 1673. It is hardly surprising that many colonials interested in obtaining the superior profits of the European market were determined to circumvent the restrictions imposed by the various trade regulations. Since enumerated articles were permitted free transit between colonies, planters eager to avoid English charges often shipped tobacco to another colony, from which it was then shipped—labeled as something else—to a foreign port. This trade grew so large that Parliament passed the Plantation Duty Act of 1673, which for the first time imposed duties on any ship transporting enumerated articles between colonial ports.

English Administrative Reform. In spite of continued passage of legislation, however, it became evident that the colonials would do all in their power to circumvent the navigation acts by whatever subterfuges they could think of. It was apparent that extending the prohibitive Navigation Acts would be of little use unless methods were developed to enforce the legislation. Restrictions, to be made effective, required administrative reforms. To achieve this goal Parliament provided both regulations and penalties. Governors who failed to enforce the Navigation Acts were subject to heavy fines and removal from office. Beginning in 1660, a Committee for Foreign Plantations consisting of merchants and nobles, and authorized by the Privy Council, began to explore the governments and administrative practices of the colonies. Its purpose was to bring about better supervision and a more effective response to colonial needs. Further efforts to improve the system came in 1668, when a Council of Trade and four Privy Council committees—Foreign Affairs, Trade and Plantations, Petitions and Grievances, and Military Affairs—were appointed. Though superior to previous regulations, this system was rendered unwieldy by overlapping authority and by its only subsidiary concern with colonial affairs. The Act of 1673, however, gave the Privy Council sole responsibility for supervising colonial affairs.

The Lords of Trade. The Lords of Trade were appointed in 1675, in an attempt to overcome the lack of a central colonial administration. This regulatory group had as its purpose the channeling of information on the colonies to the Privy Council. Though the intent of the group was honorable, the twenty-four Lords of Trade were often burdened with other duties, and colonial affairs were still only a subsidiary concern. Enforcement of the navigation acts was uneven, especially as the high degree of freedom accorded the early colonies in their original charters made them nearly independent of the Crown. These colonies strenuously opposed any effort to enforce the Navigation Acts. When Edward Randolph investigated trade conditions in the colonies in 1676, he found flagrant violations of the acts on every hand, and courts unwilling to convict. This stirred a determination on the part of the British government to extend effective regulation and a uniform system of administration by the Crown.

The Growth of Colonial Markets. The growing interest of English merchants in the colonies was stimulated by the expanding profits to be obtained from the colonial trade. Though it might be thought that the English were engaged in a ruthless exploitation of their colonies, it must be remembered that mercantilism emphasized the importance of colonies as markets for manufactured goods. Obviously, colonial prosperity insured colonial purchases. Therefore, the Navigation Acts gave the colonies a secure monopoly of the English market through the enumerating articles. Certain strategic materials, particularly naval stores, received parliamentary bounties. As trade expanded, the importance of the colonies increased. Between 1660 and 1700, the value of the colonial trade increased from £600,000 to more than £1,175,000. The encouragement to colonial shipbuilding resulted in the near doubling of the English merchant marine. Finally, the protection of the royal Navy relieved the colonists from the heavy burden of self-defense. The primary intention of mercantilism was reciprocal advantage, and it generally achieved this objective. Though the revolutionists of 1776 emphasized the disadvantages of their trade relations with England, they were to express considerable dismay when, after the Revolution, these privileges were revoked.

THE COLONIAL ECONOMIES

The most direct effect of mercantilism on the colonies was to encourage them to concentrate on the production of crops that were profitable in world trade. This concentration, in turn, tended to make the individual colonies very susceptible to the vagaries of demand for their particular staple. Before long, the economy of many individual colonies became almost entirely dependent upon the production of a single product.

The Tobacco Economy. In Virginia and Maryland the fertile lands of the tidewater regions, and even the piedmont area, could produce an abundant crop of almost anything planted. Grain (especially wheat), fruit, and truck items flourished, and some of these items found their way into world trade. But it was tobacco that dominated the economic activity of the region. Tobacco, like corn, was an American plant already extensively used by the Indians before the colonists arrived. Sailors and colonials introduced it into Europe, where smoking soon became the almost-unanimous fashion. James I initially expressed only verbal opposition to the use of "the weed," but as its use became more prevalent, he placed an excise tax of a shilling per pound on it. The angered Virginians reluctantly accepted the tax, but when James limited the import of tobacco in 1620 to 55,000 pounds per year, they protested loudly. The Dutch promptly agreed to take the whole crop. The Privy Council met this threat in 1621 by issuing the Tobacco Contract, which gave a monopoly of the English tobacco market to the growers, and which also assured them that the English would buy all tobacco produced.

The tobacco farmers, influenced by the promise of large profits from their product as well as by the belief that their entire production, no matter how greatly expanded, would immediately be absorbed in the English market, increased tobacco production from 20,000 pounds in 1619 to nearly 25,000,000 pounds in 1664. Staple farming, however, tended to force concentration on a single crop. As an inevitable result, staple farmers became dependent on outside agents not only for finished products but also for foodstuffs. The tidewater dependence upon other colonies for food helped to create the economic ties which ultimately provided intimate links among the thirteen colonies. It also brought about a complex system of credit which pushed the tidewater colonists increasingly into debt to English merchants.

As the colony expanded, the need for a cash crop made tobacco king not only in the tidewater region but also in the piedmont region. But the devastating result of continued tobacco culture was inescapable: tobacco exhausted the soil of its fertility. Had the farmer rotated his crops or fertilized his soil he could have prevented this waste. But the farmer had what he considered a simpler alternative: whenever his land ceased to produce tobacco, he moved to a new tract. As a result, the center of population in Virginia moved steadily westward. And as the tobacco farmer pushed on in his ruthless search for productive soil, the once-fertile lands of the tidewater area were left exhausted, neglected, and fallow.

Rice and Indigo. The two great staple crops of South Carolina and Georgia, rice and indigo, formed the base of a complex economic system which enabled Carolinians and Georgians to earn large profits through agriculture. Each of these staples was consumed in large quantities by the cosmopolitan markets of Europe and the West Indies.

Rice, which grew abundantly in the swampy lands that bordered the ocean and tidal inlets, was marketed for consumption in the Mediterranean basin (where it was a fundamental foodstuff) and in the West Indies (where it was used to feed slaves). Provided with a magnificent harbor at Charleston through which to export the grain, the Carolinians had a further advantage in the sheltered waterways which connected the rice-producing sea-island formations and the well-watered coastal lands where rice was also grown. An ever-increasing harvest soon flowed toward foreign ports. Indigo, a source of blue dye, was grown on the higher ground of the Carolina tidewater area and provided a profitable complement to rice culture. Since indigo did not require winter care, slaves could spend that season working in the rice fields and maintaining the plantations. A further stimulation of the Carolinian economy was provided when Parliament, in 1748, offered a bounty for indigo.

The Carolina colony flourished between 1734 and 1776 as the value of Carolina produce increased more than fivefold. Between 1740 and 1776 rice exports trebled and indigo exports quadrupled. After only three or four indigo crops, a planter would have earned enough to recoup his original investment in land and slaves, so that unlike the other colonies, Carolina had surplus capital to lend at interest. Its agriculture also required large-scale farming, unlike the relatively small tobacco farms in Virginia. Though the average plantation had between 300 and 500 acres and was tended by an average of only twelve slaves, some baronial holdings did exist. Governor James Wright owned 19,000 acres which were distributed among eleven plantations and farmed by more than 500 slaves. Often, vast acreages, still covered with forest, were owned by a few wealthy planters.

In spite of her prosperity, however, Carolina was, in many ways, a disorganized and neglected community. As in Virginia, there was a sharp contrast between the desolate, exhausted tobacco farms and the luxuriant, productive plantations located on more newly settled land. A nomadic quality colored much of the colony's life, for few settlers were willing to improve land that could so easily be abandoned and replaced once it had ceased to produce easily. Moreover, the diseases that broke out continually in the Carolina swamplands discouraged most whites from actually settling these areas—although the swamplands were highly productive, and an important part of the Carolina economy. It was not unusual for a few hired white overseers to manage large slave gangs in the swamplands, while the plantation owner and his family maintained their home in the comparative ease and luxury of Charleston.

Charleston. The city of Charleston alone was enough to differentiate South Carolina sharply from Virginia. This urban hub, unique in the pre-Revolutionary South, grew rapidly to a population of nearly 7,000 in 1740, and by 1776 it had expanded to 12,000. It provided extensive commercial facilities for the expanding rice and indigo plantations, the tidewater streams permitting swift transit to the great wharves of the town, where agents of English mercantile establishments purchased the produce and prepared it for shipment. Emporiums which stocked food, clothing, furniture, and hardware provided opportunity for planters to obtain supplies for their own use and that of their slaves. Trade with the Indians brought large quantities of deerskin and other furs into the town. Even a cursory examination indicated to the visitor that Charleston served a flourishing agriculture. Its self-preoccupation, however, gave it the dangerous conviction that it swayed the course of world commerce. In its own way, Carolina shared the insularity of Virginia; it saw that the world beat a path to its door, and concluded that the world needed it more than it needed the world. Such insularity was destined to become the source of bitter problems.

Agriculture in the Middle Colonies. Unlike their Southern neighbors, the middle colonies were never wedded to a single crop. As a result they prospered as food producers for the staple crop culture of the Southern colonies and for the commercial world of New England. By concentrating upon grains and livestock, the average farmer in the Middle Atlantic region grew a marketable surplus and at the same time created a nearly self-sufficient existence for himself. Travelers crossing New Jersey in the eighteenth century invariably commented on the "gardenlike" atmosphere. The "Pennsylvania Dutch," who were remarkable farmers, made the region around Lancaster green and flourishing with agricultural produce. The heavy concentration on wheat as a money crop led many to describe the middle colonies as the "colonial breadbasket."

A Diversified Agriculture. The abundance of the region's agriculture was indicated by the value of its produce. In 1766 the value of exported wheat products exceeded £770,000, while that of such nonperishables as peas, oats, corn, and beans totaled £52,000. A lively trade in horses with the West Indies brought £37,000 between 1763–66, and meat products earned £81,000 in 1766 alone. With new developments in husbandry, constant improvements in livestock were made. And unlike the South, the middle colonies did not rapidly exhaust the fertility of the soil, but used primitive techniques of crop rotation. The grain and consumer product agriculture characteristic of the middle region soon made it the archetype of the agriculture that would eventually dominate the great river valleys of the Middle West.

Furs. Agriculture occupied only a portion of the economic endeavor in the middle colonies. From the time they were first settled, the fur trade boomed; indeed, original Dutch settlers seemed concerned almost exclusively with obtaining pelts. During the middle of the seventeenth century more than 40,000 pelts a year were sent to England from New York alone. By the end of the century the fur trade in New York had declined to barely 15,000 pelts a year, but in Pennsylvania it expanded as trappers penetrated deeper into the hidden valleys of the Alleghenies. The fur trade remained a major economic factor although it declined during each decade of the seventeenth century.

Textiles. At the very beginning of the century a vigorous textile industry began to develop. As early as 1708, seventy-five per cent of the woolens and linens consumed in New York were home-produced, and nearly every farmstead in New England produced woven goods for sale. The incentive for this development may be traced to the high cost of transporting British-made goods to the New World. Although it cost twenty per cent more to produce linens in the colonies, and fifty per cent more to produce woolens, colonial products were still cheaper than English imports.

The Hat Industry. A rapidly expanding hat industry in New York, Rhode Island, and Pennsylvania gave the English manufacturers such sharp competition that Parliament passed the Hat Act of 1732, which restricted the sale of beaver hats to the colony in which they were produced. But the lack of adequate enforcement agencies made the law ineffective. The colonial hatters also produced cheap hats for backwoodsmen and slaves.

Minerals and Related Industries. In addition to providing the necessary lumber, turpentine, tar, and pitch required by the naval interests, colonial forests supported other important industries, such as the production of charcoal. The destruction of the English forests made it imperative that charcoal be obtained from the colonies for the maintenance of England's iron industry.

Potash, made by boiling the ashes of burned hardwood trees, was another by-product of the forests. It was an essential product for the bleaching processes then used in the woolen industry. To encourage potash production, the English government placed it on the enumerated list in 1764 and paid bounties for it despite the fact that New York alone was producing 7,000 barrels per year by 1763.

The discovery of iron deposits in the hills of northern New Jersey and eastern Pennsylvania fostered the development of numerous forges and furnaces in the two colonies. By 1750 a growing colonial iron industry threatened British home industry with severe competition; and by 1775, the exploitation of colonial mineral resources had enabled the colonies to produce one-seventh of the world's iron supply, and to make more pig and bar iron from this than Great Britain herself produced. Products as diverse as Franklin stoves, pots, hardware, and peg nails flowed from the forges of the middle colonies.

While small quantities of coal, copper, and lead were also mined, the bulk of this wealth waited upon later exploitation. A small glass industry grew up in Pennsylvania and New Jersey. Tile and pottery were manufactured in New York and Pennsylvania.

With each year it became clearer that the middle colonies would eventually possess a considerable industrial plant. But each new industry placed a strain upon the mercantilist tradition, which demanded that the colonies supply raw materials, not competitive manufactured products, to the mother country.

New England Agriculture. The farmer who expected to make a prosperous living from the New England soil lived in a world of stony discouragement. Only small, isolated sections of New England—the Connecticut Valley, for instance—possessed arable land. Even there black stem rust played havoc with efforts to grow wheat. Only Indian maize grew successfully in the sparse soil of the New England colonies; but since maize required a minimum of attention, the farmer could devote his time to other enterprises. The hardy corn ear gave the New Englanders their basic cereal for both man and beast. Converted into hasty pudding, corn pone, and hominy grits, it provided hearty, though plain fare; and, as an additional advantage, it could be converted into corn liquor as well.

Consumer Agriculture. As urban centers expanded in the eighteenth century extensive truck farms developed to supply the town dwellers with vegetables. Beans, peas, squash, turnips, and pumpkins were grown in large quantities. Large orchards—especially apple orchards—were planted, and the fruit was kept for winter consumption. Cherries, plums, pears, quinces, and berries were also grown in huge quantities. Large-scale use of maple sugar and wild honey gave the New Englanders an adequate substitute for cane sugar, which was prohibitively expensive. Dairy herds supplied milk, cheese, and butter; sheep supplied wool for homespun. Each New England farm had a herd of livestock and a flock of fowl. Life for the New England farmer proved rudely comfortable; the land did not give him great wealth but it did provide him with a stable, adequate living.

Fishing. Because opportunities in farming were limited, "Go down to the sea" was the injunction received by more than one Yankee lad, and one which had ample precedent. For decades before the first settlements in New England, English, French, Dutch, and Portuguese fishermen farmed the waters south of Newfoundland. At the beginning of the seventeenth century 10,000 men and youths manned 200 fishing craft from England in the Grand Banks. Boston had an extensive export of fish as early as 1633, and in 1641 Governor Winthrop recorded the export of 300,000 dried fish. By 1700, at least 4,000 men and 600 ships from New England were engaged in fishing, and during the eighteenth century the industry continued to expand steadily.

Whaling. In 1715, Christopher Hussey of Nantucket began the first colonial hunt for the sperm whale, creating an industry which reached its zenith only in the nineteenth century. By processing their giant catch aboard ship, the whaling captains were able to extend their voyages into the South Atlantic, Pacific, and even Arctic Oceans. Whaling quickly became a thriving and most profitable business: whale oil was a vital ingredient for candle-making and lamp oil, buttons were processed from whale bone, and ambergris was used in the perfume industry. Colonial assemblies, from 1732 on, began to offer bounties of twenty shillings apiece for the construction of two-hundred-ton whalers, and in 1747 they began to double the bounty. Immediately prior to the Revolution, 4,000 men were involved in the trade. Three hundred ships sailed from such centers of the industry as Nantucket, New Bedford, Marblehead, and Provincetown.

Shipbuilding. To keep the men on the seas required ships; and this led, inevitably, to the growth of a shipbuilding industry. In addition, the English government's interest in naval stores stimulated a sizable increase in lumbering. The virgin forests of the Northeast provided white pine which was particularly useful for the making of ship masts. In the pine forests of the coastal plains tar, pitch, and turpentine were processed to meet the large demands of both seaman and settler. The rapid expansion of shipbuilding in both the middle and New England colonies heightened the demand for naval stores produced in these sections.

The industry grew with remarkable rapidity. Massachusetts Bay launched its first craft, the *Blessing of the Bay,* in 1631, and received encouragement for further shipbuilding from the Navigation Acts of 1651, 1660, and 1663, all of which contained provisions favorable to the industry. By 1676, Massachusetts alone had a fleet of seven hundred vessels ranging from six tons to two hundred and fifty tons. The colonial need for new fishing craft and coastal trade vessels was soon matched by a heavy English demand, since the extensive American forests and the growing American production of naval stores made it possible for colonial shipbuilders to construct ships at two-thirds to one-half the cost of constructing them in England. Between 1763 and 1766 New England sold seventy ships, worth a total of £49,000, to English purchasers. At the outbreak of the Revolution a third of the ships flying the British flag had been built in the colonies, while New England possessed a fleet, independent of fishing craft, of 2,000 colonial-built ships.

Lumbering. With the growth of shipbuilding, the lumber industry of New England boomed. In 1729, white pine trees with a two-foot diameter were placed at the disposal of the Royal Navy's use unless found on private property acquired before October 1692. Only white pine trees smaller than these could be cut on private property. Forest keepers were appointed to select tall pines for use as Royal Navy masts. Once the keepers had designated their selection of a tree by marking it with a broad arrow, anyone who cut it down risked a £100 fine. These officials, usually colonials, became the core of an influential patronage service loyal to the Crown. When the Swedish Tar Company achieved a near-monopoly on European sources of tar, pitch, resin, and turpentine, England began to be threatened with a shortage of naval supplies. Fearful of becoming militarily dependent upon a foreign country, Parliament in 1705 placed colonial naval stores on the enumerated list. To encourage production they offered large bounties: £4 a ton for pitch and tar; £1 for masts, bowsprits, and yardarms; £3 a ton for resin and turpentine; and £6 a ton for hemp. Though the bounties fluctuated in value and there were some brief lapses in payment, they were paid until 1774. From this source some £1,438,702 were pumped into the colonial economy.

The Triangular Trade. As the commercial fleets of New England expanded, a complex trade relationship developed. This was known as the Triangular Trade. West Indian molasses, obtained in exchange for New England dried fish, foodstuffs, and livestock, was brought to New England and converted into rum. The rum was shipped to Africa where it was traded for slaves. The slaves, in turn, were transported to the West Indies or Southern colonial plantations to be sold for molasses or Southern staples. Though Parliament tried to regulate this trade by passing the Molasses Act in 1733, colonial merchants refused to be limited by the heavy duty imposed on foreign sugar and molasses. A vast smuggling trade developed between New England and the French and Spanish Caribbean possessions. In their search for profit, New Englanders showed a thorough contempt for parliamentary decrees, especially those lacking effective enforcement agencies.

Another triangular trade developed in the north Atlantic. The foodstuffs, livestock, and lumber of the northern colonies were used to obtain sugar, molasses, and fruit in the West Indies. These tropical products were then carried to England where they were traded for manufactured goods. Trade with the Mediterranean region carried foodstuffs, lumber, and fish from New England to Lisbon and other ports where they were traded for wine and fruit. These were also traded in England for manufactured goods.

THE LABOR PROBLEM
THROUGHOUT THE COLONIES

The New England merchant who transported slaves did so in search of profit, but he was responding to a genuine need. "This country is long on land," Captain John Smith wrote in 1609, "and short on men." From the outset, all the colonies suffered from a critical shortage of labor. As a result, the early colonists were threatened with deprivation of food if each man did not work diligently. Ministers preached the virtues of hard and unremitting labor. The laborer in America soon discovered, however, that where demand exceeded supply he could insist upon, and obtain, higher wages. The immense possibilities implicit in the ownership of an independent farm lured the free white laborer away from work on another man's land. Subsequent efforts to enslave the Indian, undertaken in New England and South Carolina particularly, proved fruitless; the noble savage showed a dismaying indifference to labor, promptly deserting and returning to the forests. It became essential for the colonists to arrange for the importation of laborers in the form of indentured servants, redemptioners, convicts, or Negro slaves.

Free Labor. In New England, the labor problem was not acute on the family farms that were so prominent during the early years of settlement. Families were usually large, and each family generally found adequate manpower for its needs within its own circle. Indeed, self-sufficiency in production seemed to be the goal of most Yankee farmers. Moreover, in cases where a single family unit could not cope adequately with its own tasks, the community structure of New England made cooperative group effort possible. It was quite common, for example, for a house or barn to be constructed by an entire community. Group "barn-raisings" of this sort not only solved the labor problem, but also provided the hard-working Yankees with a welcome occasion for socializing, gossiping, and general merrymaking.

Though unskilled laborers for farms were in good supply, however, the expansion of colonial towns brought an ever-increasing demand for skilled workers. Since few European artisans abandoned their well-paying pursuits to emigrate, the few who came to the colonies could and did demand high wages. To protect themselves against such prohibitive demands, most colonists developed a considerable number of skills, the Jack-of-all-trades becoming a familiar American character. But the cost of wages still strained the limited capital resources of the colonies until the various colonial legislatures passed laws which fixed maximum wages. Even with these laws wages remained substantially higher in the colonies than in England. The abundance of well-paying jobs, and the deferential treatment that workers consequently received, did have one fortuitous result. They combined to mitigate the development of class consciousness. When free labor organized, it did so to form benevolent societies which provided sickness and burial funds for their members, or to create closed guilds in such skilled industries as shipbuilding, cooperage, and tailoring. By the eighteenth century, many workers combined farming and a craft. They had achieved a self-reliance incompatible with an aggravated class-consciousness. As one contemporary noted: "Scratch an American worker and you find a freeman."

Indentured Servants. Though the planters, farmers, merchants, and manufacturers enjoyed the skills of the free labor force, they found that free labor's independence and self-sufficiency led to instability and arrogance. They wished to have a servile labor class whose availability and manageability would not be subject to the vagaries of free labor. To create such a servile body of workers, there developed the practice of importing "indentured servants"—men and women who wanted to come to the New World but who were unable to pay the passage cost (£5 to £6). Americans in need of workers would advance the cost of passage to these people—usually members of England's impoverished class, to whom the prospect of life in the colonies was bound to appeal when contrasted with the squalor and degradation of their own meager existence—and they, in exchange, bound themselves into service for a given number of years.

Agents of the planters visited English workers who wished to make the journey. Together they drew up a contract in duplicate on a single sheet of paper which was then cut in half at the indent (from which comes the term describing the contract—"indenture"). The planter agreed to pay the servant's passage, provide the essentials of life, and pay freedom dues at the end of his term of service. In return, the servant agreed to work at the direction of his sponsor for a period of from four to seven years—the younger the servant, the longer the period of indenture. Freedom dues consisted of clothing, tools, a gun, and usually, in the seventeenth century, a small land grant which rarely exceeded fifty acres. A lively trade in indentures developed when agents began to transport workers in exchange for payment in the local staple.

Besides indentured servants, "redemptioners" also arrived. The redemptioner usually came from the Continent and agreed to try to redeem his passage costs from relatives or friends already in America. If he failed, he was sold into indentureship under conditions which were usually substantially heavier than those exacted from indentured servants who contracted their services in Europe.

England provided most of the New World's indentured servants in the seventeenth century. Although no more than 3,500 came in a single year, this number was sufficient to make one of every ten colonials an indentured servant in 1680. Switzerland, Germany, and Ireland added to the stream in the eighteenth century. More than half, and perhaps as many as two-thirds, of all white immigrants during this century were either indentured servants or redemptioners. The use of this kind of labor was not equally distributed; most of it was concentrated in the three colonies of Virginia, Maryland, and Pennsylvania.

Throughout the colonies humane limits were set to the exploitation of indentured servants. The law provided protection for their rights, though some were afflicted by harsh masters. No matter how long the indenture, every servant knew he would in time become his own master; that the skills gained in service might permit him to obtain profitable employment when he was freed; and that indenture carried no lasting stigma.

Prisoners. A less attractive source of indentured labor to the colonial farmers was the English prison population. In 1717 Parliament provided for the transportation to America of certain convicts, designated by the courts, to serve indentures of at least seven years, with hardened criminals bound out for as many as fourteen years. Lesser criminals received shorter terms or were permitted to go free if they purchased their passage to the New World. No one knows how many of these prisoners found their way to the colonies before the Revolution, though the generally accepted figure is 50,000. That they represented a threat—justified or not—to the colonials' peace of mind is obvious from the unsuccessful attempts of several colonies to bar their admission.

Apprentices. In the northern colonies artisans obtained a secure fund of labor by offering to train youths as apprentices. These young men were entered into apprenticeship by their fathers for a period that rarely exceeded four years. The apprentice contract, accompanied by a payment of several pounds, guaranteed that the youth would be properly educated for a trade. As such it kept a steady flow of skilled workers moving into such important occupations as shoemaking, tailoring, carpentering, shipbuilding, and related crafts. At the end of his apprenticeship, the pupil received a payment of clothing and money and entered into a journeymanship. Less fortunate than these youths were the children who were kidnaped for sale into indentureship. How many were so taken is uncertain, although the frequency with which "kids"—the victims of kidnaping—were mentioned in contemporary literature suggests that the number ran into the thousands.

Slaves. The lot of the indentured servant in the colonies had one saving grace: there was a specific terminal date to his labor. The plight of the human being sold into involuntary servitude was considerably more unhappy. The slave was bound to work for his master until death, unless the latter chose to manumit him. Bondage descended from parent to offspring and servitude became an inheritance.

EARLY SLAVE TRADE

As early as the middle of the fifteenth century, Portuguese sailors discovered that Negroes were available in large numbers along the west coast of Africa. Spain actively joined the slave trade when labor shortages developed in her Caribbean possessions. The Dutch gained a firm foothold in the trade in the middle of the sixteenth century and retained a substantial control of the West African markets for nearly a century. Some Englishmen engaged in the trade during the sixteenth and early seventeenth centuries, but it was not until 1672, when Charles II granted a monopoly to the Royal African Colony, that the influx of Negro slaves into the English colonies—mainly the British West Indies—truly began. Indeed, large-scale importation of slaves into the mainland colonies did not take place until the late seventeenth and early eighteenth centuries.

Introduction of Slavery. The first Negroes to arrive in Virginia were purchased as servants from a Dutch ship in 1619. At that time some twenty Negroes were sold into indentureships that averaged twenty-eight years, considerably longer than those of white servants. Nevertheless, those Negroes who completed their indentureship were permitted to participate in colonial life. Unfortunately, few Negroes had any legal proof of their indentureship; when faced with an oppressive labor shortage, their masters did not hesitate to hold them indefinitely. The first evidence for the existence of actual slavery appears in Virginia after 1640; the institution seems to have been an almost absent-minded development. The number of Negro slaves grew slowly, and was probably less than 25,000 in 1700.

Slave Codes. Many legal decisions were made in colonial America that supported belief in the Negro's inferiority, even in cases where the Negro was not in fact a slave. Runaway servants who were white received corporal punishment and had their terms of indenture increased by a year; Negro runaways were condemned to a lifetime of servitude. By 1660 Virginia law tacitly recognized that Negro slavery existed. In 1664 Maryland felt obliged to interdict interracial marriages because "divers free born English women, forgetful of their free condition, and to the disgrace of our nation, do intermarry with Negro slaves." As the economic importance of Negro slavery increased, a code of law governing slavery slowly evolved; but it was not until 1750 that Southern law generally defined slaves as chattels. The unusually harsh slave code in South Carolina, passed in that year, was justified on the grounds that "the Negroes and other slaves brought unto the people of this province . . . are of barbarous, wild, savage natures, and such as renders them wholly unqualified to be governed by the laws, customs, and practices of this province."

The number of slaves increased spectacularly after 1700, with a particular concentration in the colonies from Maryland southward. Several explanations exist for the unusual increase. In 1678, Britain opened the slave trade to all its subjects. One clause of the Treaty of Utrecht (1713), which ended the War of the Spanish Succession, granted the Asiento, or the right to supply slaves, to England. This grant permitted the English to supply the Spanish colonies with 4,800 slaves annually. Within a short time, the English had broken Dutch control of the slave trade and had shipped 30,000 slaves to the Americas. By 1715 no less than 60,000 slaves were held in the colonies, and by 1760 a total of 386,000 slaves labored on farms and plantations, nearly 299,000 of them in the Southern colonies.

Slavery in South Carolina and Virginia. South Carolina proved especially receptive to slavery since its rice culture demanded a work force capable of laboring in the hot and humid marshes where the rice was grown. By 1724 Negroes outnumbered whites two to one in the colony, a proportion that increased steadily until 1760 when Negroes made up 70,000 of the colony's 100,000 population. A substantial number of these slaves were brought from the West Indian plantations with which the Carolinians had intimate social and economic ties. A similar rise in the number of slaves occurred in Virginia. The expansion of tobacco culture made the Chesapeake planters increasingly willing to stabilize their labor force with slaves. Though slaves had numbered less than five per cent of the population of Virginia in 1671, they had increased to over forty per cent of the Old Dominion's population by 1756.

Slavery in the Northern Colonies. Among the northern colonies the

largest number of slaves were found in New York, where they farmed
the large Hudson estates, and in New York City, where they served as
menial workers. Few slaves were found in New England, largely because
its economy had little need for such labor. The lively opposition of the
Quakers to slavery kept the institution at bay in the middle colonies.

The Slave Trade. Elsewhere the influx of slaves provoked efforts at
restriction. Georgia, Virginia, Maryland, South Carolina, Massachusetts,
and Pennsylvania, fearful that Negro slaves would drive away white immigrants, attempted unsuccessfully to limit their importation. The English government disallowed these efforts, however, for fear that they
would dry up the substantial wealth poured into the empire by the slave
trade. In 1750 John Woolman, a Quaker leader, led the Friends to oppose the ownership of slaves by any member of their society. But Puritan
moral scruples did not extend to nonparticipation in the slave trade. Newport, Boston, and Salem carried on a lively trade in "black ivory" with
West Africa. Trading one hundred gallons of rum for an adult male,
eighty-five gallons for an adult female, and sixty gallons for a child, the
average slaver could purchase and transport seventy-five slaves across
the sea. The cramped quarters—slaves were squeezed into a space three
feet high between decks, with a floor space five feet long by sixteen inches
wide for each slave—inferior food, and poor hygiene killed six to ten
slaves per cargo. Such loss was considered negligible by the slave trader,
however, as those who survived brought a net profit of £300 for each
voyage undertaken.

Colonial Unease about Slavery. By 1775, the holding of slaves had
become an accepted fact of life throughout much of the South. Many
colonial intellectuals still had serious qualms about its continued existence, though few men were ready to accept total emancipation with full
equality. In *Notes on Virginia,* written in 1781, Thomas Jefferson la-
mented the existence of slavery but could conceive no solution unless the
slaves were "expatriated." Virginians could flirt with the idea of ending
slavery in the late eighteenth and early nineteenth centuries; but South
Carolinians, possessed of an agriculture built on slave labor, and confronted with a huge Negro majority, thought of slavery as necessarily en-
during. And there existed a subtle fear among the Carolinians that a
servile revolt might engulf them, a fear kept alive by the Cato Conspiracy
of 1739, in which thirty whites and forty-four slaves were killed less than
twenty miles from Charleston. References condemning the king for fostering slavery in the colonies were deleted from the Declaration of Independence when the delegates from South Carolina and Georgia protested

sharply against their inclusion. But the moral, ethical, and economic problems resulting from slavery could not be resolved successfully simply by ignoring them. Slavery, firmly entrenched in the colonies by 1775, was destined to become the irreconcilable contradiction in the American democracy.

THE START OF THE MOVE WEST

Free Land. The colonial labor problem was made even more difficult by the availability of free land. Workers who were dissatisfied with their jobs felt that a solution to their problems was to be had by moving west. By siphoning off these discontented colonials, the free land served as a safety valve; but few industries could really afford to lose large numbers of workers, no matter how discontented they might be. Many colonists who took advantage of the free land in the west, of course, were not motivated by negative influences, but by positive ones: they hoped to find fertile tracts along the frontier on which they could achieve independent status as farmers and landholders.

The desire to "strike out on one's own"—a natural tendency for the colonists—was encouraged and stimulated by land speculators who painted glowing pictures of the marvelous opportunities inherent in westward migration. Syndicates of speculators often withdrew large tracts of the most desirable land from immediate settlement; but though we might consider such speculation somewhat unethical, the practices were, on the whole, far from disreputable, and men as illustrious and upright as George Washington and Benjamin Franklin engaged in land speculation. The interest of such men, and the vast holdings of many of the colonies' finest families—such as the twenty-two million acres owned by the Penn family—whetted many an appetite and attracted the great no less than the small.

During the eighteenth century the aggressive westward movement of settlers in the British colonies precipitated Indian wars and was a major cause of the three great wars fought between the French and English on the North American continent. This steady influx of immigrants into the virgin wilderness gave the English a hold upon the western lands that insured ultimate Anglo-Saxon dominance.

The "Back-Country" Settlements. In the South immigrants in search of land settled in the "Back Country." This hilly, fertile, heavily forested region extended from the Shenandoah Valley of Virginia southward through the piedmont of the Carolinas to the banks of the Savannah

River. In 1730, only a handful of Indians dwelt in the area; by 1776, more than 250,000 settlers had poured into the region. In the colony of South Carolina, seventy-nine per cent of the white population lived in the back country. From the North, Pennsylvania Germans and the vigorous Scots-Irish penetrated the Great Valley of Virginia and traveled southwestward into the fertile river valleys of western Virginia. The settlements, which grew up wherever fertile soil existed, were often remote and isolated, connected only by old Indian trails, and it was possible to journey thirty or forty miles without coming upon human habitation.

The same phenomenon occurred farther north. The Scots-Irish poured into the twisted valleys of the Alleghenies, disregarding the rights of the Indian, and blaming the Quakers and other eastern Pennsylvanians for not protecting them from Indian disturbances which they themselves provoked. In spite of such problems, however, the lure of cheap land continued to guarantee a flow of immigrants. The vision of independence and security offered by tracts of fertile land was not to be easily dispelled by the attendant dangers.

Regional Rivalry. The frontiersman who migrated westward frequently encountered discrimination in his attempt to receive treatment similar to that given the resident of the older settlement in the east. As the move west continued, regional rivalry flared up more and more frequently. The interior counties of Virginia, though more heavily populated than the tidewater counties, were given fewer representatives in the House of Burgesses. A similar dispute divided the interior regions of Pennsylvania from the more highly developed area adjacent to Philadelphia. Complicating this dispute was the western Pennsylvanian's insistence that he was not given proper protection from the danger of Indian attacks. In North Carolina, the conviction of frontiersmen that they were being overtaxed culminated in a small scale civil war known as the Regulator Movement. From 1765 until 1771, when Governor Tryon's troops finally defeated the Regulators at the Battle of Alamance, the North Carolinian frontiersmen were in continual rebellion against eastern authority. The complaint of the westerner that he was being exploited had firm roots in the colonial experience.

The Weakening of Royal Ties. Western expansion tended to dissolve traditional ties and allegiances. The squatter, absorbed in the all-consuming task of maintaining his way of life in the face of difficulty and danger, would not concern himself with the letter of a distant law. As he moved into the interior, the influence upon him of provincial as well as royal authority diminished until it scarcely existed. Indeed, it was upon this very point of frontier disobedience that the English scheme for achieving an orderly New World empire was destined, in part, to founder.

Westward migration had a leveling effect on society as men from a variety of cultures, backgrounds, and communities repudiated their restrictive pasts and merged with one another into a more homogeneous society. In addition, the doctrines of mercantilism, which had been so basic to the easterner's philosophy, were no longer acceptable to the frontiersman. Preoccupied with personal acquisition, forced into self-sufficiency, he was no longer able to concede those economic points which his eastern brothers verbalized so glibly, namely, that a sound economy was dependent upon reciprocal give and take. The frontier spirit emerged from the premise that nothing of value is easily received, and that nothing of value should be willingly relinquished. Before the end of the eighteenth century the British would learn that an enormous number of their colonials had become frontiersmen in spirit, if not in fact.

Part Two

THE REVOLUTIONARY EXPERIENCE

Chapter 5

The Imperial Problem

The first British Empire was the result of haphazard growth. Charter, proprietary, and royal colonies were at first established without any plan for developing a central administrative apparatus. However, as the empire grew, the need for such administration became so great that the London government launched several experiments in the administration of colonial areas. The final effort in this direction triggered the American Revolution.

THE ASSERTION OF ROYAL AUTHORITY

Salutary Neglect. Between 1607 and 1763, the colonies existed as dependencies of the Crown. Although Parliament had declared in 1650 that the colonies "ought to be subject to such laws, orders, and regulations as are or shall be made by the Parliament of England," it did not participate actively in the administration of the colonies. It tried to regulate colonial commerce, but did not attempt to establish control over colonial politics. The one constant factor in colonial relations with the mother country until the eve of revolution was the royal prerogative— the right of the king to give his assent to legislation passed by the colonials; but even this authority was a gradual development in several of the colonies. It was only with the restoration of Charles II in 1660 that the Crown firmly began to assert its authority.

Bacon's Rebellion. Even as the Crown worked to strengthen its control, the colonies were the scene of increasing discontent. The Virginians, who prided themselves on having remained faithful to the Crown during Cromwell's protectorate, seethed with protest as the governor, Sir William Berkeley, exercised autocratic rule. Heavy taxes, slave discontent, Dutch intervention in the tobacco trade, and opposition to Berkeley's Indian policy finally erupted in violence. When the invasion of Virginia by Susquehannock Indians in 1675 and 1676 brought only dilatory action by the authorities, Nathaniel Bacon, a frontier settler, raised a force of approximately three hundred men, and defeated the Indians. Though suspended by Berkeley from his position as a member of the governor's council, Bacon was subsequently able to rally support in favor of his demands for administrative reform and the establishment of a new assembly. The governor's ambivalence in the face of this threat to his authority precipitated a civil war. Bacon seems even to have contemplated rebellion against Britain, but his death, in October 1676, left his supporters leaderless. Berkeley regained power, rescinded all reforms, and hanged twenty-three of his opponents. When in 1677 Charles II finally learned of the rebellion, he sent a military force under Colonel Herbert Jeffreys to replace Berkeley, pardon Bacon's supporters, and restore order. Though many of Bacon's reforms were revoked, enough were retained to give a decidedly more liberal hue to Virginia's government.

In Massachusetts Bay, the Crown intervened to compel liberalization of voting requirements and to insure freedom of Anglican worship. The Puritans met the challenge by deliberately subverting the intention of the law. In 1664 a royal commission, frustrated in its investigation by Puritan threats against prospective witnesses, concluded that revocation of the charter would tame the recalcitrant colony. The colonists replied belligerently that Massachusetts was "not obliged to the king but by civility." Such incidents led Charles II to contemplate the establishment of direct royal authority throughout the colonies.

The King and Colonial Institutions. There was, however, a major obstacle standing between the king and easy control of his new world subjects: every colony had its own legislature. Authorized to pass laws and holding strong ideas concerning their rights, these legislatures often proved reluctant to pass laws desired by the Crown, even when royal pressure was brought to bear. In 1677, Charles II decided to impose in Jamaica and Virginia, through his Lords of Trade, a system similar to that which Poynings' Act enforced in Ireland. The new act placed the responsibility for formulating laws in the hands of the governor and his council. Before the laws could be put into effect they had to be sent to

England for approval by the Privy Council, and the legislature was authorized to rubber-stamp the final version. Distance, plus the stubborn opposition of Jamaica—Virginia, failing to realize the Act's implications, placidly accepted the proposals—frustrated the program.

The Dominion of New England. Plans for colonial consolidation were well advanced when Charles II died suddenly in 1685; his brother and successor, James II, organized the Dominion of New England, but his forced abdication in 1688 brought that experiment to an end. Under William and Mary, however, a less emphatic effort to extend royal authority continued. Even crusty Massachusetts had to accept a royal governor. Not all the colonies, however, passed under royal authority: Rhode Island and Connecticut, both of which had been deprived of their charters in 1687, maintained nearly republican systems when their charters were restored after the Glorious Revolution, while Maryland, Pennsylvania, and Delaware, after brief lapses, resumed their proprietary status.

The Colonial System of Government. Every colony, no matter what its exact status, now had to legislate in conformance with English law, and to accept review by the Board of Trade. Appeals to the Privy Council were possible, but its decisions were final. In the royal colonies the governor, appointed by the Crown and bound by instructions sent from London, held the veto power. The existence of the royal colonies had a salutary effect on the charter colonies, where the governor was elected, and on the proprietary colonies, where the governor was appointed, since these authorities governed leniently for fear of provoking royal intervention. All the royal governors were aided by appointive councils except in Massachusetts, where the council was elected by the lower house. Since most council members were colonials they tended to support the colonial interest. The assembly's control of the tax power often proved crucial in disputes between the legislative and executive authorities of a colony, and as a result, uncooperative governors frequently found themselves without their salaries. The assemblies' sense of their prerogatives in the exacting and expenditure of taxes would brook no interference from the superior power of the English Parliament. The one authority they acknowledged was that of the royal prerogative. By the middle of the eighteenth century, the various colonial assemblies had assumed the role of local parliaments.

The Dimensions of Parliamentary Power. Any effort by the Westminster Parliament to enforce its will in the colonies was certain to stir up a storm of dissent. In addition, the relationship between Britain and the colonies was beginning to be complicated by the colonists' conviction that as Englishmen they had a right to participate in lawmaking, especially where laws pertaining to taxation were concerned. There existed in the colonies the as yet unarticulated assumption that governments derive their powers from the consent of the governed. Thus, the impending conflict stemmed from a further source of discontent: had Parliament the right to legislate for the colonies, or were they themselves the sole possessors of this right? Although the passage of the Navigation Acts seemed to have established Parliament's rights in the matter, the acts themselves contained a notorious and self-canceling defect: they provided no effective enforcement agencies.

The Navigation Act of 1696. Parliament made sporadic efforts to extend the scope of its economic regulations, and in 1696 passed a navigation act to control colonial trade more effectively. The act provided for the restriction of trade to ships owned and manned by Englishmen, for the extension of the authority of both customs and naval officers to regulate trade, for the suppression of all colonial laws contrary to the new act, and for royal approval of all gubernatorial appointments. For the more effective management of colonial commerce, the Lords of Trade were replaced by a Board of Trade which, besides regulating trade, supervised all colonial laws and passed upon their constitutionality. Although this power was great, one cannot say that it was abused. Of the 8,563 laws submitted to the Board, only 469 were disallowed on the grounds that they contravened parliamentary acts or the common law, violated the colonial charter or the powers of the governor, or worked to the detriment of the imperial interest.

That few colonial laws were disallowed indicates not only leniency on the part of the Board, but also care on the part of local assemblies, who wanted to avoid provoking the mother country. The assemblies took a more subtle and devious way to achieve their ends. They preferred to pass an agreeable law and then to violate it, assuming (correctly) that the English were ill-equipped to supervise enforcement.

The Woolens, Hat, and Iron Acts. Passage of the Woolens Act in 1699 provoked a sharp colonial protest. This law permitted local production of woolen goods but forbade the sale outside the colony of surplus production. It particularly affected Massachusetts, whose woolen production was such that it had a surplus to sell to the other colonies. Similar restrictions were imposed by the Hat Act of 1732. In 1750, the Iron Act, which permitted the continued production of pig iron and bar iron, and even encouraged it by making iron a duty-free item, nevertheless made it an offense, punishable by a £200 fine, to construct new mills, furnaces, or forges.

The Board of Trade and the Molasses Act. During the first two decades of the eighteenth century, the Board of Trade added to the colonials' grievances by placing major colonial staples like naval stores, rice, and furs on the enumerated list. Another source of contention was fostered by the passage of the Molasses Act of 1733, which specifically sought to aid the sugar planters of the British West Indies, who were in competition with the French West Indies, and which provided for heavy duties on foreign sugar, molasses, and rum imported into the colonies. Faced with higher costs, declining soil fertility, and the superior production techniques of their competitors, the English West Indian planters had used their strong influence in Parliament to get relief legislation at the expense of the colonies. Once again, however, regulation failed to achieve its purpose. The lack of any effective supervisory agency made it possible for the colonials to continue their large trade with the French possessions. The unwillingness of England's first Prime Minister, Sir Robert Walpole, to press for effective enforcement added to the colonial conviction that parliamentary will need not be respected. This period of "salutory neglect" encouraged colonial independence and made it unlikely that the colonies would tamely submit to interference from abroad.

IMPERIAL REORGANIZATION

"The sovereignty of the Crown I understand," wrote Benjamin Franklin. "The sovereignty of Britain I do not understand. . . . We have the same King, but not the same legislature." Franklin's statement went to the core of the colonial dispute with the mother country. George III came to believe that his difficulties with the American colonials grew from his "scrupulous attachment to the rights of Parliament." Franklin agreed that it was not George III's assertion of the royal prerogative that provoked the colonials—nearly all of them accepted it as the link between Britain and her colonies—but rather the wish of "subjects in one part of the King's dominions to be sovereigns over their fellow-subjects in another part of his dominions." To understand the American Revolution one must recognize that it was a dispute between equals, both firmly convinced that they had right on their side.

George III. Few monarchs have been more maligned than George III. His name seems inflexibly associated with tyranny, although much of the tyranny against which the colonials protested was only remotely connected with him. The actual source of colonial grievances was Parliament, whose enactments George III, as the executive designated by the British constitution, felt obliged to enforce. George's personality, which unfortunately was characterized by secretiveness, obstinacy, and determined prejudice, added weight to the widely held colonial opinion that his was the malignant influence working to unsettle traditional relationships. The frequent changes in ministries between 1763 and 1770 did little to allay colonial suspicion that George and his parliamentary ministers dominated politics. By installing Lord North as Prime Minister in 1770 George combined with his own inflexibility that of an incompetent minister, thus precluding the possibility of such compromise as might have forestalled the Revolution.

The Imperial Problem. The problem that exacerbated the relations between Britain and her colonials—the definition of the nature and scope of the imperial relationship—was not a new one. But in the seventeenth century it had been muted by the comparative weakness of the colonies, and in the first six decades of the eighteenth century the threat of the French along their northern and western boundaries had preoccupied the colonials. With the elimination of the French threat London realized that its vastly expanded empire needed more coherent direction than had previously been provided. But the consequent decision to reorganize the administration of the empire precipitated a crisis: George III was sworn to uphold the British constitution, while the colonial assemblies were equally dedicated to upholding their own constitutions. From this inflexible conflict of interests a revolution was born.

COLONIAL WARS

King William's War. For almost three-quarters of a century, the conflicts between the French and English for domination of the European continent had its parallel in the New World, where raids and skirmishes between the French settlers of Canada and the English of the colonies were frequent. When William III took an active part in the struggle against Louis XIV's efforts to extend French hegemony over Europe, Canadian settlers began a series of attacks on the English colonies. King William's War (1689–97), which was known in Europe as the War of the League of Augsburg, saw considerable damage done to both sides. When the war was ended by the Treaty of Ryswick, none of the colonial boundaries were changed, and Port Royal, which had been taken, was returned to the French.

Queen Anne's War. The French, mistrustful of English intentions, began to fortify the region west of the Alleghenies against English encroachment. War erupted again when Louis XIV placed his grandson upon the throne of Spain. Fearing that the delicate European balance of power would be upset, England joined the Netherlands and Austria in the War of the Spanish Succession. This time the colonies were beset from both north and south, by the French and Spanish, who were now united in purpose. Known in the colonies as Queen Anne's War (1703–13), the struggle found colonial opinion divided. The exposed colonies of Massachusetts and South Carolina begged for assistance, but England, more interested in the progress of the war in Europe, left both colonies to their own resources. The "neutral" middle colonies were similarly uninterested in the troubles of the two colonies. Massachusetts managed to capture Port Royal, which they had previously occupied in King William's War, with the consequence that Nova Scotia, the Hudson Bay country, and Newfoundland were ceded by France to England in the Treaty of Utrecht (1713). But in spite of the peace treaty, the colonies still lived with the threat of the hostile French on their northern flank.

King George's War. During the quarter of a century of peace that followed, French and British rivalries in the New World continued. Faced with rapidly expanding British colonies, the French sought to contain their expansion by constructing a series of forts in the Mississippi, Ohio, and St. Lawrence Valleys. The most important of these fortifications was Fort Louisbourg on Cape Breton Island. A parallel rivalry developed between the British and Spaniards as the latter protested the settlement of the Georgia colony and claimed British violations of Spanish trade restrictions in their Latin-American colonies. In 1733 the French and Spaniards entered into the Family Compact, under which they pledged to mutually oppose British territorial expansion and economic depredations.

Peace abruptly ended in June 1739, when a British smuggler, Captain Robert Jenkins, with his eloquent description of his efforts to protect British trade rights from Spanish interference, swept Parliament to a declaration of war against Spain. The fact that he had lost his ear in the effort gave the war its name—the War of Jenkins' Ear. In the struggle that followed the Spanish launched unsuccessful attacks against Georgia and the British led an equally unsuccessful joint colonial-British attack on Spain's Caribbean possessions. The inclusive struggle merged into a broader European struggle, the War of the Austrian Succession, when in 1744 the French came to the assistance of Spain. Known in the colonies as King George's War (1745–48), it involved, at first, little more than frontier raids. Then Governor William Shirley of Massachusetts organized a campaign against Fort Louisbourg. He achieved a brilliant success. The great fort was captured in mid-June of 1745 after a forty-nine day siege. Success stimulated colonial aggressiveness and an elaborate plan for an attack on Montreal and Quebec in 1747 was drawn up, only to be frustrated by the absence of expected British aid. In October 1748, wearying of war, the British and French negotiated a treaty at Aix-la-Chapelle by which Louisbourg was surrendered to France in return for Madras in southern India. New Englanders were dismayed at this cavalier surrender of their hard-won victory. The terms of the treaty suggested to some colonists that their own interests were apt to be the victims of Britain's larger imperial interest.

THE FRENCH AND INDIAN WAR

Prelude to Conflict. The Treaty of Aix-la-Chapelle merely provided a breather for the major European antagonists. Recouping their strength, both the French and British prepared for another test. In the New World, many colonials determined to assert their claims to the French-held territories. Governor Robert Dinwiddie of Virginia attempted the expulsion of the French from the Ohio Valley in 1753. In 1754 George Washington continued these efforts, first by peaceful negotiation and then by war to force the French to withdraw from the valley. At the head of the Virginia militia, he inflicted losses on the French at Great Meadows but was eventually forced to retreat into a hastily built log redoubt in the Ohio Valley, appropriately called Fort Necessity. On July 4, 1754, he was compelled to surrender. The French, now in control of the entire Ohio Valley, could afford the magnanimous gesture of permitting Washington and his militia to return home. But his action had triggered a war that was to spread to Western Europe when Britain declared war on France in May of 1756.

The Albany Convention. In 1753, the premonition that the impending struggle with France would be decisive caused the Board of Trade to order a meeting of commissioners from every colony at Albany, in order to settle a number of important differences with the Iroquois. Unified action was thus forced upon the colonies by London. But Benjamin Franklin and others hoped to use the meeting to foster a more permanent union of the colonies. At Albany he proposed a "Plan of Union" which provided for a central government consisting of a Crown-appointed president-general and a Grand Council made up of representatives chosen indirectly by the colonial assemblies and with membership made proportional to each colony's contribution to a central treasury. Although the plan had the charm of attempting to unite the two sources of accepted authority in the colonies, it did not succeed. The English feared it demanded the relinquishing of too much of their power, while the assemblies resented the loss of power it entailed for *them*. The Albany plan would have invested the new government with responsibility for Indian relations, organization of both armies and navies, regulation of further settlement, and the right to raise taxes through tariff duties. In these matters it foreshadowed the federal government that was created after the revolution. Franklin had realized that disunity between the colonies would severely hamper the war effort against the French. Now, far from beginning the war with any unity of purpose, the colonies seemed preoccupied only with petty advantage. By refusing to raise taxes and supply needed militiamen, the colonial assemblies acted as if the real enemies were their governors, not the French.

Military Campaigns. The French and Indian War began grimly when the English sent General Edward Braddock with fourteen hundred regulars to open a campaign against Fort Duquesne in April 1755. Aided by four hundred and fifty colonial militia led by Lieutenant Colonel George Washington, Braddock struggled through the wilderness to within eight miles of the fort. There he was attacked by almost a thousand French and Indians. In the Battle of the Wilderness that followed, Braddock was killed and his troops badly defeated. Washington was left to fight a holding action along the Virginia frontier. By July 1755 the French seemed yet more strongly entrenched in the Ohio Valley.

A proposed attack upon Fort Niagara failed when English naval support did not coordinate with a land attack. Atrocities were committed on both sides as Indians attacked frontier settlements. When 2,000 New Englanders captured Fort Beausejour and gained control of the region about the Bay of Fundy, at least 12,000 Acadian settlers of French extraction were forced to migrate either to the colonies (notably South Carolina) or elsewhere (primarily to Louisiana, which was French). This action, the theme of Henry Wadsworth Longfellow's *Evangeline,* was justified by Governor Charles Lawrence of Nova Scotia on the grounds that the settlers, being under Jesuit influence, were disloyal.

Concurrent with the disasters England had already suffered in America, she sustained the loss of Minorca, a strategic island in the Mediterranean, followed by the loss of Calcutta in India and by the defeat of Frederick the Great at the hands of the French and Austrians. The British plight worsened with the relentless advance of the French General Montcalm into northern New York. On August 9, 1756, he reached and captured Fort William Henry at the southern end of Lake George. Despite promises of safe conduct, the Indian allies of the French massacred some 1,000 of the 2,400 men who surrendered at the fort. Further disasters overtook the English in the autumn, when the French and their Indian allies broke into central New York and destroyed many villages.

In Britain this combination of disasters in the Old and New Worlds resulted in growing discontent with the Newcastle ministry. It was replaced in November 1756 by a ministry headed by the Duke of Devonshire. One member of the new cabinet, William Pitt the Elder, proved imaginative and determined to reverse the trend of the French conflict. When Newcastle returned to the prime ministership in the spring of 1757, Pitt assumed full responsibility for the conduct of the war. He insisted on the necessity of Britain's taking the offensive, with prime emphasis upon complete expulsion of the French from the New World. He moved the bulk of British strength to the American theater, with young and energetic men—James Wolfe, Jeffrey Amherst, and William Howe—in charge. Parliament appropriated £1,000,000 to assist the colonies in supplying this army. The French were tied down in Europe by the aggressive moves of Frederick the Great. Unable to reinforce their troops in Canada, they lost Louisbourg to a combined British naval and military attack on July 26, 1758.

But colonial actions threatened the success of Pitt's program of conquest. New Englanders, New Yorkers, and Pennsylvanians sold large quantities of food and supplies to the French in Canada, leading Pitt to conclude that without this trade France would not have been able "to sustain and protract this long and expensive war." When General James Abercromby attempted to dislodge Montcalm at Ticonderoga, and the colonials failed to supply enough troops to support his 6,300 regulars, the British suffered more than 1,600 casualties. By November 1758, however, Fort Duquesne had fallen and the French were in retreat across all of the upper Ohio Valley. In the summer of 1759 a campaign was launched to isolate the west from Quebec and to expel the French from the Lake George-Lake Champlain region. Under General Amherst these purposes were soon achieved.

The Attack on Quebec. Meanwhile Wolfe began a slow campaign directed toward the envelopment of Quebec. After many diversionary attacks he finally launched a major assault on September 12, 1759, by way of the steep paths leading to the Plains of Abraham, an undefended plateau that dominated the city. After a short battle in which both Wolfe and Montcalm were mortally wounded, the English secured Quebec. This was the turning point of the war. During the following year, Montreal, Detroit, and the remaining western strong points capitulated. The totality of the British victory was confirmed by the fall of the major French possessions in the West Indies. Despite George III's decision in 1761 to force Pitt from office, the result of the war was already certain; England had won an overwhelming victory.

The Treaty of Paris, 1763. After preliminary negotiations, which began in November 1762 at Fontainebleau, peace was concluded with the signing of the Treaty of Paris on February 10, 1763. The Treaty confirmed the existence of the first British Empire. France surrendered to England almost all her possessions in India, all of Canada (with the exception of two small islands in the Gulf of St. Lawrence), and all French territory east of the Mississippi except for the island of Orleans in the mouth of that river. Several of the French West Indies—Grenada, Tobago, St. Vincent, and Dominica—also passed to the English. From Spain, who had joined the European war on the side of France, Britain obtained the Floridas. Subsequently, the French compensated the Spaniards for their loss by surrendering to them the Louisiana territory and the island of Orleans. In only seven years England had laid the foundations of the mightiest and most extensive empire the world had ever seen, but an empire with inherent faults that were to convulse it in less than thirteen years.

THE WESTERN PROBLEM

The Treaty of Paris put an end to the period of salutary neglect. The British had created an empire haphazardly, but also at an immense cost.

The exhilaration of victory was accompanied by a widespread desire to return to peacetime pursuits and to reap the fruits of victory. Debate over how best to achieve this result rang through the halls of Parliament. Once again the old mercantilist theories were raised. Some argued that the empire should primarily provide the home country with raw materials; others argued that they should be markets to consume manufactured goods. In addition Parliament had to face the problem of a national debt that had increased by more than £58,000,000 as a result of war, in spite of annual taxation in excess of £14,500,000. It was clearly not advisable to add further to the tax burden of Englishmen, and yet equally clear that military protection had to be provided in the New World against restive Indians, dissident Frenchmen, and aggressive Spaniards. So Parliament prepared to maintain a standing military establishment in the colonies but determined that the colonies should help foot the bill. At the same time, it decided to reorganize the empire in order to insure a more efficient and less costly management.

The Proclamation of 1763. In Britain's New World empire the Indian problem quickly became paramount. In 1763 the Ottawas, under Pontiac, laid siege to Detroit and captured every other English post west of Fort Niagara. Only after two years of struggle was peace restored. The English had attempted to placate the Indians with the Treaty of Easton (1758), which assured them that the Crown had no intention of appropriating Indian lands without their consent. Now they implemented their promise with the Proclamation of 1763. It provided, first, for the organization of civil governments in Quebec, East and West Florida, and Grenada, with strong powers vested in the governor. The colonists in this region were permitted to make appeals to the Privy Council if they were opposed to his action. Provision was also made for the setting up of local assemblies with much the same powers as possessed by the older colonial assemblies. Secondly, the Proclamation declared that "it is just and reasonable, and essential to our interest and the security of our colonies, that [the Indians] who live under our protection, should not be molested or disturbed in the possession of such parts of our dominions and territories as, not having been ceded or purchased by us, are reserved to them . . . as their hunting grounds." The effect of this provision was to temporarily close the trans-Appalachian West to white settlement, and to provoke bitter complaints from the colonials as a result. The Crown had committed itself to a program of orderly western expansion. Negotiations with the Indians to obtain their assent to land cessions would precede settlement. Provision was also made for the compensation of war veterans with land grants ranging in size from fifty to five thousand acres.

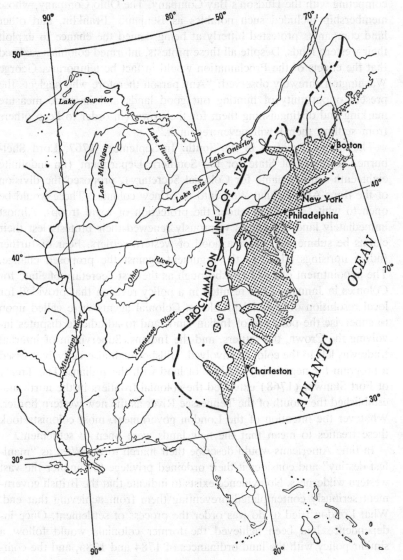

THE EXTENT OF ENGLISH COLONIAL SETTLEMENT, 1763

The Colonial Reaction. The Proclamation provoked a storm of protest in the colonies. Several, notably Virginia, ignored the temporary nature of the proclamation line and attacked it as an infringement upon their charter rights. Others saw it as an English plot to limit the colonists to the seaboard and to prevent colonial hunters and trappers from competing with the Hudson's Bay Company. The Ohio Company, whose membership included such notables as Benjamin Franklin, and other land companies protested bitterly at being denied the chance to exploit their western lands. Despite all these protests, informed colonials realized that the effects of the Proclamation would in fact be temporary. George Washington shrewdly observed: "Any person therefore who neglects the present opportunity of hunting out good lands and in some measure marking and distinguishing them for their own (in order to keep others from settling them) will never regain it."

The Indian Problem in the South. In September 1767, Lord Shelburne, Secretary of State for the Southern Department (an indefinite eighteenth-century name for Colonial Secretary), proposed the division of the trans-Appalachian West into three new colonies. These would be open to white settlement under the protection of royal troops. Almost immediately land companies vigorously renewed their protests lest their claims be submerged under a flood of western settlers. Fear of further Indian uprisings added to the argument against the proposed change. The appointment of Lord Hillsborough as the first Secretary of State for Colonies in January 1768 resulted in a policy revision that provided for local resolution of colonial problems. Colonial agents were called upon to supervise the purchase of Indian lands and to adjudicate disputes involving the Crown, the settlers, and the Indians. Supervision of internal trade was left to the colonies involved. Hillsborough also actively pressed a program for negotiating cessions of land with the Indians. The Treaty of Fort Stanwix (1768) extended the colonial frontiers in the north and established the mouth of the Tennessee River as the new western border. Whatever the intention of the London government, most colonists took these treaties to mean that the new lands were open to settlement.

In time Americans would describe their march to the West as "manifest destiny" and consider it their ordained privilege to conquer the vast western wilderness. No evidence exists to indicate that the British government seriously contemplated preventing them from achieving that end. What London tried to do was order the process of settlement. Once independence had been achieved the former colonials would follow a similar policy with the land ordinances of 1784 and 1785, and the comprehensive Northwest Ordinance of 1787. In their management of the western lands the British were clearly in the right.

THE PROBLEM OF COLONIAL TAXATION

When Parliament resolved that the colonials should bear some part of the total cost of defending the empire, it ran afoul of the colonial belief that only their colonial assemblies were authorized to tax them. The spirit of independence that more than a half century of "salutary neglect" had induced now confronted Parliament with an insoluble problem.

Colonial Assemblies and Taxation. In theory Parliament had retained the right to tax the colonies; in fact, it had surrendered this power to the colonial assemblies. The Crown's sporadic efforts to modify the taxing powers of the assemblies had met stubborn opposition. A subtle by-product of the power to tax, as Governor George Clinton of New York noted, was the control by "the ruling faction" in each assembly of "nomination to all offices." Since executive officials depended upon the assembly for appropriation of their salaries, it was not often that they chose to defy the will of the assembly. Once Parliament had launched its imperial reorganization a full-scale conflict between itself and the assemblies was inevitable.

The Revenue Act of 1764. The dispute began to take shape when Parliament passed the Revenue Act of 1764, popularly known as the Sugar Act and in fact an amendment to the Molasses Act of 1733. Its purpose was to finance garrisons to keep the western Indians in check. Parliament attempted to make the tax palatable by reducing the tax on molasses from sixpence to threepence, although it increased the tax on sugar. The colonists were forbidden to import foreign rum while British rum was admitted duty-free. Heavy taxes were also placed upon such luxury items as imported wines, silks, and velvets. From these taxes, Parliament expected to obtain £25,000 in additional revenue but it had failed to reckon with the determined opposition of the colonists. "I think Parliament have overshot their mark," warned one merchant, "and you will not, in the event, have your Expectations in any measure answered from the Provisions of the late Act." The Massachusetts General Court under the guidance of James Otis flatly argued that these "measures have a tendency to deprive the Colonies of some of their most essential Rights as British Subjects, and . . . particularly the Right of assessing their own Taxes."

The Colonial Currency Act. Despite the negative response of the colonials, the Grenville ministry pressed its program of tax reform. It proposed to limit the right of the assemblies to issue paper currency. Since Parliament had already acted in this direction in 1751, with the New England Currency Act, the ministry's decision to extend the same restrictions to all the colonies, acted on by Parliament in the Colonial Currency Act of 1764, seemed just. Furthermore, the legislative actions which made colonial paper legal tender had seemed to British creditors a deliberate effort to pay obligations with depreciated currency. The colonials, on the other hand, viewed the Currency Act as part of a monstrous plan to milk them of all hard specie. Since the Sugar Act, if enforced, would cut them off from their most lucrative source of specie—the French and Dutch West Indies—while the Currency Act would compel payment of duties in specie, their view is understandable.

The Stamp Act. Grenville, however, was flirting with a proposal that eventually shook the empire to its foundations. He proposed to institute "certain stamp duties," similar to although smaller than English Stamp taxes, which would be used to support troops in the New World. Since only a third of the moneys needed for this purpose would be raised in the colonies, the British assumed that their own expenditures in support of the troops would provide the colonies with ample specie to meet losses resulting from the Currency Act. The Stamp Act which resulted was a complex piece of legislation consisting of one hundred and seventeen sections. It provided for the purchase in specie only of stamps costing from a halfpenny to £10, to be affixed to such printed matter as newspapers, legal papers, mortgages, college diplomas, tavern licenses, playing cards, and advertisements. With the passage of the act on March 22, 1765, a system of stamp distributors was set up to collect the tax. Seeking patronage, prominent Americans such as Jared Ingersoll accepted positions as stamp distributors, and Benjamin Franklin encouraged both friends and relatives in applying for similar posts. Grenville anticipated no further difficulties.

"No Taxation without Representation." Grenville's hopes were founded in part on the fact that the colonies had accepted, albeit grudgingly, the right of Parliament to regulate their trade. He overlooked the more important fact that the navigation acts and other trade regulations had never been effectively enforced. Flagrant violation had been the consistent colonial response; and the response to the Stamp Act soon followed a similar pattern. Appealing to the unwritten principle that no person in the British Empire could be taxed by a legislative body in which he was not represented, the colonials set up a cry of "No taxation without representation." In the Virginia House of Burgesses, Patrick Henry formulated resolutions, which were subsequently approved, that only the House of Burgesses could impose taxes upon a Virginian.

Opposition to the Stamp Act. Henry's protest evoked a sympathetic response in the other colonial legislatures. The Stamp Act galvanized their fears of ultimate parliamentary intentions. Previously British authority had tapped colonial purses, but always by way of requisitions—which the colonial legislatures were free to accept or ignore. Since this new act affected most businessmen, lawyers, and journalists, the protest that ensued was highly articulate. Clergymen denounced the action from the pulpit, while countless communities issued broadsides assailing parliamentary presumption. Nonimportation agreements were made between colonial merchants who were determined to exert influence upon Parliament through affected British businessmen. Throughout the colonies, Sons of Liberty went into action to oppose the Stamp Act. In Massachusetts, Andrew Oliver, the newly appointed stamp distributor, had his life threatened and his home wrecked by a mob, and was so thoroughly intimidated that he applied for permission to resign his post. Within a short time similar demonstrations elsewhere had compelled stamp distributors throughout the colonies to resign their posts or to leave the law in abeyance.

In Boston, attacks upon officials responsible for enforcing trade regulations were commonplace. A particularly unfortunate incident was the sacking of the home of Lieutenant Governor Thomas Hutchinson with the attendant burning of a vast collection of early Massachusetts manuscripts. Efforts to punish the lawbreakers proved fruitless, since many of the most reputable citizens joined in support of the riots.

The Stamp Act Congress. Against this background of open illegality the Stamp Act Congress opened in New York on October 7, 1765. Delegates from the nine colonies chose to follow a moderate course. After eleven days of discussion they composed for the king a "declarations of the rights and grievances of the colonists in America," in which they acknowledged "alliegiance to the crown . . . and all due subordination to . . . the parliament of Great Britain," but claimed "all the inherent rights and privileges of [the king's] natural born subjects within the kingdom of Great Britain." The core of the Congress' argument was "that no taxes should be imposed on them, but with their own consent, given personally, or by their representatives," from which they deduced "that no taxes ever have been, or can be constitutionally imposed on them, but by their respective legislatures."

Repeal of the Stamp Act. British officials answered that the colonials received virtual representation in the Westminster Parliament. By this they meant that every real interest of the realm had its spokesman in the national legislature, an argument which received support when British merchants, severely hurt by colonial boycotts, flatly demanded repeal of the Stamp Act. The ferocity of colonial protest had begun to frighten British creditors, who feared that the more than £4,000,000 in colonial debts would not be repaid. As Horace Walpole subsequently recalled:

> . . . The weapon with which the Colonies armed themselves to most advantage, was the refusal of paying the debts they owed to our merchants at home, for goods and wares exported to the American provinces. These debts involved the merchants of London, Liverpool, Manchester, and the other great trading towns, in a common cause with the Americans, who foreswore all traffic with us, unless the obnoxious Stamp Act was repealed.

The Rockingham ministry, which had succeeded the Grenville ministry in July 1765, surrendered to the weight of protest and threw its support behind repeal of the act on grounds of its inexpediency. With the backing of the influential William Pitt, the act was repealed on March 18, 1768. Prior to repeal, however, Parliament, determined to assert and maintain its supremacy, passed the Declaratory Act. This asserted parliamentary supremacy over the colonial assemblies in all legislative matters, including the power of taxation. But no assertion, however strong, could make the colonials forget that in an open clash they had carried the day. Once again Parliament had retained the theory of power while surrendering its substance.

THE TRADE PROBLEM

Townshend's Ministry. The repeal of the Stamp Act was greeted by the colonials with undisguised glee. The colonial assemblies even agreed to compensate the victims of the Stamp Act riots. In Britain, the Rockingham ministry, compelled to increase domestic taxes in order to compensate for the loss of expected Stamp Act revenues, lost the support of the king and of the followers of Pitt. Forced to resign in June 1766, Rockingham was succeeded by Pitt, who then left the Commons to enter the Lords as the Earl of Chatham. Faced with large-scale want (bread riots were commonplace in England at the time), Chatham proved temperamentally unfit to handle the domestic crisis. Effective power and responsibility devolved upon Charles Townshend, Chancellor of the Exchequer, who set out vigorously to resolve the tax dilemma. The failure of his efforts to retain the wartime tax rates on land resulted in an estimated loss to the Treasury of £500,000. Since the estimated budget for 1767 was £8,500,000, Townshend had no recourse but to find new sources of revenue. Caught between the growing irritation of the English taxpayer and the obvious disinclination of the colonials to accept new taxes, he determined upon a clever—too clever, as it turned out—exploitation of what was assumed to be the widely held colonial distinction between internal and external taxation. Though confessing that he found the distinction "perfect nonsense," Townshend announced his willingness to garb new colonial taxes in the guise of duties upon American imports from England of glass, paper, paint, and tea. The total revenues to be raised by this method were not expected to exceed £50,000, a bare tenth of the amount lost through land-tax reduction, and it was intended primarily to reassure the British taxpayer that he was not alone in footing imperial bills.

Purpose of the Townshend Act. Parliament meant to use funds drawn from these new duties to meet the salaries of governors and judges in those colonies where assemblies had refused to appropriate salary payments for officials who displeased them. Massachusetts was the immediate target of this provision. Since the Townshend Act supplemented the Sugar Act and other navigation acts, Parliament decided to institute new enforcement agencies to make all these measures effective. A board of commissioners was set up in America to supervise all American customs officials, and in 1768 four new vice-admiralty courts were set up to assist in enforcing payment of duties. Rendering judgments in Halifax, Boston, Philadelphia, and Charleston, these courts seemed to complete the British intention of making trade regulation meaningful.

External and Internal Taxation. When the colonials learned of the new laws in September 1767, protests welled up again. To avoid a repetition of past violence, the more moderate colonial leaders called for a nonconsumption movement. John Dickinson, a reserved moderate, leveled an effective critique against the new British proposals in which he elaborated upon the colonial distinction between external and internal taxation. He conceded that Parliament had the right to levy taxes to regulate trade, but denied it the right to tax for revenue purposes. By this he meant that Parliament had the right to achieve the mercantilist ideal of a balanced economy and that it could suppress colonial commerce and industry in the process, but that it could not raise money to defray the costs of ordinary government since only local assemblies could authorize revenue taxes. Dickinson also noted that when the Stamp Act Congress passed its resolves, it had abolished the distinction between external and internal taxation by rejecting Parliament's right to levy any tax on the colonials.

The Colonial Protest. Remembering the effective nonimportation agreements of the Stamp Act crisis, Boston called for their revival in March 1768, but received an uncertain response from New York and Philadelphia merchants. Philadelphia eventually joined the movement, but only reluctantly.

The customs commissioners were soon convinced that they faced an impossible job in enforcing the trade regulations. Though smuggling was epidemic, only one smuggler was successfully prosecuted between 1765 and 1768. As the customs commissioners pointed out to their London superiors, "Now that the Right of Parliament to lay any taxes . . . on the Colonies is denied, we have every reason to expect that we shall find it totally impracticable to enforce the Execution of the Revenue Laws. . . ."

The Disintegration of Parliamentary Authority. In Boston, law enforcement practically ceased and near-anarchy prevailed. The seizure of John Hancock's ship *Liberty* by a British warship for suspected trade violations provoked mob action against the customs commissioners, who escaped by seeking refuge aboard another warship. The British promptly dispatched four regiments under General Gage to quell further disturbances, and the redcoats seemed to achieve their purpose. British merchants and manufacturers, however, were already suffering the pains of a diminishing trade with the colonies. In early March of 1770, all the Townshend duties except the tax on tea were revoked; the latter was retained only to uphold the principles set forth by the Declaratory Act. Even this last thin assertion of Parliamentary authority enraged the colonies. Nothing short of an acknowledgment of the exclusive power of the local legislatures would satisfy the colonials. As Thomas Hutchinson subsequently recalled:

> At first, . . . the supreme authority [of Parliament] seemed to be admitted, the cases of taxes only excepted; but the exceptions gradually extended from one case to another, until it excluded all cases whatsoever.

For all practical purposes, the colonials were asserting complete independence from the authority of Parliament.

The Boston Massacre. At first the presence of British troops in Boston provoked no violence. When the Sons of Liberty called for forceful opposition they were overruled by more temperate opinion. An uneasy peace prevailed, marred only by several minor clashes between townsmen and soldiers during the winter of 1770. But the ill feeling finally culminated on March 5, 1770, in the Boston Massacre. The available evidence indicates that the affair was provoked when a mob of young men and boys began to pelt passing troops with snowballs. In the altercation that followed two English soldiers were caught and beaten. A detachment of thirteen soldiers led by Captain Thomas Preston went to their rescue. As the mob grew in size, the Preston detachment was also attacked. Finally, when one soldier, who had been injured by a club, fired without orders, a general volley ensued. Five members of the mob were killed and six wounded. Samuel Adams promptly seized upon the incident to prove the existence of an English reign of terror in Boston. The soldiers and their captain were held for trial. John Adams successfully defended them, and all but two were acquitted. To avoid further incidents the redcoats were withdrawn to Castle William, a British fortification located in Boston Harbor. This action was promptly exploited by Samuel Adams as evidence of the superior strength of the Whig party in Boston. Contempt for the written law had now been combined with defiance of its upholders.

The Gaspee Incident. The British government's insistence that the tax on tea be continued when the other Townshend duties were repealed brought a swift demand from Boston that nonimportation be continued until total victory was achieved. With some reluctance the other port towns agreed, but when New Yorkers learned that Boston merchants were secretly importing goods they too resumed trade with England. They were quickly followed by Philadelphia and finally, officially, by Boston. With the end of nonimportation there came a swift upsurge of prosperity throughout the colonies. A deceptive tranquillity descended upon the relationship between England and her colonies. It was shattered in 1772, when colonial attacks upon royal ships attempting to enforce trade regulations culminated in the destruction of the British revenue cutter, *Gaspee*. The *Gaspee* had run aground in Narragansett Bay, near Providence, and was boarded during the night by men who wounded its commander, overpowered the crew, and burned the vessel.

The Crown responded by appointing a commission of inquiry which failed to obtain any information, although it was common knowledge that the culprits were well-known residents of Providence.

Committees of Correspondence. Further evidence of the developing rupture in the imperial relationship came when the Virginia House of Burgesses called for the organization of Committees of Correspondence to keep the colonies abreast of parliamentary actions and the individual colonial responses to them. Within a short time the newly organized Committees had ample cause for action. In May 1773, responding to the severe financial difficulties of the East India Company, Parliament passed the Tea Act. The act permitted the refunding of all duties paid on seven million pounds of tea held in East India warehouses, and authorized export of this surplus tea directly to the colonies. Parliament's expectation was that the low price of this tea in the colonies would encourage consumption and help right the fiscal affairs of the company. But Parliament failed to take into account that there were large supplies of tea already in the colonies on which full duties had been paid by colonial merchants, and even larger quantities of cheap Dutch tea which had been smuggled in. The successful sale of the cheaper and better tea of the East India Company would adversely affect a good many colonial businessmen.

The Boston Tea Party. The tea merchants of New York, Philadelphia, and Boston promptly organized to prevent the East India Company tea from being unloaded. Efforts were made in the colonies to dissuade shipowners from accepting as cargo the tea chests, and the men to whom the tea was consigned were intimidated. Despite these efforts the tea was sent to the colonies. Only in Charleston was it permitted to land. At Boston events moved swiftly as Samuel Adams compelled the three ships bringing tea to dock at locations chosen by him. Civil authority had broken down in the town and even English military and naval support proved ineffective in restoring order. On the night of December 16, a band of men disguised as Indians boarded the moored ships and dumped the tea into the harbor. This famous Boston Tea Party signaled the beginning of further resistance along the entire seaboard. Mobs prevented the landing of tea at Philadelphia, while New Yorkers dumped tea into their harbor. Any doubt that the colonials were united in their opposition to the pretensions of Parliament should have been dispelled. But the Lord North ministry chose this time to replace rule by consent with rule by coercion.

THE BRITISH RESPONSE

The Massachusetts Government Act. The impending crisis in imperial relations could no longer be ignored. The government of George III, faced with defiance of central authority by theoretically subordinate units, determined to assert its supremacy. On March 31, 1774, the king approved the Massachusetts Government Act which gave the royal governor of Massachusetts the right to appoint all inferior officers of law, converted the formerly elective council to one chosen by royal appointment, severely limited the authority of town meetings, and altered the selection of juries to ensure a more favorable hearing of royal complaints. Parliament had already passed the Administration of Justice Act which provided that royal officials charged with capital offenses in Massachusetts while carrying out their duties could be tried either in England or in another colony at the discretion of the governor. Finally, these actions were capped by the Quartering Act, which provided for the quartering of British troops in private Boston homes.

The disintegration of formal relations between England and Massachusetts focused the widespread colonial discontent. Throughout rural Massachusetts mobs of farmers drove royal officials in hasty flight to the comparative safety of Boston, while the blockaded port received such quantities of foodstuff that the Bostonians were (in the words of one British officer) "as sleek and round as robins." Yet the House of Lords refused to mitigate the restrictions of the Boston Port Act, and Edmund Burke argued in vain for repeal of the tea tax. Lord North and George III moved with increasing speed to restore royal authority. They had one final shock in store for the colonials.

The Quebec Act. On June 22, 1774, royal assent was given to the Quebec Act, which extended the boundaries of Quebec to include French-speaking settlements in the Ohio Valley and the Illinois country. A series of liberal provisions were made recognizing the Roman Catholic character of the province's inhabitants. French civil law, supplemented by English criminal law and procedure, was established. The act set up an appointive legislative council, and waived the Test Act so that Catholics could sit on this body. Though specific provision was made "that nothing herein contained, relative to the Boundary of the province of Quebec, shall in anywise affect the Boundaries of any other Colony," those colonies with claims to western land were convinced that royal authority was denying them their just claims. Moreover, the

Protestant clergy of the colonies emphatically denounced the Crown's toleration of Roman Catholicism.

THE FIRST CONTINENTAL CONGRESS

A Call for Union. As news spread of the Coercive Acts (as the Boston Port Act, the Massachusetts Government Act, the Administration of Justice Act, and the Quartering Act were known in the colonies), the Committees of Correspondence renewed their efforts to secure collective colonial action. Calls for such action went forth almost simultaneously from the New York Committee of Correspondence, from a Providence town meeting, and from the Virginia House of Burgesses. On June 17, 1774, the Massachusetts House of Representatives issued a call for a congress of the Committees of Correspondence to meet in Philadelphia early in September, its purpose to be the formulation of a more effective colonial union.

The Congress Convenes. The First Continental Congress opened on September 5, with fifty-five delegates (from every colony but Georgia) in attendance. Such radicals as Samuel and John Adams of Massachusetts and Patrick Henry and Richard Henry Lee of Virginia were present, together with conservatives like Joseph Galloway of Pennsylvania, and moderates like John Jay and James Duane of New York. For the first time men of every stripe and temperament were given an opportunity to express the depth of colonial antagonism to and fears of the Crown's authority. They quickly discovered that not even so conservative a man as Galloway was prepared to defend the old empire. Instead, Galloway introduced a Plan for Union that called for the establishment of an American government consisting of a legislative council chosen by the colonial assemblies and a President-General selected by the king. It also provided for a double veto: the American Grand Council, as the legislative council was to be called, would be authorized to veto any Parliamentary legislation affecting the colonies, while Parliament in turn could veto any of the Grand Council's legislation.

Decisions of the Congress. Instead of giving approval to Galloway's efforts at conciliation, the Continental Congress, responding to urgent pressure from the Massachusetts delegation, approved the Suffolk Resolves. These denounced the Coercive Acts and pledged the upholding of "those liberties for which the fathers had fought and bled." On October 14, the Congress issued a Declaration of Rights and Grievances which challenged, on constitutional grounds, all parliamentary legislation for the colonies. Six days later it organized a nonimportation, non-exportation, and nonconsumption committee. The Continental Congress had in effect declared economic war upon Britain. The Congress completed its labors with a volley of petitions to the king and the peoples of his various domains. Almost immediately a war of words began as colonial conservatives, fearful of the consequences the economic boycott might bring, denounced its work, only to be answered by their more radical brethren. In the developing upheaval, a moderate stance became increasingly untenable.

The British Reaction. In England, the meeting of the Continental Congress was taken as a revolutionary action. George III, suspecting the approach of a final crisis, argued that "the die is now cast, the Colonies must either submit or triumph; I do not wish to come to severer measures, but we must not retreat." Perhaps a king with greater foresight could still have salvaged something from the developing debacle. Edmund Burke, uncertain of the challenge America posed, but still seeking reconciliation, insisted that "Magnanimity in politics is not seldom the truest wisdom." He added prophetically that "a great empire and little minds go ill together." British merchants and Lord Chatham continued, during the winter of 1775, to strive for an acceptable compromise, but Parliament pressed for a showdown. Massachusetts was declared to be in a state of rebellion and steps were taken to subdue her. Two Restraining Acts forbade trade between all the colonies but New York, North Carolina, and Georgia. On February 20, 1775, Lord North, in a final effort at conciliation, offered to defer further Parliamentary efforts at taxation if the colonial assemblies would only provide the necessary funds to support British armed forces stationed in the colonies. His plan revealed the blind spot in English thinking, since now nothing would satisfy the colonials but parliamentary surrender of all taxation rights over them *and* the withdrawal of the army. As John Adams subsequently recalled, "the revolution was complete, in the minds of the people . . . before the war commenced in the skirmishes of Concord and Lexington on the 19th of April, 1775." Britain had now to decide whether to acknowledge or to subvert the independence of her colonies. By choosing the latter course she opened a war that was to end with the destruction of the first British Empire.

Chapter 6

The American Revolution

Throughout the winter and early spring of 1775, relations between Britain and New England worsened. The closing of the port of Boston brought extensive unemployment and embittered the hot-tempered workers of South Boston. Even more aggravating was the presence in the Massachusetts metropolis of thousands of troops, supported by the Royal Navy. The appointment of General Gage as royal governor brought a brief lull in the rising tension. Gage, well aware that New England tempers had been rubbed raw, wished to lessen colonial grievances. Upon assuming the governorship he immediately asked John Hancock and Samuel Adams to use their influence to keep the peace.

THE OPENING OF THE WAR

General Gage and the War's Beginning. But Gage provoked the suspicion that his efforts at conciliation were hypocritical when, on February 26, 1775, he sent a detachment of troops to Salem to seize military stores. Though unsuccessful, the foray roused the "minutemen," organizations of local militia, to round-the-clock patrols. Since British authority barely extended beyond Boston, the colonials easily accumulated arms and munitions for the local militia. In early April, Gage, under increasing pressure from both his home government and local Tories, decided to seize colonial military stores at Concord, eighteen miles from Boston.

Lexington and Concord. Gage had scarcely reached his decision before the colonials knew of it, and devised a system of signal lights to notify militiamen outside Boston of the movement of British troops.

THE AMERICAN COLONIES IN 1775

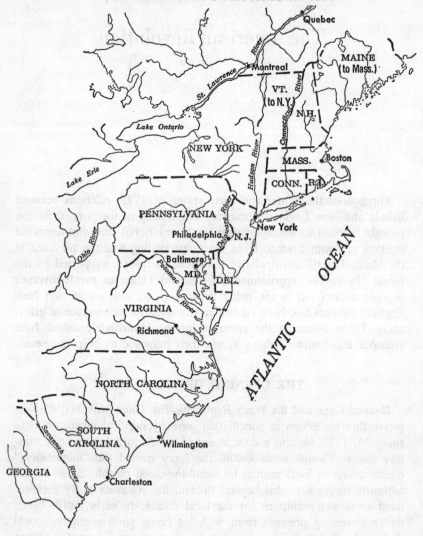

Late in the evening of April 18, 1775, eight hundred English troops began their march on Lexington. At the same time, Paul Revere and William Dawes rode through the countryside alerting colonials to the approach of the British troops. Other signals—tolling church bells, booming cannon, and rifle shots—made it unlikely that Gage's advance would go unnoticed. When the British reached Lexington, they found more than fifty minutemen under the command of Captain John Parker blocking their route through the village green. When the cry, "Disperse, ye rebels!" brought no obedience, the famous "shot heard round the world" was fired. In the ensuing exchange of fire eight colonials were killed and at least ten wounded before the remaining minutemen fled. The redcoats marched on to Concord without difficulty and destroyed the arms stores.

The British Retreat from Concord. News of the incident at Lexington brought thousands of minutemen swarming into Concord. Confronted with an unexpectedly substantial threat, the British force began to retreat toward Boston. In subsequent skirmishing the British suffered 273 casualties, the Americans 95. Only the arrival of an additional thousand troops under Brigadier General Lord Hugh Percy spared them a complete debacle. Had the minutemen been more efficiently organized, the day might well have ended with a major British disaster; but Percy managed a brilliant retreat, and the British defeat was primarily political and moral. Percy confessed that the enemy displayed a variety of "perseverance" he had not believed possible.

The Aftermath of Battle. News of the events around Boston spread with incredible speed throughout the colonies, reaching New York by the twenty-third and Philadelphia by the twenty-fourth. With the news went an urgent plea for aid. The response was immediate; thousands of troops hastened to lay siege to Boston. Massachusetts recruited an army of 30,000, Connecticut recruited 6,000, New Hampshire, 2,000, and Rhode Island, 1,800 men to help in driving the British from Boston. New York radicals, in a swift move to overcome conservative opposition, seized British military supplies; Philadelphia mobilized its manpower and manufactured powder so quickly that there existed no want for ammunition. Everywhere the response was the same—prompt mobilization. As one Philadelphia lady expressed it, "Nothing is heard now in our streets but the trumpet and drum; and the universal cry is 'Americans, to arms!'"

George III Responds. The events in Massachusetts shook Lord North, who had placed high hopes in his plan of conciliation; but they stiffened the determination of his royal master. "I am of [the] opinion that when once these rebels have felt a smart blow," George III declared, "they will submit." Rather than accept them upon any other terms, he preferred "to cast them off!" The British were determined to press the attack even at the cost of hiring mercenaries. As both sides mobilized, General Gage issued a plaintive proclamation that promised pardons for all rebels—except Samuel Adams and John Hancock—if they would lay down their arms. The proclamation was ignored.

The Collapse of Royal Authority. Everywhere revolutionary forces seized control of colonial governments as royal officials fled their posts. In Virginia, Lord Dunmore, after fruitlessly ordering the arrest of Patrick Henry, found refuge aboard a royal ship. John Wentworth of New Hampshire, confronted with an irate militia, abandoned his office early in December 1774. When Rhode Island's governor Joseph Wanton showed some hesitancy in supporting revolution he was promptly suspended by his former radical friends. By early autumn of 1775, only the governors of Georgia, New Jersey, Maryland, and Pennsylvania remained in office, and they were without effective power. A month before the final decision for independence they too departed their posts.

The Seizure of Fort Ticonderoga. As royal authority disintegrated, the colonials moved swiftly to mount an effective war effort. They invested Boston, but they were unable to press their campaign since they lacked the cannon with which to breach British fortifications. Massachusetts and Connecticut Whigs knew, however, that there were cannon at Fort Ticonderoga on Lake Champlain. A small force of no more than three hundred men, under the command of Benedict Arnold and Ethan Allen, captured the fort on May 10, 1775. From there Arnold moved swiftly to capture Crown Point and St. John's, thus putting Americans in control of the military route into Canada. And artillery was finally at hand to secure the colonials' siege of Boston.

Bunker Hill. By May 25, 1775, the aggressive intentions of the British government could no longer be denied; on that day Major Generals Sir Henry Clinton, William Howe, and John Burgoyne arrived in Boston. Gage, isolated with his 4,000 troops on the Boston peninsula by some 7,000 American militia, moved to secure his southern and northern flanks by seizing Dorchester Heights and Charlestown. When some 1,500 Americans under General Israel Putnam and Colonel William Prescott occupied Breed's Hill—incorrectly thought to be Bunker Hill—on Charlestown peninsula during the night of June 16, Gage had no choice but to attack. In the ensuing battle the British overcame stubborn

American resistance, but only after heavy losses. Gage, who had approached the battle with contempt for his colonial antagonists, learned

THE WAR IN THE NORTH 1775-1776

American Army
British Army

that only the absence of ammunition had caused the Americans to abandon their position. The British had lost 1,150 out of 2,500 men, as opposed to American losses of 400 men out of a force of 1,500. Had Gage promptly resumed the attack, the colonial lack of supplies and organization might well have enabled him to break the siege of Boston, but his heavy losses had weakened him too seriously.

When George Washington arrived at Cambridge early in July to assume command of the army, he provided the colonials with effective organization. His appointment had been unanimously approved by the Second Continental Congress on June 16, 1775. Fortunately, as Washington set to work whipping an army into shape, the British were beset with weak leadership, disease, desertion, and inadequate supplies. Early in March, American forces seized Dorchester Heights; and soon thereafter Washington occupied Nook's Hill, from which he could command Boston. On March 26, 1776, Howe, who had succeeded Gage in command, withdrew the British army by ship—along with more than a thousand loyalists—to Halifax, Nova Scotia.

Quebec. Far to the north, separate American forces under Richard Montgomery and Benedict Arnold opened a two-pronged attack upon Quebec. After early gains which included the fall of Montreal on November 13, 1775, Arnold drove six hundred miles through the Maine wilderness to reach and invest Quebec late in November. Early in December, Montgomery joined him and throughout the month they made plans for the assault upon the city. The Americans opened their attack in a blinding blizzard on December 31, 1775, only to be repulsed by the British and French under the command of General Guy Carleton. Montgomery was killed, Arnold wounded, and five hundred Americans killed or captured, while the defenders suffered only eighteen dead or wounded. Although Arnold clung to his positions about Quebec, disease and desertion played havoc with his command. The appearance of a British fleet in the St. Lawrence early in May sent the remaining Americans into a pell-mell retreat that ended only when straggling remnants found refuge at Ticonderoga. The attempted conquest of Canada had ended in disaster.

THE SECOND CONTINENTAL CONGRESS

Agitation for Independence. As the Americans came to know both victory and defeat, agitation grew rapidly for a final break with Britain. Secret discussion flared into the open with the publication of Thomas Paine's *Common Sense* on January 10, 1776. Distributed by the tens of thousands, the pamphlet argued:

> Everything that is right or reasonable pleads for separation. The blood of the slain, the weeping voice of nature cries, 'TIS TIME TO PART.'

Yet, the Whig organizers of the revolution moved toward this final step cautiously, and only after considered efforts at restoration of peace within the empire. On July 6, 1775, the Second Continental Congress, explaining the American resort to arms, pleaded: ". . . we mean not to dissolve that union which has so long and so happily subsisted between us, and which we sincerely wish to see restored." Two days later,

the same Congress sent the Olive Branch Petition to the king assuring
him of their continued loyalty and requesting royal aid in obtaining relief from unjust treatment. The king's response was to declare the colonies in a state of rebellion.

Nevertheless, as late as November 1775, the Pennsylvania Assembly
enjoined its delegates to the Continental Congress to "dissent from and
utterly reject any propositions . . . that may cause or lead to a separation from our mother country or a change of the form of this government." But Thomas Jefferson had privately concluded in the same
month that "We want neither inducement nor power, to declare and
assert a separation. It is will alone which is wanting, and that is growing
apace, under the fostering hand of our King."

The Triumph of the Whigs. The victory at Boston had assured Ameri-
cans that they could defend their independence. With this assurance
Congress began to act positively, authorizing both privateer action upon
British commerce and an embargo upon British products (February
1776). Silas Deane was instructed to enter into negotiations with the
French minister Vergennes for aid and to assure him "that there was a
great appearance that the colonies would come to a total separation."
In April, American ports were thrown open to all ships except those of
Great Britain. Simultaneously, radical forces gained control of all but
the middle colonies. South Carolina, in its new constitution, implied that
the royal tie had been abrogated by the king's aggression; North Carolina and Rhode Island instructed their congressional delegates to vote
for independence. Early in May, Massachusetts began to sound out the
trend of its town meetings on the prospect of independence. And Virginia, following the lead of Edmund Pendleton, an outspoken Whig,
voted on May 15 to call on Congress for a declaration of independence.
Only the hesitancy of the middle colonies prevented an immediate declaration of this kind. The pressure upon the Continental Congress became nearly irresistible. As John Adams expressed it, "Every post and
every day rolls in upon us Independence like a torrent."

THE DECLARATION OF INDEPENDENCE

Following the instructions of his state, Richard Henry Lee, on June
7, 1776, introduced resolutions calling for independence, the conclusion of foreign alliances, and the founding of a confederation. The extent of revolutionary sentiment was manifested when only a handful of

delegates, led by James Wilson, John Dickinson, Edward Rutledge, and Robert Livingston, opposed immediate independence. They argued that "the people of the middle colonies . . . were not yet ripe for bidding adieu to British connection" though "they were fast ripening" for a final break. The advocates of independence argued cogently that the real issue was "whether we should declare a fact that already exists." A *de facto* condition demanded a *de jure* legitimacy.

The Composition of the Declaration of Independence. Opposition crumbled at the end of June when a pro-independence delegation from New Jersey replaced the colony's earlier representatives. The Congress had delayed formal discussion of Lee's resolutions for three weeks; now a committee, consisting of Thomas Jefferson, Benjamin Franklin, John Adams, Robert Livingston, and Roger Sherman, was authorized to draw up a Declaration of Independence. On June 28, the finished document was put before the Congress. Although it had been altered verbally by Franklin and Adams, and substantively by the removal in committee of an attack upon slavery and the slave trade, it was largely the work of Thomas Jefferson. As to its objective, Jefferson himself recalled:

> . . . the object of the Declaration of Independence [was] not to find out new principles, or new arguments, never before thought of, not merely to say things which had never been said before; but to place before mankind the common sense of the subject, in terms so plain and firm as to command their assent, and to justify ourselves in the independent stand we were compelled to take.

The Declaration gained ready assent because, as Jefferson said, it proved "to be an expression of the American mind." After less than three days of debate, it was unanimously approved. Only an absent New York delegation failed to vote on July 4. And thus independence came.

WHIGS, LOYALISTS, AND THE INDIFFERENT

As John Adams pointed out, few of the men who decided on independence in 1776 expected the Declaration to "ward off calamities from this country." They expected to endure a bloody conflict. The Americans, having made their declaration, now had to make it stick, under circumstances that tested the stanchest patriot, for the unanimity expressed in the Continental Congress reflected, at best, the opinion of no more than a bare majority of the American population. Very probably, it was the expression of a minority.

Divided Loyalties. "If I were called upon to calculate the divisions among the people of America I should say that fully one-third were averse to the revolution," wrote John Adams many years later. "An opposite third conceived a hatred of the English and gave themselves up to an enthusiastic gratitude to France." As for the remainder, "The middle third, comprising principally the yeomanry, the soundest part of the nation, and always averse to war, were rather lukewarm both to England and France; and sometimes stragglers from them, and sometimes the whole body, united with the first or last third, according to circumstance." The portrait is one of divided loyalties, further complicated by numerous class conflicts that followed no national pattern but varied within individual states.

Whig and Tory. It is not possible to explain these conflicts by assigning to the colonial gentry or yeomanry either Whig or Tory sentiments. In New York the gentry, though far from united, remained loyal to England, while those of Virginia were passionate exponents of revolution. In North Carolina the upcountry yeomen, still smarting from the defeat of the Regulator movement, supported the Crown, while the lowcountry planters embraced revolution. Anglicans were loyalists; Congregationalists stood for revolution. When Quakers clung to the Crown, the Scots-Irish frontiersmen of Pennsylvania, resentful of Quaker dominance, swore by revolution. In New York, where a goodly proportion of the small farmers allied themselves with the gentry against revolution, the British remained in substantial control for most of the war. In the lower South, South Carolina had a much higher proportion of loyalists than Virginia.

The Tories and War Atrocities. The true scope of loyalist sentiment throughout the colonies is probably best illustrated by two facts: during the war no less than 75,000 Americans in a population of two million fled either to Canada or to Britain; and at no time were the Americans able to put more then 25,000 men into the field (while even these were often badly supplied). At the same time, no less than 30,000 loyalists served for varying lengths of time in the British army. Though the loyalists were ready to fight and did provide considerable assistance to the British in the Carolinas, around New York City, and along the frontier, the British never fully exploited this potential source of manpower. As the war gained momentum, loyalists caught by the revolutionaries were subjected to a variety of punishments—tar and feathers, whipping, fines, confiscation of property, banishment, and even death. They reciprocated with comparable savagery, especially along the frontier, where Tories led Indians to massacre Whig frontiersmen. The longer the war continued, the more brutal and raw it became. Somewhere between seven and eight thousand Americans, more than the number killed in battle, perished from disease and hunger on British prison ships anchored in the waters about New York. And every atrocity made reconciliation more remote and the demand for independence more insistent. The behavior of both loyalist and Whig in the developing conflict guaranteed that the losers would be compelled to accept a punitive peace. For the Whigs there would be no benevolent Britain to turn to if the war were lost; they soon realized that their fortunes and lives hung in the balance.

THE BRITISH WAR EFFORT

King and Parliament. The disunity of the American war effort raises the question of why it succeeded. The simplest explanation is the folly of George III and his ministers in alienating not only the American Whigs but also the sentiment of a considerable body of English. Although the English Whigs gave little positive aid to the Americans, they did even less to assist the Crown in its struggle to subdue the colonial revolt. The divisions within the new republic were reflected in the British Parliament. The corrupt English election of 1774 had brought to Parliament men eager to obtain royal patronage. Their votes, in return for patronage, guaranteed the king a comfortable majority. But, although the king seemed to command vast support in his efforts to restore the empire, his supporters lacked the will and tenacity to make subjugation of America a central and unwavering objective.

The English Whigs and George III. For all practical purposes, the real talent of Parliament stood in opposition to the policies of George III. Edmund Burke, who combined oratory and philosophy; Chatham, who had created an empire and lived to see its disintegration; John Wilkes, the king's anathema; Charles James Fox, glorying in his brittle brilliance; and a whole galaxy of English Whigs mocked and denounced the king for his colonial policies. Though unable to prevent his undertaking these policies, they limited the king's ability to mount the war effort necessary to subdue the colonials.

British Public Opinion. More significantly, English public opinion was divided, and this division crucially affected the military and naval leaders of the British armed forces. Such commanders as Sir Jeffrey Amherst and Lord Frederick Cavendish, both of whom had made illustrious careers in the Seven Years' War, refused active commands. In the Navy, Admiral Keppel flatly refused an American command. A deluge of petitions from merchants and from cities expressed dismay at the conflict and protested "a civil war commenced in America by your Majesty's Commander in Chief." Cambridge University was only grudging in its support of the king. The division within the aristocracy of England carried over into the lower classes. Efforts to bring the army to 55,000 men failed when recruiting met with national indifference. "People are much divided in their sentiments about the Americans," read one grim report, ". . . but the bulk of the people of England and Ireland are strongly in their interest." In the end, public indifference caused the king to hire about 30,000 German mercenaries to fight his war. The divisions in colonial sentiment were more than balanced by the open hostility of a considerable number of Englishmen to the war against their transatlantic brethren.

Strategy of War. The loss of Boston had brought British withdrawal from New England. It also brought the need for a new strategy to subdue the colonies. The British resolved to exploit the loyalist centers in South Carolina and New York. The British scheme of reconquest was initially concentrated upon the seizure of New York City and a subsequent drive up the Hudson Valley, both operations to be carried out under General William Howe. A Canadian expedition under Sir Guy Carleton was to drive south until it made a juncture with Howe's forces. Lending naval support to this operation was William Howe's brother, Admiral Henry Howe. Both men expected a negotiated settlement, and had not yet been disabused in this respect by the spring of 1776.

THE EARLY YEARS OF THE REVOLUTION

Defeat in New York. Although uncertain where the first British blow would fall, Washington thought it likely that New York City would be the immediate target. On March 18, he started moving troops into the area and ordered the men of the city to erect fortifications. The American army presented a motley appearance, with little sense of national identity, poor equipment, a thorough lack of discipline, and a tendency to confuse private advantage with patriotism. Washington was driven to plead that the soldiers sink their provincialism for the sake of the American cause. It was this army that confronted, on June 29, 1776, a fleet of more than one hundred British ships loaded with 10,000 men. General Howe led this advance force when it landed on Staten Island on July 2, and ten days later Admiral Howe arrived with an additional 150 troop transports. By August 12, the British had 32,000 men in the area of the city. During the preliminary preparations for battle the Howe brothers attempted to enter into negotiations with Washington, only to be rebuffed when they gave as the preliminary royal condition for a settlement the disbanding of all American armies and political organizations.

The Battle of Harlem Heights. The Howes opened their New York campaign on August 22, landing some 15,000 troops on Long Island. The Americans met the British attack with scarcely 8,000 troops, and those mainly raw militia commanded by the incompetent General John Sullivan. The British quickly outflanked and routed the American forces. Had General Howe shown less caution, he could probably have overrun the Brooklyn fortifications. As it was, his delay permitted Washington to retrieve the remainder of his army on the night of August 29–30, by retreating across the East River to Manhattan Island. The American commander was faced with a grim situation: his army had sustained 1,500 casualties in the Battle of Long Island and he faced the real risk of being cut off on Manhattan Island. On September 8, he decided to abandon the city to the British. Six days later Howe's forces landed on the island, swept aside the militia at Kip's Bay, and drove north until repulsed by Washington's forces at Harlem Heights. (It must be remembered, of course, that at this time the city of New York occupied only the tip of Manhattan Island; Harlem Heights was, in colonial terms, a considerable distance away.) Washington had gained a momentary respite, but he was completely on the defensive, uncertain where the British would strike next. Complicating his difficulties was the discovery that a sizable proportion of his army were "summer patriots."

Nathan Hale. As an unhappy Washington sought to extricate himself from a dangerous position, an American spy, Nathan Hale, was captured on September 21, while seeking information about the British forces on Long Island. Hale, who revealed a Spartan courage, was interrogated, found guilty of spying, dragged without ceremony to the execution post, and hanged.

In the midst of growing defeat, the example of Hale stirred American pride. Though it is not certain that Hale said "I only regret that I have but one life to give for my country," it is certain that the contemporary ballad written about his deed, asserting that the trials of war held "no fear for the brave," helped to reassure many Americans. During the weeks that followed, Americans would have great need of such reassurances.

The Retreat from New York. The moves of the American army at this time were determined in large part by the actions of the cautious William Howe. He did not attack again until early October, when he began landing forces into what is now the Bronx. Washington, faced with a flanking movement, retreated north to White Plains. Once again Howe's habitual delay prevented a swift decision, and allowed Washington to build up sufficient strength to forestall a total American defeat. But a heavy loss was sustained by the Americans when Fort Washington, on the northern tip of Manhattan, surrendered to the British on November 17 with 2,800 prisoners.

The Invasion of New Jersey. The setback shook American morale and left Washington predicting gloomily, "The loss of such a number of officers and men, many of whom have been trained with more than common attention, will I fear be severely felt. But when that of the arms and accoutrements is added, much more so, and must be a farther incentive to procure as considerable a supply as possible for the new troops, as soon as it can be done." Two days later Lord Cornwallis led a British invasion of New Jersey and compelled the surrender of Fort Lee as Washington's army retreated in pell-mell fashion. Unable to halt the British advance on Philadelphia, Washington chose to retreat in the hope that this action would lull the enemy into a false sense of security. Colonial morale sank even lower when Jersey residents appeared in captains' companies to take the oath of allegiance to the king. Disaffection spread into Pennsylvania as the war approached the Delaware River. In the middle of December, Charles Lee, an overrated American general, fell into British hands, thus adding to Washington's dismay at signs of rapid disintegration within his army. Few could deny the grim poignancy of Tom Paine's lament, "These are the times that try men's souls."

Trenton. Now desperate, Washington, on Christmas night, 1776, struck suddenly at Trenton where a large force of Hessian mercenaries were billeted. Crossing the ice-laden Delaware in snow and sleet, the Americans achieved a complete tactical surprise. They captured almost five thousand prisoners at the cost of only five American casualties. The victory brought a resurgence of hope for the revolutionaries and a swift reaction from the British, who left Philadelphia to march on Trenton. But Cornwallis, reaching Trenton on January 2, 1777, delayed his attack, while Washington moved quickly to smash the British garrison and reinforcements at Princeton. He then retreated northward into winter quarters at Morristown, New Jersey. Though all but the eastern section of New Jersey had been retaken by Washington, the state was marked with the devastation of wanton destruction of property. For the rest of the winter, except for scattered British attacks on Connecticut towns, the war remained at a standstill.

The Campaign to Split the Colonies. Farther to the north the British prepared a three-pronged attack on upstate New York under General John Burgoyne. One army was to push southward along Lake Champlain and the upper Hudson Valley, another to operate in the Mohawk Valley, and a third, under Howe, to push up the Hudson Valley. The three armies would unite at Albany.

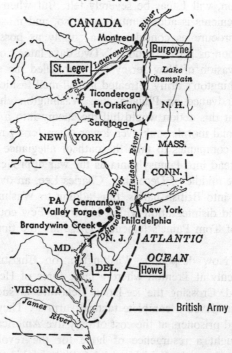

PRINCIPAL CAMPAIGNS
1777-1778

Late in June 1777, Howe withdrew his troops from New Jersey preparatory to his drive up the Hudson Valley from New York. Unfortunately for British expectations, Howe then decided on his own initiative that he could not help Burgoyne unless Washington left New Jersey to join the northern revolutionary army in obstructing the British drive from Canada. On June 17, Burgoyne and his army of 7,000, unaware of Howe's failure to proceed, launched their march toward disaster.

The Fall of Ticonderoga. The Americans suffered the first blow when Ticonderoga, overlooking the western approaches to Lake Champlain, fell in early July. Once again the American armies had to retreat, hoping to lure the enemy into a blunder. Their hopes were answered when Burgoyne made an overland advance on Fort Edward, where the Americans were encamped, rather than making his approach by way of Lake George. For twenty-four days the British army floundered through bog and stream, obstructed by trees felled in its path, to reach Fort Edward, only twenty-three miles from Ticonderoga. As Burgoyne inched along, the British force under Colonel Barry St. Leger in the Mohawk Valley reached Fort Schuyler, which barred the road to Albany, only to retreat precipitously when its Indian allies deserted. Not only was the tactical situation rapidly becoming worse, but the advancing Burgoyne had to face an increasingly critical shortage of supplies. The Americans under General Schuyler had resorted to a scorched-earth policy in opposing Burgoyne's southward march.

Saratoga. Finally made aware that Howe had failed to advance up the Hudson and planned instead to attack Pennsylvania, and increasingly aware of his own precarious position, Burgoyne resolved to push on to Albany. At Bemis Heights the two armies (the Americans now led by General Horatio Gates who had been sent to replace Schuyler because of the New Englanders' dissatisfaction with the latter's policies) met to open the momentous battle of Saratoga. A sharply fought engagement at Freeman's Farm ended in a draw, but British losses were so heavy that Burgoyne could not readily replace them. At the same time a bitter dispute over strategy between Benedict Arnold, who had served gallantly in the battle, and the commander, Horatio Gates, resulted in Arnold's removal from command.

The Surrender of Burgoyne. By early October, Burgoyne's army was in a serious plight. Only swift aid from the British forces in and around New York seemed capable of supplying the relief needed. Sir Henry Clinton, however, uneasy about his position in New York, moved with extreme caution in opening a drive on Albany. Since he met with immediate success it is possible that, had he thrown his full force into action, Clinton could have driven all the way to Albany to effect a juncture with the trapped Burgoyne. As it was, Fort Edward had fallen to the Americans, and the British, now surrounded, dug in on Bemis Heights. There, on October 7, Burgoyne's 5,000 men were attacked by Gates' 11,000. Before the day was finished, the Americans had breached his lines and Burgoyne had retreated to the heights about Saratoga. No longer able to resist, Burgoyne asked for terms. Gates was surprisingly generous. Under the Saratoga Convention of October 16, the British surrendered and were permitted to march to Boston for embarkation to Britain on condition that they not be used again to fight on the North American continent. A similar release was granted to Canadian troops. Though the war was far from ended, the Americans had won a major victory, one which established Britain's inability to subdue the interior regions of her former American colonies. And the British also learned that hopes of a loyalist uprising were futile.

The French Intervene. Once the British colonies rebelled, all Europe wondered whether a renewed war between France and Britain was in the offing. The French still smarted from their disastrous defeat in the Seven Years' War, but it was questionable whether they were prepared to identify themselves with a rebellion against royal authority. It was apparent, in any case, that the French would aid the Americans only if they were convinced that such a move was in their own clear interest. The Americans, on their part, realized from the outset that French aid and intervention might prove decisive in converting the struggle from a prospective draw to an outright victory. Beginning in 1775 Congress delegated to Benjamin Franklin, Silas Deane, John Adams, and John Jay the task of obtaining outright assistance from the French.

American Reservations on French Intervention. Though they were eager to obtain the alliance of the French, there existed a strong reservation among Americans; they did not wish to enter into any alliance which might someday involve them in any future wars in Europe. Nevertheless, well before independence was formally declared, American feelers were put out to test French sentiment on an alliance. As it was, the French had watched with increasing interest the dispute between Britain and her colonies. The central principle of French foreign policy emerged when it became clear that the destruction of Britain's American empire would permit re-establishment of the power balance upset by the total British victory of 1763.

Early French Assistance. In June 1776 France began covertly to supply the colonials with munitions and other necessities. Silas Deane, disguised as a merchant in the Indian trade, began a lively import of munitions and simultaneously ran an agency recruiting European officers to assist the American war effort. In September, Deane was joined in France by Franklin and Arthur Lee. The presence of Franklin added immense prestige to the American delegation since he enjoyed an overwhelming reputation among French intellectuals. He, as John Adams grudgingly remembered, "was considered . . . a citizen of the world, a friend to all men and an enemy to none."

The news of the American victory at Saratoga led France to decide upon open intervention. As the Comte de Vergennes, French foreign minister, expressed it, "The power that will first recognize the independence of the Americans will be the one that will reap the fruits of this war."

On January 7, 1778, the French royal council agreed to a friendship and trade treaty with the United States, and on February 6 they entered into a full alliance. With the latter treaty France committed herself to the complete independence of the Americans, and convinced the British that the time had come to seek reconciliation. But negotiations failed when the British first insisted on parliamentary supremacy and then would not acknowledge the fact of American independence. Britain's final proposals, carried by the Carlisle Commission, provided for the abandonment of a standing army in peacetime and the amendment of colonial charters only at the request of the assemblies. In addition the British agreed either to grant Americans representation in Parliament or to accept the Continental Congress as a permanent institution, and to make judicial appointments contingent on the good behavior of those appointed. Similar proposals, had they been made three years earlier, would have averted the revolution. Now they seemed a weak device to persuade Americans to relinquish a nearly attained independence.

The Campaign in the Middle Colonies. While Burgoyne floundered toward disaster at Saratoga, Howe prepared to seize Philadelphia. Anticipating ready assistance from the city's Tories, he hoped to gain control of Pennsylvania, sever the new republic, and prevent Washington from aiding Gates in opposing Burgoyne. As it was, only a strenuous campaign permitted Howe to secure control of the lower Delaware Valley by November. Extreme caution led him to launch his campaign against Philadelphia by way of Chesapeake Bay rather than directly up the Delaware. On September 11, Howe inflicted a heavy defeat on Washington at Brandywine. Further disaster struck the revolutionaries when several hundred American troops were taken unawares at Paoli, Pennsylvania, on September 21, 1777. Five days later Philadelphia fell;

and the Continental Congress, after conferring dictatorial powers on Washington, fled to Lancaster. On October 4, the American forces opened a surprise attack upon Howe's troops encamped at Germantown. After early gains, the Americans panicked and sustained heavy losses. Both forces now settled into winter quarters, the British in the comfort of Philadelphia and the Americans in the wretched misery of Valley Forge.

The Battle of Monmouth. Early in June 1778 the British, commanded by Clinton (who had replaced Howe), withdrew from Philadelphia and retreated across New Jersey. The British intended to concentrate their forces at New York to meet an anticipated joint American and French attack. Washington opened a pursuit and finally, on June 28, ordered an attack upon the British as they prepared to withdraw from Monmouth Courthouse. General Charles Lee, ordered by Washington to move against the British rear, retreated instead, permitting the British to wheel about and attack first. The ensuing battle ended in a draw. Lee was later tried by a court-martial and removed from the army. In early July, Clinton completed his withdrawal to New York without further incident.

Benedict Arnold and Major André. The arrival of a French fleet under Count d'Estaing signaled a joint Franco-American campaign against Newport, Rhode Island. The venture failed when the British sent a fleet of their own to challenge the effort. Sporadic action during the early part of 1779 brought a signal American victory at Stony Point, New York, when Anthony Wayne overpowered British fortifications guarding the west shore of the Hudson. In late August, Major Henry Lee achieved a swift victory when he overwhelmed the British garrison at Paulus Hook (now Jersey City). These events were overshadowed by the treason of Benedict Arnold, an ambitious general who put personal gain above patriotism and entered into negotiations with the British to surrender West Point, of which he was commander. His plans went awry when Major John André, the English officer with whom he had negotiated, was captured. Though Arnold escaped, André paid with his life. The treason of Arnold was symptomatic of a growing dissension within American ranks. Sporadic mutiny erupted as the Continental forces protested the paucity of their food, the absence of pay, the ragged condition of their clothes, and the seeming indifference of Congress to their plight. Only such prompt action as the execution of mutinous ringleaders in three Jersey regiments prevented these protests from getting out of hand.

THE WAR IN THE SOUTH

Having failed to subdue either New England or the middle colonies, the British now shifted their main attack to the South. The region was torn by internecine warfare made more ferocious by ruthless guerrillas who often used the guise of war to settle personal grievances. An earlier effort to capture Charleston, South Carolina, in late June of 1776, had ended in a British defeat. The British now determined upon a second drive to seize South Carolina, where considerable loyalist sentiment seemed to promise an easy victory.

THE WAR IN THE SOUTH

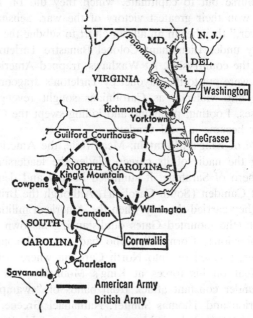

The Seizure of Georgia. As a prelude to their southern campaign, the British opened an amphibious assault on Savannah, Georgia. The state of Georgia soon passed into British hands and royal authority was quickly restored. Efforts by American militia to reconquer the lost state ended disastrously when the patriots broke ranks and fled under the disciplined attacks of the redcoats. The British, under the command of Colonel J. M. Prévost, then invaded South Carolina, whose governor offered to neutralize the state if the British would withdraw. Exploiting the obvious weakness of the Carolina militia, the British demanded nothing less than unconditional surrender. The subsequent approach of an American relief force under General Benjamin Lincoln persuaded the daring Prévost to withdraw in a campaign of swift maneuver which bluffed the superior American force. A joint Franco-American effort to recapture Savannah late in 1778 ended in failure after the allies had suffered heavy losses. The way was now clear for Clinton to open an attack in force on Charleston.

British Victories in the Carolinas. In mid-February 1780 the British landed at Beaufort and began a slow, cautious advance on Charleston. The Americans, who permitted themselves to be bottled up in the city, had no recourse but to capitulate, which they did on May 12. The British had won their greatest victory of the war. Sensing that it was "now or never," they began an all-out effort to subdue the entire colony. Tory cavalry under Lieutenant Colonel Banastre Tarleton spread terror through the countryside. At Waxhaws, trapped Americans who had surrendered were put to the bayonet by Tarleton's dragoons. Tory sentiment flared into violence as Carolinians sought revenge for former Whig excesses. Looting, pillaging, and killing swept the Carolina country; the war became a local vendetta.

The Battle of King's Mountain. Meanwhile, the American army was approaching the nadir of its career. Under the leadership of Horatio Gates, the hero of Saratoga, it stumbled hungry and demoralized into the battle of Camden (South Carolina). Although the British were outnumbered, they carried the day when the American militia fled without firing a shot (the mounted Gates outdistancing his own men in a retreat into oblivion). Cornwallis, who had assumed command of the British forces, pressed on into North Carolina where patriots inflicted a sharp defeat on his forces at King's Mountain. His overextended lines were under constant attack from bands of "swamp rats" led by Francis Marion and Thomas Sumter. Nathanael Greene, who had replaced Gates, acknowledged the superior forces of his British opponent by concentrating on a war of hit-and-run. This swift shifting of forces by the Americans finally led Cornwallis to withdraw from North Carolina into Virginia. Even as he withdrew, the Americans won a hard-fought battle with Tarleton at Cowpens. To recoup lost ground, Cornwallis moved to attack Greene at Guilford Courthouse. There he won a Pyrrhic victory that left his army demoralized and himself depressed. Greene launched a reconquest of South Carolina and Georgia. Cornwallis made his way to Virginia, leaving behind him a bloody Carolina where the Whigs spiced their reconquest with Tory and British blood.

Withdrawal to Virginia. The Virginia that Cornwallis invaded in the closing weeks of 1780 had been spared the worse excesses of the war. Occasional British attacks on the coastal areas had given the interior little idea of what the conflict was like. Nor had Virginia's governor, Thomas Jefferson, despite strong warnings from Washington, made any real effort to prepare his state for attack—a single ineptness without parallel in his career. The war that had hovered on the edges of Virginia now descended upon it in force.

The Dispute between Cornwallis and Clinton. On January 5, 1781, Benedict Arnold, now serving as a British brigadier general, captured Richmond without opposition. After thoroughly devastating the surrounding countryside and thrusting aside the Virginia militia under Baron von Steuben, Arnold settled at Portsmouth for the winter. Jefferson was heartsore at not having taken "this greatest of all traitors." In May, Cornwallis reached Virginia and soon became embroiled in a major dispute with Clinton. Cornwallis thought the British should concentrate their entire effort on subduing Virginia, and asked his rival Clinton to withdraw from New York and join him in this enterprise. Clinton refused, and Cornwallis prepared to withdraw from the area. When news of these preparations reached Clinton, he countermanded the order and directed Cornwallis to establish a post as a bridgehead in Virginia. Cornwallis selected Yorktown. While the British army dug in around their new base, the British navy lost control of the sea. The end was in sight.

"The World Turned Upside Down." At first the British did not recognize their precarious position. British cavalry rode unimpeded through the Old Dominion's interior. Tarleton's cavalry sent the Virginia legislature in flight from Charlottesville to Staunton and led Jefferson to an undignified surrender of his acting-governorship. But as Washington slowly reinforced his troops under Lafayette, who had joined the American cause in 1777, Cornwallis withdrew from the interior toward the peninsula below Richmond. Consolidating his army at Yorktown and Gloucester, he settled into a defensive position.

The Battle of Yorktown. Washington, now assisted by a French army under the Comte de Rochambeau and by the French West Indian fleet under the Comte de Grasse, relinquished his plan for an attack on New York and settled for a campaign along the Chesapeake. Since the period during which de Grasse would be able to assist such a campaign ended in October, the Americans decided it was expedient to concentrate on Cornwallis. Moving swiftly the allies had, by late September, achieved a two-to-one advantage over the trapped English. Since de Grasse had also achieved naval superiority, the British were sealed off from relief by water. Trapped, seemingly deserted by Clinton, faced with complete disaster, Cornwallis surrendered his army to the besiegers on October 19, 1781. To the strains of "The World Turned Upside Down," the formal surrender was made. Far across the ocean, on November 25, Lord North received news of the capitulation, threw up his arms, and called out time and again, "O God! it is all over!" Though more than a year would elapse before peace was finally negotiated, the war was over indeed. Freedom had come to the United States.

THE TREATY OF PARIS, 1783

By this time the Americans realized that the European powers were not inclined to look upon complete independence of all the American colonies as a basis for restoring peace. It should be noted that Vergennes was ready, in the late winter of 1781, to accept peace on the basis of the lines drawn by war. This would have left New York City, Charleston, Savannah, Maine, and much of the Northwest in British hands. The French pressured Congress unsuccessfully to instruct the American delegations at Paris—Adams, Franklin, Jay, and Laurens—to follow the advice of the French king in any peace negotiations.

The Resignation of Lord North. In Britain, the Commons resolved, on March 4, 1782, that the nation should enter into peace negotiations with the United States. Lord North resigned sixteen days later. He was succeeded by Lord Rockingham, a long-time friend of American independence, who appointed as his foreign secretary a man of similar outlook, Charles James Fox. Fox shrewdly estimated that peace negotiations could retrieve lost ground if they resulted in a split between the French and the Americans. But the sudden death of Rockingham frustrated Fox's plans; Lord Shelburne, an opponent of American independence, succeeded to the prime ministership. Negotiations reached a deadlock when Franklin demanded cession of Canada and Shelburne insisted on guarantees of payment of British-held American debts and indemnification of Tories.

American Insistence on Total Independence. Efforts at shaping a settlement were not eased by the unwillingness of the French government to require British acceptance of complete independence for all the former colonies as a pre-condition for negotiations. Only the stubborn persistence of John Jay, ably backed by the forceful John Adams, enabled the American to win this crucial point. The death of illusion rang through John Jay's somber conclusion: "If they [the British] thought they could conquer us, they would again attempt it." The American delegation emphatically insisted that America be accorded the full dignity offered to any other independent people.

The Terms of Peace. In mid-September, the British accepted this demand; and thereupon negotiations proceeded at a rapid pace. Major disputes in the concluding conversations developed only over fisheries and restitution to dispossessed Tories. Compromise resolved both problems; the Americans accepted the "liberty" rather than the "right" to fish off Newfoundland, and agreed to recommend that the various states compensate their Tories. The French and Spanish failure to capture Gibraltar in late September encouraged the British to make concessions in an attempt to break the French-American alliance. Disregarding French instructions, the Americans signed a separate peace treaty—the Treaty of Paris—leaving Vergennes to mull over the speed with which the Americans had learned the devious intricacies of diplomacy. Included in the treaty was a secret provision that, should the British retain West Florida, its boundary was to be farther north than if Spain took control of the region.

The former colonies and the mother country now faced the task of re-establishing a spirit of good relations. The crisp words of John Adams called upon the British to show "that you are sincere in your acknowledgment of American independence." The Americans, on their part, had to prove their capacity to establish a viable state and to prevent any form of external intervention by the powers of Europe.

Chapter 7

Confederation and Constitution

To achieve independence was not to justify it. A good many Americans realized that they now were confronted by a difficult test, one that would require courage and determination. To the young Alexander Hamilton, for instance, peace meant the beginning, and not the end, of exertion: "The object will be to make our independence a blessing. To do this we must secure our Union on solid foundations—a herculean task, and to effect which mountains of prejudice must be levelled!" Thirteen states and thirteen separate peoples had to become a single nation. In view of the instances of disunity that had marred the war effort, only the foolishly optimistic could feel that this objective would be easily achieved.

EVOLVING NEW DOCUMENTS OF GOVERNMENT

In 1926, there appeared a small book with a long title, *The American Revolution Considered As a Social Movement*. Its author, J. Franklin Jameson, while admitting the conservative bias of the revolution, concluded that its results had been to establish new vistas of economic opportunity, to alter class relations, to redirect intellectual and religious life, and to affect traditional methods of landholding and labor. The exact dimensions of this social revolution remain a matter for debate; nevertheless, it is true that a sizable internal revolution had occurred in America, and that this was an inescapable consequence of the disruption of empire. Both royal and proprietary governments had been overthrown, leaving all but the charter colonies of Connecticut and Rhode Island with the task of forming new state governments. The flight and expulsion of loyalists, and the destruction of royal authority, permitted a wide-scale redistribution of confiscated royal and Tory properties. Western lands which passed under American control posed two urgent questions: overlapping state claims had to be resolved, and ways to achieve an orderly distribution of these lands to legitimate settlers had to be formulated.

The Scope of Revolution. Adding to these problems was the chaos engendered by war. The destruction of property left many Americans destitute; at the same time, the war brought Americans into contact with regions and peoples previously considered remote, and encouraged economic growth to meet wartime necessity. Thus, the experiment of American independence began in a condition of near-constant flux. Time-honored traditions were subjected to the test of circumstance and, if found wanting, abandoned.

The upper-class Americans who made the revolution were thoroughly grounded in the British political tradition, with its basic assumption that the authority to govern stemmed directly from the people. Hence, the social revolution which followed in the wake of war showed a restraint which later revolutions in France and Russia, where a deep ideological gulf separated ruler and subject, were to lack. A genuinely revolutionary upheaval would have swept away whole classes. As it was, the American experiment altered the social structure only to the extent of expelling the loyalists. In Pennsylvania and Georgia, where a radical democracy temporarily established a leveling movement, traditional control was asserted by the end of the revolution. And there were striking similarities between the careers of the revolutionists who signed the Declaration of Independence. Of the fifty-five signers, sixty-nine per cent had held office in the colonial period. Of these, ninety-five per cent were to hold office in the federal republic. No less than forty per cent of all the signers were college-educated; and nearly all were the sons of wealthy families or had accumulated substantial means themselves. Accustomed to wielding power, they defended their privileges against both Britain and the American lower orders. In essence, the American Revolution was an upheaval in which the established power elite defended itself against change.

State Constitutions. With the British and their sympathizers gone, the new-born states composed new constitutions of government and inaugurated political institutions that reflected the theory of John Locke: "Men being . . . by nature all free, equal, and independent, no one can be put out of this estate, and subjected to the political power of another, without his own consent. . . ." Therefore the political sentiments which Americans set down in their new constitutions were an inheritance which they had brought with them to the new world from Great Britain. In the new world they had, in fact, adapted traditional institutions to meet the peculiar needs of the American environment. As more than one acute observer noted, America was the land in which liberty was reinvigorated by opportunity. The colonials had accepted the Lockean dictum that the possession of property justified the possession of the franchise. Since the opportunity to obtain property was readily available to most colonials, Americans had a long experience in choosing their governors. It was an experience they put to quick use when called upon to reorganize their governments after the Revolution.

Massachusetts amply demonstrated the sovereignty of the people when it decided to draw up a new constitution. Before the General Court acted, it appealed to the towns for authorization. At each step, the General Court looked to the public for guidance. When the first constitution, proposed in December 1777, lacked a Bill of Rights, the public overwhelmingly repudiated it. The delegates to the second constitutional convention were elected by all males over the age of twenty-one. Under the guidance of John Adams they came up with an acceptable document, one which insured the governed their "rights, properties, and blessings of life."

In most instances the new constitutions established legislatures with two houses, though Pennsylvania settled for one. Fear of executive power caused nine of the states to deny their governors the right of veto and to provide for annual election of their chief executives. Suspicion of *all* authority caused most of the states to provide for the annual election of their legislators. Suffrage regulations varied from the broad suffrage rights for all adult males in Georgia, Delaware, Pennsylvania, and North Carolina, to the property requirements for suffrage exacted in Maryland, New Jersey, and South Carolina. In states like New Hampshire and Virginia, either payment of poll taxes or ownership of a small freehold was required. Although the constitutions as a whole could hardly be characterized as democratic, they all made provision for representative government.

Bills of Rights. The Massachusetts Bill of Rights was preceded by that of Virginia, which had been drawn up by George Mason of Gunston Hall in the spring of 1776. It guaranteed trial by jury, freedom of the press, freedom of religion, and freedom of speech. The inclusion of such Bills in the state constitutions continued a colonial tradition that went back to the Massachusetts Body of Liberties (1641) and the Pennsylvania Charter of Privileges (1701)—the setting down of rights and privileges in black and white. Additional precedent was provided by the British Bill of Rights of 1689, a document from which the colonials had drawn a vigorous conception of their rights as Englishmen. As Americans they were not ready to settle for anything less.

Guarantees of Religious Freedom. Freedom of religion was variously interpreted in the new states. In the South the disestablishment of the Anglican Church was the primary goal. Virginia's role was critical in this respect—and it was not until 1786 that Virginia's governor, Thomas Jefferson, won his struggle for complete religious freedom. In other areas, provisions were made for varying degrees of religious freedom. In Pennsylvania, members of the Assembly had to submit to a religious test that excluded all non-Protestants. Except for Vermont and Rhode Island, New England left the Congregational Church in a privileged position. But although religious inequities persisted in various places, the current of opinion was clearly set against their continuation: sooner or later they were bound to crumble.

Emancipation of Northern Slaves. Georgia and South Carolina had forced an indictment of slavery to be deleted from the Declaration of Independence, but sentiment against slavery as an institution remained strong. The Massachusetts Supreme Court interpreted the constitutional declaration guaranteeing freedom and equality as applying to all men regardless of color. In 1780, Pennsylvania provided for emancipation of its slaves. Rhode Island followed with gradual emancipation after 1784, and Connecticut followed Rhode Island in this decision. Restrictions had already been placed on the slave trade by Delaware, Virginia, and Maryland between 1776 and 1783, and Rhode Island, in 1774, provided for the emancipation of all slaves brought within its boundaries. The agitation against the peculiar institution culminated in the Northwest Ordinance of 1787, which closed all the territory north of the Ohio River to slavery.

Provisions for Education. As restrictions on liberty and moral abuses were alleviated, a strong movement for the expansion of education developed. The constitutions of Georgia, Vermont, North Carolina, Massachusetts, and Pennsylvania vested specific responsibility for education in the state. Vestiges of English law which had never been strictly enforced in the colonies, such as primogeniture and entail, were abolished.

As extensive as these changes were, however, they grew out of accepted colonial practices, and none of them can be called genuinely radical.

THE ARTICLES OF CONFEDERATION

As the individual states experimented in democracy, the need for a more comprehensive union became increasingly evident. The possession of common political beliefs provided a promising meeting ground upon which to forge an effective union. When the colonials issued the Declaration of Independence, it was presented as "The unanimous Declaration of the thirteen united States of America." Despite the implications of this assertion, the revolutionists were careful not to excite suspicion by attempting to extend the scope of central authority. No one could forget that Britain's efforts in this direction brought about the revolution in the first place.

But war also revealed the dangers of decentralization. The Continental Congress had to supply the army, but was deprived of the right to levy taxes. The result was a paper currency system that created rampant inflation. Prices skyrocketed; public confidence in Continental currency plummeted. When Congress tried legislating price controls, they were rejected by the states as "the contrary of justice, policy, and necessity." Nor were matters helped when both the states and Congress printed money: the phrase "not worth a Continental" passed into the popular vocabulary. The added burden of military requisitions bore down upon the rickety structure of American finance. Only the desperate efforts of the able financier, Robert Morris, and the receipt of French specie, prevented a complete collapse of the Continental currency.

It is hardly surprising that the fiscal difficulties of the Congress confirmed public prejudices against central authority. Though the Articles of Confederation had been completed by November 17, 1777, the states, viewing with alarm the ineffective program of Congress, tended to reassert their sovereignty. Four years after the completion of the Articles, they were finally ratified by the states. Ratification gave Congress exclusive authority in foreign relations, together with the right to make war, to regulate admiralty cases, and to settle disputes between the states. Congress would also have the power to coin and borrow money. Representation in Congress was to be by states, with each state entitled to one vote. Decisions were by a simple majority, except in specified instances when nine votes were needed. Subverting the effective implementation of these powers was the absence of Continental control over taxation. The states jealously refused to surrender their taxing power, accepting as a cardinal principle: "The power to tax is the power to destroy." So there occurred the spectacle of Continental fiscal stability being swept away in an avalanche of paper issuances, while the states, secure in their taxing power, achieved considerable solvency.

THE CONTROVERSY OVER WESTERN LANDS

Claims of the States. The four-year delay in ratifying the Articles was due to conservative suspicion of the power assigned to the Confederation, and to the insistence of Maryland and New Jersey that Congress be vested with control of western lands. First there ensued extensive debates on the Articles in the state legislatures, chiefly over the question of limiting the central government's power. Then the legislatures of Maryland and New Jersey voiced the fears of those states that had no western land claims. These states anticipated that Virginia, Connecticut, Massachusetts, the Carolinas, and Georgia—all of whose charters placed their western boundaries at the Pacific Ocean—would possess an overweening power if their claims were acknowledged. They argued further that the western lands had been gained in a common colonial effort, and that there was no reason why some states should benefit at the expense of others. The impasse over the western lands was broken on January 2, 1781, when Virginia agreed to surrender her claims provided that all the western lands be held as a common fund preparatory to their admission into the union on a footing of equality with the original states.

Conquest of the Northwest Territory. The final disposition of the western lands, however, waited upon the completion of their seizure from the British and the Indians, and the settlement of the complex claims of western land companies. George Rogers Clark was almost solely responsible for the successful conquest of the Northwest Territory, the area lying between the rough 'V' formed by the Mississippi and Ohio Rivers, and held, before the Seven Years' War, by France. A resident of Kentucky, Clark realized that the security of the American settlements in the region could only be established by an aggressive campaign into the northwestern territories. Leading a force of less than two hundred men, Clark marched overland to seize Kaskaskia on the Mississippi River, and then turned eastward to Vincennes, completing the American conquest by early autumn of 1778. The British and their Indian allies mounted a counteroffensive that culminated in the recapture of Vincennes in mid-December of 1778. A bitter, sanguinary war ensued,

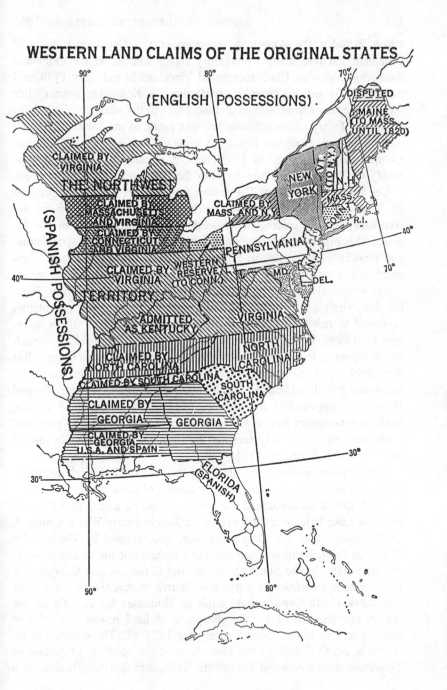

WESTERN LAND CLAIMS OF THE ORIGINAL STATES

(ENGLISH POSSESSIONS).

DISPUTED
MAINE
(TO MASS.
UNTIL 1820)

CLAIMED BY
VIRGINIA

THE NORTHWEST

CLAIMED BY
MASSACHUSETTS
AND VIRGINIA

CLAIMED BY
MASS. AND N.Y.

CLAIMED BY
CONNECTICUT
AND VIRGINIA

NEW
YORK

VT. N.H.

MASS.

CONN.

R.I.

(SPANISH POSSESSIONS)

PENNSYLVANIA

CLAIMED BY
VIRGINIA

WESTERN
RESERVE
(TO CONN.)

MD.

DEL.

TERRITORY

ADMITTED
AS KENTUCKY

VIRGINIA

CLAIMED BY
NORTH CAROLINA

NORTH
CAROLINA

CLAIMED BY SOUTH CAROLINA

SOUTH
CAROLINA

CLAIMED BY
GEORGIA

GEORGIA

CLAIMED BY
GEORGIA
U.S.A. AND SPAIN

30°

FLORIDA
(SPANISH)

which included the American massacre of the Christian Indians of Gnadenhutten and savage, retaliatory Indian attacks in the Ohio and Kentucky territories. Clark recaptured Vincennes in February 1779, and prevented the Indians from overwhelming the Kentucky frontier after their victory over frontiersmen at Blue Licks in the summer of 1782. In 1783, the Treaty of Paris finally brought peace to the frontier. Though warfare ceased, Congress faced the same difficulties that had puzzled George III's government in 1776—how to placate the Indians; how to satisfy the frontiersmen; how to keep the uncertain peace in the West.

Cession of State Claims. The Indian problem was further complicated by Virginia's insistence that her surrender of western claims be accompanied by the voiding of all western land purchases from the Indians. This proviso stirred the implacable opposition of land speculators, and especially of the Illinois-Wabash Company and the Indiana Company, whose purchases of land in the Ohio country represented investments by speculators in Pennsylvania, Maryland, and New Jersey. Fearful that Virginia's claims would supersede their own, the speculators preferred to risk their chances with a Congress, many of whose members held stock in the two companies. The speculators wielded considerable influence in the New Jersey and Maryland legislatures as well. But the surprising development of the whole affair was the genuine disinterestedness with which the Virginians, led by Jefferson and Richard Henry Lee, approached the dispute. They urged surrender of western lands as a necessary step toward cementing union. Eventually even this concession was reluctantly accepted by Maryland, which finally ratified the Articles in February 1781.

The Virginia cessions were preceded by those of New York and Connecticut. Massachusetts completed the cession of lands north of the Ohio in 1784. Connecticut retained the Western Reserve, a strip of 3,300,000 acres on Lake Erie, as a fund to reward Revolutionary War veterans. A smaller reservation, for Clark's veterans, was retained by Virginia. By 1786, the Confederation controlled the remainder of the vast northwestern territories. In the South, however, the Carolinas and Georgia saw their western territories as a potential source of revenue to retire their war debts. North Carolina sold lands in Tennessee for as little as five dollars per hundred acres; the cheapness of land resulted in sales of more than four million acres in the year 1783–84. The concurrent increase in North Carolina's tax costs to meet the need for protection of Tennessee soon convinced the eastern Tarheelers that they had made a bad bargain. Their influence was felt in 1784, when the North Carolina Assembly ceded Tennessee to the Confederation with the sole proviso that existing land titles be maintained.

This cession was promptly revoked by North Carolina when the residents of the ceded region petitioned Congress for admission to the union. The Carolina legislature, uncertain of the effect this would have upon its land claims, offered the frontiersmen better protection and improved justice. But the proponents of statehood, led by John Sevier, were able to form the rump state of Franklin which, despite the refusal of Congress to recognize it, had a shadowy existence until February 1788, when Sevier and his supporters were overturned by advocates of alliance with North Carolina. In the following year, the territory was finally turned over to Congress. A similar surrender had been made two years earlier by South Carolina. Only Georgia stubbornly refused to relinquish her claims until the first decade of the nineteenth century.

The Ordinance of 1785. With each new cession of western land, Congress came into possession of a greater empire. Determined to provide for orderly settlement, Congress authorized a committee chaired by Thomas Jefferson to plan for the administration of these territories. The result was the abortive Ordinance of 1784, which provided for the orderly transition of these territories into states. The congressional rejection of this first proposal only aggravated the problem of effective organization for the western territories. The acute fiscal problems of the Confederation led Congress to contemplate western land sales. That solution, however, required an orderly method for conducting these sales. From a debate that featured sectional differences emerged the Ordinance of 1785, which provided for the division of the Northwest lands into townships, each six miles square. These were further divided into thirty-six sections of 640 acres. Of these sections, one was set aside for the support of public education, and four for the United States. A seventh of the land first surveyed was to be used by the War Department for settlement of Revolutionary War veterans. A mixed system of disposal was employed; whole townships and individual sections were simultaneously placed on the market. Since the lowest price was a dollar an acre, comparatively few settlers could raise the $640 to purchase the minimal offering of a section. Much land thus fell prey to speculators, who purchased it with the depreciated paper currency of the Confederation.

The most notorious of these speculators was the Ohio Company, organized by General Rufus Putnam. The company bought up the scrip of veterans for a pittance, and then used it at face value to purchase western lands. Under the guidance of the Reverend Manasseh Cutler, the company entered into an arrangement with the Scioto Company, organized by public officials, members of Congress, and New York merchants. The Scioto Company was to provide a front through which western lands could be purchased without exciting public suspicion. With the full assistance of William Duer, secretary of the Confederation's Board of the Treasury, who was responsible for the sale of western lands, the Ohio Company obtained 1,781,000 acres, at an average cost of eight cents an acre in depreciated scrip. Cutler then turned his full attention to the establishment of stable governments in the region, as a likely inducement to purchasers. His efforts in this direction were aided by the general American sentiment that Congress should aid stability by organizing territorial governments.

The Northwest Ordinance. On July 13, 1787, Congress passed the Northwest Ordinance. The Ordinance provided for the establishment of no less than three and no more than five states in the Northwest Territory. It provided for three stages leading to self-government for the region. In the first period Congress would appoint a governor, secretary, and three judges to administer laws, drawn from the legislation of the established states, which best suited the new territory's needs. When five thousand adult males were residing in the territory, they would implement the second period by electing a territorial legislature. It in turn would nominate a ten-man advisory council from which Congress and the governor would choose a five-man legislative council to serve as the governor's cabinet. The territory would also send a nonvoting delegate to Congress. The third period would come when the territory achieved a population of sixty thousand. It could then apply for admission into the Union as a full state, with the same status as the original thirteen. Congress added guarantees of religious freedom, the right of habeas corpus, the upholding of common law, restriction of types of punishment, and proportional representation in the territorial legislatures. Congress also put its support behind public education, fair treatment of Indians, and the prohibition of slavery or other forms of involuntary servitude. With its passage, the Northwest Ordinance established the principles upon which the vast western territories were subsequently incorporated into the Union. The Confederation Congress had passed its most important legislation.

THE CONFEDERATION: 1781–1789

The Critical Period. In 1888, John Fiske, the historian, described the time of the Confederation as the "critical period," concluding that the American experiment in self-government reached its nadir between 1781 and 1789. From Fiske's description emerged the idea that the decision to draw up the Constitution was a response to urgent necessity. Recent scholarship has challenged Fiske's grim view, and has argued that the Confederation had established a stable peace and a viable nation at the time that it was superseded by the federal republic. Its land policy, though marred by speculative activities, was successful enough to establish a permanent precedent. The severe depression that followed the war was met, and signs of recovery were ample by 1786. Cut off from their British trade, American merchants and shippers sought markets wherever an American craft was permitted to drop anchor. The manufacturing enterprises that had existed before the Revolution grew rapidly, as larger numbers of Americans turned to consuming home products. Simultaneously, new enterprises sprang up throughout the land. Even as it approached the end of its existence the Confederation had begun to flourish.

Dissatisfaction with the Articles. Considerable discontent with the Confederation existed. Alexander Hamilton scorned the new government as "feeble and precarious," and lashed out at it as "confining the power of the Federal Government within too narrow limits." Washington subscribed to Hamilton's strictures, while Madison pressed for an amendment to compel the states to meet their obligations to the Confederation.

Other men, who had been active in the Revolution, recognized the urgency of establishing a stronger central government. They knew that America's success in 1783 had been primarily the result of the power rivalry between the French and British. Jefferson bridled at the patronizing contempt with which he was treated in Paris, and John Adams attempted in vain to persuade a condescending London government to compose a commercial treaty with the Americans and to surrender their Northwest trade posts. Spain's closing of New Orleans to American commerce also caused serious concern. And the heart of the matter was clearly the lack of power in Congress. Without centralized power America could hardly expect to command the respect of the world.

Shays' Rebellion. The men who had led the Revolution were also concerned at what seemed to be a rising threat to private property—the irresponsible fiscal behavior of an increasing number of states. Rhode Island issued depreciated paper which benefited debtors while it bankrupted creditors. In the autumn of 1786 there was panic among the propertied and commercial classes of western Massachusetts when farmers, trapped by a combination of high taxes and low prices, joined Daniel Shays in an armed rebellion. Its aim was to close the courts in Berkshire, Hampshire, and Worcester Counties, thus ending the lawsuits that threatened many farmers with foreclosure of their property. A state government, itself born in revolution, faced a revolutionary overthrow. Only the intervention of militia from eastern Massachusetts prevented the seizure of the United States arsenal at Springfield by the farmers. After urgent appeals, the Continental Congress ordered General Henry Knox to raise a force with which to check Shays. But before he could act, the Massachusetts militia under General Benjamin Lincoln (a force raised by private subscription, since the state treasury was empty) overwhelmed the rebels in the early spring of 1787. The Massachusetts authorities had the good sense to realize that their defeated opponents had been motivated by genuine grievances. The legislature reduced court costs, exempted personal property and tools of trade from debt seizure, and refused to raise taxes. They even pardoned Shays.

Nevertheless, the event had thrown a good scare into the established order. "What, Gracious God, is man," cried Washington on receipt of news of the uprising, "that there should be inconsistency and perfidiousness in his conduct?" Hamilton dismissed the participants as "villains & fools." When Massachusetts elected John Hancock to the governorship —thus neatly reversing at the polls the Shaysite defeat in the field—Madison indicted Hancock's sympathetic view of the farmer's plight as "not a little tainted by a dishonorable obsequiousness to popular follies." It was to counter the widespread feeling that this was "the mad cry of the mob" that Jefferson declared:

> I hold it that a little rebellion now and then is a good thing, and as necessary in the political world as storms in the physical. . . . It prevents the degeneracy of government, and nourishes a general attention to the public affairs.

But American conservatives felt (in the words of one Massachusetts merchant) that "the flames of internal insurrection were ready to burst out in every quarter . . . from one end to the other of the continent," and that they "walked on ashes, concealing fire beneath [their] feet." The time was ripe for a critical re-examination of the central authority, with a view to extending its scope and powers.

The Annapolis Convention. A smoldering dispute between Virginia and Maryland had long irritated relations between the two states. Maryland, which controlled the Potomac River to its south bank, taxed Virginia shipping using the river; Virginia retaliated by taxing Maryland shipping as it entered Chesapeake Bay. Relations were further strained by a varying tariff on English goods. James Madison moved in 1784 to settle the disputes by negotiation. Washington, as president of the Potomac Company, which aimed to improve river navigation, joined the conference at Alexandria. Subsequently the meeting adjourned to Mount Vernon, where the conferees agreed to support efforts toward the establishment of tariff uniformity, to press for interstate accords as a means of alleviating problems of commerce and defense, and to meet annually to discuss subsequent problems. Both the Maryland and Virginia legislatures voted their support of the Mount Vernon accord. But, as both soon learned, commercial accord between two states was meaningless unless adjacent states agreed to cooperate. So it was that Maryland called for the participation of Pennsylvania and Delaware in the accord; and Virginia took the final step by calling a convention of all the states to discuss trade problems.

The invitation from Virginia was sent out in January 1786, and designated the month of May as the time, and Annapolis, Maryland, as the place, for the convention, whose avowed purpose was to provide guidance to the Continental Congress in commercial matters. Only five states actually sent delegates, however: New York, New Jersey, Pennsylvania, Delaware, and Virginia. The states of Massachusetts, Rhode Island, New Hampshire, and North Carolina appointed delegates who failed to attend. The remaining states, Maryland being the most surprising absentee, did not bother even to appoint delegates. The convention finally settled down to business on September 11, 1786, with the aim of resolving conflicts in interstate commerce. But the New Jersey delegation proposed extending the discussion to include ways of strengthening the Articles of Confederation, a proposal which quickly occupied the attention of the assembled delegates.

Their response reflected the strongly nationalistic sentiments of those present at Annapolis. From New York came Alexander Hamilton, who had despaired of merely strengthening the Articles and now believed that nothing less than a complete reconstruction of the government was necessary. Delaware's George Read called for the absorption of the states by the national government, while Pennsylvania's Tench Coxe advocated the extension of central power to compel a more stable economic basis for union. James Madison, representing Virginia, hoped the meeting would prove "a plenipotentiary convention for amending the Confederation." But the sparse attendance seemed to preclude any fruitful outcome until Hamilton, always audacious, proposed that they recommend to the states another convention which would be authorized to discuss financial, commercial, and political problems facing the country. Since Hamilton lacked specific authorization from New York to take so radical a step, Abraham Clark of New Jersey submitted the proposal at Annapolis. It summoned a convention to meet at Philadelphia in May 1787. Despite James Madison's fears that the Annapolis convention was exceeding its powers, the proposal specifically requested that the states empower their delegates to make changes "necessary to render the constitution of the Federal Government adequate to the exigencies of the Union."

THE FEDERAL CONSTITUTION

The Philadelphia Convention. Virginia again took the lead in implementing the Annapolis proposals. After Congress timidly agreed, on February 21, 1787, to recommend revision of the Articles of Confederation, the state legislatures of Virginia, Pennsylvania, New Jersey, Delaware, and North Carolina moved swiftly to name delegates to the new convention. The full prestige of Virginia was thrown behind the convention with the appointment of a brilliant delegation headed by Washington. James Madison, the Virginian destined to influence the convention's outcome most thoroughly, intended to press for a massive reform of the Articles lest "little meliorations of the Government . . . turn the edge of some of the arguments which ought to be laid to its roots."

Connecticut, Georgia, Maryland, Massachusetts, New York, and South Carolina acted to join the convention before its opening on May 14, 1787. In June, New Hampshire agreed to take part. But Rhode Island steadfastly refused to appoint any delegates. Though twelve of the thirteen states had agreed to participate, the composition of the New York delegation did not augur well for the nationalists. Neatly checking Hamilton were two supporters of state rights, Robert Lansing and John Yates, and both meant to oppose any drastic changes in the Articles. But the presence of his protégé, Hamilton, buttressed Washington's determination to remain at Philadelphia until a new document of government was composed; and it was Washington's prestigious support that finally swung the balance in favor of a strengthened central authority.

The fifty-five delegates who gathered at Philadelphia were a distinguished lot. Ranging in age from Jonathan Dayton of New Jersey, who was twenty-six, to Benjamin Franklin, who was eighty-one, they were drawn from a class that had gained experience in colonial, state, and national government. Nearly sixty per cent had attended college; most were lawyers, merchants, or planters. Washington and Franklin provided prestige and dignity, but the bulk of the work was performed by such energetic younger members as James Madison, Alexander Hamilton, Edmund Randolph, George Mason, Gouverneur Morris, James Wilson, William Paterson, Elbridge Gerry, Rufus King, and Charles Cotesworth Pinckney. Conspicuously absent were such worthies as John Hancock and Samuel Adams of Massachusetts, and Patrick Henry of Virginia (who explained his absence by stating he "smelled a rat" in the proceedings). Thomas Jefferson and John Adams were engaged in diplomatic service abroad and could not attend.

The Virginia Plan. After electing Washington to preside over the meetings the convention went into secret session, thus permitting it to operate without substantial public interference. The heart of the subsequent discussions was set forth on May 29 by Edmund Randolph, in what was termed the Virginia Plan. It called for a thorough revision of the Articles, with the intention of strengthening the central government. It proposed a bicameral legislature: the lower house to be chosen by qualified voters in each state, with representation proportional either to free population or to the taxes contributed by the state; the upper house to be nominated by the state legislatures, and elected by the lower house. Members of either house could not serve successive terms and would possess one vote apiece. A one-term restriction was placed on the presidential office, which was vested with the executive powers previously granted to Congress. Provision was made for a Supreme Court and a federal judiciary, with the former possessing the power of judicial review. Both houses had the right to inaugurate legislation outside the competency of the individual states, and, together, the right to invalidate state laws that went contrary to the "articles of union." Amendments and the admission of new states were also provided for.

The plan provoked immediate protests from the smaller states: Connecticut, Delaware, Maryland, New Hampshire, New Jersey, and New York, all of which feared that representation by population or wealth would condemn them to an inferior position. In the ensuing debate, Roger Sherman of Connecticut proposed (June 13) the solution which ultimately settled the question of representation: "That the proportion of suffrage in the first branch should be according to the respective number of free inhabitants; and that in the second branch or Senate, each State should have one vote and no more."

The New Jersey Plan. The deep fears of the small states were expressed in a stronger form on June 15, when William Paterson of New Jersey proposed a series of nine resolutions which came to be called the New Jersey Plan. It proposed a revision of the Articles "adequate to the exigencies of Government, and the preservation of the Union," and provided for a unicameral Congress with each state possessing one vote. The reformed government would have the power to raise revenue through duties on imports, to regulate interstate commerce, and to requisition money from states in proportion to their white population plus three-fifths of their slaves. It also called for a plural executive which would operate as a Board of Directors, elected by Congress and ineligible for re-election. The power of appointment for both civil and military posts was vested in the executive. A federal judiciary appointed by the executive authority was also provided for. Of particular significance in the New Jersey plan was the proviso that all laws and treaties made by Congress were to be "the supreme law of the land."

Compromise. The conflict between the small and the large states made compromise imperative. Hamilton called for a bicameral legislature with an upper house and executive possessed of considerable power and only indirectly elected by the people. This appeal met with strong opposition. On June 19, the Virginia Plan won out over the New Jersey plan, with only the states of Delaware, New Jersey, and New York opposed. Both sides had agreed in principle, however, that the situation demanded give and take. The great compromise known as the Constitution began to take shape on July 12, when representation to Congress was agreed upon. The House of Representatives was to be elected on the basis of population, with three-fifths of the slaves being counted. On July 12, it was agreed that the upper house should consist of two senators from each state. Once the crucial problem of the composition of Congress was settled, it was relatively easy to resolve conflicts over the executive, the regulation of internal commerce, taxation, and treaty-making powers.

Memories of George III made the delegates afraid of extending too much power, or too long a term of office, to an elected executive. Thus it was specified that the President would be elected for four-year terms.

Fear of a democratic electorate resulted in the establishment of an electoral college to perform the actual election of the President. In it, each state was to be represented "equal to the whole Number of Senators and Representatives to which the State may be entitled in the Congress."

Disputes over the regulation of commerce grew out of Southern fears that Congress would use such power to destroy the slave trade. A compromise gave Congress control of "Commerce with foreign Nations, and among the several States, and with Indian tribes," but granted it the power to regulate the slave trade only after 1808. The question of slavery also provoked dispute over the basis for federal taxation. The North demanded a tax system based on population while the South wanted one that would be based on the wealth of the respective states. The South feared inclusion of its slave population for tax purposes. Congress also obtained the power, formerly held by the states, to coin money.

On September 17, all but three delegates (Elbridge Gerry of Massachusetts, and Edmund Randolph and George Mason of Virginia) agreed to sign the new, federal Constitution.

Checks and Balances. The Constitution, as adopted, was a consummate expression of the checks and balances system derived from the political theory of such seventeenth-century British liberals as John Locke and James Harrington. The executive was vested with the veto power co-jointly with one third of the Congress. However, Congress could override the presidential veto with a two-thirds vote. Although not stated explicitly, the Supreme Court was assumed to have the power to declare a law unconstitutional. The new document reflected the considered fear of the delegates that an uninhibited democracy would tend to destroy the civil rights of a minority. As James Madison expressed it: "There is no maxim . . . which is more liable to be misapplied, and which, therefore, more needs elucidation, than the current one, that the interest of the majority is the political standard of right and wrong." Only the House of Representatives was chosen by a direct popular vote. Even Thomas Jefferson believed that such a method was "inferior," though the fact that the lower house had the power of taxation caused him to support it in this instance.

The Bill of Rights. Jefferson, writing from Paris, expressed to Madison his concern over the Constitution's lack of a Bill of Rights; but Madison believed that "these parchment barriers" were subject to constant violation "by overbearing majorities in every State." He thought a national majority would be no less apt to violate civil rights, but he supported a national bill of rights when he concluded it was necessary for ratification. The overwhelming preoccupation of the founding fathers was with individual liberty and the possible tyrannies of an uncontrolled majority. The new constitution committed "the majority of the Community" to protect the defenseless individual and his property. But, concerned with more than the bare economic rights of the individual, Madison defined "property" to mean not only "that domination which one man claims and exercises over the external things of the world, in exclusion of every other individual," but also "every thing to which a man may attach a value and have a right; and *which leaves to every one else the like advantage.*" Possessing grave doubts about the perfectibility of the human character, the founding fathers worked for, and achieved, a balance between individual rights and necessary governmental powers. The Constitution did not specify whether the new central government or the states possessed sovereign power, though by making the Constitution the "supreme law of the land" it implied the subordination of the states. The exact implication of this definition was to manifest itself in the subsequent dispute over the strict or loose interpretation of the Constitution.

Ratification. The real struggle over the Constitution began when the Convention submitted it, on September 20, to the Confederation Congress. Despite the efforts of some Congressmen to censure the Convention delegates, Congress voted on September 28 to submit the Constitution to the states for ratification. This left the document's fate in the hands of nine states; the Convention had decided it would become effective only after that number had approved it.

As the fate of the Constitution hung in doubt, a sizable protest movement, which became known as the Anti-Federalists, was organized. Its most prominent spokesmen were Patrick Henry, Samuel Adams, and Richard Henry Lee, who voiced the fear that under the Constitution the well-born would dominate the government to the detriment of the common man. The most telling of the Anti-Federalist arguments was voiced by Richard Henry Lee:

> Our object has been all along to reform our federal system, and to strengthen our government . . . but a new object now presents. The plan of government now proposed is evidently calculated totally to change . . . our condition as a people.

Lee posed the conflict as one between "little insurgents, men in debt, who want no law, and who want a share of the property of others" and "more dangerous men, with their servile dependents," who "avariciously grasp at all power and property." It was to the faction in between that the Anti-Federalists made their appeal, for they made up "the weight of the community; the men of middling property, men not in debt, on the one hand, and men, on the other, content with republican governments, and not aiming at immense fortunes, offices and power."

Any effort to estimate accurately the relative strength of Federalist and Anti-Federalist factions is hazardous, although it is generally conceded that the Federalists were probably fewer in number. But the Federalists met this deficit by the caliber of their leadership. James Madison, Alexander Hamilton, and John Jay joined in composing the *Federalist,* eighty-five essays defending the Constitution, in order to persuade the uncertain state of New York to ratify the document. With unusual candor, the three authors set forth the pessimistic view of human nature that had guided the founding fathers. Madison argued in paper number fifty-one that the system of checks and balances included in the Constitution might "be a reflection on human nature," but he concluded, "what is government itself, but the greatest of all reflections on human nature [for] if men were angels, no government would be necessary." Far from assuming that the intent of the Constitution was to prepare for a leveling movement, the Federalists took the position that government should provide the political institutions within which the natural talents and diversity of interests of the American society could find fullest expression.

The ratification conventions began to act when, on December 7, 1787, Delaware unanimously approved the document. Pennsylvania moved swiftly to ratify the Constitution by a margin of two to one on December 15; its speed was a tribute to the ruthless efficiency of the Federalist Party, which had thus prevented any effective, organized opposition by the Anti-Federalists. New Jersey ratified without opposition on December 18. Georgia, exposed to the constant threat of a hostile Indian and Spanish attack, saw in the Constitution greater security, and ratified unanimously on January 2, 1788. Two days later, Connecticut voted for ratification by more than three to one. Maryland added its support by a vote of almost six to one in late April of 1788.

But opposition to the Constitution was vigorous in Massachusetts, where resentment engendered by Shays' Rebellion still smoldered. Conservatives naturally favored ratification in the belief that a strong union would prevent similar outbreaks. The Anti-Federalists in the state strongly suspected that the proposed changes were a device of their enemies, designed to foist upon them a government detrimental to their interests. Only skillful maneuvering by the federal element in the convention secured ratification, by a narrow margin, in early February of 1788. (Most interesting of all was the lure used to gain the support of John Hancock; he endorsed ratification when he was given a tentative promise of support for either the presidency or vice-presidency.) On May 23, 1788, South Carolina quietly added its support by a vote of more than two to one. With this action, ratification by only one more state was needed to make the Constitution effective. In June, a reconvened ratification convention met in New Hampshire, and, overcoming its original doubts, subscribed to the Constitution.

Despite the requisite support of nine states, complete success was not certain until Virginia, the motive power behind the new Union, ratified. After a brilliant debate which gave full expression to the Federalist and Anti-Federalist positions, Virginia voted to ratify the Constitution on June 25, 1788. The uncommon eloquence of the Anti-Federalists had been matched by that of Madison and John Marshall; the Federalists had oratorically outgunned their opponents. Virginia's decision, together with the threat of New York City to secede and join the new union, finally broke the strongly Anti-Federalist bias of New York. On July 25, by a three-vote margin, New York ratified the Constitution.

North Carolina and Rhode Island alone remained as stubborn holdouts. In late July of 1788, despite the recent decision of New York and the example of its neighbor Virginia, North Carolina overwhelmingly rejected the Constitution. But the North Carolina Federalists, by strenuous effort, succeeded in reversing this decision the following year. Rhode Island stubbornly held out until May 28, 1790, when energetic pressure by its neighbors finally secured ratification. The second phase of the great experiment was under way.

Part Three

THE EARLY REPUBLIC

Chapter 8

The Federalist Republic

The ratification of the Constitution launched a new experiment in government. The men who had brought about the Revolution, the Confederation, and the Constitution now had to make a success of the new republic. George Washington took stock of his political and economic inheritance when he reached New York in late April of 1789 to be inaugurated: the old Confederation had bequeathed to him a foreign office headed by John Jay, assisted by three clerks; a diplomatic corps consisting of John Adams in London and Thomas Jefferson in Paris; a Treasury Board without funds; a War Secretary who supervised an 840-man army; a staff of twelve clerks who wondered when they would next be paid; a vast, uncertain debt; a minuscule revenue; and no credit. During the first decade of the new federal government's tenure, this unlikely inheritance was transformed into a working and durable republic.

WASHINGTON AND THE NEW REPUBLIC

The census of 1790 indicated that there were now almost 4,000,000 Americans, all but a few of whom resided within a hundred miles of the Atlantic seaboard. But already the restless pioneer had breached the Allegheny Mountains. By 1796, the original thirteen states had been joined by Vermont (1791), Kentucky (1792), and Tennessee (1796). The virtually imperial domain of the United States was bounded on the north by the uncertain border with Canada, and on the south by the even less clearly defined boundaries of Spanish Florida and Louisiana. The

West was still largely the realm of the Indian, but already the curiosity of pioneers was being stirred by rumors of untold wealth and boundless land.

Strong sectional antagonisms had developed between the staple-crop South, the commercial East, and the backwoods West. Especially aggravating to the Northern states was the constitutional provision giving the South the right to claim representation in Congress for three-fifths of its slave population. Frontiersmen viewed the new federal government with suspicion as it seemed to threaten new taxes. Despite some uneasiness over the future of a nation thus divided, no one doubted that the United States had the human and natural resources necessary for success. The problem was to mobilize these resources in support of the national interest. At this juncture, the Americans were fortunate enough to have at the helm George Washington, a man whose character seems to have had Olympian proportions.

Washington as President. No one who met Washington came away unmoved. One contemporary recalled a "tall, upright, venerable figure" characterized by "a seriousness in his manner which seemed to contribute to the impressive dignity of his person, without diminishing the confidence and ease which the benevolence of his countenance . . . inspired." He added, "So completely did he *look* the great and good man he really was, that I felt rather respect than awe in his presence." His prestige was a valuable asset, as was his determination "to commence the administration, upon a well adjusted system, built on tenable grounds, [rather] than to correct errors or alter inconveniences after they shall have been confirmed by habit."

A single objective governed his behavior and his administration: the happiness of his fellow citizens. Although "unpracticed in the duties of civil administration," he brought to his high office a steady practicality which "united knowledge of men and things, industry, integrity, impartiality, and firmness." He used his prestige to persuade two exceptionally able and yet very different men—Hamilton and Jefferson—to accept high office in his cabinet. And although Jefferson was eventually to leave the group, unable to accept Hamilton's pre-eminence, he remained long enough to give vital help in enabling institutions of the new government to achieve stability. "In general," Jefferson could declare as early as 1791, "our affairs are proceeding in a train of unparalleled prosperity."

By the end of his first term, Washington had succeeded in establishing three administrative departments: State, Treasury, and War, and had secured executive control of appointments to their top posts. A customs and internal revenue agency was in operation; national credit had been put on a stable basis; an effective army had been organized; a vigorous diplomatic service was stationed abroad; postal service extended to the farthest reaches of the republic; a federal judiciary enforced its decisions throughout the country. With the growing rivalry between Hamilton and Jefferson there had come into existence a vigorous, though ill-defined, party system. Washington, whose private sympathies were Federalist, insisted upon remaining aloof from partisan politics. In the formative years of the republic he made the presidency a symbol of national unity, and had established executive autonomy. Partisanship he left to others.

HAMILTON AND HIS ADMINISTRATIVE SYSTEM

The Creation of the Treasury Department. The Treasury Department was established by Congress on September 2, 1789, by legislation which (unlike that setting up the State and War Departments) did not permit the President to add to the Secretary's duties or to direct him in the implementation of those duties. Although Congress made the Secretary subject to removal by the President, it also obliged him "to make report and give information to either branch of the legislature . . . respecting all matters referred to him by the Senate or House of Representatives." Congress thus established the Treasury Department and its Secretary as second in importance to the President, allowing them to occupy a unique place in the new government. Under the guidance of Alexander Hamilton, the department played a critical role in establishing the new republic.

Hamilton candidly accepted the paramount importance of his department in putting the new republic on a firm financial base. The Treasury's importance was made manifest in the size of its administrative staff, which consisted of assistant secretary, controller, treasurer, auditor, register, thirty clerks, and nearly a thousand customhouse officers and internal revenue agents. The State Department (four clerks, a messenger, and an office keeper) and the War Department (three clerks) were dwarfish by comparison. The significance of the Treasury Department's activities and its fund of patronage insured that it would dominate the new government. The secretaryship was an alluring post for an ambitious man; and Hamilton was very ambitious.

In Hamilton's view, the Treasury was "the most arduous department in the public administration in a new government, without the guidance of antecedent and precedent." It was therefore necessary for him to "trace out his own path, and to adjust for himself the import and bearings of delicate and important provisions in the Constitution and in the laws." The post was an immense challenge to his creativity. Highly suspicious of the argument for states' rights, he believed in a strong central government which would "govern well." Time and again, he insisted that "American liberty and happiness had much more to fear from the encroachments of the great states, than from those of the general government." In the Treasury, he worked ceaselessly to prove his point.

Hamilton brought to his labors an administrative genius which was founded on a passion for order, exactness, detail, and accuracy. In a nation unaccustomed to effective implementation of customs and tariff payments, Hamilton created a customs service that proved a model of dispassionate honesty. He worked relentlessly to make the Constitution an effective instrument by adding, wherever possible, to the effective power of the federal government. In time, his activities were to divide the Federalists and bring into existence a political opposition.

Fiscal Policies. Hamilton's great achievement was the formulation of the fiscal policies which guided the republic during its early history and which permanently established the tone of federal fiscal responsibility. He inherited from the Confederation a twofold difficulty—how to obtain sufficient revenue, and how to stabilize American credit. These problems were interdependent. As an underdeveloped country, America was heavily dependent on foreign loans; and the large outstanding debts of both the states and the central government had undermined American credit abroad. It was necessary immediately to fund the old debts and put them on a self-liquidating basis, in order to restore American credit abroad. A further complication arose out of the extensive domestic debt. Much of it had been originally contracted in a period of rampant inflation, by veterans and farmers who had since sold their holdings to investors and speculators for a fraction of their true value. Representatives of the original holders argued that their clients were being unfairly deprived of proper compensation.

The Report on Public Credit. In his Report on Public Credit, Hamilton set forth the system which he believed would secure the national finances. Questioning whether the provincial attachments of the average American could be diverted to the support of the new central government, he argued that a direct appeal would have to be made to educated professional and businessmen, all of whom "thought continentally." He rejected the idea that the new government should do anything less than fully redeem outside obligations. "A government which does not rest on the laws of justice," he warned, "rests on force." By fully meeting its inherited obligations the new government would establish its credit and attract to its support the very people who could extend credit in the future. To implement his proposal, he suggested the funding of the entire debt by converting the outstanding interest payments of $13,000,000 into principal. He meant to give the federal finances a stability and reliability which would make them "an article of faith."

As part of his campaign to diminish the power of the states, he further proposed that the federal government assume responsibility for outstanding state debts. With almost Machiavellian calculation, he saw assumption as a device to wed the state creditors to the new government while vesting exclusive taxing power in the federal authority: the price for federal assumption of their debts would be the surrender, by the states, of their right to tax. But Hamilton overlooked the fact that he was asking states with small debts to surrender their taxing power in the interest of their more deeply indebted brethren. Thus, Maryland, North Carolina, and Georgia took a relatively strong position against federal assumption. Pennsylvania, with a modest debt of two millions, took an ambiguous position; but New York, New Jersey, Massachusetts, and South Carolina, all heavily in debt, were strongly in favor of the move. In fact, only one representative from New England voted against assumption. Virginia, having reduced her debt by half through the use of depreciated paper money and the sale of Kentucky several times over, saw no reason to accept assumption. Indeed, most Virginians believed, quite wrongly, that the federal government was in debt to Virginia, and thus had the impression that assumption would give their state no evident advantage. The immediate result of the funding and assumption proposal was to precipitate a savage debate that led several New Englanders to contemplate secession.

Only the intervention of Jefferson, at the request of Hamilton, finally resolved the impasse. Jefferson agreed to a compromise which obliged the federal government to pay outright grants to states such as Delaware, which had no debt, and Virginia, which had a comparatively small one. In addition, Hamilton agreed to transfer the national capital from New York to Philadelphia for a ten-year period, after which time it would be located in the District of Columbia.

Thus, Hamilton's plan was accepted. The immediate result was to send the national debt soaring to over $75,000,000. Servicing of the debt consumed almost 80 per cent of the federal expenditures, while interest payments on the national debt between 1790 and 1800 covered more than

40 per cent of national revenues. But Hamilton viewed the development with equanimity; it had wedded foreign and domestic creditors to the new government.

The First Bank of the United States. Putting the national credit on a balanced basis was the first step in an extensive program of fiscal reform that included the creation of a central bank and an adequate circulating medium. Thus Hamilton, in January 1791, proposed the establishment of a corporation called the Bank of the United States. The bank would function as the major depository of government funds, as the agent of the Treasury in domestic and foreign fiscal activities, and as a control upon state banking. It would be further authorized to issue bank notes, redeemable in specie and receivable for government payments, as the principal national currency.

As conceived by Hamilton, the proposed bank was a mixed corporation combining government and private initiative. Ownership of twenty per cent of the stock and the appointment of five of the twenty-five directors were vested in the government. The remainder of the stock was offered for sale to the investing public. A debt limit of $10,000,000 in excess of deposits was placed upon the bank, and frequent reports to the Secretary of the Treasury were stringently required. Once again Hamilton combined governmental necessities with an effort to draw private enterprise into full support of the new republic. Investors were permitted to purchase up to three-quarters of the new stock with government bonds. Hamilton shrewdly anticipated that this would boost the price of government securities while firmly binding the interests of the new bank to those of the federal government.

Stubborn opposition to Hamilton's bank flared up in Congress. Agrarian-minded congressmen feared that the proposed entry of the federal government into banking would create a second "engine of corruption," analogous to the Bank of England. To these hot suspicions of the proposed bank, James Madison added his own doubts concerning its constitutionality. Moving away from his earlier call for strong government, he now proposed to strengthen the states against this expansion of the federal authority. After a bitter floor fight, the House approved the bank by a sectional vote of 37 to 20. All but four of the votes in favor came from north of the Potomac. Washington, unsure of his ground, asked Hamilton, Jefferson, and Attorney General Edmund Randolph for advice as to whether Congress had the constitutional power to charter corporations. Jefferson and Randolph, in voicing strict construction, argued in the negative. But Hamilton set forth the argument in favor of a broad construction of the Constitution. Basing his stand on an interpretation of the "necessary and proper" clause, he argued that the bank was needed for the collection of taxes, trade regulation, and common defense; and he persuaded Washington to approve the measure. The first Bank of the United States, and a momentous precedent, had been established. Henceforth the federal government could use all "necessary and proper" means to achieve constitutionally authorized ends.

Report on Manufactures. Once the bank was firmly under way, Hamilton turned his attention to the problem of industrializing the United States through a program of government aid to private business. In December 1791 he submitted to Congress the Report on Manufactures, in which he drew attention to the fact that American private enterprise had prospered wherever protected from foreign competition by state duties. Federal action, he argued, would have even more beneficial results. He also noted that foreign restrictions on American exports, together with the obvious productivity of American agriculture, made it imperative that the government foster industry to absorb the burgeoning supply of raw materials. Pessimistic about the willingness of American mercantilists to risk their wealth in the hazards of manufacturing, Hamilton proposed that the government stimulate their appetites with protective tariffs, industrial bounties, exemption from duties on essential imports, and a system of rewards for labor-saving inventions and improvements in the quality of industrial goods. This plan, he argued, would also heal sectional discord: the South would supply raw materials to Northern factories, receiving manufactured goods in return.

Once again Madison and his supporters expressed dismay. Hamilton's use of the "necessary and proper" clause led Madison to protest: "If not only the means, but the objects are unlimited, the [Constitution] had better be thrown into the fire at once." Again their protests were unavailing, for Congress chose to include all of Hamilton's recommendations, with the sole exception of industrial bounties, in the Tariff Act of May 1792.

Determined to achieve his ends by every method at his disposal, Hamilton now funneled his energy into the organization of the Society for Useful Manufactures. He hoped to demonstrate in Paterson, New Jersey, where the great falls of the Passaic River promised ample water power, that the arguments of his Report on Manufacturing were feasible. But he failed to lure private capital into his manufacturing venture at Paterson, since American enterprise was still firmly concentrated on commerce, with its guarantee of a quick and easy profit. Nevertheless, the indomitable Secretary of the Treasury had drawn with exactness for a predominantly agricultural country an image of the industrial, urban society that was America's future.

HAMILTON AND JEFFERSON

The Agrarian Republic. As Hamilton's schemes unfolded, Jefferson took an increasingly vigorous role in opposing them. Though responsible for ending opposition to Hamilton's proposals on the national debt, Jefferson afterward came to believe that he had been tricked by his colleague in the cabinet; and he did not mean to be tricked a second time. Jefferson, firmly committed to the ideal of an agrarian republic, could not view the extension of federal power with equanimity. "Cultivators of the earth," he believed, "are the most valuable citizens," and in them he founded his vision of the republic's future. They were, he believed, "the most vigorous, the most independent, the most virtuous, and they are tied to their country, and wedded to its liberty and interests, by the most lasting bonds." Between Hamilton, who looked to the affluent and influential man of means, and Jefferson, who looked to the sturdy, yeoman farmer, a clash was inescapable.

The two men had been bare acquaintances when Jefferson entered the State Department in March 1790. Both apparently expected that they would work together amicably, and Jefferson, as has been mentioned, helped to overcome the opposition to Hamilton's debt plans. At that time, if his private correspondence is an accurate guide, Jefferson viewed settlement of the controversy over funding as necessary to the preservation of the Union. His subsequent charge that "I was most ignorantly & innocently made [by Hamilton] to hold the candle" must be viewed against the background of his political estrangement from Hamilton. Relations between the two men steadily deteriorated when Hamilton began to intervene in the conduct of foreign affairs, an action which Jefferson hardly appreciated, and the break became open when Hamilton proposed establishment of the bank.

As the bank dispute raged, Jefferson's opposition to a strong central government became more emphatic. He stated that the "natural progress of things is for liberty to yield and government to gain ground," and feared that this was all too fully apparent in the career of Hamilton. In opposition to Hamilton's plans for federal participation in the development of national resources and power, Jefferson proposed a laissez-faire policy which would allow the private individual to pursue his own well-being. To proposals for the establishment of a federally inspired Agricultural Society and for a road-building program assisted by the federal government, he remained adamantly opposed. As a slaveholding planter, he subscribed to the notion that the farmer alone possessed the "substantial and genuine virtue . . . the focus in which [God] keeps alive that sacred fire, which otherwise might escape from the face of the earth." With the abundance of land at the disposal of Americans, Jefferson believed that for generations to come the nation could be kept a secure agrarian paradise. The serpents endangering paradise were the manufacturers, whom he considered "the panders of vice, and the instruments by which the liberties of a country are generally overturned."

The stylistic sophistication which characterized Hamilton's reports to Congress added to Jefferson's concern. "The accounts of the United States," he declared, "ought to be and may be made as simple as those of a common farmer, and capable of being understood by common farmers." The vision of a simple government ministering to the needs of simple folk, and characterized rather by its absence than its presence, filled Jefferson's mind. To Hamilton, one need hardly add, this vision was appalling.

The Feud. The debate between Hamilton and Jefferson soon extended itself into departmental business. Convinced that Hamilton intended a strong central government, Jefferson resolved to frustrate his plans by circumscribing his influence. Early in the spring of 1791, the death of Nicholas Eveleigh, Comptroller of the Treasury, gave Jefferson the opportunity to open his attack. Jefferson backed Tench Coxe for the post, in opposition to Hamilton, who pressed for the appointment of Oliver Wolcott. In the end, Washington chose Wolcott. A similar struggle ensued over the position of Postmaster General; Jefferson supported Tom Paine, while Hamilton backed Timothy Pickering. Again Hamilton won the day. The Secretary of State then advocated transfer of the Post Office from the Treasury to the State Department. He candidly confessed to Washington his fear "that the department of treasury possesses already such an influence as to swallow up the whole Executive powers."

To placate Jefferson, Washington relinquished the Mint (rather than the Post Office) to the State Department. Hamilton viewed this development with considerable dismay, feeling with some justice that the Mint, as a link in the nation's currency system, belonged logically in the Treasury. By August 1793, Jefferson was considering an attempt to divide the Treasury into a customs and internal tax office. But any such effort was doomed to failure by the solid Federalist majority in the Senate. Frustrated in his efforts to limit Hamilton's influence, Jefferson now shifted his attack to the floor of Congress and into the public journals.

With the cooperation of Madison, a hostile congressional committee, the forerunner of a formal opposition party, was selected to investigate Hamilton's management of funds. John Beckley, clerk of the House of Representatives, fed scurrilous rumors about Hamilton to Jefferson, whose good judgment had deserted him, and who now described Hamilton's career as "a tissue of machinations against the liberty of the country which . . . has heaped its honors on his head." To provide a more effective agency for these attacks, Madison and Jefferson arranged to have Philip Freneau, the radical poet of democracy, edit a newspaper called the *National Gazette,* which would carry the attack upon Hamilton to the public. Hamilton replied in kind with a series of letters published in the *Gazette of the United States.* Washington, mortified, protested against "the seeds of discontent, distrust, and irritations which are so plentifully sown."

FOREIGN POLICY

But Washington unwittingly aided the conflict by consulting the entire cabinet on all matters except those related to the Treasury. This gave Hamilton an opportunity to extend his activities into the domain of Jefferson without fear of a similar intrusion into this own departmental business. In the realm of foreign affairs, the two men were divided by Hamilton's strong sympathy for Great Britain and Jefferson's equally strong feelings toward France. When Britain proposed that the United States permit her troops to cross American soil should she find herself at war with Spain, Hamilton readily assented; but Jefferson seized upon the proposal as an opportunity to remind the British that, seven years after the signing of the Treaty of Paris, they still refused to relinquish their western posts to the Americans. The antagonism between the two men was sharpened by their differing views on the French Revolution.

French aspirations for liberty excited a widespread sympathy in the United States. "The liberty of the whole earth was depending on the issue of the contest," Jefferson later wrote, "and . . . rather than it should have failed, I would have seen half the earth devastated." To Hamilton and his supporters, the French revolution seemed increasingly an anarchistic attack on property, individual rights, and world peace. They felt certain that if the excesses of the revolution went unchecked, they themselves, as men committed to the stability of property and authority, would eventually feel the headsman's ax. France's decision in the winter of 1793 to proclaim herself a republic, declare war on Britain, and send Edmond Genêt as minister to America, precipitated a major crisis. For once both Jefferson and Hamilton agreed on ends—the preservation of American neutrality—though not on means.

Under the treaty of alliance negotiated in 1778, the United States had agreed to help France retain her West Indian possessions, and to permit French warships the use of American ports. In 1792 Hamilton argued for the temporary suspension of this treaty on the grounds that the permanence of the new French government was not yet secured. He also opposed the reception of Genêt, fearing that it would be tantamount to recognition of the French republic and would thus compel the United States to honor the 1778 treaty. Jefferson preferred to let circumstance determine the policy of the American government toward the French revolutionists. He suggested that the United States, rather than discuss the implications of the treaty, leave its intentions ambiguous. He hoped, thereby, to force both belligerents to bid for continued American neutrality. Once again the two men disagreed about the interpretation of the Constitution; Hamilton assumed that in the absence of Congress the President had the right to declare neutrality, while Jefferson contended that only Congress possessed the needed power.

Washington steered a course between the positions of the two men. He received Genêt and refused to suspend the treaty, but he also declared that American neutrality would be applied impartially to the belligerents. Many Americans, mindful of French assistance during the Revolution and eager to aid a new sister republic, protested against this "desertion" of the French. They charged that the evil influence of Hamilton had led the President astray. The Secretary answered this charge by reminding his critics that France had acted out of self-interest in her aid during the Revolution, and that America could hardly be expected to do less.

Citizen Genêt. The young French minister, Edmond Charles Edouard Genêt, bursting with revolutionary doctrine, meant to guide the United States into forthright support of his embattled republic. He considered American proclamations of neutrality to be formalities only, behind which he could work to make the country a base for the conquest of Canada, Florida, and Louisiana, and he hired George Rogers Clark to organize an expedition against the latter territories. He also expected to use American ports as bases from which privateers would attack British shipping. Both Hamilton and Secretary of War Henry Knox flatly refused either financial or military assistance to Genêt's schemes; but the outspoken sympathy of Americans for the new French republic kept the minister's expectations high. When Jefferson took the vivacious Frenchman into his confidence, he provided the country with an anomalous spectacle: its Secretary of the Treasury was keeping the British fully informed of state secrets, while its Secretary of State did the same for the French.

The French decision to throw open their colonial ports to American shipping added to the weight of pro-French sentiment in the United States. Thereupon Jefferson, using much the same justification employed earlier by Hamilton when he agitated for aid to the British attack upon Louisiana, agreed to assist Genêt's plans for an attack on Florida, Louisiana, and Canada. Jefferson anticipated that this would resolve the irritating issue of the northern frontier posts, and would open the Mississippi to American shipping. Genêt, now thoroughly convinced that Jefferson was in effect his aide-de-camp, commissioned twelve American privateers which seized no less than eighty-five merchantmen, some in American territorial waters. These ships were brought into American ports and sold by French consuls.

As the French minister took ever more aggressive actions, Washington and Hamilton became increasingly alarmed. Because of the damage to their merchant fleet, the British contemplated drastic retaliatory measures, made all the more ominous by the British minister's conviction that the Americans had lost all ability to control the cocky French minister. Only the desperate efforts of Hamilton prevented the British from taking immediate action. In August 1793, Genêt, aware of the growing official displeasure, demanded that Washington convene Congress so that it could choose between the stand of the President and the demands of the French minister that America abandon its neutrality. Genêt threatened to appeal directly to the American public if his wishes in this respect were not complied with. Jefferson, dismayed, undertook to check the French minister while maintaining friendly relations with the French republic. "Hot-headed, all imagination, no judgment, passionate, disrespectful & even indecent towards the President," was his new estimate of Genêt. The emergence of the Jacobins as the dominant party in Paris resolved the administration's dilemma: Genêt was ordered home. Finding the prospect of the guillotine unattractive, Genêt asked for, and was granted, asylum. Thus ended a dangerous incident in the young republic's history.

Even as the Genêt affair came to its ironic conclusion, Jefferson, convinced that Hamilton had usurped the conduct of foreign affairs, submitted his resignation (effective as of December 31, 1793). As Jefferson retired and the administration struggled to steer an even course, the British resolved upon an attack against the French West Indies; and as a complement to this joint naval-military action in the Western Hemisphere, the London government, on November 6, 1793, issued an Order in Council which authorized British commanders to seize all neutral ships supplying produce to, or transporting produce from, the French islands. The obvious target of this action was the American merchant marine, which carried the bulk of this trade. The ensuing seizure of some 250 American ships caused a rapid deterioration in relations between Britain and the United States.

The Northwest Frontier Posts. Further antagonisms were provoked by the ambiguous policy of the British military in retaining outposts along the northern American frontier. The British denied encouraging hostile incursions by the Indians into American territory, but supplied the Indians with arms and powder. In a series of savage outbreaks during 1790 and 1791, the Indians inflicted heavy losses along the Northwest Frontier. The further refusal of the British to withdraw from the Northwest territory during the spring of 1794 made war seem inevitable. Even the revocation, in January 1794, of the November 1793 Order in Council failed to lessen tension between the two countries. It was only the intervention of Hamilton in March 1794 that finally ended the drift toward war.

Jay's Treaty. Hamilton persuaded Washington to send Chief Justice John Jay (a strong Federalist) to London, as minister plenipotentiary. Though Edmund Randolph was the new Secretary of State, the Secretary of the Treasury drew up Jay's instructions. In them, Jay was directed to obtain British withdrawal from the Western outposts, reparations for losses inflicted upon American shipping, compensation for slaves removed from the United States when the British army withdrew in 1783, and a commercial treaty. Jay, suave and sophisticated, moving easily in British society, viewed his task as one of friendly settlement rather than conference-table dispute. This simplified his negotiations with Lord Grenville, the British foreign secretary, who made it emphatically evident that the key to settlement was complete American neutrality. Jay was obliged to surrender the American conception of freedom of the seas, and to accept clauses in the treaty which employed the British definition of contraband, accorded Great Britain the most-favored-nation treatment, closed American ports to the warships and privateers of

Britain's enemies, and secured privately held British debt in America from confiscation. In addition, the United States agreed to redeem debts held by British creditors and defaulted by American citizens.

In return for these concessions, the British agreed to withdraw from their Northwest posts by June 1796, to pay compensation for damage inflicted on American commerce, and to grant American ships the right to conduct restricted commerce with India. Small American craft were permitted to trade with the British West Indies, so long as the products obtained were consumed only in the United States. The treaty was conspicuously silent on the issue of the abducted slaves; his abolitionist sentiments made it almost impossible for Jay to demand that Britain pay for having freed slaves.

When the terms of the treaty became known to the American public, the response was a burst of outraged indignation. Only after bitter debate was the necessary two-thirds vote of confirmation obtained in the Senate. So many effigies of Jay were burned in the United States that he concluded he could find his way across the country by their light. Washington, who was unsure of the treaty's merits, had his dilemma resolved through revelations concerning his Secretary of State. Randolph had divulged state secrets to the French minister Fauchet, and had tried to obtain bribes from the same source for several Republican politicians. Fearful of war with Britain and American subordination to France, Washington signed the treaty on June 25, 1795. It still had to run the gantlet in the House of Representatives, where efforts were made to kill the appropriation needed to make the treaty effective. But this opposition was overcome in April 1796.

Thus, relations between the United States and Great Britain took a turn for the better; but domestic politics remained agitated, as supporters of Jefferson bewailed the American abandonment of neutrality. They neglected to note the inability of the United States to garrison many of the Northwest posts abandoned by the British in June 1796—an inability which scarcely augured well for the United States should it go to war.

Pinckney's Treaty. While John Jay was still trying to resolve the Northwestern Frontier disputes, American attention was directed toward the equally turbulent Southwestern Frontier. Spanish control of Louisiana and New Orleans hindered American use of the Mississippi River, and Americans vainly demanded compensation for Spanish depredations against American commerce. As matters turned out, however, Jay's treaty aided the solution of America's problems in this region.

Although Spain was allied with Great Britain in the war against

France, a succession of military disasters convinced the Spaniards that a negotiated peace with France was imperative, and a secret settlement was arrived at. On August 7, 1795, the treaty of peace was published in Madrid; but, fearful that England would seek revenge for this betrayal, Spain now struck up friendly relations with the United States. Thomas Pinckney, an affable, judicious South Carolinian, was already negotiating with Manuel de Godoy, the Spanish king's first minister, when news reached Spain of the secret treaty negotiated with Britain by Jay. Fearing that it was the forerunner of an anti-Spanish alliance between the Anglo-Saxon powers, Godoy decided to give the Americans evidence of Spain's good intentions. He was prepared to concede to them the right of navigation on the Mississippi, and to establish the border of Florida at latitude 31°, without an alliance or reciprocal guarantees of territory by either party. From that moment until October 27, 1795, when the treaty was finally signed, there existed no doubt that the Americans had obtained a considerable concession at a small price. All Spain received in exchange was a brief delay before her final surrender of the Louisiana territory to France, and its subsequent sale to the United States.

DOMESTIC AFFAIRS

As the United States slowly negotiated settlements with Britain and Spain, domestic affairs were overshadowed by an insurrection in western Pennsylvania.

The Whiskey Rebellion. A dispute originated in a decision undertaken by Congress, at the behest of Hamilton, to institute an excise tax on distilled whiskey. Hamilton, though aware that excises had always provoked opposition, believed that the tax was necessary to meet the burden of the state debts assumed by the government. Now, Western farmers, unable to export their wheat to market by way of the Mississippi, had traditionally distilled their grain in order to transport it to market; and the perennial Western currency shortage made whiskey a common medium of exchange. It was inevitable, therefore, that Hamilton's tax of twenty-five per cent on the net price of a gallon of whiskey should provoke rumbles of discontent throughout the West.

For three years this discontent remained stifled; then, in the summer of 1794, violence erupted in four western Pennsylvania counties. Mails in Pittsburgh were robbed, excise officers were terrorized, and federal courts were kept from acting. Pittsburgh joined the insurrection when threatened with attack by insurgents from the surrounding counties, and federal troops guarding the excise inspector for western Pennsylvania were compelled to surrender. Efforts at persuading the insurrectionists to surrender peacefully having failed, Washington called upon the states to raise an army of almost 13,000. He acted swiftly for fear that the insurrection might spread throughout the West. Upon the appearance of this formidable force, the rebels scattered to their homesteads. Only twenty prisoners were captured, and two were convicted of high treason. Both were pardoned by Washington on the grounds that one was a "simpleton" and the other "insane." So ended the first formidable challenge to federal authority, but it had served to bring a substantial accession of strength to the Republican opposition. And the Federalists were already beginning to engage in intramural warfare.

THE PRESIDENCY OF JOHN ADAMS

The Election of 1796. By 1796, Washington, disgusted by mounting attacks from Republican sources, had decided to relinquish the presidency. In January 1795, Hamilton had withdrawn from the cabinet, though he continued to exert considerable power as a frequent adviser to Washington and the new cabinet. The worsening of party faction was evident in the ludicrous charge now leveled by extremist Republicans that Washington had been a secret traitor during the Revolution. For Washington the presidency had become an intolerable burden, one to be dispensed with as soon as possible.

The Federalists had decided to back John Adams for President in 1796. Stubborn and stuffy in his opinions and prejudices (many contemporaries thought the two indistinguishable), Adams was certain to prove an unmanageable President. The campaign itself was a quiet affair, the various state legislatures choosing the electors. Hamilton supplied the excitement when he decided to relegate Adams to another term as Vice-President. Since the Federal Constitution stated only that the candidate with the largest number of electoral votes became President, and the one with the second largest number Vice-President, Hamilton planned to secure the election of Thomas Pinckney by withholding from Adams some Federalist votes in the Electoral College. The decision of New England electors to withhold their votes from Pinckney frustrated Hamilton's design. Thomas Jefferson ran only three votes behind Adams, and thus became Vice-President.

Jefferson promptly set to work to widen the breach between Adams and Hamilton. Only the intervention of Madison prevented Jefferson from writing to Adams contrasting his own respect and esteem with the treacherous behavior of Hamilton. Madison felt it would be wiser to allow the Federalists to cut their own throats—something which they were obligingly preparing to do.

The Republicans had steadily gained strength until they usually dominated the House of Representatives even though the Federalists kept a tenuous control in the Senate. There was still a large enough group in Congress committed to neither party to keep the ultimate issue of dominance unsettled. In the end, however, the sharp rivalries within the Federalist party, which centered upon the ambitions of Hamilton, gave the Republicans a victory by default.

Hamilton v. Adams. When Hamilton withdrew from Washington's cabinet in January 1795, he retained considerable power and influence in the administration. Washington, who had grown dependent upon his young friend, soon turned to him for advice on nearly every issue. The members of the cabinet were no less dependent. Oliver Wolcott, now Secretary of the Treasury, looked to Hamilton for guidance on almost every aspect of Treasury policy. A cursory examination of the two men's correspondence indicates that Hamilton was *de facto,* if not *de jure,* the master of the Treasury. In matters concerning foreign affairs and defense, Hamilton's opinions were brought to the attention of the administration. Timothy Pickering, soon to be Secretary of State, illustrated the relationship succinctly when he requested of Hamilton: "Will you have the goodness to express your mind? . . . Will you indulge me with your sentiments on all the subjects of this letter?" In addition, a constant stream of advice flowed from Hamilton to the Federalist leadership in Congress. Such a comprehensive influence was certain to disturb the incoming President, already touched to the quick by his narrow electoral victory and suspecting that Hamilton had shared in the effort to supplant him with Thomas Pinckney. Most of all, however, Adams distrusted the pro-British sentiments of Hamilton which, together with Jefferson's Gallophilism, he considered a threat to American neutrality.

Of one thing everyone who knew Adams was certain: he would never accept the idea that he was another man's puppet. Under such circumstances it was a disaster for Adams to retain Washington's cabinet. As protégés of Hamilton, they looked to him for advice, especially when Adams pursued policies increasingly objectionable to the former Secretary of the Treasury. The paramount importance of foreign policy at this time made the divergences between Adams and his cabinet even more evident.

In August 1796, Washington withdrew James Monroe as minister plenipotentiary in Paris, and replaced him with Charles Cotesworth Pinckney, whom the French refused to recognize. Both Hamilton and Adams independently arrived at the conclusion that the new administration should attempt to resolve its French difficulties with a special mission. On May 31, 1797, Adams nominated Francis Dana, John Marshall, and Pinckney to perform the task. But the failure of the mission (on which Elbridge Gerry replaced Dana) made war between the United States and France seem imminent. To meet this contingency, Congress, in the late spring of 1798, authorized an army of 10,000, and called upon the President to commission officers. Adams promptly designated Washington lieutenant general in command of the new force. Hamilton now expected to be made second-in-command, a position for which Washington favored him. But both men were informed by Secretary of State Pickering that Adams had "a disinclination to appoint Colo. Hamilton in what we [Washington, Hamilton, and Pickering] think is his proper station."

Neither Hamilton nor Adams showed any willingness to step aside in the dispute, and Washington threatened to resign. When the cabinet threw its support behind Washington and Hamilton, a shaken Adams resolved the conflict by dating the commissions of Henry Knox, Charles Pinckney, and Hamilton on the same day and leaving it to Washington to decide who had seniority. Adams was too shrewd not to realize that he had sustained a defeat and that his cabinet had been caught in an equivocal posture, torn between their duty to support their chief and their loyalty to the foremost Federalist.

Adams and France. Adams had resolved upon a foreign policy which emphasized the complete neutrality of the American nation. He agreed with his son, John Quincy Adams, that "it must always be our unequivocal interest to remain neutral" and to seek "a good understanding with the nations which have an interest similar to ours, that is a neutral interest." He viewed the French Revolution as apt to lead to a catastrophic bloodletting which would end in military despotism. Unlike Hamilton, however, he saw no advantage in allying the United States to Britain. He suspected that his two great rivals, Jefferson and Hamilton, would end up damning him. "At the next election England will set up Jay or Hamilton, and France, Jefferson, and all the corruption of Poland will be introduced," Adams predicted to his wife shortly after his inaugural, "unless the American spirit should rise and say, we will have neither John Bull nor Louis Baboon."

The XYZ Affair. Relations with France reached a pitch of tension when the Pinckney, Gerry, and Marshall mission failed in March 1798. Congress was shortly afterward notified by Adams that the three commissioners had been approached by three French agents, designated X, Y, and Z, who notified them that relations with France could be improved if (1) a $250,000 bribe were paid to Talleyrand, the French foreign minister, (2) the French government were lent twelve million dollars, and (3) an apology were obtained from President Adams for the harsh comments he had directed toward the French government. When news of these demands reached America, it gave rise to the curt slogan, "Millions for defense but not one cent for tribute." Adams suddenly found himself engulfed with well-wishers. Congress overcame its previous lethargy and energetically set about building up the woefully weak American defenses.

All that had happened, particularly the frequent French attacks on American shipping, seemed to point toward war. The Federalists, eager to exploit popular antagonism toward France, looked to Adams to mobilize public opinion behind such a conflict, but Adams fully recognized that the United States lacked the means with which to fight. Over the strenuous opposition of the Republicans, who generally favored the French, Adams managed to obtain congressional authorization for the construction of a twenty-seven-ship fleet. In addition, Congress authorized the issuance of six per cent bonds to cover any private contribution made toward construction of a ship. The result was an avalanche of private funds.

The "Unofficial" War with France. By 1799, American warships and privateers were waging an aggressive war against armed French shipping in the Caribbean and Atlantic. Abroad, Napoleon's threatened invasion of England fizzled, and a British fleet under Nelson inflicted an overwhelming defeat on the French in the Battle of the Nile. But Adams was careful to keep an unofficial naval conflict with France from mushrooming into open warfare. He feared that such an event would thrust the United States into the British camp, a course he viewed as contrary to America's interests. At the same time, frequent British attacks upon American shipping and the impressment of American sailors were exacerbating relations between the two countries, and soon Adams realized that much of what he protested against in French behavior was being practiced in an equally unpleasant form by the British. If the United States could not afford a war with France alone, then a war with both the French and British was unthinkable. (And Adams recognized that Britain's naval strength made her a far more dangerous antagonist.) With sturdy realism Adams worked for peaceful settlement with Britain, while unofficially fighting to compel one from France; and on the domestic front he sailed a delicate course between the demands of the Hamiltonians for open war with France, and the Jeffersonian efforts to worsen relations with Britain. But his political position became steadily less tenable. A dangerous breach was opening, not only between himself and Hamilton Federalists, but also with the Republicans.

ADAMS AND THE REPUBLICANS

It was Adams' misfortune to be the first President with a vigorous party opposition. The Republicans, who had taken shape as a group in the aftermath of the debates between Hamilton and Jefferson, were able by 1796 not only to mount a near-successful challenge in the Electoral College, but also to gain dominance in the House of Representatives. Adams and his party lived with the uncomfortable knowledge of Republican ascendancy. It is understandable, therefore, that the Federalists sought a way to reduce the power of their political antagonists. They seized upon the war fever which followed the XYZ revelations to launch what many Americans, especially the Republicans, thought to be a "reign of terror."

The Naturalization Act. On June 18, 1798, Congress approved a naturalization act which provided that no one should be admitted to American citizenship unless "he shall have declared his intention to become a citizen of the United States, five years . . . before his admission" nor until "he has resided within the United States fourteen years." This act severely modified the earlier naturalization act of 1795, which had made the total period of residence five years. The obvious intention of the act was to hamper harvests of strength reaped by the Republican party among newly enfranchised immigrants. "If some means are not adopted to prevent the indiscriminate admission of wild Irishmen & others to the right of suffrage," wrote the die-hard Federalist from Massachusetts, Harrison Gray Otis, "there will soon be an end to liberty and property." The prominence of such immigrants as Albert Gallatin and Matthew Lyon in the Republican Party made the attack even more pointed. Had the Federalists responded to the request of the Massachusetts General Court and five other state legislatures, a constitutional amendment denying public office to all immigrants would have been adopted.

The Alien and Alien Enemies Acts. On June 25, 1798, and again on July 6, 1798, Congress extended the scope of its attack on the Republicans. On the first occasion, the Alien Act gave the President the power to deport "all such aliens as he shall judge dangerous to the peace and safety of the United States." The Alien Enemies Act specifically extended a similar set of provisions to aliens who were citizens of any country with which the United States found itself at war. Though never enforced, these acts persuaded some Frenchmen resident in the United States to return to France. A substantial number of aliens, particularly foreign-born Republican journalists, hastened to obtain naturalization papers.

The Sedition Act. On Christmas Day of 1811, John Adams delivered himself of the thought that the Sedition Act of 1798 had been "constitutional and salutary, if not necessary." But of all the acts passed during the Federalist repression, no act has come to have a more heinous reputation. The act made anyone who wrote, published, or spoke anything "false, scandalous, and malicious . . . against the government of the United States" punishable with heavy fines ranging up to $2,000, and imprisonment for as much as two years. But it strongly modified the more repressive features of the common law on libel. Common law did not permit truth as a defense nor require that malicious intent be proved, and it left it to the judge to determine whether the writing under consideration was libelous. The Sedition Act made truth a defense, required that malice be proven, and provided for a jury trial. The Act had substantially incorporated within its text the findings of the jury in the John Peter Zenger case of 1735. In that year Zenger, the printer and publisher of the *New York Weekly Journal,* had been tried for ostensible libel against New York's Governor William Cosby. A brilliant defense prepared by Andrew Hamilton, a Philadelphia lawyer, and James Alexander, the *Journal's* editor, had emphasized that *"Truth* ought to govern the whole Affair of Libels." Despite the instruction of Chief Justice De Lancey that anything which had "scandalous" implications was a libel even if true, the jury acquitted Zenger. The act, moreover, was considered a temporary war measure; its fourth section provided that it would lapse automatically on March 3, 1801. Some contemporaries of the event and some historians have agreed with Adams' conclusion that the Act was "remarkable for its lenity and humanity: No honest man need to dread such laws as these."

The Republicans took a much dimmer view of the Sedition Act's intent. Few of them were prepared to subscribe to the Federalist dictum

that "to punish licentiousness and sedition is not a restraint or abridge-
ment of the freedom of speech or of the press." It is true, however, that
many Republican editors had confused criticism of administration policy
with personal vilification of the Federalists. Such absurdities as the
charge that Washington had been a secret traitor during the Revolution
found their way into news columns. At the same time, the Federalists
were equally guilty of wholesale condemnation of their opponents, as-
cribing bloodthirsty conspiracies to them, and using language like Noah
Webster's when he described the Republicans as "the refuse, the sweep-
ings of the most depraved part of mankind from the most corrupt nations on earth." Had the Sedition Act been impartially applied in the flood
of charge and countercharge that now engulfed the nation, Alexander
Hamilton would have been brought before the courts.

Twenty-five people were arrested under the act, and ten were convicted. The four leading Republican newspapers were attacked, and such
prominent Republican editors as Benjamin Franklin Bache, Thomas
Cooper, James Callender, and William Duane were arrested. The last
three were convicted under the act; only death from yellow fever spared
Bache a similar fate. Particularly active in pressing the charges were
Pickering and Justice Samuel Chase, whose flagrantly anti-Republican
views ultimately led to Republican impeachment proceedings against
him. The most famous victim of the Sedition Act was Congressman
Matthew Lyon of Vermont, who had achieved considerable notoriety by
spitting full in the face of Theodore Sedgwick, a Federalist congressman,
on the floor of Congress. His chief crime, however, was the publication
of supposedly slanderous attacks upon Adams. For this behavior, Lyon
was imprisoned for four months and fined $1,000. His outraged constitu-
ents returned him to Congress while he was still in jail. The Federalists
had created a martyr, and had driven the normally individualistic Republicans into a united stand against the Sedition Act. They had also
precipitated a counterattack by Jefferson and Madison; and a constitutional doctrine was now set forth, the validity of which would be tested,
eventually, in civil war.

The Virginia and Kentucky Resolutions. Jefferson, confronted by bitter Federalist attacks upon the Republicans, had not hesitated to reply in
kind. He bluntly referred to the federal government as a "foreign jurisdiction" and urged Virginia to prevent its inhabitants from appealing to
federal courts when doubt existed about their jurisdiction. The Alien
and Sedition Acts convinced him that a plot was under way to establish
a powerful central government that would override state authority. To-

gether with Madison he composed a response that went far toward asserting the supremacy of state power over federal government.

On November 16, 1798, John Breckinridge presented to the Kentucky legislature a series of resolutions composed by Jefferson. Although qualified by Breckinridge, their essential purpose was to advocate the doctrine of nullification: any federal law which a state considered a violation of its constitutional rights could be declared unconstitutional—that is, null, and void. The Virginia Resolutions, composed by Madison, were not so radical; they left the task of dealing with federal aggression to a convention of the states, though they added that "the states . . . have the right and are in duty bound to interpose for arresting the progress of the evil" of federal acts which the state deemed unconstitutional. Although both sets of resolutions were delivered to state legislatures, they brought from the seven Northern states an outraged protest that it was the task of the Supreme Court, not of the states, to determine the unconstitutionality of federal laws. Since the justices of the Supreme Court were all Federalists, Jefferson and his fellows did not view this assertion with enthusiasm. On February 22, 1799, Jefferson reiterated his position in a new set of resolutions. He now concluded that the rightful course for Kentucky when confronted with unconstitutional federal actions was "a nullification of those sovereignties, of all unauthorized acts done under color of that instrument. . . ." The actual effect of all three measures was limited. The Alien Act expired on June 25, 1800; the Sedition Act passed into the limbo of repealed acts on March 3, 1801; and the Republicans repealed the Naturalization Act shortly after Jefferson's inaugural.

THE COLLAPSE OF THE FEDERALIST PARTY

Intra-Party Conflict. Of the Federalist leaders only John Marshall, soon to be appointed Chief Justice of the Supreme Court by Adams, had opposed the Alien and Sedition Acts (though Hamilton had given them only qualified support, suspecting that their political consequences were apt to go against the Federalists). But the semblance of unity which this gave the Federalists was an illusion. Even as the controversy over the acts continued, Adams precipitated a major conflict within his party when he decided, without consulting his cabinet, to send William Vans Murray, the American minister to Holland, to France in order to negotiate a settlement. The Federalists, stunned at this display of independence by Adams, finally persuaded the President to send instead a three-man commission consisting of Murray, Oliver Ellsworth, and Patrick Henry. Hamilton's influence on the administration had been severely shaken since Adams, in choosing to act independently of his cabinet, eliminated any possibility that the advice of the former Secretary of the Treasury would prevail. Adams' mistrust of his cabinet could scarcely have been more complete. As he later recalled, "If I had called the heads of department together, and asked their advice, I knew from past experiences that their answers would have been flat negatives. . . ." Relations between Adams and his subordinates had reached a permanent impasse.

For more than a year an uneasy peace in the administration was maintained; but in May 1800, Adams demanded McHenry's resignation, dismissed Pickering, and finally exploded in outrage against Hamilton and his minions, going so far as to offer uncomplimentary reflections on Hamilton's origins. He concluded that his rival's ambitions had undermined the Federalist party. By removing McHenry and Pickering he established beyond question the subordination of the cabinet to the President. But he had acted too late. As the election of 1800 approached, the Federalists were divided and distracted. The Republicans, scarcely a very solid party themselves, seemed a model of unity by comparison.

The Election of 1800. As the election approached, Adams found himself in the rough environment of the new federal capital, Washington. Compelled to live in an unfinished White House, plagued by mosquitoes and humid heat in summer and damp cold in winter, the irascible Adams viewed his plight with skeptical detachment. "What course is it we steer," Adams asked, "and to what harbor are we bound?" He posed his question in the midst of seeming Federalist triumph. In the congressional elections of 1798 and in the elections of 1799, the Federalists had registered major advances. The congressional delegations of such Republican states as Virginia, the Carolinas, and Georgia were substantially Federalist. But the Republicans had worked hard to recoup their losses. In Virginia, the Republican legislature revised the vote for electors from a district-wide to a state-wide basis. They meant to secure a unanimous vote for Jefferson in his home state. In Pennsylvania, Republican governor Thomas McKean ruthlessly applied the spoils system to state government; no Federalist remained where a deserving Republican could be found. In New York, Aaron Burr applied his political genius to the organization of a Republican machine. One of his associates described Burr as "a man whose intrigue and management is most astonishing." Against this display of energy, the Federalists presented a singular portrait of divided counsel, bitter rivalry, and a curious reluctance on the part of leading Federalists to aid their party by standing for office.

The Federalists' loss of the New York legislature augured badly for them. Since the state's electors were chosen by the state legislature, it meant the loss of the electoral votes that had elected Adams in 1796. To compensate for this loss, the Federalists nominated a ticket consisting of John Adams and Charles C. Pinckney, with the latter expected to draw South Carolina's votes to the Federalists and thus provide the support needed to replace New York. These maneuvers collapsed when Hamilton decided to dump the incumbent. After first feeling out Federalist sentiment and discovering that a sizable part of it supported Adams, Hamilton, bent upon rule or ruin, issued a "Letter from Alexander Hamilton Concerning the Public Conduct and Character of John Adams" which described Adams as vain, disgusting, and jealous, with the use of other uncomplimentary adjectives as well. Adams' response was succinct—he called Hamilton "a bastard"—and the division had become irreparable. Such leading Federalists as Theodore Sedgwick and Harrison Gray Otis concluded that the time had come for them to withdraw from politics.

Having suffered the lash of Republican libel, the divided Federalists, as the election of 1800 approached, turned the full vitriol of their pens on the Republican candidate, Jefferson. Jefferson pursued a restrained course; he remained at Monticello while his supporters worked to prove that both Hamilton and Adams were opponents of American institutions. From October to December, the states chose their electors. As the electoral votes were counted, it became apparent that the Federalists still had a chance of winning. A united party might have won; a party more fully aware of the power of patronage might have avoided losing South Carolina's support—liberal Republican patronage promises secured its votes for Jefferson—and still have won.

When the votes were counted, Jefferson and his running mate Aaron Burr had both received seventy-three electoral votes; John Adams had obtained sixty-five, while Pinckney, his running mate, had sixty-four. The one remaining vote had gone to John Jay. The Federalists had denied one vote to Pinckney to insure that he would not obtain the presidency instead of Adams. The Republicans, however, had blundered in this respect. The Constitution provided merely that the candidate with the largest number of electoral votes should become President. As it was, Jefferson and Burr were tied. The election went into the House of Repre-

sentatives where the Constitution provided that a state's vote would be
cast by a majority decision of its representatives. Since the Federalists
controlled six states and had divided control in two states, they could
prevent the election of either Republican—and over the bitter opposition
of Hamilton they contemplated throwing their support behind Burr.
They hoped to break the Republican ranks and secure themselves from
"the fangs of Jefferson." Hamilton pressed for the election of Jefferson,
his old rival, insisting that Burr had the inclinations of a Caesar whereas
Jefferson, despite his democratic fanaticism, would conserve the established order. But the Federalists, ignoring the urgent protests of Hamilton, persisted in a course that threatened to complete the Federalist
debacle. Hamilton saw himself in "the awkward situation of a man
who continues sober after the company are drunk." Burr did nothing to
simplify their task, to coöperate by private word or deed. The wily New
Yorker was playing a shrewd game. He assumed that support from his
fellow Republicans would come only if they despaired of Jefferson's election and that, should he align himself with the Federalist plot, he would
turn the Republicans irrevocably against him. Efforts by Federalist
congressmen to obtain from Jefferson a public commitment to uphold
the Federalist administrative system proved equally fruitless. Nevertheless, Jefferson assured Senator Samuel Smith of Maryland privately that
his intentions were conservative. On February 16, 1801, when this fact
became known, Federalist opposition to Jefferson collapsed. With the
triumph of the Virginian, the Federalist party ceased to be a serious
political threat; but the administrative machinery built by Hamilton and
his fellows endured.

Chapter 9

The Jeffersonian Republic

American historians have often called the election of Thomas Jefferson a "revolution." It scarcely qualifies for so emphatic a description. As Hamilton predicted, Jefferson as President was very much inclined to temporize, to accept the established order. Once in office, he hastened to assure his Federalist opponents that they had no need to fear for the future. "All . . . will bear in mind this sacred principle," he declared in his inaugural address, "that though the will of the majority is in all cases to prevail, that will, to be rightful, must be reasonable; that the minority possess their equal rights, which equal laws must protect, and to violate which would be oppression." He went on to add, "We have called by different names brethren of the same principle. We are all republicans—we are all federalists." The sound and fury of a decade of political rivalry ended not with a bang but with an appeal to reason. The Republicans, who had gained control of Congress (they held sixty-six of the one hundred and six House seats), could have undertaken a program of massive change, but they were content to manage an established government.

JEFFERSON IN OFFICE

Thomas Jefferson. The man who succeeded to the presidency in 1801 was a complex personality. The secretary of the British legation subsequently described him as "a tall man, with a very red freckled face, and gray neglected hair; his manners good-natured, frank, and rather friendly, though he had somewhat of a cynical expression of countenance." Soft-spoken, shy, he was most at ease in the company of his family. Indifferent to his appearance, he thought nothing of wearing "a blue coat, a thick gray-colored hairy waistcoat, with a red underwaistcoat lapped over it, green velveteen breeches with pearl buttons, yarn stockings, and slippers down at the heels." To even the friendliest of eyes his appearance was that of "a tall, large-boned farmer." The range of his interests was extraordinarily broad. Architecture, music, science, philosophy, language, and belles-lettres all came within the scope of his genius. Yet an air of paradox surrounded Jefferson the statesman and politician: an aristocrat, he gave eloquent testimony to the virtues of democracy; a gifted conversationalist, he was a wretched orator; a painter of the agrarian dream, he, more than anyone, was responsible for securing the permanence of Hamilton's governmental plan.

Jefferson was able to write "We hold these truths to be self-evident: that all men are created equal," and he hated slavery. Yet he could see no solution for the slavery problem other than the expatriation of the Negro, since between the white and black races "there exist real distinctions which nature has made." In his first inaugural address he called for a "wise and frugal government, which shall restrain men from injuring one another, which shall leave them otherwise free to regulate their own pursuits of industry and improvement, and shall not take from the mouth of labor the bread it has earned." Four years later, confronted with an expanding revenue and declining governmental obligations, he considered assigning surplus revenue to the improvement of "rivers, canals, roads, arts, manufactures, education, and other great objects." Yet when similar suggestions had been made earlier by Federalists, he indicted them as "a bottomless abyss for money . . . and the richest provision for jobs to favorites that has ever yet been proposed." Opposed to a government of large powers, he pressed Albert Gallatin, his Secretary of the Treasury, for liquidation of the First Bank of the United States in order to supply bankers with the patronage that would make them good Republicans. Contradiction permeates Jefferson's career and accounts, too, for his greatness, which was that of a man ever ready to accommodate his principles to change, never allowing the past to dominate the present.

Jeffersonian Democracy. The philosophies of the first President to take office in the nineteenth century were, in many respects, the distilled essence of all that the eighteenth century had considered most admirable, most virtuous. Jefferson's was to be a democracy founded on reason, on simplicity, on man's innate dignity and capacity for conducting himself sensibly. His purpose is perhaps best summarized in his own words: "I have sworn upon the altar of God eternal hostility against every form of tyranny over the mind of man." Jefferson had an inflexible faith in the future of the republic, and an undying conviction that Americans of his own time were ready to make of the republic an eminently workable, almost utopian democracy. But he was not purely and simply an idealist.

Jefferson knew that an ideal government could not be achieved without practical policies. He knew the value of giving office to men sympathetic with his cause and helpful to his interests, and used patronage accordingly. Realizing that economic stability was a prerequisite for a successful government, he determined to eliminate the national debt. But in spite of the revenues they provided, and in spite of his essentially frugal temperament, Jefferson revoked the hated excise on distilled liquors, recognizing that in some cases dollars had to be sacrificed in order to gain the support of citizens. His belief in man's ability to help his fellow man did not prevent him from pursuing a policy of neutrality in relations with the unstable governments of Europe; for he recognized (like Washington) that the stabilization of the American democracy would require the full and exclusive attention of its government.

Circumstances beyond his control dictated that Jefferson's vision of "rational," negative government should never be realized. Yet Jefferson never lost his determination to pursue, wherever possible, a shrewd political course imbued with principles of simplicity, frugality, dignity, and optimistic conviction.

Albert Gallatin and Hamiltonian Practice. Had the differences between Jefferson and Hamilton been in fact irreconcilable, the most immediate consequence of Jefferson's inauguration would have been the dismantling of Hamilton's system. No such action occurred. This was due in part to Jefferson's acceptance of the established system's utility, and in equal part to the character of Jefferson's Secretary of the Treasury, Albert Gallatin. Swiss-born, Gallatin had migrated to the United States in 1780. Before 1790 he moved across the Allegheny Mountains and settled at Pittsburgh. An active Republican, he soon achieved nationwide notoriety through his role in the Whiskey Rebellion. Though Gallatin used all his influence to moderate Western expressions of discontent, the Federalists regarded him as an extreme radical. In Jeffersonian circles he acquired a reputation as an advocate of modest and frugal government, and it was this that led Jefferson to make him Secretary of the Treasury.

From the outset, the relationship between the two men was that of mentor and student. Jefferson, who had little knowledge of financial affairs, relied upon Gallatin to shape and administer fiscal policies. Sharing many of the qualities that made Hamilton a great administrator, Gallatin also had the latter's wide-ranging interests. He carefully supervised other governmental departments to enforce sound fiscal practices, effect savings wherever possible, and thus eventually bring about a reduction in taxes. He shared wholeheartedly Jefferson's insistence that everything possible be done to reduce the public debt. "We shall never see," Jefferson concluded, "another President and Secretary of the Treasury making all other objects subordinate to this." Between them they set to work to liquidate the national debt of $82,000,000.

While a congressman and senator Gallatin had protested against the increase of executive power at the expense of the legislature; as Treasury chief, he did not hesitate to press executive influence upon Congress. Since he had an extraordinary rapport with members of Congress, he was able to obtain much of the legislation that he thought imperative. Even the Federalist minority gave little opposition to his requests. To some extent this reflected an awareness on the part of the Federalists that Gallatin was confirming rather than repudiating Federalist practice, but another, more subtle reason was the role Gallatin played in preventing the wholesale removal of Federalist officeholders. Jefferson had often reasserted the sentiments he once conveyed to a Pennsylvania physician: "Of the thousands of officers . . . in the United States, a very few individuals only, probably not twenty will be removed; and these only for doing what they ought not to have done." Gallatin took Jefferson at his word and refused to allow the spoils system to penetrate the Treasury. At every opportunity, he encouraged the development of a nonpolitical civil service. But Jefferson's lesser supporters demanded patronage, with demand invariably exceeding supply, and Jefferson complained with bleak accuracy: "If a due participation of office is a matter of right, how are vacancies to be obtained? Those by death are few; by resignation none. Can any other mode than removal be proposed?" The fuel of parties, as Jefferson and the other Presidents of the nineteenth century discovered, was patronage. Only a man with the talent and integrity of a Gallatin could withstand the pressure for removals.

On issues far more important than patronage, Gallatin stood at odds with Jefferson. The Virginian carried into the presidency his hostility to the Bank of the United States, and thus came into unavoidable conflict with a Secretary of the Treasury who defended the bank and praised its achievements in raising the value of United States stock, providing the government with needed banking facilities, and speeding the circulation of money. Gallatin declared that "It is equally the interest of this Department, and of the Bank of the United States, mutually to observe the most liberal spirit of accommodation towards each other." The Secretary's stance met with presidential indignation. "This institution is one of the most deadly hostility existing against the principles and forms of our constitution," Jefferson declared, and he went on to demand that efforts be made toward abolishing the bank. Gallatin stubbornly and successfully defended the established relationship. Necessity overcame political ideology and the bank survived.

THE FEDERAL JUDICIARY

An even more immediate enemy of the triumphant Jeffersonians was the Federal judiciary. In the waning months of the old order, the Federalists had passed the Judiciary Act of 1801, which created twenty-three new judicial offices and substantially altered the judicial system. It reduced the Supreme Court to five members, and relieved the justices from the onerous task of circuit-riding. In the future the Court would render its decisions from the confines of a small chamber in the basement of the Capitol. Circuit Courts had their jurisdiction extended to cover debts of $400 or more and, in all but one of the six circuits, three judges were appointed to hear cases. The Act left the retiring John Adams with the delightful task of appointing numerous judicial officials through whom the Federalists could secure supremacy in the national judiciary. Of the many appointments which Adams made, none proved more important than that of John Marshall as Chief Justice of the United States. Under the guidance of this formidable Virginian, the Supreme Court became the bulwark of property rights. The preponderance of Federalist judges among Adams' appointments caused Jefferson to protest being left with a choice "either to execute the government by my enemies, whose study it would be to thwart and defeat all my measures, or to incur the odium of such numerous removals from office, as might bear me down." Even before his inauguration he had decided to undo his predecessor's handiwork. He had not, however, reckoned with the shrewdness of his leading antagonist—John Marshall.

John Marshall. A rough-hewn, yet cool and logical rustic who did not hesitate to promulgate laws where none existed, Marshall harbored an intense dislike for Jefferson. He feared that his fellow Virginian intended to "embody himself with the House of Representatives." He suspected that "By weakening the office of President, he will increase his personal power." He described Jefferson as a man seeking to "diminish his responsibility," working to undermine "the foundation principles of the government," and one whose "morals . . . cannot be pure." Jefferson reciprocated in kind. He described Marshall and other Federalist leaders as "men who were Samsons in the field and Solomons in the council, but who have had their heads shorn by the harlot England." The antagonism between the two men was not sweetened when Marshall proposed, a bare two weeks before he was appointed Chief Justice, that the House of Representatives leave the Jefferson-Burr election unsettled until March 4, 1801. This would have left both the presidency and the vice-presidency vacant until Congress determined by law how to fill the offices. It would have completed Jefferson's discomfiture at the election of 1800.

The Impeachment of Chase. Jefferson approached court removals indirectly. Justice Samuel Chase, who had made flagrantly partisan attacks upon Republicans from the bench, was his first target. No man seemed more vulnerable, and the House of Representatives impeached him without ado. In the trial before the Senate, Marshall was called as a witness. Aware that Jefferson, with John Randolph, an eccentric Virginia Congressman, as his agent, intended to use the conviction of Chase as precedent for a move against himself, Marshall was a model of decorum. He deferred respectfully to the Congress and staged a performance which left Randolph eulogizing him. When Congress failed to convict Chase, Marshall knew he had won the struggle to free the Court from political reprisals. Jefferson acknowledged as much when he terminated his attacks upon the Court.

Marbury v. Madison. In the closing hours of his administration, John Adams signed a commission appointing one William Marbury as Justice of the Peace in the District of Columbia. When Jefferson took over the office of President he found that a number of commissions, among them that of Marbury, had not actually been delivered. Jefferson decided to withhold them. Simultaneously, he revealed publicly his purpose: he meant to appoint as many respectable Republicans as he could to judicial office, since these would be "the only shield for our republican citizens against the federalism of the courts." Marbury, who was one appointee whom Jefferson did not intend to honor with office, then sued under the Judiciary Act of 1789 to obtain a writ of mandamus which would require James Madison, Jefferson's Secretary of State, to deliver the appointment. Jefferson anticipated that the Court would issue the writ, but he was prepared to ignore it. Such behavior would almost certainly undermine the prestige of the Supreme Court, which lacked the power to enforce its decision. And Jefferson was not prepared to have Marshall decline the test.

The Chief Justice settled the issue by declaring that Congress, when it vested the Supreme Court with the power to issue a writ of mandamus (in the Judiciary Act of 1789), had granted an unconstitutional power. This meant that Marbury could not sue before the Supreme Court, and that he was thereby denied relief. But Marshall then added the gratuitous information that Marbury was legally entitled to his appointment. With devastating precision he drove his point into the heart of Jefferson's attack, and simultaneously asserted, for the first time, the Court's power to subject legislative actions to review and to pass upon their constitutionality. Jefferson could hardly protest, since he had notified Madison at the time of the ratification of the Constitution that "I like the negative given to the Executive, conjointly with a third of either House; though I should have liked it better, had the judiciary been associated for that purpose, or invested separately with a similar power." Nevertheless, the Supreme Court used its immense new power gingerly. (It was not until 1857, in the Dred Scott Case, that the Court again chose to invalidate federal legislation.) But the power was there, to be exploited whenever the Court saw fit.

The Composition of the Marshall Court. During the thirty-four years that Marshall presided over the Court, he seemed to dominate its existence. Some contemporaries even referred to it as the "Marshall Court." Jefferson added to the legend by describing him as a "crafty chief judge" who dominated his "lazy or timid associates." But such a description of the Court implies that the five associate justices who served before 1807 and the six who served after that year were nonentities. To dismiss them as such is to ignore the extensive political and judicial experience that the fifteen associates had before they reached the Court. Nine had served in their state legislatures and six in Congress; five had held federal administrative posts and five had filled similar state posts; eleven had had previous judicial experience. Several were self-willed men, hardly likely to submit tamely to management. The explanation for Marshall's seeming dominance of the Court lies in his determination to establish a harmonious Court in which judicial dignity would be maintained.

Marshall deplored more than once the "indecency of judges cutting at each other" lest the Court suffer a "loss of reputation." He realized that by maintaining the image of a united Court he added to its authority. His most remarkable achievement was to preserve this judicial stance in a Court which, after 1805, was infiltrated by Republican appointments. Although, by 1808, only three of the seven justices were Republican, the poor health of Chase and Cushing frequently compelled their absence, thus giving the Republicans an effective Court majority. When Madison appointed Joseph Story of Massachusetts and Gabriel Duvall of Maryland to the Court in 1811, the Republicans gained a majority of five to two. Still, for all practical purposes, Marshall and the Republicans remained in rapport; the Chief Justice was rarely obliged to dissent.

Marshall worked to mediate differences between Justices Joseph Story and Bushrod Washington, who supported the exclusive assertion of national power, and Justice William Johnson, who argued the concurrent assertion of power by the states. The Chief Justice approached problems pragmatically as he sought to keep the Court united, wishing to avoid extremes and to achieve decisions which would command comprehensive rather than exclusive assent. This was particularly true of decisions which limited the power of the states to pass laws "impairing the obligation of contracts." Carefully guided by Marshall, the Court denied in New Jersey *v.* Wilson (1812) the right of a state to alter a tax-exemption clause in a land grant; in Dartmouth College *v.* Woodward (1819) the power of a state to interfere with a privately endowed college charter; in Sturges *v.* Crowinshield (1819) a similar effort of a state to alter a private contract; and in Green *v.* Biddle (1823) state efforts to impinge upon land-titles obtained through an interstate grant. By the time the Court had completed its labors on this subject "the obligation of contract" had achieved an almost sacrosanct position. Though divergences existed—primarily expressed by Justice Johnson, with varying support from Justices Brockholst Livingston, Thomas Todd, and Gabriel Duvall—a coherent opposition never formed. Marshall's dominance of the Court was, therefore, less a matter of his overwhelming control than an expression of his shrewd management. He never allowed a snap decision to endanger the majesty of the Court.

The Economic Decisions. The third paragraph of Article I, Section 8 of the Constitution provides: "The Congress shall have power . . . to regulate commerce with foreign nations and among the several States, and with the Indian tribes." Marshall's Court interpreted this clause in such a way as to provide the basis for a constant extension of the federal power. The direction of the Court's decisions had been foreshadowed by its determination to bar easy impingement on private contracts. Since these threats came from the states, the major result of the contract decisions had been to limit state power. In the McCulloch v. Maryland, Cohens v. Virginia, and Gibbons v. Ogden decisions, the Supreme Court added severe further limits to state power while expanding the scope of federal government.

In the McCulloch v. Maryland decision (1819), which grew out of the efforts of the state of Maryland to tax the federally chartered Bank of the United States, the Court flatly decided that the federal government had the right to charter a bank, and that implementation of such power overrode previous state action. As Marshall put it:

> The question is, in truth, a question of supremacy; and if the right of the States to tax the means employed by the general government be conceded, the declaration that the constitution, and the laws made in pursuance thereof, shall be the supreme law of the land, is empty and unmeaning declamation. . . .

The Cohens v. Virginia decision (1821) was given when the Cohen brothers appealed a conviction in a Norfolk court for illegally selling lottery tickets in Virginia. They argued that an act of Congress in 1802 had authorized such sales. This raised a question as to whether the federal judiciary was superior to state courts. The Supreme Court's response was an emphatic *Yes*. Chancellor James Kent, then Chief Justice of the New York Supreme Court, summarized the impact of the decision when he wrote:

> It is a very clear & masterly Piece of Logic with irresistible conclusions. It shows that the judicial is coextensive with the Legislative power of the Union, & that the Government is Supreme as far as the Constitution goes, & as far as the Government is empowered to act, & that the Judicial is bound to decide on *all cases* arising under the Constitution & laws of the Union, whoever may be the Parties to that case—That *Construction* of the Constitution is to be adopted which will consist with the words & promote its general Intention—The U.S. are a *Nation* & *one People* as to all cases & Powers given by the Constitution—Every *principal Power* carries with it all those incidental Powers which are necessary to its complete & effectual Execution.

But the Court's ultimate declaration of the superiority of federal to state power was given in Gibbons v. Ogden (1824). The original litigation grew out of the exclusive right granted by the New York legislature to Robert Livingston and Robert Fulton to navigate by steamboat the waters of New York State. Subsequent to the original grant, the power passed to Aaron Ogden, who sued to prevent Gibbons from operating a steamboat between New Jersey and New York under a federal coasting license. The New York courts enjoined Gibbons from operating in New York waters and Gibbons then appealed to the Supreme Court.

The issues raised by the case were twofold. It posed a question as to whether the commerce clause invalidated the power of a state to grant an exclusive right to navigate its waters. It also renewed the conflict between defenders of state rights and the proponents of a strong federal authority. The Court asserted that, under the commerce clause, an act of Congress dealing with such matters takes precedence over any state statute on a similar subject. As Marshall expressed the issue, the power of Congress to regulate commerce "is complete in itself, may be exercised to its utmost extent, and acknowledges no limitations other than are prescribed in the Constitution." The decision established that the purpose of the commerce clause was to protect commerce "from the embarrassing and destructive consequences resulting from the legislation of so many different States, and to place it under the protection of a uniform law." Though the implications of this decision were not realized until after the Civil War, Marshall and his Court established a power the dimensions of which are still being explored by the federal government.

TERRITORIAL EXPANSION

The Closing of the Port of New Orleans. Jefferson had long dreamed of an agrarian republic whose boundaries would expand to the western oceans. This expansion would secure vast acreages with which to endow future generations of farmers. It would also eliminate the danger of America's becoming involved in the embroilments that shook the peace of Europe. Nevertheless, the territories west of the Mississippi were not an urgent matter so long as they remained the possession of a weak Spain. In 1796, however, Spain ceded the vast Louisiana Territory to France, in the secret treaty of San Ildefonso. News of the transfer left Jefferson and the West profoundly shocked: Napoleon's aggressive designs seemed now to stand on the very threshold of the American nation. The matter was further complicated when, in 1802, the Spanish administrative official still responsible for the port of New Orleans closed the port to Americans. Westerners promptly threatened war against the Spanish Louisiana authorities, and the Federalist opposition called for an army of 50,000 with which to seize the port.

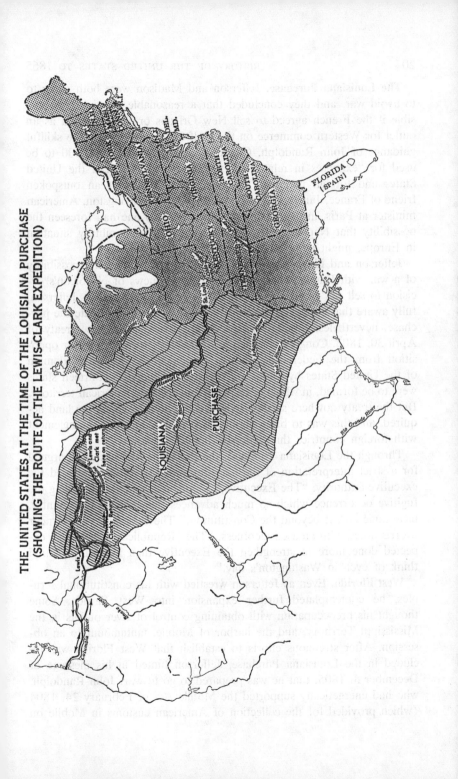

THE UNITED STATES AT THE TIME OF THE LOUISIANA PURCHASE
(SHOWING THE ROUTE OF THE LEWIS-CLARK EXPEDITION)

The Louisiana Purchase. Jefferson and Madison were both eager to to avoid war, and they concluded that a reasonable solution was possible if the French agreed to sell New Orleans or West Florida as an outlet for Western commerce on the Gulf of Mexico. Under the skillful guidance of John Randolph, Congress appropriated $2,000,000 to be used for "expenses in relation to the intercourse between the United States and foreign nations." Jefferson then dispatched an outspoken friend of France, James Monroe, to aid Robert R. Livingston, American minister at Paris, in negotiating the purchase. No one had foreseen the possibility that Napoleon, confronted with a critical military situation in Europe, might agree to sell the whole territory.

Jefferson and his cabinet were actually contemplating the possibility of a war with France when they first received news of Napoleon's decision to sell the whole region for the price of $15,000,000. Jefferson, fully aware that he lacked the constitutional power to negotiate the purchase, nevertheless urged Congress to approve the purchase treaty of April 30, 1803. Congress acceded to his request, with only minor opposition from the Federalists, and so expanded the territorial domain of the United States by about 140 per cent. Ultimately, thirteen states were to be formed, in whole or in part, from the new American territory. But the treaty nowhere strictly delimited the boundaries of the land acquired, and this was to bring about the kind of American entanglement with foreign countries that Jefferson hoped to avoid.

Through the Louisiana Purchase, the President who had once argued for a strict interpretation of the Constitution enormously expanded the executive authority. "The Executive," Jefferson admitted, "in seizing the fugitive occurrence which so much advances the good of the country, have done an act beyond the Constitution." The Federalist Gouverneur Morris noted with amused aloofness, "The [Republicans] have as I expected done more to strengthen the Executive than Federalists dared think of even in Washington's day."

West Florida. Even as Jefferson wrestled with his constitutional scruples, he contemplated further expansion into West Florida. Some thought his preoccupation with obtaining control of river outlets in the Mississippi Territory, and the harbor of Mobile, tantamount to an obsession. After strenuous efforts to establish that West Florida was included in the Louisiana Purchase, Jefferson hinted in his message of December 5, 1805, that he was prepared to go to war. John Randolph, who had energetically supported the Mobile Act of February 24, 1804 (which provided for the collection of American customs in Mobile on the assumption that the Louisiana Purchase included West Florida), was prepared to support the proposal. To his dismay, Randolph learned that what Jefferson really wanted was two million dollars to *buy* the territory. Outraged, convinced that Jefferson was displaying both duplicity and cowardice, Randolph broke with the Republicans to follow an independent course in politics. Since Spain stubbornly refused to sell Florida, the issue was left for final settlement until a decade later.

JEFFERSONIAN FOREIGN POLICY

American Neutrality. Though Jefferson identified himself with a pro-French policy during the Federalist period, he soon made it clear that, as President, he stood for making "neutrality the ground of gain to [our] country," and that he was prepared to do anything reasonable to keep the peace. "We are friendly, cordially and conscientiously friendly to England," he declared. "We are not hostile to France," he added. By this policy of avoiding entangling alliances, he expected to escape having "as much to swallow from [France and Britain] as our predecessors had. . . ." To the strong he accorded a respectful aloofness; to the weak, a display of firm determination.

The Barbary Coast War. Shortly after Jefferson assumed the presidency, he was compelled to face the prospect of war with the Barbary Coast pirates. Accepting European practice, the United States under Washington and Adams had paid tribute to the beys and deys of Northern Africa as insurance against piratical attacks upon American commerce. When Tripoli decided to demand increased tribute in 1801, Jefferson resolved to send four warships to the Mediterranean Sea to protect American commerce. The Bey of Tripoli responded by cutting down the flagpole before the American consulate—the Barbary method of declaring war—and shortly afterward, dispatched warships to blockade the Straits of Gibraltar.

A small American fleet under the command of Commodore Edward Preble seized Tangier and forced the Emperor of Morocco to accept American terms, but the Tripolitans captured one of his vessels and enslaved its crew of almost three hundred men. The administration promptly established a special Mediterranean fund, with which to finance the war. During the summer of 1804, Preble effectively blockaded the Tripoli coast. William Eaton, an American adventurer, staged an unsuccessful *coup d'état* against the reigning Bey of Tripoli. Obtaining the reluctant support of Jefferson, Eaton returned to Egypt, where he raised a force of several hundred Arabs and Greeks with whom he marched five hundred miles, to capture the Tripolitan town of Derne. Only the availability of American naval and marine support saved the Eaton force from a massacre; but the successful invasion of his homeland convinced the Bey of Tripoli that a peace treaty was required. The final treaty (1805) restored payments to about what they had been before the Bey had raised his tribute charges, but the Americans agreed to pay an additional $60,000 ransom for the captured American sailors. So ended the Barbary Coast War.

The Napoleonic Wars. As the Napoleonic Wars swept the European continent, Jefferson found it ever more difficult to avoid involvement. Frequent seizures and confiscations of American ships and impressment of American sailors by the British navy made it seem likely that the United States would find itself at war with Great Britain. Between 1805 and 1806, no less than 120 American ships were taken by British forces. When repeated American protests had been ignored, Congress, on April 18, 1806, passed the nonimportation act. By severely limiting British imports, they hoped to persuade the British to relent in their interference with American trade. But the Americans were tilting against windmills. Each antagonist in the British-French struggle used every means available to lessen the economic potential of the other. When the British instituted a blockade of northwestern Europe, Napoleon responded with the Berlin Decree blockading "the British islands." Britain answered with an extended blockade of all French ports, as well as those of French allies. The Paris government replied with the Milan Decree of December 17, 1806, which declared that every neutral ship searched by the British automatically became enemy property. This proved particularly painful to American merchants, since it denied them access to Continental ports at the same time that it made their ships liable to seizure, even when acts of British search were beyond American control.

The Embargo. Jefferson, trying to find a solution to the American dilemma, obtained authorization from Congress (December 22, 1807) to impose an embargo on all American vessels trading with foreign ports. The Jeffersonians saw this as the only practical alternative to war. Any active defense of American rights would have committed the country to a war with the greatest naval power in the world, or the most powerful land power, or both (with the latter a distinct and frightening possibility, since both Britain and France had violated American commercial and political rights). Having committed himself to restraining American commerce, Jefferson was willy-nilly engaged in an internal struggle with domestic interests reluctant to accept the cost of the embargo.

From the outset, Jefferson made it clear that his intention was "to keep our seamen and property from capture, and to starve the offending nations." He also admitted that the national defenses were grievously weak, though not that this situation stemmed directly from the Jeffersonian passion for economy and debt reduction. At the behest of Jefferson and Gallatin, the navy had been cut down to small gunboats whose primary function was to protect ports from attack. Jefferson committed himself to restoring freedom of the seas but he (and his successor) systematically reduced naval and military expenditures; and the embargo was at least partly a device to circumvent the costs of creating a defense organization that would be capable of forcing international respect. It also revealed the overwhelming desire of Jefferson and his supporters to keep the peace at almost any cost. The idealism that underlay these hopes was eloquently expressed by Albert Gallatin even as he left it behind:

> I had conceived that our distance from the European world might have prevented our being involved in the mischievous policies of Europe, and that we might have lived in peace without armies and navies and without being deeply involved in debt. . . . I had conceived it would have been our object to have become a happy and not a powerful nation, or at least no way powerful except for self-defence.

Jefferson discovered that his advisers viewed the embargo with dismay. Gallatin bluntly told his mentor, "In every point of view, privations, sufferings, revenue, effect on the enemy, politics at home, etc., I prefer war to a permanent embargo." But the presidential response was one of stubborn persistence, and Jefferson even pressed for a strengthening of the act. On January 9, 1808, Congress placed all coasting vessels under bond, to prevent sailings to foreign ports. Similar restrictions were placed on fishing and whaling vessels. A program of heavy penalties was instituted to enforce the embargo. On March 12, 1808, a third Embargo Act was passed to permit small supply vessels to transport goods without payment of bond, but it also added new penalties to strengthen the act. The slightest hint that exceptions to the act might be made brought a deluge of mercantile petitions to the President, who commented: "I imagine they will come in bales every day." In the face of repeated violations, Jefferson proposed even more drastic penalties. From April 25, 1808, all sailings, no matter what the size of the ship, its cargo, or its destination, required the supervision of a revenue officer during the loading process. Only presidential authorization permitted sailings from American ports adjacent to foreign territory. Naval craft were ordered to inspect all suspicious ships. And the decision of Congress to adjourn after passage of the third act left Jefferson to maintain the experiment unhindered. "Congress," he promptly declared, "has just passed an additional embargo law, . . . which, if we act as boldly as I am disposed to do, we can make . . . effectual." With equal forthrightness, he admitted that the major victim of the program would be the commercial interests. "I set down the exercise of commerce, merely for profit," he wrote Gallatin, "as nothing when it carries with it the danger of defeating the objects of the embargo."

But the great experiment carried within it the seeds of a primary dilemma. Since many of the staple supplies consumed within the United States were transported by coastal vessels from one point on the eastern seaboard to another, the prohibitions placed on the coasting trade threatened to starve America before they reduced Great Britain. As the results of the embargo became apparent in America, local pressure was brought to bear on the authorities in a number of ports, forcing serious modifications to be made in the embargo restrictions. Jefferson responded with the proposal that communities guilty of violation be themselves placed under a blockade. Congress, well aware what the political consequences of such proposals might be, granted instead a new enforcement act (January 9, 1809) to instruct enforcement agents for more effective application of the law. Enforcement was not made easier when it was suspected that Republican merchants were granted exemptions denied known opponents of the administration. Indeed, almost all commercial interests, Republican or not, employed subterfuge and open defiance to frustrate enforcement of the embargo.

The New England Merchants. As news of the administration's embargo spread along the Atlantic seaboard, New England and New York merchants and shipowners felt the cold breath of ruin on their necks. Boston went into open defiance. From both that great port and the thousands of inlets and bays that dot the New England shore, vessels sailed loaded with contraband cargo. It was not unusual to find a ship authorized to sail to Norfolk arriving in Lisbon—driven there, of course, by the "stress of weather." Though Philadelphia and Southern ports were less defiant, Jefferson received ample evidence that the embargo was abused even in these citadels of Republicanism. Along the vast northern frontier, smuggling became a large-scale enterprise. Behind much of this open defiance lay the increasingly large profits to be made from the successful transport of a cargo either into or out of the country. Yet the actual volume of smuggling should not be exaggerated. On the whole, the embargo proved moderately successful. Large amounts of shipping lay idle at American wharves, while in more than one port, and especially in New England, the surface placidity of the scene masked the bitter fury of the merchants.

New Englanders contemplated tearing a leaf from Jefferson's own book as they explored his doctrines of nullification and secession. As the cost of Jefferson's experiment mounted, the Massachusetts General Court ominously warned that continuation of the policy would endanger "our domestic peace, and the union of these States." The governor of Connecticut flatly refused to provide state militia to enforce the embargo. Ships violated the restrictions in full awareness that state authority would be used in their defense. And the impending political consequences made the Jeffersonian contingent in Congress unwilling to press the experiment further. Fearful of civil war, and with his supporters in a "kind of panic," Jefferson, on March 1, 1809, signed a bill repealing the embargo. So ended "a noble and magnificent effort." Three days later Jefferson surrendered the presidency to James Madison.

JEFFERSON IN RETIREMENT

The prominent public man who retired to Monticello in 1809, at the age of sixty-six, had had his fill of politics. No longer obliged to accommodate his principles to necessity, he devoted his time to the management of his private affairs and to private comments on the course of the world. "I am tired of practical politics," he mourned, "and . . . the total banishment of all moral principle from the code which governs the intercourse of nations."

With the end of political ambition, Jefferson renewed his friendship with John Adams, opening a classic correspondence. In it he wondered whether the natural aristocrats among men, so designated by their "virtue and talents," might not provide the best governors of mankind, and succeed in countering the steady degeneration of decency. He hoped that the young American would find in himself the capacity to sympathize with the oppressed wherever found. He dreamed of a nation where necessities were available to all and luxury known to none. To Adams he wrote, "My temperament is sanguine. I steer my bark with Hope in the head, leaving Fear astern." From the perspective of more than seven decades of life he was still able to write: "I am not among those who fear the people. They . . . are our dependence for continued freedom." He greeted the prospect of change with equanimity, arguing that "laws and institutions must go hand in hand with the progress of the human mind." And always he believed in the American dream, the vision of an America "destined to be a barrier against the returns of ignorance and barbarism." In a moment of rhapsodic vision, he foretold:

> What a colossus shall we be when the southern continent comes up to our mark! What a stand will it secure as a ralliance for the reason and freedom of the globe! I like the dreams of the future better than the history of the past.

On July 4, 1826, fifty years to the day after the signing of the Declaration of Independence, Thomas Jefferson died, followed within a few hours by John Adams. He left as his legacy a uniquely American hope: that his Declaration of Independence signaled the beginning of the triumph of reason, the beginning of a time when the world would recognize "the palpable truth, that the mass of mankind has not been born with saddles on their backs, nor a favored few booted and spurred, ready to ride them legitimately, by the grace of God." In moments of stress and doubt Americans have again and again had recourse to the words and ideals of Jefferson who, as he aged, grew ever more hopeful.

Part Four

THE SECTIONAL REPUBLIC

Chapter 10

The Era of Good Feelings

The so-called "Era of Good Feelings" opened with war and closed with the collapse of the Jeffersonian party. The era marked the emergence of an America self-assured in its foreign relations, dedicated to the politics of universal enfranchisement, and stirring with dynamic capitalism. A superficial glance would seem to confirm the idea that all was tranquil as the Americans waxed fat in their boundless wealth.

MADISON AS PRESIDENT

James Madison. For the twenty-four years between 1801 and 1825, a succession of Virginians occupied the presidency: Jefferson, Madison, and Monroe. Of these, only Jefferson achieved genuine greatness in the conduct of his office. His successor, James Madison, had a genius for political theory but revealed a marked deficiency as President; he proved incapable of acting upon the political principles which he had so eloquently postulated in the *Federalist Papers*. Although capable of subjecting the major problems of his day to an acute and perceptive analysis, he was less successful in finding solutions for them.

Jefferson left to Madison many problems that seemed to defy solution, among them the wreckage of the embargo policies. To compel a more just treatment of American commerce by the European belligerents, Jefferson had signed three days before the end of his presidency the Non-Intercourse Act, which permitted American merchants to trade with any country other than France or Britain. France and Britain were each given the choice of accepting continued severance of their trade with America or resumption of trade when they ended their restrictions on American commerce.

The Erskine Agreements. George Canning, the British foreign minister, swiftly directed his minister at Washington, David Erskine, to enter into talks with the new administration, and it seemed that Madison was about to obtain by negotiation what Jefferson had struggled for nearly three years to bring about by coercion. Erskine agreed to settle with the new administration the long smoldering controversy over the *Chesapeake* affair (the British warship *Leopard* had attacked the American frigate *Chesapeake* in the early summer of 1807 after the American commander refused to permit his ship to be searched for deserters), and both countries agreed to repeal their trade restrictions. Madison proudly announced that the United States and Britain would resume amicable trade relations.

These high hopes were quickly dashed, however, when Canning denounced the treaty, and removed Erskine for having exceeded his instructions. To compete the humiliation of the Americans, Napoleon renewed his seizure of American ships. He justified his action by charging that the Non-Intercourse Act was a severance of commercial relations with France.

Macon Bill Number 2. Still hoping that economic coercion would resolve American difficulties, Nathaniel Macon, chairman of the House Committee on Foreign Affairs, first proposed (unsuccessfully) that all French and British imports be carried in American vessels. He then successfully proposed on May 1, 1810, Macon Bill Number 2, which provided that should either France or Britain revoke their trade restrictions on American commerce, the United States would resume nonintercourse with the remaining culprit. It was obvious that the Americans were desperately playing the two major opponents against each other. What Madison and his advisers had not foreseen was the possibility that this policy would be used by one of the belligerents to provoke a war between the United States and the other antagonist. In early August, 1810, the American minister to Paris was informed by the Duc de Cadore, the French foreign minister, that his government intended, on November 1, 1810, to revoke the Berlin and Milan Decrees—(1) if Britain revoked its blockade of the Continent, or (2) if the United States compelled the British to respect American commercial rights. Madison promptly threatened to invoke the Non-Intercourse Act against Britain within three months unless the Orders in Council were repealed. Britain ignored the threat; Napoleon restored his order to seize American ships; and on March 2, 1811, Congress restored non-intercourse with Britain. Less than two years after his inauguration, Madison found his country drifting towards war.

THE WAR OF 1812

The Causes of War. On the diplomatic level, the developing conflict was discussed in terms of impressment, seizure at sea, freedom of the seas, and Orders in Council, but no group opposed war more than the shipping and merchant interests who seemed most affected by these actions. The truth was that the ports of the Northeast, despite French and British interference, were making large profits, and wished to continue making them. It was the frontiersmen and Southern planters that supplied the chief pressure for war. Along the northern frontier Americans looked longingly toward Canada, and dreamed of despoiling the Indians of fur and land. The Southern planters looked with equal fervor upon the Spanish provinces of East and West Florida, and upon the Alabama and Mississippi lands of the Creek Indians. Quickened by the greed for land, men distant from the seaboard saw war as the fulfillment, rather than the destruction, of their dreams.

Tecumseh. Throughout Jefferson's administration, petty fighting between Indians and frontiersmen had enlivened the two frontiers. In the Northwest, William Henry Harrison, the Indian-hating governor of the Indiana Territory, used any means available to despoil the Indians of their land. When Tecumseh, Chief of the Shawnees, and his brother, the Prophet, attempted to forge an Indian Confederation in the remaining northwestern territories, Harrison went to war and, at the battle of Tippecanoe on November 7, 1811, which took place while Tecumseh was visiting tribes in the South, Harrison utterly routed the leaderless tribe. When Harrison informed the government in Washington that the Indians had received arms from Canada, he gave force to the demand that the British territories to the north be incorporated into the United States.

Expansion into Florida. Equally insistent were American claims to Florida. No respectable Jeffersonian ever conceded that West Florida, bordering on the Mississippi, was not included in the Louisiana Purchase. When in 1810 the American settlers residing in West Florida revolted against Spanish rule and declared themselves incorporated into the United States, Madison accepted incorporation. Pressure for the seizure of East Florida increased until, in midwinter of 1811, Congress gave preliminary authorization for seizure of the territory. Bellicose frontiersmen viewed British intervention in American commerce as a personal affront. The belligerent nationalism and expansionism which raced through the interior of America permitted energetic young frontier congressmen known as "war hawks" to press for war.

The Declaration of War. Two such war hawks, Henry Clay of Kentucky and John C. Calhoun of South Carolina, channeled American war fever. They demanded war as an assertion of "the honor and independence of [their] country." Against the nearly unanimous opposition of New England and the Middle Atlantic States, the Westerners and Southerners had their way. On June 1, 1812, Madison asked for war against Great Britain. Three days later the House of Representatives, with a vote of seventy-nine to forty-nine, complied. On June 17, the Senate, by a vote of nineteen to thirteen, confirmed the proposed adventure. Ironically, on June 16, 1812, the British government had repealed the odious Orders in Council which had disrupted American commerce. So began a war without an evident cause.

A Nation at War. The United States could hardly have chosen a more inauspicious moment to go to war. The national defenses were in a scandalous condition. The Jeffersonians viewed a standing army and navy as "inconsistent with the principles of republican Governments, dangerous to the liberties of a free people, and generally converted into destructive engines for establishing despotism." As a result, the War Department lacked even the rudiments of a system of war management. The Secretary of War had only a dozen clerks with whom to arrange procurement of supplies, mobilization of manpower, and supervision of strategy. Complicating the problem of mobilization were the vast distances across which supplies and men would have to move. Only rivers and wretched roads existed to provide the necessary routes.

Mobilization for War. As the war began, even the exact state of the nation's army was confused and unknown. The Inspector General, who was supposed to know how many men were in the service, openly admitted his ignorance. Perhaps slightly more than 6,700 men garrisoned some twenty-three different forts and posts. The great port of New York was guarded by less than 900 men. The proposed strategy of war included a plan for a swift conquest of Canada. It ended in a disastrous repulse that was foreshadowed when Madison, authorized by Congress to raise 50,000 volunteers, obtained the services of barely 10,000. Anticipating disaffection among western Canadians, Americans under William Hull had invaded Upper Canada; there they were met by the British under Major General Isaac Brock, and after brief skirmishes, retreated to Detroit, where they were surrounded. On August 12, 1812, they surrendered. The energetic Brock then moved swiftly across Ontario to Niagara, where he defeated American forces under Stephen Van Rensselaer. An American attempt to capture Montreal ended in a fiasco when the American militia refused to cross the border into Canada. In 1813, only the minor gains of Captain Oliver Hazard Perry, who defeated British naval forces on Lake Erie (September 10, 1813), and the victory of William Henry Harrison at the Thames River (October 5, 1813), prevented the American war effort from degenerating into utter futility.

The Management of War. The management of the war exposed the limited competence of Madison and his advisers. Secretary of War William Eustis became so concerned with minor details that he lost track of major principles. James Monroe, ambitious and eager to gain a reputation in the War Department by successfully prosecuting the war, hoped to add appointment as Secretary of War to his secretaryship in the State Department. When Madison appointed John Armstrong, a New York politician, to succeed Eustis, Monroe seized every opportunity to snipe at the new secretary, despite the fact that Armstrong revitalized the army command. But no amount of energy could overcome the incompetence of most field commanders, or the inability of the Treasury to meet the cost of supplying the army or of paying the militia.

The Burning of Washington. The defeat of Napoleon in 1814 released the full might of Britain to challenge the United States. In London, a scheme for a four-pronged attack upon the United States was planned: British forces would attack in the North in Maine; at Plattsburgh, New York; in the Chesapeake region in the Middle States; and at the mouth of the Mississippi in the South. Of these attacks, the movement against Washington had the greatest demoralizing effect on the government. The British landed unimpeded below Washington on August 23, 1814. Madison, taking his position as Commander-in-Chief of the Army and Navy literally, wandered along the American lines, while Secretary of War Armstrong flatly refused to take any measures to protect the capital from attack. Secretary of State Monroe directly interfered in the conduct of the battle, without informing the commanding general of his actions. To complete the chaos, the commanding general,

William Winder, displayed absolutely no capacity for leadership. It is hardly surprising that Washington fell with little more than token resistance. Twenty-four hours after the British had landed, the White House and other public buildings were put to the torch, while Madison and the government fled ignominiously. Only the repulse of the raid on Baltimore relieved the national gloom.

The War at Sea. If the army was hardly fit to mount a war effort, the navy was in a state of utter demoralization as a result of the Jeffersonian passion for economy. Fleets of gunboats, designed for defensive warfare, were deemed by Jefferson the only suitable instrument of American naval policy. The minute navy was managed by the Secretary of the Navy, Paul Hamilton, and thirteen clerks. At the advent of war, Hamilton remained preoccupied with problems of economy and took no measures to improve the navy's strength. In January of 1813, William Jones, a capable and energetic Philadelphia merchant who had replaced Hamilton, applied himself with an intense sense of purpose to naval business. He accepted the idea that if America were to possess an adequate naval establishment, future naval development would have to concentrate upon the construction of ships of the line. These ships would provide both defensive and offensive action.

Proposals for naval reform, no matter how urgent, do not resolve established deficiencies in a time of war. Individual ships, like the *Constitution, Essex,* and *Hornet,* did win notable victories; the navy captured no less than 165 British craft; and privateers seized more than 1,300 prizes. But when British naval power was released from the European war effort, American war craft were swept from the seas. By 1814 the coast was completely blockaded, and British marauders landed at will along the sprawling American coastline. To encourage the growing disaffection of New England, the British navy winked at the movement of ships in and out of New England harbors. As the war approached its third year, the American cause flagged; defeat and sectional discord prevailed.

Mr. Madison's War. The war had hardly begun when the presidential elections of 1812 were held. DeWitt Clinton of New York, heading a coalition of dissident Republicans and Federalists eager for peace, gained 89 electoral votes to 128 for Madison. Every Northern state but Pennsylvania and Vermont voted for Clinton. The vote signaled a growing disaffection for the war in segments of the nation which at first only hampered the war effort, and later threatened disunion. New England openly opposed the invasion of Canada, flatly refused to appropriate or lend money for the war effort, defied efforts to raise the militia, and actually sold supplies to the British blockaders and armed forces in Canada. Public journals throughout the region contemptuously dismissed the war as "Mr. Madison's War." When a British force occupied Bangor, Maine, on September 1, 1814, the inhabitants of northeastern Maine took an oath of allegiance to the still-reigning King George III.

The Hartford Convention. Sectional disaffection reached its climax in the early autumn of 1814 when Massachusetts and Connecticut announced the withdrawal of their militia from federal jurisdiction. In October, Massachusetts issued a call for a convention of the states at Hartford to discuss further action toward halting the war. Talk of state rights, nullification, and secession was rife. From the Jeffersonians came vigorous protests against this threat to the Union, though few persons noted that New England was appealing to the doctrines of the two great Republican patrons—Madison and Jefferson. The evidence strongly suggests that New England was preparing to withdraw from the Union and was only retrieved from this step by news of the formal ratification, in February 1815, of the treaty ending the war. But the Federalist party was ruined; its name became synonymous with "treason."

The Search for Peace. The war had hardly started when efforts to restore peace were begun, both at home and abroad. The Russian Czar, fearful of any diminution of the British war effort against Napoleon, approached John Quincy Adams, then American minister to St. Petersburg, as early as September 1812, to offer the good offices of Russia as mediator in the war. Madison, whose natural caution had returned as soon as war actually began, promptly accepted the offer. He designated Adams, Albert Gallatin, and James A. Bayard as American commissioners at peace talks. The British overcame their original reluctance, and proposed direct negotiations. Madison, determined to involve the "war hawks" in the prospective parley, added Henry Clay and Minister to Sweden Jonathan Russell to the American delegation. On August 8, 1814, negotiations opened at the Hotel des Pays Bas in Ghent, Belgium.

The Treaty of Ghent. At first the British pursued a hard policy. They angrily charged the United States with a program of aggrandizement in Florida and the Mississippi Valley. "It is notorious to the whole world," they stated, "that the conquest of Canada, and its permanent annexation to the United States, was the declared object of the American government." The American delegation privately recognized the truth of the charges, and the painful news of American reverses added to their discomfiture. Working for the Americans, however, was the profound war weariness of the British nation. London viewed the prospect of more sacrifice and additional charges to an already staggering war debt without enthusiasm. A lagging trade and the stymied peace negotiations with France at Vienna also worked to make the British government seek a reasonable settlement. When the Duke of Wellington expressed unwillingness to lead a military expedition into the United States, and further informed Lord Liverpool, the British Prime Minister, that he considered the cabinet's territorial demands unjust, the British abandoned all thought of continuing the war. Negotiations thereafter proceeded rapidly; on December 24, 1814, the Treaty of Ghent was signed. It made reference neither to the conflicts over navigation of the oceans nor to territorial changes; it merely returned conditions to the pre-war status quo. The war had been a draw.

The Battle of New Orleans. Had transatlantic communications been in a less primitive state, the culminating American victory would never have been fought. The Battle of New Orleans was fought on January 8, 1815, fifteen days after the signing of the Treaty of Ghent. The British had viewed the attack upon New Orleans as part of their general campaign to force a peace by discrediting the American federal government. It was also felt that by occupying the city the British claim to free navigation of the Mississippi River would be strengthened. What had not been foreseen was that Andrew Jackson, leading a force of pirates, New Orleans Creoles, their slaves, and some one thousand Kentuckians, would rout the British; and this with but a handful of American casualties. The battle, though fought after the treaty ending the war had been signed, lifted American spirits and made Andrew Jackson a national hero. The war's over-all effect was one of psychological stimulation. As Albert Gallatin assessed its results later:

> The war had been productive of evil and good, but I think the good preponderates. . . . Under our former system we were becoming too selfish, too much attached exclusively to the acquisition of wealth, above all too much confined in our political feelings to local and state objects. The war has renewed and reinstated the National feelings and character which the Revolution had given, and which were daily lessened. The people now have more general objects of attachment with which their pride and political opinions are connected. They are more American: they feel and act more as a Nation, and . . . the permanency of the Union is thereby better secured.

THE UNSETTLED SOUTHERN FRONTIER

Florida. The war of expansion in the North and South had ended without expansion. The military power of Britain had put Canada beyond American grasp, but the weakness of Spain made another effort to secure East Florida attractive. The successful seizure of West Florida had been preceded by Congress' issuance of the No-Transfer Resolution of January 15, 1811. It had pointedly declared:

> Taking into view the peculiar position of Spain and her American provinces; and considering the influence which the destiny of the territory adjoining the southern boundary of the United States may have upon their security, tranquillity, and commerce: Therefore,
>
> Resolved, by the Senate and House of Representatives of the United States of America in Congress assembled, that the United States, under the peculiar circumstances of the existing crisis, cannot without serious inquietude see any part of the said territory pass into the hands of any foreign Power; and that a due regard to their own safety compels them to provide under certain contingencies, for the temporary occupation of the said territory; they, at the same time, declare that the said territory shall, in their hands, remain subject to a future negotiation.

The question, therefore, was not whether, but when, Florida would be fully annexed to the Union.

Warfare in Florida. Some of the most brutal warfare of 1812 had occurred along the southern frontier where the British had encouraged the Indians to attack American outposts and settlements. No less than 250 men, women, and children had been massacred by Indians at Fort Mims, Alabama. And Andrew Jackson had made a considerable reputation for himself before the Battle of New Orleans by brutally suppressing the Indians in response. British efforts to stir up a slave insurrection in Florida had accentuated American fears. Florida in the hands of an enemy was an unendurable threat.

The Arbuthnot and Ambrister Affair. Once the war had ended, Britain abandoned efforts to extend her control in Florida. Spain made scarcely any effort to reassert her control. For all practical purposes, the territory was in the hands of British soldiers of fortune, Indians, and escaped slaves. Colonel Edward Nicholls, a British officer who had organized the Creek and Seminole Indians during the war, now turned to inciting the Seminoles against the Americans to the north. He was aided by three other British adventurers named George Woodbine, Alexander Arbuthnot, and Robert C. Ambrister. These four men unwittingly supplied the United States with justification for a drastic intervention. Spain had pledged in 1795 to keep Indians within her territory at peace with the United States; she had hardly carried out this promise, and the result was a mounting series of claims against Spain for damage wrought by Indian raids. The renewed raids only worsened the already deteriorating situation.

The Intervention of Jackson. The chaos was made to order for General Jackson. Proud, imperious, ruthless, he viewed the border raids with growing anger. Behind him stood the frontier traditions of hunger for land and hostility to the Indians. Taking Florida was for him, therefore, an article of faith and an act of patriotism. When orders came from Secretary of War Calhoun to suppress further Seminole raids from Apalachicola, with specific instructions "to adopt the necessary measures to terminate a conflict which it has ever been the desire of the President, from motives of humanity, to avoid," Jackson responded with alacrity. He immediately proposed to Monroe that all of Florida be seized and held as "indemnity for the outrages of Spain upon the property of our Citizens. . . ." Moreover, he proposed to carry out this project "without implicating the Government." All Jackson wanted was a single sign "that the possession of the Floridas would be desirable to the United States, and in sixty days it will be accomplished." When Monroe made no explicit response, the precipitous general was allowed to draw his own conclusions.

Seizure of Florida. Jackson acted swiftly. With a force of three thousand men he swept through Northwestern Florida. Arbuthnot and Captain Ambrister, both deeply implicated in Indian raids, were captured, tried by court-martial, and executed. The British government, despite strong objections at home, accepted the fate of their unsavory subjects without protest. But when news reached Washington of Jackson's action, a serious dispute shook Monroe's cabinet. Secretary of War Calhoun countermanded Jackson's order to General Gaines to occupy St. Augustine, and insisted that the government repudiate Jackson. Secretary of the Treasury Crawford joined Calhoun in his stand, hoping to destroy Jackson as a possible presidential candidate. The supporters of Henry Clay joined in the clamor; and soon the entire cabinet, with the one critical exception of Secretary of State John Quincy Adams, supported Calhoun's proposal that Jackson should be "the subject of investigation by a military tribunal."

Monroe and Jackson. Jackson was saved by the weight of public opinion and the diplomatic realities of the situation. Monroe, an assiduous cultivator of public favor, hardly wished to alienate the populace. He also agreed with the vigorous arguments of Adams that to repudiate Jackson would only encourage Spain to renew its claim to Florida. Adams further justified the general's action as a necessary response to the inadequacies of Spanish government in Florida. "If the question is dubious," he protested, "it is better to err on the side of vigor than of weakness—on the side of our own officer, who has rendered the most eminent services to the nation, than on the side of our bitterest enemies, and against him." Finally a compromise settlement was reached —the American force would be withdrawn when Spain provided forces sufficient to keep the Indians in check. Jackson's behavior was justified as necessary to keeping the peace in Florida. As John Quincy Adams soon learned, Andrew Jackson had made an indelible impression on Madrid. The Spaniards were reconciled to the loss of Florida, and wanted now to obtain the best terms.

The Transcontinental Treaty of 1819. "The events which have occurred in both the Floridas show the incompetency of Spain to maintain her authority," Monroe explained by letter to Jackson. Withdrawal was necessary, therefore, to provide Spain with a face-saving device preliminary to final negotiations. Monroe and Adams did not intend to allow the Spaniards to escape the consequences of their weakness. Spain had decided Florida was irreparably lost; but she meant to save as many of her Pacific Coast possessions as possible. Such was the essential basis of the Transcontinental Treaty that the two countries ratified on February 22, 1821. In it, Spain ceded Florida to the United States, and defined the western boundary of the United States along the Sabine, Red, and Arkansas Rivers to latitude 42° and thence westward to the Pacific. The treaty provided the basis for further dispute by leaving the future of Texas to subsequent discussion. Before this problem could be settled, Mexico achieved independence from Spain and final settlement was left to another war.

THE MONROE DOCTRINE

The Growth of Latin-American Independence. James Monroe had watched with deep sympathy the struggle of the Latin-American countries for independence. It was a clear identification of Latin-American aspirations with those of his own nation. John Quincy Adams, his

Secretary of State, viewed developments in Latin America differently. The restoration of peace in Europe posed the dire possibility of a collective European effort to restore Spain's control over her dwindling empire. Adams thought the best course open to the United States was one of neutrality. He sturdily supported his father's hope that "our Government will stand fast in its impregnable fortress, neutrality." Particularly uncertain were Britain's attitudes toward Latin America. The Monroe administration suspected that Britain's leading intention was to secure advantageous trade conditions in the Southern Hemisphere, but was uncertain whether she would join with the other European monarchs to restore the authority of Ferdinand VII of Spain over his rebellious subjects. Lord Castlereagh, the British foreign minister, did not propose to clarify the issue for the Americans until it suited Britain's purposes.

British Aims in the Americas. The British aimed to achieve two objectives: supremacy over the seas, and a stable power balance in Europe. The suicide of Castlereagh led to the accession of George Canning to the Foreign Office. Unlike his predecessor, who had sought to maintain a power balance in Europe through a system of European alliances, Canning thought Britain should remove herself from direct European entanglements while reducing, whenever possible, the power of her continental rivals. One such course he saw in Britain's acceptance of the freedom of Latin America. This meant not only that Spain should lose power but also that any other European power should be prevented from replacing her in the newly independent South American countries. Canning saw one impediment preventing a steady amelioration of British-American relations: the United States seemed to be developing an interest in the annexation of Cuba. As it was, neither Britain nor the United States wished to see a country stronger than Spain occupy the rich island. To eliminate this possibility, Monroe considered proposing to the British a joint renunciation of expansion into Cuba. The political future of the island came in doubt in the summer of 1823 when Spain, torn by civil war, was occupied by French armies. In reply to urgent American inquiries about British intentions, Lord Liverpool assured Washington that his government intended neither to seize the island nor to permit a change in the island's control.

British-American Rapprochement. It seemed to John Quincy Adams that this was the moment for a British-American rapprochement. He sounded out the British minister in Washington on whether the time had not come "for the United States and Great Britain to compare their ideas and purposes together, with a view to the accommodation of great interests upon which they have hitherto differed." George Canning promptly seized upon this proposal as the prelude to an unofficial understanding between the two countries concerning foreign intervention in Latin America. "The force of blood again prevails," he publicly announced, "and the daughter and the mother stand together against the world." To France, Canning sent the flat demand that she abjure "any design of acting against the [Latin-American] colonies by force of arms."

Monroe turned to Jefferson and Madison for guidance on the momentous proposal for a British-American concert. Jefferson promptly urged acceptance of the proposal, since it would make the United States sure of "keeping out of our land all *foreign powers,* of never permitting those of Europe to interfere with the affairs of our nations." Madison added his assent, contending that "With the British power and navy combined with our own we have nothing to fear from the rest of the nations. . . ." He added further that "in *the great struggle of the Epoch between liberty and despotism,* we owe it to ourselves to sustain the former in this hemisphere at least."

John Quincy Adams and the Monroe Doctrine. It remained for Adams to dissent. He argued for America taking an independent American stand, which would avow "our principles explicitly" to the world rather than coming in "as a cockboat in the wake of the British man-of-war." As the administration was guided toward an independent course of action by Adams, Canning, who had decided to interpose British power between Latin America and Europe with or without American support, viewed Washington developments philosophically.

Formulation of the Monroe Doctrine. In a series of cabinet meetings, the American position slowly emerged. The forceful Secretary of State, Adams, argued for a positive assertion of American principles derived from "those upon which our own Government is founded, and, while disclaiming all intention of attempting to propagate them by force, and all interference with the political affairs of Europe, to declare our expectation and hope that the European powers will equally abstain from the attempt to spread their principles in the American hemisphere, or to subjugate by force any part of these continents to their will." Adams stubbornly opposed any extension of the statement to include European conflicts, insisting it be made "an American cause. . . ." In the end his will prevailed. The final statement, which was included in President Monroe's annual message to the Congress of the United States on December 7, 1823, has come to be known as the Monroe Doctrine. It set forth the singular proposition "that the American Continents, by the free and independent condition which they have assumed and maintain, are henceforth not to be considered as subjects for future colonization by any European Power." Monroe, though pledging noninterference with existing European colonies and dependencies, pointedly observed: "We owe it, therefore, to candor and to the amicable relations existing between the United States and those powers to declare that we should consider any attempt on their part to extend their system to any portion of this hemisphere as dangerous to our peace and safety." It confirmed America's isolation from European entanglements, and its determination to achieve domination of the Western Hemisphere.

Britain and the Monroe Doctrine. At first Canning viewed the American assertion as presumptuous, but upon reflection saw it as a positive advantage to Britain. "The effect of the ultra-liberalism of our Yankee co-operators on the ultra-despotism of [the Holy Alliance]," he privately confessed, "gives me just the balance that I wanted." Some time later he proclaimed to Parliament, "I called the New World into existence to redress the balance of the Old." The independent American course had been confirmed. The United States could be sure that the power of the British navy would sustain the Monroe Doctrine even as the United States remained true to the "great rule of conduct" of Washington's Farewell Address:

> The political system of the United States is . . . extra-European. To stand in firm and cautious independence of all entanglement in the European system, has been a cardinal point of their policy. . . . It may be observed that for the repose of Europe, as well as of America, the European and American political systems should be kept as separate and distinct from each other as possible.

A century of isolation had been inaugurated; the United States had achieved the security within which it could pursue its continental destiny.

Chapter 11

March to the West and Policies of the 1820s

Between 1803 and 1853, the United States extended its physical boundaries from the Mississippi River to the Pacific Ocean, and the American people settled the Ohio, Mississippi, and lower Missouri Valleys. The lure of cheap land coupled with a transportation revolution provided the incentive for resettling and made vast migrations possible. And as the Western population grew, it subtly disoriented American politics, for it shifted the locus of political power from the eastern seaboard to the states which were emerging in the vast interior. Of primary significance was the development of turnpikes, of steamboats, and of canals. The goal of establishing a national transportation network was approaching fruition in 1820, and provided adequate communications between East and West.

THE EARLY TRANSPORTATION REVOLUTION

The Patterns of Settlement. The great historian Frederick Jackson Turner, seeking an analogy with which to explain American westward expansion, compared it to the flow of water, which follows the path of least resistance. This image enabled him to explain why vast stretches of land remained unsettled while land further west possessed flourishing communities. The path west usually followed the river bottoms of valleys, especially those that provided gaps through the mountain ranges separating the eastern coast from the great river valleys of the Ohio, Mississippi, and Missouri, and those with gaps through the

Rocky Mountains that barred the way to the Pacific coast. As early as the mid-eighteenth century, a traveler noted that there existed "the Great Wagon Road . . . through Virginia to Philadelphia distant 435 Miles." It followed old Indian trails through the Susquehanna and Shenandoah Valleys, terminating in the Piedmont of South Carolina. Until the American Revolution the flow of westward settlement had been largely southwestward.

The Turnpike Movement. At the time America achieved her independence, a network of roads bound the states together. Most were country roads that led from farms to nearby villages, usually conveniently located on a navigable stream. These roads were frequently mere ruts, supplemented in swampy places by "corduroy roads" that consisted of logs laid side by side. Bridges were uncommon, most river crossings being ferries or fords. Though these primitive roads provided a national means of communication, there was considerable agitation for the construction of state supported through roads. As a result of this agitation, a system of turnpikes, roads subsidized by tolls and chartered by the state to private stock companies, was developed. Some, like the Lancaster Turnpike in Pennsylvania, had been built upon already existing roads—in this case, the old Philadelphia-Lancaster-Pittsburgh road, first constructed during the French and Indian War. Farther south, running from Baltimore and by way of Washington up the Potomac Valley to Cumberland, Maryland, ran the Cumberland Road. In 1815 Congress, prompted by James Madison, who urged "the great importance of establishing throughout our country . . . roads and canals . . . executed under national authority," authorized the construction of the National Road, which was to run from Cumberland to Wheeling along the Ohio River.

The States and Turnpikes. In the final decade of the eighteenth century, New England launched a turnpike construction program that soon crisscrossed the region with good roads. After the War of 1812, New York extended its turnpike system from the border of Massachusetts to Buffalo, supplementing the Hudson and Mohawk route to the West. No less than 2,400 miles of turnpike were constructed by 1832 under Pennsylvania charter. Some 550 miles of similar road crossed New Jersey, providing speedy transit between New York and Philadelphia. In the South, though considerable agitation for roadbuilding existed, construction lagged. Westward migrants from the South passed either through the Cumberland Gap along the Wilderness Road into Kentucky, or farther south through the Saluda Gap into Tennessee. Under the Turnpike Act of 1817, Virginia after some delay completed in the 1840s the Staunton and Parkersburg Road and Northwestern Turnpike. South Carolina, less venturesome, constructed a number of causeways across the swampy coastal plain, and a road linking Columbia and Charleston.

Financing Turnpikes. In New England, New York, and New Jersey, turnpikes were financed with private funds; but in Pennsylvania, nearly one-third of the $6,000,000 expended by 1822 came from state funds. South Carolina and Indiana subsidized and owned their turnpikes; Virginia, Ohio, and Pennsylvania, though chartering private firms, invested state funds in turnpike stock. Most Southern and Western states agreed to match private funds with state appropriations. The exact amount of public funds appropriated for turnpikes is unknown, since counties and municipalities, whose records are no longer available, assisted their construction with local funds. The unwillingness of the public to pay tolls, however, dealt a deathblow to turnpike construction, and by the 1830s much of the turnpike system had been abandoned, or incorporated into the state-operated road system.

The Erie Canal. Canals were small in dimension and had had little success up to the end of the War of 1812. Then, in an act of foresight, the New York legislature in 1817 authorized the construction of the Erie Canal. This project called for the building of a 364-mile canal, running through the still unsettled wilderness between Albany and Buffalo. Under the guidance of DeWitt Clinton, engineering difficulties were overcome, and in 1825 the canal was completed. As each section of the canal was opened, it attracted phenomenal traffic; and in the first year of full operation, the canal earned tolls of more than half a million dollars. Traffic on the canal continued to increase until 1880.

Canals Elsewhere. New York's success with the Erie Canal triggered nationwide canal construction. Three types of canals were constructed: those designed to provide water routes between the Tidewater and upcountry in states along the Atlantic Ocean; those which linked Eastern waterways with the Ohio Valley or the Great Lakes; and those which connected the Mississippi-Ohio Valleys with the Great Lakes. Construction was particularly heavy in Pennsylvania, Ohio, and Indiana, but the high costs—not only of building but of operation—in addition to inadequate traffic prevented most of these canals from making profits. And in the West, the coming of the railroad provided devastating competition. Public funds had been used to subsidize much of the heavy cost of canal construction, but New York's experience with the Erie

Canal proved that a state could raise large sums for public works through the sale of state bonds. The states were joined in their effort by the federal government, which prior to 1860 made grants of 4,000,000 acres of public lands to canal companies, and invested $3,000,000, largely in the Chesapeake and Ohio Canal. By 1840, a public and private expenditure of $125,000,000 had been made to build 3,326 miles of canal.

The Steamboat Era. The difficulty of transportation determined that early settlement in America be near water. Oceangoing craft were frequent sights in tidal streams, but adverse currents restricted much of the traffic to downstream movement. Crude rafts and flatboats were also commonplace, transporting interior produce to the ocean ports. In the Mississippi-Ohio system, vast quantities of goods were moved by these primitive methods to New Orleans. But such trips were time-consuming; a 1,950 mile trip from Pittsburgh to New Orleans, for example, usually took four months. The obvious dependence of the nation on water transportation at the beginning of the nineteenth century provided a strong incentive to develop craft that could move against the current and attain greater speed than that provided by the current.

Robert Fulton and John Stevens. In the last decade of the eighteenth century, experiments by John Fitch and William Henry demonstrated that the application of steam power to river craft was technically feasible. It was not until 1807, however, that Robert Fulton proved the commercial feasibility of steamboats on the Hudson River, and in 1809, John Stevens proved as much on the Delaware River. Fulton organized with Robert Livingston, under a New York charter, a company which obtained exclusive rights to navigate New York waters with steamboats. Stevens settled for plying the waters in and around Philadelphia.

Western Steamboats. In 1811, a successful steamboat journey from Pittsburgh to New Orleans inaugurated the era of Western steamboats. From a total of seventeen steamboats in 1817, the number had increased by 1855 to 727, providing service not only on the Mississippi and the Ohio, but also on their tributaries, and by 1860 steamboats were plying some 2,200 miles up the Missouri to Fort Benton, Montana. The frequent fluctuations of the river water levels, the often shallow flats, and the existence of numerous sandbars made the development of a peculiarly Western craft necessary. The inventive genius of Henry Shreve, Oliver Evans, Daniel French, and Stephen H. Long ultimately produced such a vehicle: a stately, but light, wooden steamboat that could navigate in as little as thirty inches of water. Until the eve of the Civil War these craft transported much of the bulky freight and many of the passengers in the West and South, but railroads during the '50s were making heavy inroads, and the heyday of the steamboat was passing.

GROWTH OF WESTERN TERRITORIES

Federal Land Policies. Even before the Constitution had been composed, the Northwest Ordinance provided for the steady organization and admission into the Union of western territories as states. Subsequently, the federal government expanded the agencies through which to dispose of its lands, altered policy so as to attract the maximum number of purchasers, and worked to minimize difficulties with the Indians. The task of maintaining peaceful relations with the Indians obliged the federal government to negotiate treaties with the tribes under which the Indians relinquished their title to western lands.

Indian Policy under the Federalists. The relations between the Indians and the whites had been justly characterized by Henry Knox, in 1787, as governed by "deeply rooted prejudices, and malignity of heart . . . reciprocally entertained . . . by the Whites and Savages." To prevent frequent warfare, it was felt that a strong public hand would be needed. The War Department supervised Indian affairs, with territorial governors serving as the superintendents of Indians. Normally, day-to-day relations with the Indians were managed by post commanders on the frontier. Since much of the Indian trouble grew out of sharp trade practices with the tribes, Congress in 1790 authorized the licensing of traders to deal with Indians, and in 1796 established government trading houses. The 1790 act forbade the sale of Indian lands except those obtained by a treaty of the United States, and in 1793 settlement on Indian lands was forbidden. The military was expected to enforce these provisions.

Indian Policy under the Jeffersonians. By 1830 the Eastern tribes had become submissive, their fate dependent on the national conscience. The insatiable demand of the white man for land led to numerous treaties under which the Indians steadily ceded lands. As late as 1825, however, 130,000 Indians residing in the states and territories claimed over 77,000,000 acres of land. Nevertheless, in the first three decades of the nineteenth century, whole tribes were being relocated west of the Mississippi. The federally authorized trading posts, despite excellent service, were liquidated on June 3, 1822, as sentiment for a free competitive society grew. During the Jeffersonian era efforts were made by the government to draw the Indians into "civilization." In 1793 and 1802 the federal authority inaugurated programs which gave Indians useful domestic animals, farm implements, and gifts of goods and money. But it was not until 1819 that the government launched a program of education to make the Indians literate and to teach agricultural techniques to the boys and domestic arts to the girls. Particularly receptive were the Cherokees of Georgia, who had adapted themselves to an agrarian existence.

Jackson and the Indian. Indian policy was swiftly reversed under Jackson, who held the opinion that the best Indian was a dead Indian. The 33,000,000 acres held by the Southern tribes were an irresistible lure to white settlers. When Georgia refused to recognize Cherokee rights and pressed them to sell their lands, Jackson supported Georgia. He bluntly refused to enforce the Supreme Court decisions in Cherokee Nation *v*. State of Georgia (1830) and Worcester *v*. Georgia (1832), which upheld Cherokee rights. Instead, Jackson called for a policy which would expel the Indians to the west of the Mississippi River. What followed was a tragic experience in which the Indians were defrauded on all sides after having been deprived of their home. When the Creek Indians opposed their removal from Alabama, they were rounded up, put in chains, and marched away. When the Sac Indians in Illinois rebelled in the Black Hawk War of 1832, they were swiftly suppressed; but the Seminoles, under the young chief Osceola, launched the Seminole War, which plagued Florida from 1835 to 1838. Jackson and Van Buren pursued a policy, however, which ultimately removed nearly all the Indians from territory east of the Mississippi.

Administration and Sale of Western Lands. The policy of land disposal launched by the Ordinance of 1785 inaugurated direct sales of public lands by the government. Before 1789, over 4,000,000 acres had been sold to the Ohio Company, the Scioto Company, and to John Cleves Symmes, largely for speculative purposes. Hamilton established that land sales had as their purpose the earning of revenue for the federal government. In 1796, sales of as little as 640 acres were authorized, but the income from land sales failed to produce the expected revenue. The Land Act of 1800 established local land offices under the jurisdiction of registers, whose task was to conduct and regulate land sales. The intention of the government under the Federalists was to administer these lands preparatory to their sale to private owners;

and the Republicans continued and expanded this policy, which they viewed as a guarantee of a vigorous yeomanry.

The Credit System of Land Sales. The Land Act of 1796 had authorized the sale of land upon a down payment of five per cent, with full payment due within the year. But public pressure resulted in the extension of full payment to five years, and subsequently postponed payments were permitted for those who could not meet even that time period. By 1820, almost $22,000,000 was due the federal government on previous sales, and after July 1, 1820, only cash sales were accepted, with minimum prices of $1.25 an acre for tracts as small as eighty acres. Between 1787 and 1825 some 19,000,000 acres were sold (out of almost 262,000,000 acres under federal control). This vast domain led to demands that land be given free to anyone who settled upon it and improved it over a five-year period. This proposal, first broached in 1838, was to prove the keystone of the Homestead legislation of 1862.

The Preemption Act of 1841. Prior to the Homestead Act, however, Congress, bowing to Western pressure, had legislated to simplify land sales. Under the guidance of Henry Clay, efforts had been made to distribute the proceeds of land sales among the states. Seeking to insure distribution, Clay had proposed the Preemption Act of 1841, which gave settlers the right to "squat" on 160 acres of land until it was opened to settlement, and then permitted them to purchase their holdings at minimal government prices. Though Clay's distribution proposals were rejected by Tyler, Thomas Hart Benton continued to agitate for further liberalization of land policy. He proposed that unsold land be subjected to the graduation principle, under which the price of land would be steadily reduced the longer it remained unsold. Before graduation was instituted, however, the Mexican War was fought, and vast new accessions of territory complicated the disposition of land. In 1849 the Polk administration recognized the difficulty by transferring the regulation of land policy from the Treasury Department to the newly established Interior Department. It was not, however, until the Civil War that any further innovations in land policy were made.

Migration to the West. When the western lands were offered for sale a vast migration began. By 1810 the Mississippi and Ohio Valleys had a population of more than one million. By 1820 population of the same region had reached more than two million, and by 1840 it exceeded six million. Between 1810 and 1821, six new western states were formed: Louisiana (1812), Indiana (1816), Mississippi (1817), Illinois (1818), Alabama (1819), and Missouri (1821). Population increases between 1820 and 1830 ranged from a modest 22 per cent in Kentucky to 185 per cent in Illinois. Many in the new population were migrants from adjacent states. The northern areas of the Middle West were settled by Yankees and upstate New Yorkers; in the Deep South, most settlers came from the Carolinas and Georgia. Exceptions existed along the great rivers that drained the interior valleys. Natchez, Mississippi, had a sizable settlement of Pennsylvanians; New Orleans attracted New Yorkers and Irish immigrants; the lower Middle West received a steady influx from the upper South. By 1830, one out of every four Americans lived west of the Appalachians.

These Americans had abandoned the amenities of the East in the hope of achieving a self-sufficient economic independence. Compelled to overcome the western wilderness, they added to the qualities of the staid, settled East the dynamic, vigorous qualities born in the West. The pioneer's westward progress marked the advance of a people's hope that on the untamed frontier a better America would be established.

The Frontier. Migration westward meant that the society of the United States was in perpetual flux. In the older settlements along the eastern seaboard, time had worked to mitigate the rough crudeness of original settlement. A sophisticated, often complex, society had been created, and in the aftermath of the War of 1812 the rudiments of an industrial society had been established as well. Deprived of their normal commercial activities, New Englanders and other Easterners had turned to manufacturing. Thomas Jefferson had grieved: "Our enemy has indeed the consolation of Satan on removing our first parents from Paradise: from a peaceable and agricultural nation, he makes us a military and manufacturing one." But as the citizens of the East became more sophisticated, as their society became more complex and cosmopolitan, the homely tradition of simple virtue was reborn in the West. The new settlements were founded in reaction against the complications of a manufacturing society; and with their return to the land as a source of sustenance, the pioneers returned to the homely, humble virtues which the East had begun to neglect. The over-all effect of the frontier was to give American society a dynamic mobility. The ambitious man could pull up stakes and seek out a new and better future, while the abundance of American wealth made it possible for the poor man of today to achieve tomorrow's fortune.

The American Purpose. Mobility also gave American life a peculiarly urgent vitality. "No sooner do you set foot upon American ground than you are stunned by a kind of tumult," observed de Tocqueville; "a confused clamor is heard on every side, and a thousand simultaneous voices demand the satisfaction of their social wants." The American seemed to know that he was participating in a great social and political experiment. Elsewhere, Jefferson observed, opinion might be that "the object of a government is . . . to confer the greatest possible power and glory upon the body of the nation," but in the United States the national aim was "to ensure the greatest enjoyment and to avoid the most misery to each of the individuals who compose it." To one bemused British observer, the United States was "an organized anarchy."

ECONOMIC DISLOCATION

The First Bank of the United States. In 1811 the charter of the First Bank of the United States expired. After a desultory debate in Congress, efforts to renew the charter were defeated. The United States was obliged at the outset of the War of 1812 to deal with the many state and private banks that were eager to assume the functions of the defunct First Bank —especially the functions of deposit. At the forefront of opposition to renewal were the Eastern capitalists who found that, through their ability to influence banking legislation in their states, they could earn advantageous profits. Agrarians were almost as vigorous in defense of renewal. They charged that opponents of the Bank wished "to compel the United States to use their banks as places of deposit for their public monies." The added charge was made that many of the individual members of state legislatures who had instructed their congressional delegations to vote against rechartering were bank stockholders influenced by sheer personal greed.

Fiscal Collapse during the War of 1812. Albert Gallatin, who had witnessed the dissolution of the bank with misgivings, subsequently described the effects of its disappearance:

> The creation of new state banks was a natural consequence of the dissolution of the Bank of the United States. And, as is usual under such circumstances, the expectation of great profits gave birth to a much greater number than was wanted. . . . That increase took place on the eve of and during a war which did nearly annihilate the exports and both the foreign and coasting trade. And, as the salutary regulating power of the Bank of the United States no longer existed, the issues were accordingly increased much beyond what . . . circumstances . . . rendered necessary.

Between 1811 and 1816 the value of bank notes in circulation increased from $28,000,000 to $68,000,000. The obvious import of this development was a steady depreciation in the value of currency. When the British seized Washington, banks throughout the country, except those in New England, suspended specie payments. The result was a crazy quilt of currency values throughout the nation. In Boston the quoted value of the dollar was 100 cents and in New York 93 cents, while in Washington it was 75 cents. Public confidence waned. Congress authorized bond issues of $61,000,000 between 1812 and 1814, but only $45,000,000 worth was sold, and most of that for less than par value. The credit of the federal government had reached bottom. At one point in the war the Department of State's funds were so low that it was unable to pay even its stationery bill.

The Establishment of the Second Bank of the United States. By war's end the pressure for restoring the bank was growing. James Madison argued for it as necessary to restore "an uniform national currency." Under the guidance of John C. Calhoun, Congress approved the chartering of the Second Bank of the United States and on April 10, 1816, Madison approved the act. The old Jeffersonian dismissed protests against the bank's constitutionality "as being precluded . . . by repeated recognitions, under varied circumstances, of the validity of such an institution, in acts of the legislative, executive, and judicial branches of the government."

Early History of the Second Bank. The charter of the restored bank provided that one-fifth of its $35,000,000 capital was to be subscribed by the government, and that five of its twenty-five directors were to be appointed by the President of the United States. To meet charges that the first bank had been dominated by foreigners, the remaining directors were to be chosen by stockholders resident in the United States. The bank was responsible for the receipt and disbursement of federal funds. Since all notes and deposits paid into the bank had to be made in specie, it was able to compel other banks to maintain specie reserves. The further proviso was made that no one could refuse the bank's notes, which were made receivable for government obligations. This had the effect of expanding the national currency. Unfortunately, the bank early fell into the control of speculators and politicians. The bankrupt William Jones was made president of the bank and charted an "enlarged, liberal, and useful" course. It liberally distributed credit.

The Depression of 1819. The boom conditions that immediately followed the war seemed to justify the course taken, since a war-ravaged

Europe had enormously expanded its demands for American agricultural produce. But within a short time, however, bumper crops had seriously depressed the market and the swift recovery of European agriculture affected the American markets even more. American industry, though protected by the Tariff of 1816, was driven from the market when the British began to dump a glut of manufactures that plagued them. The generous disposition of bank credit merely delayed the inevitable collapse of the overextended economy. When the bank inaugurated a policy of loan contraction in 1819 and reduced its loans from $41,000,000 to $31,000,000, it forced an even more drastic contraction among the state banks. Total issuances were reduced from $100,000,000 in 1817 to less than $45,000,000 in 1819. Numerous banks suspended specie payments, and extensive business failures accompanied the decline in credit extension. William Jones was unceremoniously removed from office and replaced by Langdon Cheves, a South Carolinian attorney, who learned to his dismay that the bank's "power had been so completely prostrated . . . that [it] was on the point of stopping payment." Only rigid economy and a thorough shaking out of the banking system spared the bank from collapse.

From the perspective of the bank's future, the development in the West and the South of the feeling that it served only the interest of wealthy Easterners was unfortunate. But the shaky frontier economy and limited capital resources of the newer regions made the bank's contraction measures most acutely felt in the West and South and resentment grew quickly. The distribution of the bank's stock added to the sense of frontier grievance. New England, New York, Pennsylvania, Maryland, and South Carolina held 208,011 shares as opposed to the 21,619 shares held in the remaining Southern and all the Western states. Even foreign holdings, which totaled 40,412 shares, were more extensive. It was not difficult to persuade Westerners and Southerners that they were being milked for the favored few. This major source of sectional discord, the Bank of the United States, had begun to fester.

KING COTTON AND THE SOUTH

Cotton Culture in the South. Rarely has a technological innovation influenced the course of a region's history more profoundly than did the invention of the cotton gin in 1794. It is doubtful whether slavery could have remained economically viable without it. Most certainly it shaped the course of Southern history, making the South the pre-eminent supplier of raw cotton for the swiftly expanding textile industries of Great Britain, western Europe, and the North. The uneasy conscience of the South was soothed by the huge profits drawn from cotton crops that increased from 3,000 bales in 1790 to more than 5,000,000 bales in 1859. The insatiable demand for "white wool" received further impetus when short-staple cotton superseded the long-staple cotton of the Sea Islands during the first two decades of the nineteenth century. The new cotton, hardy and inexpensive, rapidly spread across the interior regions of the South. It is uncertain whether this new cotton culture required slave labor to produce it; but it provided a rationale for maintaining the institution. Unable to believe a Negro the equal of a white man, the Southerner sought for, and found, a confirmation of the permanence of Negro slavery. As the Southern planters moved into the Southwest, they carried slavery along with them.

The Aristocratic Ideal. Less obvious as a distinguishing factor was the aristocratic tradition that pervaded the South. The politics and society of the region were dominated by comparatively few families, often intermarried and almost unanimously dedicated to the preservation of slavery —not because they approved of slavery itself, but because they feared that any change would undermine the system of privilege to which they were accustomed. "I am an aristocrat," John Randolph of Roanoke had bluntly proclaimed. "I love liberty, I hate equality." Anything threatening the status quo could provoke such a bitter response.

The Missouri Compromise. An event that was the precursor of change was the proposal of James Tallmadge, congressman from New York. On February 13, 1819, he offered an amendment to the Missouri Enabling Bill providing for Missouri's admission to statehood. It provided:

> That the further introduction of slavery or involuntary servitude be prohibited, except for the punishment of crimes whereof the party shall have been duly convicted: and that all children born within the said State [of Missouri] after the admission thereof into the Union shall be free, but may be held to service until the age of twenty-five years.

Whatever the congressman's motives, his amendment struck a responsive chord throughout the North and West, where there existed an ill-concealed hostility to the constitutional provision that granted the South representation for three-fifths of its Negro slaves. These sentiments were displayed in the strictly sectional vote by which the House of Representatives approved the amendment. It scarcely mattered that the Senate refused to subscribe to the House's vote; both North and South erupted into a violent and revealing debate. Thomas Jefferson described it as "a fire-bell in the night" which "awakened and filled [him] with terror." Somberly, he prophesied that it would prove "the knell of the Union."

Reaction to the Compromise Debate. Jefferson feared that the issue once joined would "never be obliterated." As a Southerner, he was prepared for the end of slavery provided that the emancipated Negroes were removed from the South. But his hopes represented a passing viewpoint. Northerners, many of them genuinely horrified, heard Southern congressmen extol the virtues of the institution and claim that slavery redeemed not only the slave but the enslaver. The Bible was invoked in the argument: "The Scriptures teach us that slavery was universally practiced among the holy fathers." John Quincy Adams, in the privacy of his diary, unburdened himself of the thought that if the Union were ever to dissolve, it would be on the question of slavery that it should break. The conflict was resolved with a compromise (the Missouri Compromise) that admitted Missouri as a slave state and Maine as a free state. It also closed the remainder of the Louisiana Purchase north of latitude 36° 30' to slavery. For the moment the issue was at rest; at no point had anyone proposed the outright abolition of slavery. But the issue, once raised, could only be muted, not ended. As Jefferson noted, "This is a reprieve only, not a final sentence."

THE ADMINISTRATION OF JOHN QUINCY ADAMS

For almost a quarter of a century, Virginians had filled the presidency. By 1820 the Jeffersonians had irretrievably shattered the Federalist Party. Only the withholding of one vote prevented Monroe from obtaining unanimous electoral support. Superficially, one would have had to conclude that Monroe had great popular support; in fact, he was the legatee of monumental indifference. It was his fate to preside over the regrouping of the political parties. In their moment of absolute triumph, the Jeffersonians began their rapid slide toward disintegration.

Monroe and the Collapse of the Jeffersonian Party. For eight years, Monroe strove to be President for all the people. His efforts, though laudable, were disastrous for his party. He deprived it of an issue, a platform, or a slogan with which to mobilize the voter. The collapse of the Federalists left the Jeffersonians with the only prospective presidential candidates—John Quincy Adams, John Caldwell Calhoun, Henry Clay, William Crawford, and Andrew Jackson. All sought the presidency as Republicans. As they struggled toward their goal, they fragmented the

Republican Party. The presidential caucus had traditionally chosen the President, but when called upon to perform its function in 1824 it succeeded only in revealing the near-anarchy that plagued the Republican Party. William Crawford, the bulky Secretary of the Treasury, though the nominal choice of the Virginia regency and the ultimate choice of the presidential caucus, had all the opposition focused upon him. By using rumors, innuendoes, and distorted facts, Crawford's opponents eliminated him from the race. Calhoun suffered the same fate from too intimate an identification with the South. Known as a man of Southern principles and Northern policies, he was mistrusted by all. In the end only the suave Clay, the dour Adams, and the enigmatic Jackson had a real chance of election. As it turned out, no one candidate gained the necessary electoral majority, and the election was thrown into the House of Representatives for final settlement.

The Election of 1824. So divided was the electorate in 1824 that it might be best described as the "Election of Undecided Feelings." Jackson had obtained a slight plurality over his opponents, but he had nowhere near a majority. Nevertheless, he believed himself to be the only candidate who could be considered popularly chosen. His supporters in Congress watched with anger as Henry Clay, excluded from the race as low man, threw his support to John Quincy Adams. It was enough to make the Secretary of State the President-elect. On February 9, 1825, thirteen states cast their votes for Adams; seven states voted for Jackson; and four states backed Crawford. The result was constitutional but unpopular. The unhappy Adams accepted his election as hardly "satisfactory to my pride or . . . just desire, with perhaps two-thirds of the whole people adverse to the actual result." Nor were the unhappy supporters of Jackson to let Adams forget the circumstances of his election.

The Corrupt Bargain. The new President had always viewed life as an extended exercise in rigorous morality. No man could so justifiably claim as he that his was the existence of a moral athlete. Anticipating election as a reward for service, he had been compelled to electioneer, to make deals, to promise patronage, and to converse with his moral inferiors. Desperately wanting public recognition, he had never learned how to court public affection. He had both the virtue and the vice of unyielding principle. And having won the game, he was overwhelmed with a sense of guilt, and seemed almost to believe the Jacksonians' charge that he had won election through a corrupt deal.

The Appointment of Clay. The charge had originated when Adams had appointed Henry Clay to the State Department after the election. It is true that supporters of Jackson, Crawford, and Adams had all courted Clay's support and all three undoubtedly were prepared to pay a good price for his backing. But it was Adams who, on January 9, 1825, succeeded in coming to an understanding with Clay in which Clay had agreed to use his influence among his congressional followers to build support for Adams. Though the State Department was not specifically promised to Clay, his subsequent appointment was a natural reward for his sturdy efforts on behalf of Adams. The two men were in essential agreement on one thing: a military man, especially one with the impulsive habits of Jackson, was ill-equipped to fill the presidency. They were not alone in their unease: Jefferson had warned, "I feel much alarmed at the prospect of seeing General Jackson President. He is one of the most unfit men I know of for such a place." Such was the Republican judgment of the man who was destined to later revolutionize American politics.

Adams' Policies. Adams struggled to remove the cloud under which his administration was born. He organized his cabinet to include supporters of most of the major figures in the recent election. Only supporters of Jackson were conspicuously absent. But of equal consequence was Adams' failure to appoint men truly committed to his own cause. He justified his course by stating that appointments should be yielded "to talents and virtue alone" rather than to those "who bore the badge of party communion." It was a plea for his own acceptance. His inaugural address made that impossible.

Adams and the Doctrine of Positive Government. In a nation dominated by a growing spirit of laissez-faire, Adams had the temerity to call for a widening of the scope of governmental activity. With eloquent precision he reminded the nation that "liberty is power; that the nation blessed with the largest portion of liberty must in proportion to its numbers be the most powerful nation upon earth, and that the tenure of power by man is, in the moral purposes of his Creator, upon condition that it shall be exercised to ends of beneficence, to improve the condition of himself and his fellow-men." From this proposition he deduced a call for a "career of public improvement." From all sides came unwarranted charges of tyranny, usurpation, monarchy, and neofederalism. The Sage of Monticello saw in Adams' proposals an effort to revive a moribund federalism which would abandon "the feelings and principles of '76," erect "an aristocracy, founded on banking institutions, and moneyed incorporations" and ride roughshod "over the plundered ploughman and beggared yeomanry." The charge of corruption was further supplemented with another accusation that foresaw Adams striving to erect a "despotism of the worse tendencies." Adams responded that his single goal was to put the strength of the nation behind a program of public improvements; still he was indicted as a traitor to the Jeffersonian inheritance. He perversely refused to take the one step that might have saved him. No man was to be removed from office "for merely preferring another candidate for the presidency." Like his father before him, he retained cabinet members, such as Postmaster General John McLean, who were known to be bitterly hostile to him. His administration was doomed to frustration.

THE RISE OF THE JACKSONIANS

Opposition to Adams. The clamor against Adams brought together a group of men in search of a leader. Prominent among them was Martin Van Buren, who in New York State had fought against debt imprisonment and for extension of the suffrage. An articulate but opportunistic advocate of the small farmer and the poor and a leading spokesman for Crawford, he had determined to destroy Adams although he had not decided to support Jackson. He struck first at Adams' decision to have the nation participate in a Pan-American Conference called by Simón Bolívar. Although Adams took care to promise that no alliances were contemplated, and that participation in the Panama Conference was directed toward establishing friendly relations with the newly independent Latin-American countries, the Senate chamber soon resounded with attacks upon the presidential motives. More than one Southern Senator saw the whole affair as a thinly disguised abolitionist plot. John Randolph, ever mercurial, charged anew that Adams and Clay had corruptly bargained for the presidency. The result was a comic duel between Randolph and Clay. Relations between Adams and his Vice-President, John C. Calhoun, soon came to the breaking point. The President suspected that the South Carolinian wished him ill and hoped to attain the presidency at his expense. What he failed to realize was that he was out of step with his time, that a host of opponents were manipulating and taking advantage of public sentiment.

The Elections of 1826. Those who opposed Adams took heart from the elections of 1826. Both the Senate and House consisted of majorities hostile to the administration. The election of DeWitt Clinton, an outspoken Jacksonian, to the New York governorship, convinced Van Buren and the New York congressional delegation that open identification with Jackson was in order. From the West a veritable army of Jacksonians descended on Washington to take their seats. In Kentucky, even Clay had suffered heavy losses. Within his own camp, Adams heard mutterings of discontent when, in his Third Annual Message, he failed to speak out for the passage of a protective tariff.

Jackson and the Tariff of 1828. Everyone knew that sentiment outside the South was strong for a high tariff. Van Buren, laboring to construct an effective coalition between Southern planters and Northern Republicans to assure Jackson's election in 1828, knew he had to reconcile the divergent positions of the two groups. Extensive agitation by manufacturers who favored the tariff made longer delay impossible. The wily New Yorker urged Jackson to keep a discreet silence on the subject, and to make only pontifical references to his earlier desire for "judicious examination and revision of the tariff." It allowed his supporters to place their own interpretation on the Tennessean's intentions.

While Jackson remained above the dispute, his congressional supporters went to work weaving a tariff law that would gratify Pennsylvania, Ohio, and New York Jacksonian supporters of a tariff, and punish the New England supporters of Adams. By placing heavy duties on raw wool, molasses, hemp, and unprocessed iron, they hoped to compel the New Englanders to vote against the tariff lest it raise exorbitantly the cost of their raw materials. The Jacksonians expected to have it both ways: they could claim that they had supported a protective tariff but had been defeated by New England. But these expectations were blasted when the New Englanders decided that a bad bill was better than no bill at all. The result provoked the outraged South Carolinians, who viewed tariffs as anathema, to dub it the Tariff of Abominations. The administration learned that everyone accepted it as a New England measure; and the Jacksonians took care to spread the word that "Jackson will repeal the Tariff."

The Election of 1828. The Tariff of Abominations was but the last in a series of errors that overwhelmed Adams and his administration as the next election approached. The dour New Englander, incapable of optimism, had already concluded that "General Jackson . . . will be elected." Adams sensed that no matter what his previous services had been, he could never compete with the glamorous military reputation of his adversary. He also understood—albeit only dimly—that his appeal for an active government went contrary to a national feeling that preferred for its government (as Jackson had put it) "a plain system, void of pomp, protecting all and granting favors to none, dispensing its

blessings, like the dews of Heaven, unseen and unfelt save in the fresh-
ness and beauty they contribute to produce."

The Rachel Jackson Issue. The national electorate had a genuine
choice, but extraneous issues clouded the campaign. Scandalous rumors
were spread, charging that Jackson and his wife had lived in adultery. It
hardly mattered that Jackson had married Rachel Robards in 1791
thinking that she was already divorced from her first husband, or that
he had promptly remarried her when they learned that the divorce was
granted in 1793. The general learned that his opponents were determined
to win, no matter what the cost. It was a harsh price for Jackson; his beloved Rachel, he believed, overwhelmed by the rumors, lost her will to
live and died. The old general neither forgave nor forgot.

The Meaning of Jackson's Victory. Jackson was riding the crest of a
revitalized political life. To the polls there flocked an expanded electorate, freed from restrictive electoral qualifications and allowed by state
legislatures (save in two states) to vote directly for a candidate, and,
most importantly, provided with a real choice between opposing political
philosophies. Three times as many people voted in 1828 as had voted in
1824. Jackson carried the country with 647,276 votes to 508,604 for
Adams. Only New England, New Jersey, Delaware, and Maryland remained loyal to the incumbent. Adams wearily and bitterly wondered
why he had been so totally repudiated. He fled the capital rather than
watch the triumph of his rival, and wondered whether the Adams family
were doomed to preside at the collapse of old political parties and to
leave the inauguration of new departures to its foes. Thus the last Jeffersonians passed into the shadows to watch their opponents come forth
to claim the sun.

Chapter 12

Jacksonian Democracy

Inauguration day, March 4, 1829, saw an unprecedented tumult in Washington. A horde of office-seekers besieged the President-elect in his hotel and pursued him into the White House. Untold thousands of plain citizens had come for a look at the new President, whose military prowess had already made him a myth. A leading society matron recalled the day in vivid detail:

> Orange punch by barrels full was made, but as the waiters opened the door to bring it out, a rush would be made, the glasses broken, the pails of liquor upset, and the most painful confusion prevailed. . . . Wines and ice-creams could not be brought out to the ladies, and tubs of punch were taken from the lower story into the garden, to lead off the crowd from the rooms. On such an occasion it was certainly difficult to keep anything like order, and it was mortifying to see men, with boots heavy with mud, standing on the damask satin chairs, from their eagerness to get a sight of the President.

Daniel Webster's prediction that when Jackson reached Washington he would "bring a breeze with him" had been amply borne out. Some critics thought that he had brought a tornado. The era of the common man had been inaugurated.

JACKSON IN OFFICE

Andrew Jackson. Tall, angular, crowned with a shock of white hair, the new President brought into the White House a reputation for violence, unthinking action, and ignorant prejudices. He was not unaware that many people viewed him—as he expressed it himself—"as a savage . . . who allways carried a scalping knife in one hand and a tomahawk in the other, allways ready to knock down, and scalp any and every person who differed with me in opinion." Jackson's lack of formal education was reflected in John Quincy Adams' description of him as a "barbarian who could not write a sentence of grammar and hardly could spell his own name." Notorious for fierce eruptions of simulated rage, he was a man who unnerved foe and friend alike. Few people knew or claimed to know him well. Yet, he conducted himself with a courtly grace which belied the myth surrounding him.

A product of the frontier, Jackson had witnessed and participated in the Revolutionary War along the Carolina frontier. When still a youth, he was subjected to brutal treatment while imprisoned by the British; he had also witnessed the death of his mother and a brother from the smallpox contracted in a British prison camp. An orphan at thirteen, he migrated to Tennessee where he raised himself to a position of local eminence, and achieved the status of a self-made aristocrat. He was a living example of the great American dream: that America was a land of opportunity in which the common man could, through application, achieve success. He brought with him the aura of the frontier where, living in a state of liberty, the talented man could win recognition commensurate with his ability. He symbolized the destruction of privilege and the restoration of that equality which was the natural state of man. He was both the fulfillment and the confirmation of American expectations.

Liberal Democracy. Where John Quincy Adams had sought a government of expanding powers, Jackson worked to reduce the role of government to the bare constitutional necessities. He assumed that government governs best when it governs least. He favored frugal economy in government and steady reduction of the debt. Whenever possible, he labored to expand the responsibilities of local government. In short, he thought of himself as a Republican dedicated to the maintenance of that party's traditional values.

Jacksonian Supporters. To a considerable degree, Jackson drew his support from the same sources that had put Jefferson in the White House. His greatest following was in the West and the South, in the poorer farming regions of the Middle Atlantic states, and in the large cities of the East. Voters were attracted to him for a multitude of reasons. The nationwide fame of Jackson was skillfully fused with the exploitation of local grievances. Debtors and cheap money advocates viewed with favor Jackson's suspicions concerning the Bank of the United States. The same issue brought him support from the banking communities of New York and Boston, both resentful of the power of Nicholas Biddle and his favored institution. Local bankers, and the supporters of state banks, who were severely restricted by the regulatory functions of the Philadelphia Bank, added to the Jacksonian entourage. Enraged by the Tariff of Abominations, many Southern planters gave him diligent support. The Jacksonian appeal to equal rights brought the poorer farmers and the urban workingmen flocking to his standard. And a not inconsiderable number of intellectuals lent their pens and lecterns in support of Jackson's laissez-faire values. His was a coalition that embraced the intensely political Martin Van Buren, the coldly analytical John C. Calhoun, the dogmatic bullionist Thomas Hart Benton, the political editor Francis Preston Blair, the ambitious entrepreneur Amos Kendall, the old Federalists, Roger Taney and James Buchanan, and, at least in 1828, the shrewd financier Nicholas Biddle. It was a coalition of strength—but of weakness as well; it would begin to crumble the moment the administration began to legislate.

The Kitchen Cabinet. From its start, the new administration was dominated by Jackson himself. Although everyone expected his poor health to limit him to one term, and many expected him to be led rather than to lead, he swiftly set to work expanding the power of the executive branch. The cabinet was quickly subordinated to a group of advisers known as the Kitchen Cabinet. Pre-eminent in it was Secretary of State Martin Van Buren who, after years spent in the rough and tumble of New York politics, provided intelligent political advice. Almost as prominent was Amos Kendall, the Fourth Auditor of the Treasury, who concealed Jackson's deficiencies as a grammarian by composing many of his state papers. He used intrigue and a vitriolic pen in pressing Jackson's policies. No less vigorous in this respect was the Second Comptroller of the Treasury, Isaac Hill, who added the sharp edge of class partisanship to the Jacksonian rhetoric. At the helm of the Washington *Globe,* the party journal, was Francis Preston Blair, whose sharp pen spared no enemy and canonized all friends. Major William B. Lewis, who had dedicated his life to making Jackson President, was a constant companion. In his capacity as Second Auditor of the Treasury, Lewis, who lived at the White House, devoted his shrewd politics to the advancement of his mentor. Others, such as Roger B. Taney, Edward Livingston, James Hamilton (the son of Alexander Hamilton), and Senator Hugh Lawson White, found their way into the presidential circle. The President drew advice from each of them as administration policy was slowly hammered out, until no one could know for certain who was immediately responsible for the result.

Jacksonian Policy. The new administration had pledged economy in government; it therefore worked to reduce expenditures. Federal spending, which had exceeded $16,000,000 in 1828, was reduced to scarcely $15,000,000. Jackson also strove to revitalize the federal bureaucracy. Long tenure had filled many offices with inefficient men, though most office-holders were able and conscientious. Countless supporters of Jackson who desired these posts created an almost irresistible pressure for removal. More than one Jacksonian assumed that all who did not actively support his administration would be removed, and Jackson soon complained that for every vacancy there were five hundred applicants.

Jackson and Patronage. The expectation of wholesale removals filled the great body of officials with dread. But much of the fear was unwarranted. In the first eighteen months of his administration, Jackson removed only 919 office-holders, of a total of 10,093. Although specific evidence is lacking, it is probable that not more than twenty per cent of the office-holders were removed during Jackson's eight years. Nevertheless, a firm principle was being established; in the future, incumbent office-holders could expect to be replaced by partisans of a newly victorious chief executive. Rotation in office became the rule, and provided much of the locomotive power of American politics. The spoils system, as it was known, also had the less distinguished effect of depriving the public service of both efficiency and prestige. As Gideon Welles, who was later to become Secretary of the Navy in Lincoln's cabinet, noted at the time, "Office-seeking and office-getting was becoming a regular business, where impudence triumphed over worth."

The Eaton Affair. The inability of the administration to gratify all of its supporters was soon painfully evident. There simply were not enough offices to bestow on all seekers; the Kitchen Cabinet caused jealousy in the official cabinet. The presence of Van Buren in both cabinets convinced the supporters of Calhoun that a plot was afoot to promote the ambitious New Yorker to the presidency over the South Carolinian. All the tinder of discord was gathered; only a spark was needed to set off an explosion. This spark was provided by the marriage of Secretary of War John H. Eaton to Margaret "Peggy" O'Neill Timberlake on January 1, 1829.

Peggy O'Neill was the daughter of a Washington tavern owner whom Jackson knew. She had been previously married to a navy purser, who four months before her marriage to Eaton had committed suicide. Nasty rumors circulated that Timberlake had taken his life in desperation over his wife's entanglement with Eaton. The marriage confronted Washington society with the painful question of whether it would receive Mrs. Eaton. Floride Calhoun, the Vice-President's wife, supplied a swift answer; she and the other ladies of the cabinet would have nothing to do with the "scarlet Jezebel." All the courtly instincts of Jackson were aroused. "I never war against females," he had declared when his beloved Rachel was under attack; now he meant to protect Mrs. Eaton from wagging tongues. The husbands of the cabinet found themselves caught in the cross fire of domestic and presidential wrath. Only the widower Van Buren rode above the storm; he arranged entertainments for Peggy, and took every opportunity to offer her his arm. He also took care to identify the Calhouns as the culprits behind the difficulty; and Jackson's prejudices were fastened upon the aloof South Carolinian.

Calhoun and Nullification. Presidential ire over the Eaton affair further reduced the cabinet's influence. As Jackson relied increasingly on Van Buren and the Kitchen Cabinet, the regular cabinet took on the appearance of a ceremonial organization. John C. Calhoun fought back with all the skill he could muster. Already at fundamental odds with proponents of a protective tariff—in the South Carolina Exposition of 1828 he had set forth the doctrine that a state had the right to interpose its authority to prevent enforcement of federal acts—Calhoun openly disagreed with Jackson on distribution of federal funds among the states once the national debt had been paid. He proposed that the cost of public lands be reduced, his obvious intention being to create a political alliance between the South and West, with the East indicted as aiming to deprive the West of its natural inheritance. Senator Robert Y. Hayne of South Carolina led the attack, while Daniel Webster defended his section with eloquence. The Massachusetts Senator charged that Hayne's patronizing references to the Hartford Convention were hardly defensible since Hayne's own state espoused similar premises in its present stand. New England had, Webster further contended, risen above sectional or state selfishness to espouse Union. He denounced nullification as a bankrupt and futile doctrine and concluded in a stunning peroration: "Liberty and Union, now and forever, one and inseparable." These were sentiments that captivated Jackson.

Jackson and Calhoun. Jackson's suspicions concerning the nullifiers had reached a critical state. At a Jefferson birthday celebration, he threw down the gauntlet: called upon to deliver a toast, the President proposed,

"Our Federal Union. It must be preserved." Calhoun accepted the challenge; "The Union—next to our liberty the most dear," he firmly replied.

Relations between the two men deteriorated rapidly as Jackson insisted that Calhoun explain his demand, made in 1818 as Secretary of War, that General Jackson be censured for his conduct in Florida. Encouraged by Van Buren and his supporters, Jackson distorted the Calhoun attack upon Peggy Eaton into a covert attack upon the memory of Rachel Jackson. The South Carolinian found his hopes for the presidential succession fast waning.

The Collapse of the Original Cabinet. Deprived of the bulk of his patronage, removed from control of the party organ when Francis Preston Blair replaced Duff Green (who had been a Calhoun supporter) as editor, Calhoun suffered total defeat in the spring of 1831, when Van Buren maneuvered reorganization of the cabinet. When the shrewd Secretary of State and Eaton resigned, they permitted Jackson to ask for the resignations of all but Postmaster General William Barry, the others being identified with the Calhoun interest. Van Buren was appointed Minister to the Court of St. James's.

Faced with the expulsion of his supporters from the administration, Calhoun announced the final rupture of relations between himself and Jackson and declared himself a presidential candidate for 1832. Strenuous opposition to the stubborn President erupted in Virginia, South Carolina, Tennessee, Mississippi, and Pennsylvania. Van Buren had won a total victory, but at the price of total disruption of the coalition which had elected Jackson in 1828.

Henry Clay and the American System. The opponents of Jackson looked increasingly to Henry Clay for political guidance. Clay's "American System," in which he advocated a program of positive federal aid for the advancement of capitalism, appealed to national pride. It proposed protective tariffs to build up American industry on the assumption that expanding industry would increase national wealth and encourage the growth of urban population, which in turn would be a reliable market for American agriculture. Clay also advocated internal improvements subsidized by public funds, the employment of income from the sale of public lands for that purpose, and the maintenance of the Bank of the United States. Jackson had little real reason to disagree with Clay's proposals on internal improvements; indeed, his administration had pursued an active program along just these lines. But the President could never resist striking out at an enemy scheme for political advancement, least of all one offered by Henry Clay.

The Maysville Veto. Jackson's opportunity came when the bill authorizing construction of the Maysville Road reached his desk. The road had been planned as part of the Cumberland Road, and was meant to provide a twenty-mile highway connecting Maysville and Lexington, Kentucky. To the considerable surprise of Congress, Jackson vetoed the bill, arguing that "if it be the wish of the people that the construction of roads and canals should be conducted by the Federal Government, it is not only highly expedient, but . . . necessary, that a previous amendment of the Constitution, delegating the necessary power and defining and restricting its exercise with reference to the sovereignty of the States, should be made." The immediate intent of the Maysville Veto was, of course, to embarrass Henry Clay, in whose state the proposed project was located. Since Jackson had approved intrastate improvements elsewhere, Clay had no alternative but to accept it as a personal rebuff and as marking the administration's decision to focus its attack upon his American System in the developing campaign of 1832. Clay accepted the challenge.

THE BANK WAR

Bank Policy. The Second Bank of the United States had been chartered in 1816 for a period of twenty years. Despite the vagaries of its first years, the appointment of Nicholas Biddle to its presidency in 1823 made it a mainstay of the national banking system. Since it was permitted to issue up to $35,000,000 in notes that were receivable for federal government dues, it brought into effect a considerable enlargement of the national currency. In addition it served as a useful adjunct to the Treasury as the intermediary in the selling of government bonds and in the conduct of other government activities. By swift transfers of currency and credit, it proved a boon to business. By frequently presenting outstanding notes of the state banks for payment, it compelled these lesser institutions to maintain a liquid backing for their currency issuances. As the depository for government funds, it was able, by extending these deposits for short term or demand loans, to keep the currency from contracting too quickly whenever large payments were made into the government accounts. Although it rarely made more than a fifth of the nation's bank loans, issued more than twenty per cent of the national currency, or held more than a third of the national bank deposits and specie, even in 1830 when at the peak of its prosperity, the bank was of such dimensions that it effectively dominated and regulated the national banking system. Had its political power not been effective, it is unlikely that the attack that Jackson mounted against it would ever have occurred.

Nicholas Biddle. The dispute that shook the country over the bank between 1830 and 1834 was traceable, in large part, to the personality of Nicholas Biddle, president of the bank. Imperious and brilliant, he dominated the bank's policy. Unlike Jackson, he was sophisticated, well-educated, and prone to condescension when dealing with his intellectual inferiors. On the assumption that he and the bank were above politics, he made the grievous mistake of informing Samuel D. Ingham, the Secretary of the Treasury, that the bank directors "acknowledge not the slightest responsibility of any description whatsoever to the Secretary of the Treasury touching the political opinions and conduct of their officers —that being a subject on which they never consult and never desire to know the views of any administration." Jackson took particular note of this statement, viewing it as further proof of the arrogance of the "money power." It hardly mattered that Biddle viewed the bank as an institution whose first responsibility was to the nation, or that he had written:

> The great object, . . . , to which the Bank has for many years directed its anxious attention, has been to identify itself thoroughly with the real business of the country and . . . to bring down these exchanges to the lowest cost. . . . By such an effort the Bank has thought that it assumed its true and federal character as the great channel for the intercommunication for the business of the Union; and that leaving to local institutions as much as they desired or could accomplish of the local business in every section of the Union, its more appropriate sphere was the general communication between them all.

Given the Jacksonian antipathy for concentrations of power, a conflict over the bank was certain to come. By 1832, Jackson had concluded that the "monster" should not be rechartered in 1836. The fiscal communities of New York and Boston were prepared to support the President's decision. They expected to inherit the functions of the bank.

Motives behind the War. The bank never forgot its dependence on the politician. Biddle, who supported Jackson in 1828, took care to appoint Democrats to the Boards of Directors of the various bank branches. Knowing Jackson's concern with liquidation of the national debt, he had proposed ways to expedite this end. But frequent presidential references to the bank as a "hydra of corruption" drove him to the reluctant conclusion that nothing short of the bank's destruction would placate Jackson. Biddle calculated that the frequent favors dispensed to influential politicians by the bank might stay the blow. Daniel Webster, who served

as the bank's legal counsel, borrowed large sums from it which were subsequently liquidated as payment for services rendered. Henry Clay, William Seward, and Amos Kendall were but a few of many politicians who
had accepted favors from the bank. It was upon the advice of Webster
and Clay that Biddle decided to try to recharter the bank in 1830 before
the original charter expired.

The Move to Recharter. To minimize the chance of a Jacksonian
counterattack, the new charter, which was to run for fifteen years, was
designed to meet some of the strongest presidential criticisms. It limited
the number of branches the bank could establish, modified its real estate
holdings, gave to Congress the power to restrict small note issuances,
and gave to the President the right to appoint a member of every branch's
board of directors. Since Jackson desired establishment of a bank tied to
the Treasury and deprived of the power to issue notes or make loans, it
was suspected that he was seeking to convert the bank into a source of
patronage. Efforts to frustrate the President's intention failed since he
had reached an unyielding determination to have his own way.

Congressional Support for Rechartering. Biddle's decision to press
the rechartering seemed sensible at the time. The Jacksonian faction in
Congress was deeply divided, and more than a third favored rechartering. When the bill reached the Senate it was passed by a vote of 28 to
20; the House followed with a vote of 107 to 85. The sectional appeal
of the bill was reflected in the votes cast by the South and Southwest
against rechartering; only three Senate votes were obtained for the bill
in this region. In the West, the vote was reversed; only Missouri, Illinois,
and Kentucky (all of which cast divided votes) opposed the measure.
In the East, Isaac Hill of New Hampshire, the two New York senators,
and one from New Jersey were alone in the opposition. Jackson's enemies thought they had boxed the Old General in: if he were to veto the
bill, he would run the risk of antagonizing Pennsylvania, within whose
boundaries the bank was located; if he were to approve the bill, he
would appear ludicrous after his prolonged denunciation of the bank.

Jackson and the Bank. Jackson recognized the political implications
of the attack, and, true to his natural pugnacity, prepared for a fight.
"The Bank is trying to kill me," he declared, "but I will kill it." Aban-
doning the traditional reluctance of the President to wield the veto
power, he, with the assistance of Roger Taney, Amos Kendall, and Levi
Woodbury, drew up a veto message that castigated the bank. The institution was denounced as an unconstitutional threat to liberty, as an in-

fringement on state rights, and as the tool of foreigners. The final, slashing attack appealed to the leveling instincts of democracy:

> Many of our rich men have not been content with equal protection and equal benefits, but have besought us to make them richer by act of Congress. By attempting to gratify their desires we have . . . arrayed section against section, interest against interest, and man against man, in a fearful commotion which threatens to shake the foundations of our Union.

Against such injustice, the Jacksonians proposed a government which (as Jackson put it) "would confine itself to equal protection, and, as Heaven does its rains, shower its favors alike on the high and the low, the rich and the poor. . . ." They had, in the words of an editorial appearing in a Jacksonian journal, invoked "idealism against lucre and . . . human rights against property rights." It was, in fact, the rebellion of the self-made man against restrictions, against limits, and against privilege in which he did not share.

After the Veto. The veto message was also a campaign document. Everyone recognized that the critical issue of the 1832 campaign had been formulated. Jackson, who to some had seemed to lack the physical stamina to survive one term, meant to win re-election, and *Jackson and Death to the Bank* was to become the rallying call of the Democrats. In opposition were William Wirt, the Antimasonic candidate, whose primary issue was the threat Masonry presented to American institutions; and the slate of Henry Clay and John Sergeant, the National Republican candidates, who attacked spoils, the veto power, and the failure to recharter the bank. To accentuate the opposition's dismay, Van Buren, an eminently shrewd politician, was chosen as Jackson's running mate. The result was an overwhelming victory for Jackson and Van Buren. No matter how wrongheaded Jackson's attack upon the bank was, Jackson appealed to the powerful leveling instincts of the American democracy. When the ballots were finally counted, the Democrats had 219 electoral votes to 49 for Clay. Old Hickory believed he had received carte blanche to complete the destruction of Biddle's "monster."

Removal of Deposits. Though the bank had four years of its charter to run, Jackson, with the complicity of Taney and Kendall, determined to undermine the "monied oligarchy." The assault began at a cabinet meeting, in November 1832, when Jackson announced his conviction that the bank was insolvent, and proposed withdrawal of federal deposits. When Congress, after investigation, declared the bank to be solvent, Jackson publicly dismissed the report. Assisted by Roger Taney, he developed his case for removal of federal deposits. From Amos Kendall came the news that bankers in Baltimore, Boston, New York, and Philadelphia were eager to receive the deposits, and that the time had come to act. Only one obstacle remained: neither Secretary of the Treasury Louis McLane nor his successor, William J. Duane, was willing to acquiesce in this drastic maneuver, since both feared that the result would be a skyrocketing inflation. McLane and Duane were swiftly dismissed and replaced by Taney, and almost immediately the steady flow of government funds into "pet" banks located in various cities throughout the country was begun.

The U. S. Bank Contracts. As the deposits were relocated, the government drew upon its account with the Bank of the United States. Biddle responded with the decision to contract, to call in loans, and to limit discounts of notes. This course was clearly necessary if the bank were to retain its liquidity. But in addition the now thoroughly aroused Biddle and his political mentor, Henry Clay, saw in contraction a weapon to force rechartering, since the steady reduction of credit would cause a great stringency in the money market. Indeed, as the contraction proceeded, a flood of petitions poured into Congress and an endless number of deputations waited upon Jackson. The response they obtained from the President was firm: the course was set. If they wanted relief, they were instructed to "go to the Monster, go to Nicholas Biddle."

Jackson and Biddle. The Philadelphia banker had miscalculated. For although his contraction policies caused real economic distress, they did not cripple national finances; and Biddle had unwittingly demonstrated to the public the validity of Jackson's charges that the power of the bank was excessive. The economic duress was a consequence of "monster monopoly," Democratic politicians thundered—and their message found a ready audience. Far from intimidating Jackson, the bank's policy confirmed his wisdom in shifting deposits to private banks.

Biddle had exhausted his stratagems; he was defeated and he knew it. In 1836 he began an ill-starred venture when his bank was rechartered by Pennsylvania as the United States Bank of Pennsylvania. Caught first in the depression following the panic of 1837, and then in a disastrous effort to corner the cotton market, Biddle resigned his post as president in March 1839, and in 1841 the bank was declared bankrupt. Biddle spent the remaining days of his life in various courts fighting charges of criminal conspiracy. When he died on February 27, 1844, at the age of fifty-eight, a newspaper reported that he had spent his declining years brooding "with smiling face and stifled groans over the wreck of splendid blasted expectations and ruined hopes." His career served as a monumental warning of the dangers involved in crossing swords with the dogmatic Old General who flaunted the executive power with contempt for precedents and no fear of rebuke.

THE NULLIFICATION CRISIS

The Tariff of 1832. John Quincy Adams had earned a unique distinction after his departure from the presidency when on November 1, 1830, the constituents of his home district elected him to the House of Representatives. As chairman of the Committee on Manufactures, it was his responsibility to draw up a new tariff. Far from sharing the protectionist views of Clay, Adams agreed with the administration that a reduced tariff was needed, one which would provide reasonable protection to Northern manufacturers while placating those Southerners who felt that the tariff of 1828 had been excessive. The result was the tariff of 1832, which returned the level of duties to those established by the tariff of 1824. On July 14, 1832, Jackson signed the bill into law. Despite its nod to the South it opened a major crisis with Calhoun and the nullifiers who wanted free trade. The usual stubborn opposition of South Carolina to the tariff was again evident in its decision not to support either of the two major candidates for the Presidency.

The Doctrine of State Interposition. Calhoun composed a lengthy disquisition, "On the Subject of State Interposition." Its central proposition was that "The Union, of which the Constitution is the bond, is a union of States, and not of individuals." He drew from this the conclusion that the state had the final say on whether its citizens would obey an act of Congress. Where Marshall had enunciated the power of judicial review, Calhoun proclaimed the doctrine of state review. To complete the symmetry of his proposal, the South Carolinian denied that the federal government had the power to compel obedience. Although the state power thus asserted was designated "nullification" by Calhoun, it was in fact the entering wedge of the principle called secession.

Nullification of the Tariff. For South Carolina the election of 1832 was a test of whether nullification or Union would prevail. The state legislature which was convoked by Governor James Hamilton on November 19, 1832, consisted of 136 nullifiers and 26 proponents of Union. It promptly called a special convention which declared that neither the tariff of 1828 nor the tariff of 1832 would be enforced in

South Carolina after February 1, 1833, and bluntly warned that the use of federal force would be interpreted "as inconsistent with the longer continuance of South Carolina in the Union." A specific threat of secession had been made against the federal government, and it was not likely to pass unnoticed by a President who was notoriously quick to take offense.

The Force Bill. Jackson, however, remained calm. Privately he expressed the conviction that Calhoun and his followers were insane; he publicly described the South Carolinian position as "strange" since it provided no appeal from the state's decision. Jackson made his own position unmistakably clear in a Proclamation to the People of South Carolina on December 10, 1832:

> The laws of the United States must be executed. I have no discretionary power on the subject; my duty is emphatically pronounced in the Constitution. Those who told you that you might peaceably prevent their execution deceived you; they could not have been deceived themselves. They know that a forcible opposition could alone prevent the execution of the laws, and they know that such opposition must be repelled. Their object is disunion. But be not deceived by names. Disunion by armed force is *treason*. . . . On your unhappy State will inevitably fall all the evils of the conflict you force upon the Government of your country. It can not accede to the mad project of disunion, of which you would be the first victims. Its First Magistrate can not, if he would, avoid the performance of his duty.

To implement his intentions, Jackson threw his support behind a "Force Bill," which provided for the raising of additional military forces and increased the government's power to enforce tariff collections.

Tariff Reduction. The use of federal force was balanced with a promise to alleviate the primary South Carolinian grievance. With the assistance of Secretary of the Treasury Louis McLane, a tariff bill was drawn up by Gulian C. Verplanck of the House, which reduced tariff rates substantially and held out the promise that rates would be curtailed by a full fifty per cent in 1834. Although Jackson had assumed an attitude of belligerence, he and his administration knew that application of the Force Bill without tariff reduction might provoke disruption of the Union. Indeed, South Carolina had even nullified the Force Bill.

The Compromise Tariff of 1833. An unexpected ally came to the assistance of Jackson in the person of Henry Clay. Eager to recoup his lost prestige after his disastrous defeat in the presidential election of 1832, Clay proposed a compromise tariff on February 12, 1833, which provided for a gradual reduction of all tariffs to twenty per cent *ad valorem* over a ten-year period. By 1842, the highest tariffs would be at twenty per cent. Despite considerable discontent the tariff obtained approval; it passed the House on February 26, 1833, by a vote of 119 to 85, and the Senate concurred on March 1, by a vote of 29 to 16. Once again, the sectional alignment appeared. The South solidly favored Clay's compromise tariff; New England and the Middle Atlantic region generally opposed it; and the West was divided in its attitude. The great challenge to federal authority was momentarily forestalled—but not terminated. The "firebell in the night" that Jefferson had so dreaded had again rung ominously.

THE EMERGENCE OF PARTIES

As the nullification crisis waned, Henry Clay and John C. Calhoun entered into an alliance of convenience. The force that united them was "King Andrew," whose effective extension of executive power seemed to them to threaten the proper balance of legislative and executive relations.

The Democratic Party. Under the shrewd management of Martin Van Buren, now Vice-President of the United States, a disciplined political organization emerged: the Democratic Party. It stood for liberty and equality, and championed the cause of every man. The Democratic message was as wide as the human imagination. It stood for the poor against the rich, attracting to its support the small farmer, the independent fisherman, the hired laborer, the Irish immigrant, and the modest Southern planter. Its denunciation of monopoly privilege attracted the state banker and commercial capitalist (as opposed to the industrial capitalist). By supporting free or nearly free homesteads and free schools, the Democrats attracted the Western farmer and the frontiersmen. Above all, the towering figure of Jackson, the disciple of republican virtue, served to unite about his standard all believers in the virtues of the agrarian republic. The party's most potent appeal lay in its promise of opportunity to all and privilege to none. The Jeffersonian ideal had been resurrected.

The Jacksonian Persuasion. In the Supreme Court, which had numerous changes in personnel, Chief Justice Taney and the six associate justices appointed by Jackson gave judicial support to democratic premises in their emphasis upon individual as opposed to monopoly property rights. In the Charles River Bridge *v.* Warren Bridge decision (1837) the Court struck a damaging blow against monopoly rights and extended the scope of individual enterprise. Jacksonian intellectuals like William Leggett, Robert Rantoul, Jr., George Henry Evans, and Theodore Sedgwick argued for complete equality. They opposed the corporation, arguing for total liability on the part of all stockholders; they denounced paper currency and supported specie currency; and they supported free trade and advocated a completely equalitarian society. Their philosophic bias was that of complete laissez-faire. The only rights that a workingman could claim from society were, according to Rantoul: "(1) The right to his faculties, and the products of their use; (2) the right to choose the terms on which he will employ his time; (3) the right to steady wages at the highest going rate; (4) the right to education; (5) the right to respect; (6) the right to advancement in life." But all these rights were individual, and had to be obtained and maintained through individual effort. Any external combination or effort to effect them was morally indefensible. To make the point emphatic, the definition of "a worthy hard workingman" was expanded to include such diverse personalities as the Philadelphia banker Stephen Girard, Isaac Newton, Benjamin Franklin, George Washington, William Shakespeare, and Robert Fulton, among others.

The Whiggery. As Jackson provided the inspiration for the Democrats, so anti-Jackson sentiment spurred the organization of the Whig party after 1834. The Whigs owed their name to James Watson Webb, editor of the New York *Courier and Enquirer,* who sought to stigmatize the rule of "King Andrew" as an effort to restore the despotism of George III, and to dignify Jackson's opponents by implying that they drew their inspiration from that monarch's revolutionary opponents. The new party appealed to industrialists, to factory labor, to small-town businessmen, and to farmers who viewed their occupation as a business enterprise. In the South it appealed to the urban commercial classes, to those of unionist sentiments, and also to the Louisiana sugar planters who eagerly welcomed the benefits of tariffs. Disgruntled Democrats also joined the Whigs. Twenty-eight of the forty-one Democrats who had voted in Congress for rechartering of the Bank in 1832 were confirmed members of the Whiggery by 1836.

The Whig and Democratic Parties Contrasted. The new conservative party viewed with suspicion the Democratic Party's appeal to the degraded—the poor farmer, the tumultuous city folk, the underdogs of society—men to whom the Whigs felt they owed an example but not equality. The Democrats held that opportunity was an individual endeavor; the Whigs held that failure was an individual responsibility. Unlike the Democrats, they saw the immense possibilities for national economic development. Where Jackson's policies led inevitably to the accentuation of state rights, those of the Whigs fostered the growth of the federal authority. The Whigs' economic vision transcended that of the Jacksonians; its knowledge of the democratic tendencies of American society was inferior.

The Specie Circular of 1836. The attack upon privilege culminated with the issuance of the Specie Circular of 1836. It was the climax of Jackson's campaign against issuances of paper currency below twenty dollars; the circular's purpose was to "revive and perpetuate those habits of economy and simplicity which are so congenial to the character of republicans." To effectuate this purpose, only specie would be accepted for land purchases after July 11, 1836. Inflationary speculation in western lands immediately came to an end. Between 1834 and 1836, nearly 38,000,000 acres of land had been sold by the federal government. But most of the payments for this land were based on uncertain bank credits, often extended without adequate backing. With the disappearance of the regulatory activities of the Bank of the United States, currency had increased from $124 million to well over $200 million; loans had nearly tripled between 1832 and 1836; and land sales were part of a speculative bubble maintained only by the constant issuance of paper credit.

The End of Land Speculation. Jackson's purpose in issuing the Specie Circular had been to impress upon the public the obvious superiority of specie as currency; instead, he succeeded in pricking the bubble. Specie, attracted by large profits, moved westward, unbalancing the normal distribution of currency. It became increasingly apparent that sufficient specie did not exist to meet the needs of the economy throughout the United States. Not only Whigs but also Jacksonians expressed a growing awareness that some means of expanding the national currency would be required. A presidential pocket veto frustrated proposals to make currency of bank paper issued by banks that did not issue small notes. Since the average purchaser of land could not meet government specie requirements, he was driven by necessity to purchase from profit-hungry speculators.

Retirement of Federal Debt. The fiscal structure of the nation received a further jolt when the federal government finally retired the national debt in 1836. Money continued to pour into the Treasury with no one knowing how to dispense it once it had been received. The surplus approached $21 millions. Politicians of both parties realized that this treasure trove had immense possibilities in a presidential election year. Under pressure from the states Congress agreed, in June, 1836, to distribute all but $5 million to the states in proportion to their Congressional representation. The decision stimulated further the raging inflation. But the Jacksonians had gained renewed popularity as a result of the surplus distribution, at a time when Jackson was determined that Van Buren should succeed him.

The Election of 1836. Jackson's influence in the Democratic Party easily secured a unanimous nomination for Van Buren when the party met in Baltimore on May 20, 1835, despite the fact that Alabama, Tennessee, and Virginia viewed the nomination of the New Yorker with marked distaste. The Whigs had four candidates: William Henry Harrison, Hugh Lawson White, Daniel Webster, and Will P. Mangum. Since each candidate had strong backing in a particular section—Harrison in the Northwest, Webster in New England, White in the Southwest, and Mangum in South Carolina—the Whigs hoped to throw the election into the House of Representatives. The two major candidates, Harrison and Van Buren, disagreed on whether to distribute the proceeds of land sales. Van Buren opposed distribution as well as internal improvements at national expense. He stood against a restoration of the bank, while Harrison left the question unsettled. Van Buren also announced his support of a gold currency. But in the end the election proved to be a national referendum in which the major question was whether one approved or disapproved the actions of Andrew Jackson. The response was a modest triumph for the Old General's heir. Van Buren won, with 170 electoral votes to 124 for the combined opposition; but his popular majority was only 25,688 out of 1,505,290 votes cast. The Jacksonians retained control of the Senate, but in the House factionalism left effective control with conservative Democrats. Jackson departed for Tennessee, convinced that his policies had been vindicated. But he left an unexpected legacy: two reasonably well-defined political parties, the Democrats and the Whigs.

VAN BUREN AS PRESIDENT

The Heir. Martin Van Buren had earned as a result of his political machinations the sobriquet of Little Magician. Short, plump, and smiling, his tact and suave manners made him a leading social figure in Washington. Several Whigs noted that in spirit, if not in politics, he was one of them. But his pleasant qualities were balanced by a multitude of defects. Some Democratic opponents charged that he acted without sufficient thought; more often he was indicted as a vacillator; and nearly all of his opponents noted his stubbornness in acknowledging error. A self-made man, he had the confidence of the self-made. Moreover, where Jackson had held to a policy of laissez-faire out of stubborn prejudice, Van Buren pursued it with the fervor that only an idealogue firmly convinced of his correctness feels. He had recently become a member of the radical wing of the Democratic Party, known as Loco Focos, and, as has been noted, he believed in hard money, noninterference of the government in the economy, and in the sanctity of private property. He stated his position when he notified Congress:

> All communities are apt to look to government for too much. . . . But this ought not to be. The framers of our excellent Constitution and the people who approved it with excellent and sagacious deliberation acted at the time on a sounder principle. They wisely judged that the less government interferes with private pursuits the better for the general prosperity . . . its real duty . . . is . . . to leave every citizen and every interest to reap under its benign protection the rewards of virtue, industry, and prudence.

Origins of Economic Collapse. Van Buren was doomed to live in the shadow of his great predecessor, a situation succinctly summarized by Thomas Hart Benton's remark that "the rising was eclipsed by the setting sun." He pledged to uphold the policies of Jackson and to maintain a program of noninterference in the institution of slavery. He did not intend to rock the ship of state. Unfortunately, the consequences of Jacksonian economic policies were already manifest in the winter of 1836–37. The skyrocketing issuance of paper currency and the unrestricted granting of loans had created a spiraling inflation. Land sales continued at a breakneck pace, encouraging borrowing in which thirty per cent interest rates were not uncommon. The rickety structure had come tumbling down shortly after the issuance of the Specie Circular. As one contemporary recalled it:

> The Specie Circular was issued without warning, and the splendid lie of a false credit burst into fragments. . . . Gen. Jackson was no fairy; but he did some very pretty fairy work, in converting the bank bills back again into rags and oak leaves. Men worth a million were insolvent for two millions: promising young cities marched back again into the wilderness. . . . The frolic was ended, and what headaches, and feverish limbs the next morning!

The Impending Crisis. The chaos had been compounded by the destruction of the Bank of the United States. Once its restraint upon issuances of paper by state banks had been lifted, generous credit extension had undermined even the soundest of banks. Another shattering blow came with the onslaught of depression in Britain. Cotton prices tumbled from 17½ cents to 13½ cents a pound. Foreign investors who had poured vast sums into internal improvements sponsored by the states curtailed their investments and sought to recoup their losses. The drain of specie from circulation accelerated. And as banker, merchant, investor, and creditor struggled to save themselves from the depression by contracting credit, the crisis deepened.

The Depression of 1837. Van Buren perversely refused to recognize the signs of crisis. In his inaugural address he praised the expanding economy and predicted an acceleration of the boom; one month later, a full-scale depression had begun. Business failures, forced sales of farms and plantations, factory closings, and spreading unemployment signaled the end of the great boom. The New York banks, faced with a run on specie, suspended specie payments on May 10, 1837, a measure promptly duplicated by banks throughout the country. The President resigned himself to a long period of recovery in which the government would pursue a negative policy by allowing the economy to regain its own health. The Whigs made haste to lay the blame at the door of Jacksonian fiscal policies—where, indeed, it belonged.

Political Effects of the Depression. In the 1837 election, the Jacksonians suffered disastrous losses. In the 128 member New York State Assembly, Democratic strength was reduced from 94 to 27. The pro-bank faction within the Democratic Party broke with the hard money faction. The alliance of the bank supporters with the Whigs brought them frequent legislative victories and foreshadowed catastrophe for the Democrats in the presidential election of 1840. Supporters of Van Buren charged that bankers were conspiring insidiously to undo the gains of Jacksonian reform. Van Buren refused to be intimidated. Even with overwhelming pressure for revocation of the Specie Circular, he clung stubbornly to his support of hard money. When the banks suspended specie payment the government was left with a serious dilemma. Under the law the banks had become ineligible for government deposits since they had to be redeemed in specie. The crisis was complicated by fears that the Treasury would be unable to meet its regular expenses as revenue receipts declined.

Van Buren and the Depression. On September 4, 1837, Van Buren called an emergency session of Congress to solve the economic difficulties of the government. The President made it clear to Congress that he intended to continue the war upon banks when he proposed a law which threw into bankruptcy those banks that suspended specie payments. He also proposed to retain the undistributed Treasury surplus to meet the expected deficit of 1837. But the bulk of his address was devoted to a proposal for the establishment of an Independent Treasury in which the government would keep its receipts. The divorce of private and public funds would be complete. At no point did Van Buren suggest that the government had a responsibility to aid in the economic recovery of the nation; and this permitted the Whigs in Congress to charge that "public policy" had as its object "the convenience of Government" and left "the people to shift for themselves."

The Independent Treasury. The Whigs and conservative Democrats responded to the President's requests by supporting proposals for postponement of the surplus distribution. But they fought proposals for the Independent Treasury. To their chagrin, Calhoun, anticipating the disintegration of the two national parties, threw his support behind the proposal. In fact, he proposed to strengthen the Independent Treasury by gradually making all government disbursements and receipts payable in coin, notes, bills, and paper issued by the federal authority. The Independent Treasury promised to provide a stable currency. It also permitted the Democrats to escape the charge that they were dominated by banks; indeed, it permitted them to charge the Whigs and their allies with being the true minions of repressive banking. But against the Whig charge that they were callous toward the plight of the suffering masses, the Democrats could only respond that the banks were responsible. When the votes were counted, a coalition of Whigs, conservative Democrats, and some Western Democrats defeated the Independent Treasury by a vote of 120 to 106.

Van Buren did not abandon hope. The banks resumed specie payments in May 1838, but when business conditions worsened in the autumn of 1839, there were renewed suspensions. The obvious instability of the nation's banks permitted Van Buren to renew his campaign for establishment of the Independent Treasury. After narrow passage of the bill in June 1840, Van Buren signed it on July 4, 1840. Deleted from the final draft was the specie clause, which would have restricted payment of obligations to the federal government to specie. At best, the Treasury provided a means to administer government funds uniformly.

It did not give the government effective control of the national currency but left this critical power to the states.

Land Policies under Van Buren. Reckless speculation in Western lands had convinced thoughtful Americans that reform of federal land policies was imperative, but there was no agreement on how best to achieve these reforms. The Whigs and most Eastern Democrats wanted to distribute proceeds from land sales to the states. Westerners advocated restriction of land sales to actual settlers, taxation of land as soon as it was sold, permanent pre-emption to secure the rights of squatters upon land they had improved, graduation of land sales to permit reduction of prices on land that remained unsold, and surrender of federal lands to state control. The leading spokesman for the Western viewpoint was Thomas Hart "Old Bullion" Benton of Missouri, who, like Van Buren, advocated a hard money policy. Van Buren, eager to obtain backing for his Independent Treasury, supported Benton's proposals. Over the opposition of both the Whigs and Calhoun, who wanted the federal government to cede its lands to the states, Van Buren obtained a pre-emption bill in 1836, and in 1840 the bill was extended until 1842.

The Canadian Revolution of 1837. Domestic difficulties had their complement in difficulties along the northern border. Late in 1837, William Lyon Mackenzie and Louis J. Papineau led an abortive revolt in Canada to establish Canadian independence from Great Britain. Both men fled to the United States where they received a warm reception. Within a short time a considerable number of Americans had flocked to the insurgents' standard. Open preparations for the invasion of Canada started along the northern frontier, and the American press and public platform rang with promises that the incorporation of Canada into the Union was under way. Neither the Canadian government nor the Canadian citizenry viewed the prospect with enthusiasm.

The Caroline Affair. The insurgent base had been established on the Canadian Navy Island in the Niagara River. The *Caroline* was an American steamer which transported supplies from the American side of the river to the island. Her voyages were abruptly halted on December 29, 1837, when Canadian soldiers crossed the Niagara River, killed an American citizen, and seized and burned the *Caroline*. Outraged Americans promptly organized raids into Canada, and avenged the *Caroline* by seizing and burning the Canadian steamer, *Sir Robert Peel*. Finally Canadians who had fled Canada during the abortive uprising of 1837 organized a government in exile at Cleveland, Ohio, in September 1838.

British-American Relations under Van Buren. As relations between

Britain and the United States deteriorated, Van Buren pursued a cautious policy. As an American, he sympathized with Canadian aspirations for freedom. As President, he warned that American citizens captured on Canadian soil would have to face the consequences. To prevent further frontier marauding, he dispatched General Winfield Scott to the border. With only a small force at his disposal, Scott managed to persuade Americans to desist from further aggressions. But relations were further aggravated by the arrest of a Canadian deputy sheriff, Alexander McLeod, on November 2, 1840, after he boasted in a New York tavern that he had killed the American citizen when the *Caroline* had been seized. Only the acquittal of McLeod by a New York Court prevented war from breaking out between Britain and the United States.

The "Aroostook War." The irritation between the Canadians and Americans was increased by the dispute over the border between Maine and Canada. At issue were some 12,000 square miles of timber land. Earlier efforts to resolve the dispute had collapsed when Maine protested a decision by the King of the Netherlands which awarded about 8,000 square miles to the United States and the remainder to Canada. A small conflict, the "Aroostook War," broke out between Maine and the adjacent Maritime Provinces of New Brunswick and Nova Scotia. By 1838, Maine had sent troops to seize the disputed region. The Canadians responded in kind. Congress authorized Van Buren to call up 50,000 volunteers and expend $10,000,000 for defense. But the wily New Yorker, unwilling to complicate the nation's grievous economic difficulties, sent Scott to settle the dispute. Once again the general managed to soothe ruffled feelings, and Maine agreed to withdraw from the Aroostook region until the dispute could be negotiated. There the issue rested when Van Buren entered his unsuccessful campaign for re-election in 1840.

THE ELECTION OF 1840

Harrison and Van Buren. The Whigs had strong reason to expect that they would sweep the presidential polls in 1840. Unwilling to jeopardize their hopes by nominating a well-known Whig, they had settled for an unknown general, William Henry Harrison, who promised to give the party the same popular appeal that Andrew Jackson had given the Democrats. To balance their ticket, they nominated for Vice-President the conservative John Tyler of Virginia, a believer in state rights. The Democrats quickly renominated Martin Van Buren but could not decide on a candidate for Vice-President. That issue was left to the states. The Democratic platform reaffirmed the traditional Jacksonian hostility to internal improvements at national expense and the party's commitment to a government of limited powers. The platform denounced assumption of state debts, restoration of the bank or protective tariffs, and denied the power of Congress to interfere with slavery. It pronounced itself in favor of the Independent Treasury and against naturalization restrictions. As one newspaper observed, "It was noteworthy for what it was against rather than what it was for."

The Campaign of 1840. The Democrats displayed little optimism in the campaign; and the Whigs, anticipating the certainty of victory, plunged enthusiastically into the contest. Although they argued for a uniform currency, land distribution, and limitations on executive influence, the Whigs spent most of their time creating the myth of the Hero of Tippecanoe, William Henry Harrison, the old gentleman of North Bend, Ohio—he was sixty-seven—who would bring the traditional virtues back to Washington. The stern qualities of the Whig general were depicted in vivid contrast to the "dissipation" of the incumbent Van Buren. The President was accused of eating off gold plate, wallowing in champagne, and indulging in French extravagance. As the Democrat lolled in mansions, it was claimed, Harrison sat outside a log cabin, taking a swig of cider and talking on a level with the common man.

The Triumph of Democratic Politics. Huge parades of men carrying replicas of log cabins and rolling barrels of cider became the hallmark of the Whig campaign. Cries of "Van Van Van Van Van is a used-up man man man man man," shook the quiet of American streets. Banners, bonfires, busts of "Old Tip" in plaster of Paris, and constant use of the slogan "Tippecanoe and Tyler too" kept the campaign in turmoil. As one Democrat, observing the Whig hullabaloo, observed about his own party, "We have taught them to conquer us!" By the time the campaign ended, George Templeton Strong, a proper New Yorker, complained:

> I'm beginning to wish this affair ended; the novelty of the thing is over and I'm tired of humbug, lying, spouting, swearing, O. K. [Old Kinderhook, Van Buren's birthplace], and the Old Hero. Nothing but politics. The newspapers crowd out their advertisements for mendacious "returns" that nobody believes, the walls are papered three deep with humbug, banners and inscriptions dangle over every street, mass-meetings are held in every groggery. . . . If the North River were actually on fire . . . or if the continent of Europe were to sink in the sea, the papers wouldn't be able to find room for the news.

The Voting and the Parties. The Whigs won a sweeping victory. Harrison carried nineteen states as opposed to seven for Van Buren, and received 53 per cent of the popular vote. Both houses of Congress were Whig. But the election had a larger significance: almost a million additional votes had been cast. This was truly a mighty democratic upsurge. The election of 1828, which has often been considered the apex of the growth of democratic participation in government, was actually less democratic than this election. Four out of five adult white males had gone to the polls. In twenty-one of the states voter participation exceeded records established in pre-1824 elections. In fourteen states voters established participation records that were not to be exceeded again during the ante-bellum period. Whereas Jackson had attracted to the polls men accustomed to voting either in state or national elections, 1840 brought hundreds of thousands to the polls who had never previously cast a ballot in any election.

To the dismay of the Jacksonians, the new democracy had overwhelmed them. It also marked the culmination of the major Jacksonian achievement: the final emergence of two well-defined parties. To win a national election both parties would have to fight long and hard. Time and again it would be a handful of votes located in a state with a strategic electoral majority that would make the difference. And both parties would have to seek a stirring issue to gain a majority in the future, a future foretold by the ominous appearance of a new party—the Liberty Party—which stood for the abolition of slavery. In 1840, it polled a mere 6,225 votes; four years later, it commanded 61,999 votes, enough to swing New York, and the election, to James K. Polk.

Chapter 13

A Nation of Sections

The Constitution had been composed in order to establish a more nearly perfect Union. It had attempted to resolve the competing authority of federal and state government through compromise, by assigning to each an ill-defined sphere of power. The result had been to leave both teetering on the edge of indecision or threatening dispute. The Union, created by compromise, sought to resolve continuing difficulties by further compromises. Every American politician had to operate within a system that placed a premium on moderation. As the nineteenth century progressed, and circumstances changed, it became increasingly apparent that the political party, the vehicle of compromise, was unable to perform its function. By midcentury the nation found itself divided by sectional rivalries. Between 1850 and 1860 the politicians would make desperate efforts to achieve a successful compromise with which to hold together a disintegrating Union.

THE TYLER ADMINISTRATION AND MANIFEST DESTINY

Manifest Destiny. John L. O'Sullivan, a New York editor, in 1844 had described America's progress to the Pacific Ocean as her "Manifest Destiny." He gave voice to the American conviction that the nation's natural boundary is the Pacific Ocean. As everyone knew, he claimed, "the swelling tide of our population must and will roll on until that mighty ocean interposes its waters, and limits our territorial empire."

And O'Sullivan was not a visionary radical in thinking this way. Even so eminent a conservative as John Quincy Adams anticipated that "the world shall be familiarized with the idea of considering our proper dominion to be the continent of North America." De Tocqueville warned of the approaching day when "the Anglo-Americans alone will cover the immense space contained between the polar regions and the tropics, extending from the coasts of the Atlantic to those of the Pacific Ocean." America's expansion westward was deemed inevitable; and each new accession of territory, in addition to "proving" the validity of Manifest Destiny, seemed also to lend conviction to a second widely held concept, namely that the Anglo-Saxon-American breed should naturally meet with success where the French and the Spanish had met only with failure. Implicit in Manifest Destiny was the added conviction that America was the recipient of divine aid in her westward quest. When, in 1846, the United States made her final westward leap at the expense of Mexico, the American expansionist had a ready explanation: "Providence called upon us to regenerate her [Mexico's] decadent population." What few Americans understood was that the way west would also lead to the final crisis of the Union.

John Tyler. William Henry Harrison had barely succeeded to the presidency when his health began to fail. Beset with office-seekers, harassed by the claims of the Whigs, he found escape in death only thirty days after claiming the presidency. His successor, John Tyler, found it immediately necessary to establish the principle that the Vice-President succeeds to the full authority of the presidency rather than to serve as an acting President until a new election. Tyler, a state-rights Democrat and the archetype of the Virginia gentleman, also claimed leadership of a Whiggery that expressed considerable antipathy for a strong executive. Moreover, this brought him into conflict with the ambitions of Henry Clay who did not propose to relinquish his dominance within the Whiggery, or his hopes for 1844, to "His Accidency" John Tyler.

Battle within the Whig Party. When the new President, in his brief inaugural address, gave no indication that he intended to step down after his inherited tenure had expired, Clay set to work to exploit his congressional powers to insure his own nomination in 1844. He easily secured the repeal of the Independent Treasury by the Senate as part of a plan to establish a Third Bank of the United States. When Tyler realized that the clever Kentuckian had isolated him from Whig leadership in Congress, he responded by vetoing the bill establishing the new bank. Subsequent efforts to modify the bank bill so as to meet the objections of both Clay and Tyler met with a second presidential veto. It became obvious that the incumbent and his rival were both intent upon securing party dominance.

Tyler and Reorganization of the Cabinet. Tyler, now fully aware of Clay's power among Whigs, decided to establish a new party with himself at its head. To implement his decision, he determined to remove everyone but Daniel Webster from the cabinet, and replace them with either anti-Clay Whigs or conservative Democrats. Clay, also eager to complete the Whiggery's break with Tyler, pressured the cabinet to resign. On September 11, 1841, the cabinet members resigned and Tyler reconstructed his cabinet without a single Clay supporter, appointing to the position of Postmaster General a long-time Clay antagonist, Charles A. Wickliffe of Kentucky.

The Tariff of 1842. In the resulting political stalemate, only a modified protective tariff, passed in 1842, conformed with the Whig pledges of 1840. Several factors determined the passage of a new tariff, most important among them being the rapid rise of the government debt, and the sharp drop in tariff rates scheduled for July 1, 1842, by the Compromise Tariff of 1833. Indeed, the awkward wording of the 1833 Tariff left genuine doubt whether any tariffs at all could be collected after that date. Tyler conceded the need for a tariff whose rates would be higher than twenty per cent of the products' actual valuation, and one whose primary objective would be to provide federal revenue and only incidentally protection for home products; but if such a tariff were passed, he made it clear that he would adamantly refuse to accept distribution of land receipts among the states. In the resulting struggle between Clay and Tyler, the President wielded the veto so effectively that though the 1842 Tariff restored rates to the level of 1832, distribution was a dead issue. It was hardly surprising that, among Clay Whigs, Tyler was contemptuously referred to as "Judas Iscariot."

The Webster-Ashburton Treaty, 1842. Daniel Webster, an Anglophile, had remained in Tyler's cabinet, hoping to secure peace with Great Britain. Of particular urgency was settlement of the boundary line between Canada and the United States. A compromise line was drawn from Lake Superior to the Lake of the Woods (Minnesota), and a realignment favorable to the United States was made of the New York and Vermont borders. The more difficult problem of the Maine-New Brunswick border was also settled by compromise. The existence of a map (showing a red line supposedly drawn by Benjamin Franklin) that gave the disputed territory to Britain persuaded supporters of Maine's claim to accept compromise—a compromise that was made considerably more palatable by federal payment of $150,000 each to Maine and Massachusetts in lieu of their claims on the lost territory. All told, the United States received 7,000 of the 12,000 square miles in dispute. The treaty also pledged both countries to suppress the slave trade, and established a useful extradition agreement. Perhaps of greatest significance, it inaugurated a precedent whereby the United States and Great Britain negotiated future disputes.

Tyler and Texas. While Webster negotiated a peaceful settlement of disputes with Britain, Tyler adopted an aggressive policy on the future of Texas. It was this policy that he hoped would provide him with a rallying point for a third party in 1844. When Webster, unwilling to sever his relations with the Whiggery, finally withdrew from the cabinet on May 8, 1843, Tyler appointed Abel P. Upshur to the State Department. This enthusiastic proponent of slavery saw in the annexation of Texas a renewed opportunity for the South to retain political parity within the nation. In addition to his desire for sectional advancement, Upshur was guided in his efforts by his fear of British expansion into the region if the United States were to refrain from taking action on the matter. Andrew Jackson threw his immense prestige behind annexation, though his traditional antagonist, John Quincy Adams, warned that annexation would preface dissolution of the Union. When the explosion of a cannon aboard the warship *Princeton* on February 28, 1844 killed Upshur, Tyler appointed Calhoun, another ardent proponent of annexation, to replace him.

The Democrats and Texas. As Tyler battled with the Whigs, many Democrats chaffed under the leadership of Martin Van Buren. Men like Lewis Cass, Robert J. Walker, James Buchanan, and James K. Polk supported a vigorous policy of expansionism, with particular emphasis upon the annexation of Texas. When Van Buren publicly announced his opposition to annexation, the expansionist wing of the party decided to deny him a third Democratic nomination. The support of annexation by state-rights Democrats, led by Tyler and Calhoun, suggested that Texas would be the issue upon which the Democrats could ignore their differences and present a united front in 1844.

The Election of 1844. When in the spring of 1844 Clay also expressed a qualified opposition to the annexation of Texas, the issue seemed dead. Though the Whigs dutifully endorsed Clay for the nomination, the Democrats repudiated Van Buren rather than renounce agitation for the annexation of Texas. When it became clear at the Baltimore convention of

May 1844 that Van Buren would never obtain the two-thirds vote needed for nomination, the Democrats settled for the nomination of the dark-horse James K. Polk. The expansionist wing of the Democratic Party won a total victory in which they committed the nation to "the reoccupation of Oregon and the reannexation of Texas at the earliest practicable period." In order to prolong the issue, the Democrats in Congress permitted the defeat, on June 8, 1844, of a treaty annexing Texas. As Jackson suspected, Texas and President-making had become hopelessly entwined. The controversy led Silas Wright, the New York spokesman for Van Buren, to the conclusion that "our Union was never so much in danger as at this moment."

The Campaign of 1844. In a hard-fought, often nasty contest, Polk edged through to a narrow electoral victory. Exploiting Clay's opposition to expansion, the Democrats pledged their party to the annexation of both Texas and Oregon. Clay attempted unsuccessfully to undo the damage by announcing himself to be in favor of the acquisition of Texas—provided it could be obtained without a Mexican war. On Election Day, Polk's narrow victory by 5,106 votes in New York defeated Clay. (That the decisive number of votes should have been so small was caused largely by the appeal in New York of the anti-slavery Liberty ticket, which had polled 15,814 of the state's votes.) The new President seemed to have restored the old Jacksonian coalition.

POLK'S ADMINISTRATION

Polk's Policies. The South thought that Polk had been elected by its own votes and it meant to have a full reward. Under the guidance of Tyler and Calhoun, a joint resolution inviting Texas to join the Union passed Congress. The day before Polk's inauguration, the invitation was forwarded to Austin, Texas. This action permitted the taciturn, determined Polk to divert his energy to completing his own policy of expansion and reform. Convinced of the correctness of his goals, he set about pushing through Congress a four-point program which provided for tariff reform through rate reduction, the restoration of the Independent Treasury, the settlement of the Oregon dispute with Britain, and the establishment of the American claim that the border between Texas and Mexico was marked by the Rio Grande, some hundred miles south of the Nueces River, the border claimed by Mexico. He also meant to establish the moderate Democrats as the dominant force within the party. The latter course disappointed both the Calhoun and Van Buren factions, but it assured Polk that he would be master in his own house.

The Tariff of 1846 and the Independent Treasury. With the assistance of his shrewd Secretary of the Treasury, Robert J. Walker, Polk maneuvered the tariff of 1846 through Congress. Despite a Senate split in which Vice-President George M. Dallas was compelled to cast the deciding vote, a tariff was passed which established the *ad valorem* principle as the basis for maintaining low rates, and which drove most Pennsylvania Democrats into opposition. The tariff convinced Eastern Democrats who represented industrial constituencies that Polk was working to gratify Southern demands. Shortly afterward, the Independent Treasury was also approved by a largely partisan vote. Though supposedly a hard money measure, it permitted payment of government obligations not only in specie but also in treasury notes, a move tantamount to the establishment of a federally backed paper currency.

The Warehousing Act. Supplementing the tariff and treasury bills was the Warehousing Act. This gave importers the right to deposit imported goods under government bond until such time as they were needed for consumption. This freed the commercial interests from having to tie up large amounts of money in tariff payments until they were able to reclaim their investment quickly. Most important, the Tariff of 1846 committed the United States to a modified free trade policy in the hope that by allowing European, and particularly British, manufacturers easy access to the American market, reciprocal access would be obtained for American farm produce.

The Oregon Territory. Polk's program of domestic reform, though important, was insignificant in comparison with his territorial program. Of particularly pressing concern was the future of the Oregon Territory. Since 1818, it had been under the joint occupation by Britain and the United States, but in 1827 a proviso was added to the treaty which permitted either power to end joint occupation after a year's notice. The fur-trading wealth of the region attracted the interest of the Hudson's Bay Company, while its agricultural promise lured several thousand Americans to the Willamette Valley, south of the Columbia River. During the election of 1844, Democratic campaigners declared that the days of joint occupation were numbered. "Fifty-four forty or fight" was the inflammatory slogan which announced the Democrats' intention to secure the entire region for the United States. Polk accentuated the problem when he announced in his inaugural address that the American title to Oregon was "clear and unquestionable."

The Oregon Negotiations. Since every administration after that of Monroe had announced its willingness to settle for latitude 49° as an Oregon boundary, Polk and his Secretary of State, James Buchanan, offered a similar compromise to the British in July 1845, but deleted the crucial clause assuring both parties free navigation of the Columbia River. When the proposal was turned down by Pakenham, the British envoy, tension mounted. In his annual message to Congress in 1845, Polk declared his intention to terminate joint occupation. Party antagonisms reappeared when Northwestern expansionists, guided by Senators Lewis Cass of Michigan and Edward A. Hannegan of Indiana, demanded total annexation, while Southern Democrats, under the leadership of Calhoun, called for conciliation leading to a compromise settlement with Britain. The Southerners recognized that the United States could hardly afford war with both Britain and Mexico; they therefore proposed to surrender Northwestern claims; and they found ready allies in the Whigs, whose commercial interests made them view war without enthusiasm. This South-Whig alliance succeeded in adding to Polk's order terminating joint occupation of Oregon by British and American troops the pious hope that the dispute would be settled peaceably.

The Oregon Settlement. Powerful commercial and financial interests in the North threw their weight behind a peaceable settlement. Their primary concern was to obtain control of such promising western ports as San Francisco and Puget Sound. Given a choice between war for California and war for the northern reaches of the Oregon Territory, Polk chose the former. In Britain, the Peel Ministry, eager to advance free-trade policy, decided upon compromise; they agreed to accept Polk's proposal without insisting upon free transit of the Columbia River. On June 15, 1846, five days after Polk submitted the British proposal to the Senate, it was approved. Only fourteen Northwestern expansionists opposed the decision. The United States, already at war with Mexico, turned its full attention to winning that conflict.

THE MEXICAN WAR

The offer of statehood to Texas hastened conflict with Mexico. The southern republic, ridden by debt and internal corruption, had nevertheless resolved to fight the moment Texas and the United States consummated annexation with the entrance of American troops into the new state.

Invasion of Mexico. To meet concentrations of some 8,000 Mexican troops on the Rio Grande, Polk ordered General Zachary Taylor with about 4,000 troops to move up to the Nueces River. Between the two armies stretched one hundred miles of disputed territory. When Taylor crossed to the south side of the Nueces, he was engaging in a deliberate show of force designed to dissuade the Mexicans from warlike action. Polk hoped to persuade the Mexicans to accept a peaceful settlement of the Texas border and then to lure them by generous cash offers into selling their western lands, including California, to the United States. When Taylor moved his army from the Nueces to the Rio Grande in late March 1846, the Mexicans protested vigorously. Late in April, a small American cavalry detachment was ambushed by a large Mexican army north of the Rio Grande. When news of this clash reached Polk on May 9, he decided on war to satisfy national aspirations.

Seizure of the California Territory. When Congress confirmed his request with minor opposition, Polk then made it clear that he intended to take the California territory and the intervening regions in order to satisfy American claims against Mexico. American forces moved swiftly to seize the northern areas of the Mexican Republic. General Stephen W. Kearny occupied Santa Fe in New Mexico on August 18 and then continued his march on California. Naval and army detachments captured San Francisco on July 9, 1846, and Los Angeles on January 13, 1847. In less than a year the Americans had conquered an imperial domain of almost a million square miles.

The Campaign in Northern Mexico. Taylor's forces drove the Mexican army steadily backward into the interior of their country. At Palo Alto and Resaca, American arms won tidy victories that culminated in the capture of Monterrey after a four day battle (September 20–24, 1846). As a result of these victories Taylor, whose nickname "Rough and Ready" soon became a household term, although never previously identified with a party, seemed a growing political threat to Polk. The President attempted to subvert the general's popularity by sending General Winfield Scott to launch an amphibious attack upon Vera Cruz. Since Scott was a Whig, Polk hoped to split the Whigs should they decide on a general as their 1848 candidate. He also followed a devious course with the exiled Mexican dictator Santa Anna; he offered to restore him to control of Mexico if he would agree to peace. The wily Santa Anna accepted the offer, returned to Mexico where he took power from the floundering Paredes administration, and proceeded to prosecute the war with vigor. He attacked Taylor at Buena Vista (February 22–23, 1847)

EARLY SETTLEMENTS IN CALIFORNIA, IN THE SOUTHWEST, AND TEXAS

GULF OF MEXICO

Sabine River

Houston (1836)

San Antonio (1734)

Austin (1836)

TEXAS

Red River

Boundary Claimed by Mexico after 1836

Nueces River

Missouri River

Arkansas River

Platte River

Rio Grande

Pecos River

Treaty with Spain, 1821

Santa Fé (1609)

El Paso (1659)

U.S.-MEXICAN BORDER (Defined by Transcontinental Treaty with Spain, 1821)

MEXICO

Gila River

Tucson (1776)

Colorado River

San Diego (1769)

Los Angeles (1781)

Santa Barbara (1782)

CALIFORNIA

Monterey (1770)

San Francisco (1776)

PACIFIC OCEAN

and was repulsed with heavy losses. But the battle had the unexpected effect of convincing Taylor, who had been compelled to relinquish troops for Scott's amphibious assault, that he had been callously betrayed by the administration. He applied for leave and returned to the United States less in the role of general than in that of presidential candidate.

Vera Cruz and Mexico City. Scott launched his invasion of Mexico on March 9, 1847. Within twenty days Vera Cruz was compelled to surrender. Scott resolved to duplicate the feat of Cortes and ordered his army to advance on Mexico City. After reaching Puebla, only seventy miles from the capital, on May 15, Scott halted while he built his force to almost 12,000 men. In August he abandoned his lines of communication and marched upon the capital. Despite opposition by an entrenched Mexican army of 30,000, Scott entered and occupied the city on September 14, 1847. Santa Anna's government disintegrated; the shooting part of the war was over.

The Treaty of Guadalupe. Polk occupied himself with the task of concluding an advantageous peace. Though an expansionist, he opposed Secretary of the Treasury Walker's extreme demands for the annexation of all Mexico. Instead, he delegated the task of negotiating the peace to Nicholas Trist, a conscientious Virginian, who Polk thought could be depended upon not to exceed his instructions. Trist was authorized to offer the Mexican government $30,000,000 for cession of New Mexico, Lower and Upper California, and the right of transit across the isthmus of Tehuantepec. If the Mexicans failed to cede Lower California, the price was to go down five million, and if they refused a Tehuantepec passage the price was to drop by another five million. The Mexican government finally agreed to negotiate, and met with Trist at Guadalupe-Hidalgo on December 28, 1847. Since Polk had by that time taken offense at the Mexican delay in opening negotiations, he instructed Trist to press for larger cessions and smaller payments. Trist received subsequent instructions from Polk to terminate negotiations entirely, but, encouraged by Scott and the British consul, he decided to continue them. On February 2, 1848, the Treaty of Guadalupe-Hidalgo was signed. The treaty established the Rio Grande as the southern boundary of Texas and ceded California and New Mexico to the United States; in return, the United States agreed to pay Mexico $15,000,000 (another $5,000,000 had been deducted for the prolongation of the war) and American claims of $3,250,000 against Mexico were assumed by the American government.

Ratification of the Treaty of Guadalupe. The Whig capture of the House of Representatives in 1846 had brought increasing criticism of

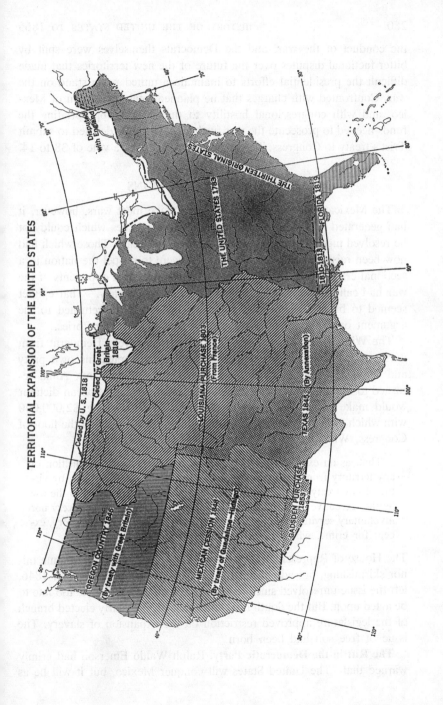

TERRITORIAL EXPANSION OF THE UNITED STATES

THE THIRTEEN ORIGINAL STATES

THE UNITED STATES 1783

FLORIDA 1819

1810-1813

LOUISIANA PURCHASE 1803
(From France)

TEXAS 1845
(By Annexation)

Ceded by U. S. 1818

Ceded by Great
Britain 1818

Disputed
with England

OREGON COUNTRY 1846
(By Treaty with Great Britain)

MEXICAN CESSION 1848
(By Treaty of Guadalupe Hidalgo)

GADSDEN PURCHASE
1853

the conduct of the war, and the Democrats themselves were split by bitter factional disputes over the future of the new territories that made difficult the presidential efforts to maintain a united party stand on the war. Confronted with charges that he planned total annexation of Mexico, and with congressional hostility to the idea of appropriating the funds needed to prosecute the war further, Polk finally decided to submit Trist's treaty to Congress. The Senate approved it by a vote of 38 to 14.

THE CRISIS OF SECTIONS

The Mexican War was officially ended. Like most wars, however, it had generated problems and raised troublesome issues which could not be resolved merely by the ratification of a peace treaty. Those which had now been raised by the war with Mexico were to propel the nation to a sectional crisis. Many people would later recollect that opponents of the war had called Polk "The Hangman of the Confederacy." That epithet seemed to be grimly accurate when North and South returned to the argument over the extension of slavery into the new territories.

The Wilmot Proviso. David Wilmot, an anti-slavery Democrat from northern Pennsylvania, created the issue that disrupted his own party and brought the Republican Party into being. When Santa Anna returned to Mexico, Polk, who thought the return of the Mexican dictator would make peace likely, asked Congress to appropriate $2,000,000 with which to inaugurate negotiations. When the bill reached the floor of Congress, Wilmot offered an amendment which provided:

> That, as an express and fundamental condition to the acquisition of any territory from the Republic of Mexico by the United States, by virtue of any treaty which may be negotiated between them, and to the use by the Executive of the moneys herein appropriated, neither slavery nor involuntary servitude shall ever exist in any part of the said territory, except for crime, whereof the party shall first be duly convicted.

The House of Representatives approved the amendment after some minor skirmishing, but adjournment of the Congress on August 12, 1846, left the issue unresolved since the measure reached the Senate too late to be acted upon. But the South now knew that the popularly elected branch of the legislature approved restriction on the expansion of slavery. The issue of free soil had been born.

The Rift in the Democratic Party. Ralph Waldo Emerson had grimly warned that "The United States will conquer Mexico, but it will be as the man who swallows the arsenic which brings him down in turn. Mexico will poison us." By 1848, the Democrats had ample reason to suspect that this had proved true—at least in respect to their party. Polk had known little but success, and yet each step forward seemed politically a step backward. The Van Buren wing of the party, convinced that the administration had deliberately worked to prevent the re-election of Silas Wright as governor of New York in 1846, and deprived of their major candidate for nomination in 1848 by Wright's untimely death, was bitter. Alienated from the Southern Democrats, Van Buren decided that Northern Democrats should stand against further expansion of slavery. The popularity of the issue in the North was evident when eight Northern legislatures passed resolutions supporting the Wilmot proposal. Southerners viewed this development with stark hostility, and insisted that their full rights in both party and nation be respected. The antipathies that thus divided the Democratic party were well diagnosed by Gideon Welles:

> It has appeared to me for several years that a derangement of parties was inevitable . . . that the party organization was perverted, and . . . we must sooner or later be involved in difficulty. The aggressive spirit of the southern democrats . . . their arrogance which has led them to believe that they alone are qualified to direct the democratic party . . . their patronizing airs to *their* "allies" the northern democrats, some errors and too great concessions on the part of the north, could not otherwise than cause a reaction if there is a salutary corrective in the public mind.

When the Democrats gathered at Baltimore on May 27, 1848, to nominate a presidential candidate, the rift in their party came into full public view.

The Democrats in 1848. The primary intention of the Democrats was to seek out a moderate candidate acceptable to all factions. Lewis Cass seemed to meet the qualification. An energetic expansionist, a dedicated temperance man, and an Anglophobe, he had also opposed the Wilmot Proviso. Since it seemed likely that Zachary Taylor, who was a Louisiana slaveholder as well as a general, would receive the Whig nomination, Cass' nomination would give the Democrats an opportunity to eliminate a divisive issue from the campaign. With only minor opposition, he gained the Democratic nomination on the fourth ballot. To assuage the Van Buren faction, the Democrats nominated General William O. Butler for Vice-President. Since no New York delegation had been seated as a result of a dispute between "Barnburners" (the Van Buren faction) and

"Hunkers" (the conservative faction), this effort at pacification proved inadequate.

The Whigs in 1848. The Whigs promptly nominated Taylor. Since he believed that the Polk administration had failed to give him the support that his military genius warranted, he relished the idea of punishing the Democrats. His lack of any previous political identity enabled him to stand forth as the candidate of all the people: "Rough and Ready" would run *above* issues. In the end, it was the belief that Taylor would divert normally Democratic votes to the Whig ticket that decided his nomination by the Whigs.

The Free Soil Party. Although the Democratic platform made its traditional bows to the Jacksonian opposition to banks and promised to support hard money, it avoided a commitment on free soil. The Whigs avoided a platform altogether, and for the so-called Conscience Whigs, stubbornly opposed as they were to slavery, Taylor's nomination proved unbearable. Rather than support him they called a convention of free-soilers at Buffalo. A parallel movement developed in the Democratic Party, where supporters of Van Buren rejected the Cass ticket. Gideon Welles, John Van Buren, David Wilmot, and Preston King led a rebellion compounded of antipathy for Cass, commitment to free soil and distaste for slavery, and a desperate desire to capture control of the party machinery. In late June, this group of radical Democrats nominated Martin Van Buren for the presidency at Utica, New York. Subsequently, these dissidents gathered at Buffalo to join with other disgruntled elements to form a new party consisting of free-soilers, abolitionists, radical Democrats, Conscience Whigs, homesteaders, advocates of internal improvements, and "Working Men of New York" (an organization of New York small businessmen). A compromise ticket was nominated which consisted of Martin Van Buren and Charles Francis Adams; their platform was "free soil, free speech, free labor, and free men."

The Election of 1848. In the ensuing three-cornered race, Taylor emerged narrowly triumphant. The Van Buren defection in New York had thrown the state to the Whigs; otherwise it might have gone to Cass and given him the victory. Still, the newly elected President had won by a plurality, with Van Buren receiving the balance between the two major candidates. The 291,000 votes cast for the Free-Soil ticket indicated a surprising upsurge of antislavery sentiment. It also indicated that Americans felt a surprising affinity for generals in the White House, so much so that the Whigs failed to gain control of Congress even as they elected the President. From all sides came the prediction that American political parties stood at the edge of massive reorganization. Within two years the Whigs would be well on their way toward dissolution; the Democrats were to have a mere decade longer before they too suffered a similar fate.

THE COMPROMISE OF 1850

National Debate over Slavery. The election of 1848 had made it abundantly clear that the future of the new territories gained by Polk would not easily be decided. Even as preparations were made to transfer power to Taylor, the House of Representatives witnessed such frequent discussion of slavery that one congressman protested, "From morning to night, day after day and week after week, nothing can get a hearing that will not afford an opportunity to lug in something about negro slavery." Efforts to still the issue only provoked extremists on both sides to press the harder for a solution favorable to themselves. Antislavery congressmen proposed that new territories be organized in California and New Mexico which would be closed to slavery. An even more direct attack proposed that the slave trade be prohibited in the District of Columbia. Southern congressmen, under the leadership of Calhoun, composed an "Address of the Southern Delegates in Congress to their Constituents," in which they warned that the Northern effort to monopolize the new territories for free soil was the opening gun in an effort to abolish slavery. The Southern response ranged from the warning of the governor of Virginia that acceptance of the Wilmot Proviso would indicate "the day of compromise will have passed, and the dissolution of our great and glorious Union will become necessary and inevitable" to the open appeal of the South Carolinian fire-eater, Robert Barnwell Rhett, for the withdrawal of his state's congressional delegation from Congress. For better or worse, the South showed increasing willingness to accept Calhoun's conclusion that "the alienation between the two sections had . . . gone too far to save the union."

The Search for Compromise. Southern Whigs and conservatives expressed alarm at the prospect of disunion and sought means to settle the worsening dispute over free soil. Such disputes had traditionally been settled by compromise, a procedure tantamount to the avoidance of fundamental issues in the hope that time would salve indignant feelings. But events now conspired to propel the controversy forward. The discovery of gold in California sent thousands of settlers rushing to the new land. Without waiting for congressional sanction, a California convention met in September 1849, organized a state, drew up a constitution forbidding slavery, elected senators, and pressed for admission to the Union. Texas expressed increasing alarm at the prospect of the establishment of a New Mexico territory when her boundary line with that territory was unsettled. The almost evenly divided House of Representatives, where a handful of Free-Soilers held the balance of power, was the scene of a bitter fight to elect a Speaker of the House. Only after three weeks of wrangling, interspersed with threats of disunion, did the Democrats manage to elect Howell Cobb, a Georgia aristocrat, to the speakership.

Clay's Proposals for Compromise. The Senate also now seemed hopelessly divided. The presence of such luminaries as Clay, Webster, and Calhoun could not dim the fact that the future belonged to William Seward of New York, Salmon P. Chase of Ohio, and Jefferson Davis of Mississippi. It remained for Clay and Webster, however, to contrive one final compromise. The Compromise of 1850 marked their last great victory and ended an age born in the Compromise of 1820. Subsequent efforts at compromise would be doomed.

On January 29, Clay, having obtained guarantees of Webster's support, proposed "a series of resolutions . . . which . . . together . . propose an amicable arrangement of all questions in controversy between the free and slave states, growing out of the subject of Slavery." These provided that California would be admitted as a free state; that New Mexico would be organized with the question of slavery unsettled; the western boundary of Texas would be drawn to the advantage of New Mexico but with the federal government assuming the Texas debt as a compensation; that the District of Columbia would retain slavery so long as Maryland supported it, but that the slave trade in the District would be abolished; and a new, effective fugitive act would be enacted, with Congress admitting that it had no control over the domestic slave trade.

Calhoun and the Compromise. The Compromise appeared inadequate to Calhoun. He charged that its provisions continued, as had previous compromises, the surrender by the South of its equality with the North. The old confederation had slowly given way to a unitary state that constantly advanced the interests of the North. Calhoun demanded restoration of the old order: the South should be accorded equality in the territories; there should be an end to antislavery agitation; and constitutional amendments should be ratified which would permit the South to veto acts detrimental to her interests.

Webster and the Compromise. Webster argued the case for the Union. A faithful nationalist, he asked whether the federal government had not accorded full consideration to the rights of the South. The annexation of Texas alone had been adequate evidence of the favorable accord given the South. If, as Calhoun insisted, the North outstripped the South, its advantages came not from federal action but from free labor and free institutions. He argued that the North could afford patience with the South since slavery was an institution that was doomed to wither away. The concessions proposed by Clay were temporary; in time the North was destined to win. Webster had unwittingly confirmed Calhoun's contention that further compromise meant the gradual but peaceful elimination of slavery from the South.

The Collapse of Opposition to the Compromise. William Seward exposed the deep-seated dilemma. He indicted the proposals as immoral. To impose chains upon another human being made a mockery of American pretensions to being either "true Christians or real freemen." Despite these sharp expositions of the conflicting viewpoints, a compromise was hammered out under the guidance of John Bell of Tennessee, Lewis Cass of Michigan, and Stephen Douglas of Illinois. The death of Calhoun in the early spring of 1850 removed the most serious obstacle to compromise and permitted moderate Southerners to speak of it as "the interposition of God to save the country." Then, when agreement seemed at hand, President Taylor intervened. He took the extreme position that slavery could expand no further. He proposed to admit California as a free state, to support any bill passed, no matter how harsh it might be on slavery, and to hang anyone who chose to challenge the result. Once again death intervened. On July 9, 1850, Taylor died of cholera. His successor, Millard Fillmore, was an open supporter of compromise. Efforts to rally Southern opposition to compromise collapsed at the sparsely attended Nashville Convention which was held on June 3. Though originally organized to defend Southern rights, delegates at the convention admitted that most Southerners were ready and eager for compromise. Even normally belligerent South Carolina advocated moderation. By late July, the Compromise of 1850 had become law.

The Aftermath of Compromise. The Compromise of 1850 inaugurated a period of calm, though few thoughtful people believed that the controversy had been permanently settled. As one Southern congressman noted, Southerners feared "that nothing [they] could do, short of general emancipation, would satisfy the North." To gaunt Abraham Lincoln that diagnosis seemed accurate. "The free States carry on their government on the principle of the equality of men," he wrote. "We think slavery is morally wrong," he added, "and a direct violation of [that] principle. . . . It is the only thing that threatens the Union. It makes . . . for

. . . an 'irrepressible conflict.'" For the remainder of the decade, a generation would struggle to avoid the implicit logic of an issue that seemed to preclude further compromise. Though issues other than slavery divided North and South, only the future of the slave seemed insolvable.

Chapter 14

The Tumult of Reform

It is fair to say that reform has been to America what revolution has been to Europe; and the fundamental mythology of American reform movements, like the mythology of European revolution, has remained remarkably stable through the nineteenth and twentieth centuries: the United States has had to struggle to keep its nearly perfect society pure, and to strive for a fuller perfection of its society. This has involved a constant struggle to eliminate abuses when discovered, and to restore lost innocence. It has rarely been assumed that the structure of American society is corrupt; frequently, though, it is claimed that daily practice has somehow resulted in social abuse. The prime assumption of American reform has always been that tinkering with society, rather than revolutionary upheaval, would resolve the difficulty.

THE REFORMER

The Reform Temper. Reformers have never constituted more than a handful in American society, but they have compensated for their deficiency in numbers with vigorous agitation, generated by a stubborn persistence that has overcome the most serious obstacles. Invariably they have supported their reforms with an allegiance that has defied all odds. And as this would imply, there has run through American reform a strain of unyielding moral principle which has given reformers the conviction that no matter how unpopular their agitation may be, they have the power of right on their side. To abandon the cause has always carried with it something akin to the risk of losing one's immortal soul. Faithful adherence to the moral imperative carries with it not only personal salvation but also the awareness that one has given an added dimension to the divine purpose.

From Unitarianism to Transcendentalism. The formidable doctrines of Puritanism had steadily weakened after the Revolutionary War. New England intellectuals had in growing numbers drifted into Unitarianism, a sect which rejected the Trinity, maintaining that God was unipersonal. Under the guidance of the gifted William Ellery Channing, the Unitarians were "illuminated with the idea of the absolute immutable glory of the Moral Good; and reverence for conscience [as] the key to . . . human destiny and duty." Every man, Channing taught, possesses "an element truly Divine, and worthy of all reverence." From such a belief, it was but a short step to Transcendentalism. Within the tradition of free-thinking inspired by the Unitarians, the Transcendental faith flourished. It taught that the seeds of eternal truth were contained within the soul itself, and that a soul awakened by love and knowledge exhibited divine attributes. The Transcendental concept of God was suffused with the tender and compassionate love of Jesus Christ. In 1838 the leading American Transcendentalist, Ralph Waldo Emerson, addressing the students of the Harvard Divinity School, enjoined ". . . in the soul, then, let redemption be sought." It was an injunction that was followed.

The Transcendental Faith. In the fourth, fifth, and sixth decades of the nineteenth century, the certitude of the reformer was augmented by the Transcendental values, based, as they were, in the autonomy of the individual. "The world is nothing, the man is all," preached Emerson. And his Concord companion, Henry David Thoreau, added: "Every man is the builder of a temple, called his body, to the god he worships, after a style purely his own. . . . We are all sculptors and painters, and our material is our own flesh and blood and bones." The reformer was enjoined to "enjoy an original relation to the universe," and to cease to "grope among the dry bones of the past, or put the living generation into masquerade out of its faded wardrobe." Sublimely self-confident, prepared to question and repudiate the past, the reformer went his way. And in an equalitarian democracy, he believed that a single right man could constitute a majority of one. Such beliefs promised to unsettle the status quo.

The Scope of Reform. The reformers in 1830 found multitudinous abuses in need of correction: prison conditions, education, the status of women, the evils of alcohol, the depravity of slavery, and the indifference of society to these evils. But the fervor they produced can be explained only by the profoundly religious cast of education in the first decades of the nineteenth century. In the mind of the educator, the inculcation of religious and moral values took precedence over intellectual training. Most institutions of higher education operated on the principle that their purpose was to teach commonly-held principles of Christianity and morality. Public education was no less rigorously defined and controlled by religious precepts. Until 1827, the Protestant ministry of Massachusetts retained responsibility for the supervision of public schools and faculty. But as America labored to adjust itself to a pluralistic society, the public system of education lost its sectarian hue while retaining a general body of Christian belief. Furthermore, the democratic tenor of American life was reflected in the position that publicly supported institutions of education should be publicly controlled. The American student was thus conditioned to think in terms of moral values; and as a result reform and morality were so interfused that the average reformer assumed that he had the support of eternal truths which defied refutation. It soon became apparent that reform doctrine omitted possibility of compromise. When reformers turned to political action, they undermined the system of compromise that had maintained the Union.

Religious Ferment. As Transcendentalism made inroads among American intellectuals, rural New England, upstate New York, and the shores of the Great Lakes were swept by novel religious doctrines. The extent of the religious excitement earned for the region the name "Burned-over District." Typical was the Millerite movement which had been inspired by William Miller, a Vermont farmer, to expect in 1843 the second coming of Jesus and the final judgment. The movement reached a climax on October 22, 1843, when the second coming failed to materialize. In the cold dawn of October 23, the Millerites lost their faith.

More fortunate were Joseph Smith's followers, the Latter-day Saints, better known as the Mormons. They had followed Smith until his murder in 1844, and then Brigham Young, who led them to a new home on the shores of Utah's Great Salt Lake.

Contemporary observers of certain sects noted that their literal interpretation of the Bible attracted the poor and ill-educated, who gained emotional release in the intense excitement of the camp meetings as well as gratification from membership in a unique sect.

The Utopian Communities. While the average American in the mid-nineteenth century valued a rugged individualism, a small number of intellectuals experimented in communal living, hoping that a harmonious and collective endeavor would solve world problems. No less than fifty of these experiments were launched before the Civil War, inspiring Emerson to comment: "We are all a little wild here with numberless projects of social reform. Not a reading man but has a draft of a new community in his waistcoat pocket." Among the more spectacular of these experiments were John Humphrey Noyes' Oneida Community, Bronson Alcott's Fruitlands, and the Transcendentalists' Brook Farm, in all of which efforts to build a happy idyl on earth came to naught. In each, religious idealism, governed by a touching humanitarianism, expressed itself through a Christian Socialism that aspired to restore a simpler life. Though the Oneida Community knew some success, the Alcott and Transcendentalist experiments ran afoul of the unwillingness or inability of their members to devote as much energy to labor as to intellectual endeavor. As Louisa May Alcott recalled in *The Transcendental Wild Oats,* her father and his followers had sought to regain paradise, but had failed, leaving behind "the lost Paradise, lying white and chill in its shroud of snow."

Experiments in Utopian Socialism. European experiments in socialism also gained an American audience. Aware of the social dislocations that resulted from industrial growth, American and European reformers hoped to resolve them by experiments in Utopian Socialism. In Britain, industrialist Robert Owen had established the New Lanark experiment, but his desire to achieve a better environment in which to continue his experiment led him to establish, in April 1825, a socialistic community at New Harmony, Indiana. Its success was ephemeral, because as soon as Owen returned to England, the community fragmented into near-anarchy as each member struggled to have his own unique ideas prevail.

The doctrines of Charles Fourier, the French socialist, also gained an audience, and a number of so-called Phalanxes, experiments in co-operative living, were launched, but failed. Though sponsored by Horace Greeley and Albert Brisbane, the Phalanxes could not overcome the incorrigible individualism of their membership. The proclivity to experimentation, however, even though unsuccessful, provided the atmosphere in which reform flourished, for Americans were becoming accustomed to challenging the most hoary traditions, and ready to explore the most unlikely proposals for change.

THE ESSENTIAL EDUCATION

Religion and Education. Education at the beginning of the nineteenth century was firmly founded on religious precepts. The young student learned in his primer that "In Adam's Fall We Sinned All" and that "The idle Fool is whipt at School." Guilt and punishment were intertwined. Education, however, was almost exclusively the prerogative of boys; girls learned just enough so that they could copy a few lines of simple prose and sign their names. The development of the common school system, however, gave primary emphasis to pragmatic education. Noah Webster, shortly after the Revolution, set the prevailing tone by rejecting both religious domination of, and European approaches to, the school curricula. He insisted upon the secularization of education, and worked to provide the necessary textbooks. The classics were to be read in the vernacular, not in the original. The Protestant mind, which had insisted upon the translation of the Bible, now insisted upon making the entire legacy of human knowledge available to the common man.

Democracy and Education. The spread of democratic practices in politics brought recurrent demands that education be democratized. The creation of an intellectual elite was rejected in favor of the systematic cultivation of the hearts and intellects of all Americans. The establishment of true equality required, first, the establishment of an intellectual equality. The common school provided more than an education; it secured democracy. To insure the maintenance of public education, both the federal and state governments took care to provide land for the necessary schools, even though the poverty of a region often kept anything but the rudiments of an education from being provided. Nevertheless the one-room schoolhouse, badly heated, poorly ventilated, unattractive, and staffed by undereducated and underpaid teachers, symbolized the nation's dedication to learning.

Horace Mann and Reform. By 1830 there was a growing demand for improvement of educational facilities, curricula, and teachers. In 1834 James Wadsworth, New York's commissioner of education, had secured a normal school for his state. Massachusetts, under the guidance of Horace Mann, its superintendent of education, established a normal school at Lexington, Massachusetts. Mann achieved distinction as the leading educational reformer in America, fighting for improved buildings, textbooks, and libraries. To encourage the teaching profession he urged higher salaries obtained from higher taxation. Teaching methods were subjected to constant scrutiny, the object being to secure the best education possible for children. In his *Common School Journal* and in his annual reports to the state legislature, Mann set forth with clarity his conception of education. Learning was, he insisted, the foundation stone of the republic:

> If we do not prepare children to become good citizens—if we do not develop their capacities, if we do not enrich their minds with knowledge, imbue their hearts with the love of truth and duty, and a reverence for all things sacred and holy, then our republic must go down to destruction, as others have gone before it. . . .

Other School Reformers. Mann was not alone in his struggle. In Connecticut and Rhode Island, Henry Barnard agitated successfully for similar reforms. Thaddeus Stevens led the fight in Pennsylvania for the establishment of state-supported public schools. By 1834 the fight had been won, and Pennsylvania began to provide more facilities for education. Stevens' arguments were used in 1838 in New Jersey to reach a similar result. Under the guidance of the Free School Society, the public system of education was opened to all in New York City. And subsequent public pressure on the New York state legislature brought about the establishment in the 1840s of "union districts" to enable rural areas to cooperate in the establishment of "union schools." By 1860, school reform had widespread acceptance. Even the South had launched campaigns for the extension of education to all without regard for the ability to pay. Education had been converted into a right rather than a privilege, a responsibility of the community rather than of the individual.

Prison Reform. No less a concern of the community than education was the problem of rehabilitating criminals, though this phenomenon was almost exclusively in evidence in the Northeast. As early as the Revolutionary period, agitation which drew heavily on the proposed prison reforms of the great Italian penologist Cesare Beccaria had attracted the attention of Benjamin Franklin. Many reformers found Becarria's emphasis on using prison to rehabilitate criminals, rather than to punish them, sensible and congenial. In Pennsylvania, New York, and Massachusetts, new prisons were designed to provide prisoners with the correct environment in which to develop a mental and spiritual attitude conducive to reform. At Auburn and Sing Sing, New York, and at Cherry Hill, Pennsylvania, workshops were provided in which to teach prisoners a trade. Though some doubt existed as to whether adults could be reformed, none questioned that children could be educated to a better existence if an improved environment were provided. The latter effort was made at reform schools, in which stringent discipline was maintained, but in which compliance was rewarded by special favors. At the Boston House of Refuge, the Reverend E. M. P. Wells established a system of self-government in which the boy inmates were taught self-reliance and responsibility.

The Reform of Insane Asylums. For centuries the insane had been treated as animals, but the reformer of the early nineteenth century took for his premise that the mentally afflicted were human, and that, as such, they too possessed a spark of the divine. Their condition could be alleviated, it was believed, if men would apply to it the scrutiny of reason. The traditional treatment had been to lock the insane in barred rooms, cages, jail cells, or outhouses, and they were often neglected and condemned to a life of misery. The effort to alleviate their lot was inspired by the gentle Dorothea Dix, whose sympathy had been aroused when she discovered several insane persons confined in a cold, dreary room at the East Cambridge House of Correction. With passionate intensity she informed residents of Massachusetts that insane persons in the Commonwealth were kept "in cages, closets, cellars, stalls, pens! Chained, naked, beaten with rods, and lashed into obedience!" Under the resulting public pressure, the General Court of Massachusetts authorized construction of a hospital for the insane at Worcester. This inspired Miss Dix to carry her campaign for state-supported insane hospitals successfully throughout the nation. This single, frail woman gave ample proof of the power of feminine determination, and her behavior accentuated the growing demand that women be accorded an equal place in society.

A WOMAN'S PLACE

The Early Status of Women. At the beginning of the nineteenth century, a woman's place was almost exclusively in the home, though even before the Revolution there had been some who voiced discontent with their status. Abigail Adams, wife of John Adams and mother of John Quincy, had warned her husband in the days immediately preceding the Revolution that "if particular care and attention are not paid to the ladies, we are determined to foment a rebellion, and will not hold ourselves bound to obey the laws in which we have no voice or representation." Despite such protests, an unmarried woman was made the ward of male relatives, while a wife was considered part of her husband's chattel. As late as 1850 in most states a husband possessed the right to inflict corporal punishment on his wife. Although women were active in church and school activities, they rarely participated in political or social life. Most foreigners commented upon the absence of feminine touches in American society. America was distinctly a man's world.

Women as Agitators. No facet of their secondary status escaped the notice of energetic women. The low quality of female education led Catharine Beecher, Emma Willard, and Mary Lyon to establish academies for the education of girls. Margaret Fuller, whose free-thinking father had given her a man's education, fought and argued for the admission of women into the professions; intellectual recognition for women commensurate with their abilities was her goal. Susan B. Anthony spoke for an increasing number of women teachers when she protested against the "absurd notion that women have not intellectual and moral faculties sufficient for anything but domestic concerns." It seemed implausible to her that women, if their intellect were deficient, should have the responsibility for "educating our future Presidents, Senators, and Congressmen." Harriot K. Hunt and Elizabeth Blackwell gained admission into the medical profession after surmounting the hostility of men. The admission of Antoinette Brown to Oberlin College in 1847 proved a small but significant step toward the opening of higher education to women.

The Women's Rights Movement. Feminist agitation came to a head in 1848 when Lucretia Mott and Elizabeth Cady Stanton convened a women's rights congress at Seneca Falls, New York. In a declaration similar to the nation's Declaration of Independence of 1776, but in which the offending culprit was altered to read "man" rather than "George III," the assembled women indicted "man" for having endeavored "in every way he could, to destroy [woman's] confidence in her own powers, to lessen her self-respect, and to make her willing to lead a dependent and abject life." It would be seventy years before equality was achieved, but the struggle had been firmly launched.

TEMPERANCE

The fight to destroy Demon Rum has had an extraordinary impact on the United States. Its history reveals an aspect of American life which is infrequently noted—the often unpleasant willingness of Americans to assume the role of their brothers' keepers. What might be dismissed as presumptuous interference elsewhere has often been elevated to civic duty in America, where reform frequently has led to efforts to legislate moral attitudes. The prevalence of liquor consumption, however, made the first efforts to achieve temperance unlikely to succeed. The loneliness of the American frontier made liquor a welcome release, and even the heartiest of prohibitionists admitted that "ardent spirits were used as a preventive of disease." Alcohol was also regarded as a necessary celebratory beverage. There could not be a harvest, a barn-raising, a housewarming, a log-rolling, a husking bee, a quilting bee, a wedding, a christening, or a funeral without the aid of liquor. Liquor even served as a medium of exchange in isolated portions of the West and South.

The Temperance Message. A less determined set of reformers might have despaired of success, but nineteenth-century temperance advocates were infused with sublime confidence. Originated by the clergy, the campaign against intemperance grew throughout the first three decades of the nineteenth century. It was emphasized that the elimination of the millions of dollars annually spent on liquor would enable the breadwinner to provide better food and clothing for his family. Correlations were made between intemperance and crime in order to demonstrate that the one led inevitably to the other. Prisons, reform schools, workhouses, and poorhouses were assumed by temperance advocates to be the ultimate destination of the drunkard. According to the reformers the exclusively temperate life alone could provide the dignity of republican virtue and the nobility of Christian purity.

The Organizing of Temperance Reform. In February 1826, Dr. Justin Edwards convened a meeting of the American Tract Society at Boston to organize the American Society for the Promotion of Temperance. Soon a flood of journals and pamphlets, all preaching temperance, covered the nation. At public meetings efforts were made to obtain pledges from the participants to give up liquor; Sunday schools instructed their charges both in the articles of faith and on the sinfulness of intoxicating beverages. Within three years more than a thousand temperance societies, with a total of one hundred thousand members, had been activated; by 1833, there were 4,000 locals and 500,000 members, and in the following year membership had doubled. Only the South seemed impervious to the onslaught of the campaign.

Disagreement among the Reformers. The crest of success brought with it unexpected problems. The ultraprohibitionists wanted condemnation not only of hard spirits but also of wine and malt beverages. Majority sentiment within the prohibitionist societies refused to support this extended denunciation. The extremists also pressed, unsuccessfully, for condemnation of "the traffic in ardent spirits" as *"morally wrong."* By

1836, the movement had split between the moderate position which advocated moral suasion and the ultra view which demanded legislation to check consumption of liquor. What had been launched as a voluntary campaign to persuade the individual to surrender a bad habit had given birth to an effort to impose goodness through political action.

Temperance in the 1840s. Renewed temperance agitation came in the early 1840s, when a group known as the Washingtonians adopted camp meeting and revival practices to persuade imbibers into relinquishing the habit. At huge rallies young children circulated through the crowds to obtain signatures for "cold water pledges." Poetry and song were also employed. Preachers passionately intoned the effects of drinking from "the cursed bowl," and led audiences in singing the maudlin sentiments of "Father, Dear Father, Come Home with Me Now." In thousands of churches, parish halls, and playhouses, audiences sat enraptured by the dramatization of Timothy Shay Arthur's *Ten Nights in a Barroom and What I Saw There*. Reformed drunkards took the evangelical circuit to exhort others to follow their path. Irish immigrants, who had achieved a certain notoriety for their drinking habits, received the temperance guidance of Father Theobald Mathew, a gentle Irish priest who had arrived in the country in 1849. Although divided, the temperance movement stood upon the verge of its most substantial ante-bellum success.

The Effect of the Dow Law. Between 1830 and 1840, regulation of the liquor trade was established in several states. By 1845, one hundred towns in Massachusetts had exercised local option to terminate liquor sales. In 1846, under the leadership of the redoubtable Neal Dow, Maine instituted state wide prohibition. The successful passage of the Dow Law provoked similar campaigns in other states. Vermont followed the lead of Maine in 1852, and was in turn followed by Rhode Island and by the Minnesota Territory in the same year; by Michigan in 1853; and by Connecticut in 1854. The relentless reformer, Gerrit Smith, brought about the same result in New York, and Iowa, Wisconsin, New Hampshire, Illinois, Indiana, Tennessee, and Delaware joined the ranks of the dry states in 1855. But prohibition was invariably followed by second thoughts; states frequently repealed prohibition as swiftly as they had established it. Furthermore, many sincere temperance men doubted whether legislation would provide the promised radical and nearly instantaneous cure. Fragmented among a host of societies, distracted by antislavery agitation, the effort to reform drinking habits had practically been reduced to a whisper by 1860.

THE ABOLITIONIST MOVEMENT

Early Antislavery Agitation. Of all the varieties of reform agitation initiated before the Civil War, none revealed more fully the nature of the reformer, or had a more powerful impact upon the history of the United States, than the movement for the abolition of slavery. Throughout the eighteenth century, constant and sharp attacks were made upon the institution. Two Quakers, John Woolman and Anthony Benezet, had denounced the immorality of the practice during the middle of the century, and Benezet was the first to set forth a comprehensive program of emancipation. When the statement condemning George III for vetoing colonial antislavery acts was stricken from the Declaration of Independence, Benezet concluded that "these blessings were only meant to be the *rights of white men,* not of *all men.* . . ." But the proponents of abolition did secure the exclusion of slavery from the Northwest Territory in 1787; and between 1776 and 1804, the seven Northern states provided for either immediate or gradual emancipation.

The American Colonization Society. Even in the states of Delaware, Virginia, and Maryland, lively discussion threatened to undermine the institution. Only in the Deep South was slavery secure from attack. It remained for the Upper South to support most consistently the American Colonization Society, which sought to resolve the question by returning freed slaves to Africa. The movement's supporters saw in the emancipated slave a vehicle to carry knowledge of Christ to the African heathen. Despite extensive preachments and considerable agitation, the movement returned barely 8,000 former slaves and free Negroes to Liberia during the forty years before the Civil War.

The Leading Abolitionists. As efforts to end slavery continued, a growing, increasingly articulate abolitionist press appeared in Northern and border states. Typical of the early abolitionists was Benjamin Lundy, Quaker born, who insisted that Christians had a grave moral responsibility to exert themselves for the abolition of slavery. In 1828, Lundy was joined by William Lloyd Garrison who soon added a uniquely savage note to the indictment against slavery. "The whole scope of the English language," he declared, "is inadequate to describe the horrors and impieties of slavery, and the transcendent wickedness of those who sustain this bloody system." His journal, the *Liberator,* achieved attention that made him the best known of abolitionists. The most effective response to antislavery appeals came, however, not from New England but from the old Northwest.

In Ohio, Charles Finney and Theodore Dwight Weld obtained the support of the wealthy and courageous reformers, Arthur and Lewis Tappan, in their efforts to establish at Oberlin College a seminary which would admit Negro students. Soon a growing number of young preachers, trained in evangelical methods at Oberlin, rode the western circuit preaching against slavery. The success of abolitionists in Britain in securing the passage of the British emancipation law in 1833 accelerated the efforts of American abolitionists to obtain the same goal in the United States. Although the movement for abolition appealed only to a comparatively small number of agitators, it provided a fulfilling release for its advocates. Slavery was an issue that allowed for no easy moderation; it instilled in its opponents the conviction that "the vow which we have given for freedom and humanity is registered in heaven."

Disagreement among the Abolitionists. As often happened in reform movements, increasing ideological differences among the abolitionists caused a separation between factions in 1840. Garrison, who preached immediate action by way of civil disobedience, insisted upon combining antislavery agitation with agitation for other reforms. He also repudiated all political action, and denounced the Constitution as an evil compact. It followed logically that all political institutions drawing their existence from the "cursed document" were also damned. The Weld-Finney faction, under the leadership of former slaveholder James Birney, demanded political action as a means of abolishing slavery. Rather than accept this direction, Garrison chose to disrupt the movement. From 1840 abolitionists took two diverging paths, following either the radicalism of Garrison or the Liberty Party of Birney. The most effective agitators found their way into the Birney movement. In 1844, the Liberty Party polled 60,000 votes for Birney in his presidential bid. The men who founded the Liberty Party were to give the Republican Party its antislavery hue in 1854.

Religion and Slavery. The evangelical Protestant sects were in the forefront of the agitation against slavery. The Methodists took a strong stand during the first decades of the nineteenth century against the continuance of slavery by making it sinful for church members to hold slaves; but in 1836 Southern Methodists counterattacked by insisting that the General Conference of the Church pronounce slavery a blessing and not a curse. Despite bitter opposition from abolitionist ministers, the Conference circulated a pastoral letter advising against further discussion of slavery, and denouncing abolitionist activity by Northern ministers. In 1844, the issue finally divided the Methodist Church into a

Northern and Southern Church. A similar fate awaited the Baptists when, in 1845, the Southern Baptists seceded to form independent organizations for home and foreign missions. The dispute lasted longer in the Presbyterian Church, which underwent final disruption only shortly before the Civil War. Religious disunity cast an ominous shadow over the future of political union. In a nation deeply committed to moral verities, it was not unreasonable to wonder whether a people divided by opposing convictions on the morality of slavery could long remain united.

The Southern Defense of Slavery. If the North viewed slavery as an evil, the South defended it as a positive good. When called upon to reconcile slavery with Christianity, Senator Smith of South Carolina responded promptly that "Christ himself gave sanction to slavery," and he added, "He [Christ] admonished them to be obedient to their masters; and there is not a word in the whole of His life which forbids it. . . . Christ came to fulfill the law, not to destroy it." This argument was supported by the Old Testament as well, since ". . . the Scriptures teach us that slavery was universally practiced among the holy fathers." The South had joined the North in mobilizing God in defense of their stand on slavery.

Once the sanctity of slavery had been confirmed, Southerners argued that it was a social advantage. George Fitzhugh set forth a theoretical defense in his *Sociology for the South, or the Failure of Free Society,* in which he asserted that slavery, rather than freedom, was the social norm. Arguing that a hierarchical society proved most beneficial for all, Fitzhugh frankly espoused the enslavement of Northern laborers by the factory owner and the creation of vast landed estates worked by white serfs. In his *Cannibals All! or Slaves without Masters,* he advocated reopening of the slave trade. Others argued that slavery provided the basis for the completely Christian society. Edmund Ruffin touched both the pocketbooks and psychic fears of the Southerner when he argued the economic profitability of slavery and its success in settling the race problem of the South. Despite these defenses, the tempo of attack increased both from within and without, and the Southerner, unable to ignore these attacks, consoled himself with the ultimate assurance that the world, no matter what its sentiments, had to accept its dependence upon the South, for cotton was king.

The South under Attack. Attacks upon slavery drew the Southern charge that the dispute was not (in the words of one Southern newspaper editorial) one between "abolitionists and slaveholders" but between "atheists, socialists, communists, red Republicans, Jacobins on the one side, and the friends of order and regulated freedom on the other." It followed that neither freedom of the press nor of speech should be permitted the minions of destruction. Newspaper editors like Cassius Clay found that criticism of slavery brought suppression of their journals. Southern institutions of higher learning found that academic freedom did not include freedom to pronounce forthright judgments on slavery; criticism of the practice justified dismissal from a faculty. Northern schoolteachers resident in the South came under increasing supervision as Southerners suspected they were agents of abolitionism.

Slave Uprisings. Periodic waves of fear swept the South as rumors of impending slave insurrection were spread. Though the actual number of such uprisings was small, and though Southerners insisted that their slaves were content, two major incidents unsettled the South in the ten years between 1822 and 1831. Denmark Vesey, a free Negro, organized in 1822 an unsuccessful insurrection in Charleston, South Carolina, in which several thousand Negroes were involved. An uprising was scheduled for June 16, 1822. Before it could be launched, the authorities struck. One hundred and thirty-one arrests were made: Vesey and thirty-six other Negroes were executed, forty-three were transported, and forty-eight were whipped. South Carolina lowered a curtain of secrecy around the event, and instituted stricter surveillance of its slaves. In August 1831 Nat Turner, a slave mystic, led a small group of slaves in an insurrection that terrorized Southampton County in Virginia. In less than seventy-two hours, more than sixty white men, women, and children were murdered. A thoroughly frightened South instituted severe penalties to repress anyone who distributed antislavery literature or spoke out against the institution. The tension made Southerners increasingly antagonistic to criticism, and even less certain as to the desirability of remaining within the Union when that Union tolerated attacks upon her economic and social system. An increasingly receptive audience subscribed to Fitzhugh's blunt conclusion that "free society is a failure."

Hinton Helper and The Impending Crisis. An occasional Southerner, unable to abide the silence imposed on him within the South, went North to speak his mind about the peculiar institution. One such man was Hinton Helper, a nonslaveholding North Carolinian whose book, *The Impending Crisis and How to Meet It,* denounced slavery as a plague on the South. He saw it as a systematic exploitation not only of the slave but of the poor whites. "The stupid . . . masses, the white victims of slavery," Helper protested, "believe whatever the slaveholders tell them, and thus are cajoled into the notion that they are the freest, happiest and most intelligent people in the world." Northerners seized upon the book as a guide to true class conditions in the South. It argued that the bulk of the Southern whites, nonslaveholders as they were, might be persuaded to abandon the political leadership of the planter aristocrats. (Ironically, many of Helper's views, had they been fully presented, would have been wholly unpalatable to Northern abolitionists; he was later to write three racist novels attacking the Negro for inherent inferiority. But in its text, based primarily on economic theories, *The Impending Crisis* made many assertions which provided the abolitionist movement with ammunition. And, as the work of a Southern white, its antislavery position was of inestimable value to the Northern cause.)

Fugitive Slaves. Despite Southern insistence that the slaves were content with their lot, no single irritation caused greater Southern protest than the constant, though numerically small, flight of slaves to Northern or Canadian sanctuaries. This exodus belied Southern pretensions and revealed the existence of Northerners who, despite the constitutional provision for the return of fugitive slaves and the Fugitive Slave Law of 1793, were prepared to break the law. The "underground railroad" operated by these Northerners spirited escaped slaves across Ohio, Indiana, and Illinois. Particularly active in the operation of these escape routes were Midwestern colleges like Oberlin, Knox, and Western Reserve, all of which gave practical application to their abolitionist sentiments. By 1830 similar routes crisscrossed the East, with Boston becoming a center for slaves who escaped by boat. The main goal of the escapees was Canada, whose government refused to surrender them. Though the dimension of this effort was considerably smaller than has been supposed, Southerners viewed it as further evidence of Yankee aggression.

The Effect of the Fugitive Slave Law. Southern irritation was often matched by Northern outrage when fugitive slaves were seized in the North. When the Compromise of 1850 instituted a stringent fugitive slave act which obliged Northerners to assist in the capture of escapees, the saintly abolitionist Joshua Giddings protested:

> Let me say to Southern men: it is your privilege to catch your own slaves, if anyone catches them. . . . When you ask us to pay the expenses of arresting your slaves, or to give the President authority to ap-

point officers to do that dirty work, give them power to compel our people to give chase to the panting bondman, you overstep the bounds of the Constitution.

Within a year of its passage the Fugitive Slave Law was deliberately flaunted. In 1851, an escaped slave named Shadrach was helped to escape from federal jurisdiction by a group of New Englanders, among whom were such notables as Theodore Parker, Wendell Phillips, and Samuel Gridley Howe. Efforts to convict those most directly involved failed. The law was similarly flaunted in places as distant as Syracuse, New York, and Oberlin, Ohio. In Christiana, Pennsylvania, a slave pursuer was killed. State legislatures interposed "personal liberty laws" which indicted slave catchers as kidnapers and denied them the use of local police and judicial facilities. It quickly became apparent that where the slavery issue was concerned a good part of the nation held a thoroughly anarchistic view of the law. Henry David Thoreau described it as a law that "was born and bred, and has its life, only in the dust and mire, on a level with the feet; and he who walks with freedom . . . will inevitably tread on it, and trample it under foot." The logic inherent in such an appeal to a higher moral law now asserted itself for the antislavery reformer, as man's duty to his conscience transcended his allegiance to the upholding of civil law. The appeal to conscience permitted every man to take upon himself the responsibility of exercising judicial review. Upon the rock of conscience, even the Constitution would be broken.

John Brown and His Raid. In an atmosphere supercharged with emotion, only a simple dramatic incident was needed to illuminate the depth of the national division over slavery. Such an event was provided by the strange, fiery John Brown whose antislavery sentiments amounted to a monomania. Aided by Theodore Parker, Gerrit Smith, F. B. Sanborn, T. W. Higginson, and Frederick Douglass, he plotted a slave insurrection which would open the door to a wholesale escape of slaves from their bondage into the mountains of the South. Whether the various participants fully understood the violence implicit in the plot is uncertain. With their assistance, and that of George L. Stearns, Ralph Waldo Emerson, Bronson Alcott, and Rockwood Hoar, Brown raised more than $4,000 to finance his scheme.

Harpers Ferry. Brown's plan was to attack the federal arsenal at Harpers Ferry, Virginia; it would be the first step in the overthrow of slavery. "I knew there were a great many guns there that would be of service to me," he explained, "and if I could conquer Virginia, the balance of the Southern States would nearly conquer themselves, there being such a large number of slaves in them." On the night of Sunday, October 16, 1859, Brown launched his attack. Leading a force of twenty men, he quickly seized control of the arsenal and its several millions of dollars' worth of arms and munitions, took as hostages Lewis W. Washington (a local planter and great-grandnephew of the first President), a farmer, his son, and ten slaves. Ironically, the first casualty was a free Negro who was mortally wounded by the invaders when he tried to investigate the noise at the bridge seized by Brown's men. By morning, a citizen of Harpers Ferry had been killed, numerous others were prisoners at the arsenal, the express train to Baltimore had been halted in the station, and telegraphic communications severed.

The Defeat of John Brown. News of the strange happenings at Harpers Ferry spread during the day, especially after Brown permitted the express train to continue its journey. By midmorning, both Washington and Richmond knew that a slave insurrection had started at Harpers Ferry. Militia and volunteers cut a strangely inactive Brown off in the arsenal. Federal troops under Brevet Colonel Robert E. Lee also moved on the town. In the fighting that ensued, most of Brown's party were either killed or wounded. As the news spread that John Brown had headed the attempted revolt, both North and South expressed dismay. Brown, who had sustained minor injuries, was tried by Virginia for treason. Without realizing it, Virginia gave him the chance to translate his defeat into a triumph. He presented himself to the court as a man who wished only to aid the weak and poor children of God. When the judge who was to condemn him to death asked him if he had anything to say before sentence, Brown answered with eloquence:

> I see a book kissed, which I suppose to be the Bible, or at least the New Testament, which teaches me that all things whatsoever that man should do to me, I should do even so to them. . . . I endeavored to act up to that instruction. I say I am yet too young to understand that God is any respecter of persons. I believe that to have interfered as I have done, as I have always freely admitted I have done, in behalf of his despised poor, I did no wrong, but right. Now, if it is deemed necessary that I should forfeit my life for the furtherance of the ends of justice, and mingle my blood further with the blood of my children and with the blood of millions in this slave country whose rights are disregarded by wicked, cruel, and unjust enactments, I say, let it be done.

With these words the abolitionists received a martyr. His earlier declarations that "slaveholders had forfeited the right to live" and that he accepted the shedding of blood as necessary to his insurrection's success no longer mattered. For those who sympathized with his intention—and many shared the conclusion of the New York *Tribune* that Brown and his band "dared and died for what they felt to be right, though in a manner which seems to us fatally wrong"—Brown seemed a stone tossed by God into the black pool of slavery.

The Execution of John Brown. When Brown went to the gallows on December 2, 1859, church bells tolled from Concord to Chicago. Throngs gathered in Northern towns and villages to deliver prayers for him. Southerners had tapped the depth of Northern feelings on slavery, and well might they wonder whether the Northern bells tolled the knell of Union.

THE LEGACY OF REFORM

For good or for ill, ante-bellum reformers had defined the dimensions of the abuses that marred the American dream. They compelled the nation to look upon social injustice and they proposed solutions. They refused to allow the American conscience to continue its undisturbed sleep. They delivered a manifesto of conscience which stated that the abuses of society were the responsibility of the individual. With uncompromising clarity, they told a republic of free men that the price of freedom is individual responsibility. Unfortunately, although they recognized the price of a free society, they failed to plumb the depths of the problems with which they dealt. It was sufficient for them to know that wrong existed and that they had right on their side, for they were convinced that so armed they could not fail to triumph.

The Literary Dissent. As the reformer struggled to reconstruct the world about him, America witnessed an explosion of literary genius unmatched before or again in the nineteenth century. Edgar Allan Poe, Nathaniel Hawthorne, Herman Melville, Walt Whitman, and a host of lesser lights wrote poetry, short stories, and novels which were major contributions to the literature of the English language. And they explored themes that were peculiarly American. With harsh exactitude, Hawthorne defined the dilemma of the American writer who would write romance: Europe alone provided the "poetic or fairy precinct, where actualities would not be so terribly insisted upon as they are . . . in America." Imagination alone permitted flight from the omnipresent realities of America. "No author, without a trial," Hawthorne groaned, "can conceive of the difficulty of writing a romance about a country where there is no shadow, no antiquity, no mystery, no picturesque and gloomy wrong, nor anything but a commonplace prosperity in broad and simple daylight."

The Theme of Innocence. As Hawthorne suggests, the American lived in a world where the illusion existed that a primeval innocence had been regained. Yet, from the pen of Melville came the great novel, *Moby Dick,* which told of the American Ahab's struggle to master the elements. In the vast American wilderness, he seemed to say, "lonely death" followed "lonely life." The American slaughtered the desolation of the frontier, only to be recaptured by a relentless past in which the ancient corruption of mankind reasserted itself. The theme of innocence-lost agitated even the jubilant poetry of Walt Whitman, who wrote:

O you singer solitary, singing by yourself, projecting me,
O solitary me listening, never more shall I cease perpetuating you,
Never more shall I escape, never more the reverberations,
Never more the cries of unsatisfied love be absent from me,
Never again leave me to be the peaceful child I was before what there in
   the night,
By the sea under the yellow and sagging moon,
The messenger there arous'd, the fire, the sweet hell within,
The unknown want, the destiny of me.

But the Americans of mid-century made the gallant fight, hoping to redeem what they thought to be the last best hope of mankind: their America.

Chapter 15

The Two Nations

In the mid-nineteenth century the growing industrial revolution pointed up the existence of two "nations" within each of the more progressive national states. In 1845, Benjamin Disraeli described the two figurative nations in England as being founded, one on industry, urbanization, and the exploitation of the working classes, the other on agriculture, the farmhouse and village, and established relations between squire and tenant.

Applying this concept to the United States at the middle of the century, one finds an important difference: the budding industry of America was based upon the championing of individual freedom, while a considerable portion of agrarian America seemed increasingly committed to preserving the institution of slavery. Between North and South a marked disagreement over fundamental principles served to demarcate an increasingly sharp boundary. Simultaneously, railroad construction rapidly increased, providing the foundation of a rapidly expanding national economy. Thus America revealed a contradictory image, with political disunity paralleled by the conditions for economic integration. The vast influx of immigrants (largely from Ireland and Germany) subsequent to 1845 accentuated political dislocations, but also supplied a large and growing reservoir of labor upon which industry, especially in the North, could draw. If a single word were needed to describe America's economic and political situation at the middle of the nineteenth century, the word would be *flux;* but as with most one-word generalizations, extensive analysis and explanation are required before the term *flux* may be fully and accurately comprehended in its present application.

THE SOUTHERN NATION

In 1850, the fifteen states that comprised the cotton kingdom could hardly have been called a coherent entity. In the Upper South, as Calhoun recognized, loyalties had become increasingly muted as the nineteenth century wore on.

Poor Whites and Southern Aristocrats. The tiny state of Delaware actually had fewer slaves in 1850 than it had had ten years earlier. It seemed only a matter of time before the border areas would become free. As large numbers of Northerners settled in St. Louis, resentment flared against domination of Missouri by a handful of slave oligarchs. Similar conflicts existed in Kentucky and Tennessee; in the latter state, Andrew Johnson voiced the antagonism of the poor whites for Southern aristocrats. Throughout the South there were increasing signs of a burgeoning class conflict between the slave oligarchs and the yeomen farmers. Only the antipathy of the yeomanry to the Negro prevented an even more extreme conflict. All Southern whites seemed to agree upon one thing: the Negro had to be kept in subjugation. Often resentful under the domination of the wealthy slave owners, nonslaveholding whites were nevertheless kept in check by an overriding fear that disunity in the ranks of the whites would serve to advance the blacks to equality. In the end it was as a solution to the race problem rather than as a source of profit that slavery commanded a Southern consensus.

The Slave Population. In 1860, ownership of more than 3,600,000 slaves was concentrated in the hands of barely 384,000 slaveholders out of a total Southern population of more than 8,000,000 whites. But even these figures are deceptive. Some three hundred slaveholders owned more than two hundred slaves each; twenty-three hundred were masters of one hundred or more slaves; less than two hundred thousand owned more than ten slaves each; and seventy-seven thousand owned only one slave apiece. The concentration of wealth in the upper classes of Southern society permitted three-tenths of one per cent of the white population in Alabama, for instance, to own almost 130,000 slaves, one-third of all the slaves in that state, together with nearly a third of all cultivated lands and almost two hundred and fifty million dollars of the state's seven hundred million dollars in assessed valuation. The system had already created an opulent class, small in number, living among an overwhelming majority of depressed whites and slaves.

The South and Cotton. The census returns of 1860 indicated that in less than ten years the number of Southerners who drew their livelihood from some aspect of the plantation system had declined from one in three to one in four. Of this number only two hundred and fifty thousand enjoyed the full fruits of plantation life. The now legendary plantation was, therefore, the exception rather than the rule in the South. It provided a goal toward which the ambitious Southern youth aspired; but, by 1850, access into the ranks of the plantation elite had become nearly impossible. Profits from the plantation system remain a matter for acute debate, even today. While a number of plantation owners cleared $50,000 on a single crop, the average planter found that his staple, cotton, governed in price by distant and often indecipherable fluctuations of the market at Liverpool, provided only bare sustenance. And the system was wasteful: land was farmed until it was exhausted; the black laborer was often misused. The planter dismissed such charges with the argument that the Negro, not the land, was his true investment.

The Limitations of Slavery. Frederick Law Olmsted, a Northern observer traveling through the South shortly before the outbreak of the Civil War, noted that Southerners frequently described slavery as a blight. "The Negroes are the weight continually pulling us down," complained one Southern housewife. "Will the time *ever* come for us to be free of them?" Slave conditions varied. On the larger plantations adequate, though rude, provision was made for them. Self-interest dictated such action since each slave constituted an investment with a cash valuation in the plantation roll book. Rather than risk the lives of their slaves, owners often hired white workers, usually Irish immigrants, to do the dangerous work of draining swamps and loading heavy bales of cotton on riverboats. There also existed a widespread custom of paternalism toward slaves which caused more than one mistress of a plantation to complain that instead of having the care of only one family, she was "the nurse, physician, and spiritual adviser to a whole settlement of careless slaves." More than one observer noted that the system was conducive to wholesale prodigality.

The Abuses of Slavery. But slavery also lent itself to vicious abuse. Fanny Kemble, an English actress of wide fame, recalled that "every Southern woman to whom I have spoken on the subject has admitted to me that they live in terror of their slaves." To keep slaves subjugated, laws were passed which denied slaves the opportunity to learn to read.

Night patrols roamed the countryside to make certain that the slave kept in his cabin and curfew was imposed on free Negroes and slaves alike. Mere misdemeanours were punished by flogging; capital crimes led almost invariably to lynch law, with roasting at the stake a frequent punishment. The sale of slaves split families and destroyed the most elemental base of personal stability for the Negro. The occasional sadistic master had his slaves utterly at his mercy. Slavery degraded not only the slave but also the master. Its corruption permeated every layer of Southern life. Most detrimental to the democratic ideal was the insidious association that came to be attached in the South to the word "free." One young Southerner complained:

> We have got to hating everything with the prefix free, from free Negroes down and up through the whole catalogue—free farms, free labor, free society, free will, free thinking, free children, and free schools—all belonging to the same brood of damnable isms.

The Economic Decline of the South. As the South drew apart from its association with the rest of the country, it expressed increasing alarm at its declining economic importance. Whole areas of the Virginia and Carolina tidewater had reverted to overgrown wilderness, while concentration on staple crops obliged the South to import large quantities of food. And the available supply of slaves retarded the introduction of farm machinery. The self-sustaining agriculture of the North, with its emphasis on careful husbandry, farm machinery, and scientific usage of the land, had scarcely any parallel in the South. Few travelers failed to make an adverse comparison between Northern and Southern agriculture. The absence of industry in the South made the region wholly dependent upon outside manufacturers. An Alabama journalist protested:

> Our slaves are clothed with Northern manufactured goods, have Northern hats and shoes, work with Northern hoes, ploughs, and other implements, are chastised with a Northern-made instrument, are working for Northern more than Southern profit. The slaveholder dresses in Northern goods, rides in a Northern saddle, . . . patronizes Northern newspapers, drinks Northern liquors, reads Northern books, spends his money at Northern watering places. . . . In Northern vessels his products are carried to market, his cotton is ginned with Northern gins, his sugar is crushed and preserved with Northern machinery; his rivers are navigated by Northern steamboats, his mails are carried in Northern stages, his Negroes are fed with Northern bacon, beef, flour, and corn; his land is cleared with a Northern axe, and a Yankee clock sits upon his mantelpiece; his floor is swept with a Northern broom, and is cov-

ered with a Northern carpet; and his wife dresses herself in a Northern looking-glass; . . . his son is educated at a Northern college, his daughter receives the finishing polish at a Northern seminary, his schools are supplied with Northern teachers, and he is furnished with Northern inventions and notions.

Southern View of the North. Perversely, many Southerners drew the wrong conclusion from this relationship, assuming that it indicated the Northern need for a market rather than an involuntary Southern dependence. Though many Southerners preached the urgency of developing home industry, there existed an insurmountable obstacle: the Southern association of industry with Yankee pettiness and lack of chivalry. A South Carolina planter complained:

> Free society! we sicken at the name. What is it but a conglomeration of greasy mechanics, filthy operatives, small-fisted farmers, and moonstruck theorists? All the northern and especially the New England states, are devoid of society fitted for well-bred gentlemen. The prevailing class one meets with is that of mechanics struggling to be genteel, and small farmers who do their own drudgery, and yet are hardly fit for association with a southern gentleman's body servant.

The Southerner assigned to the Northerner a status beneath that of slaves. The bond of sentiment wore thin; the bond of affection had long since snapped.

THE NORTHERN NATION

Changes in Northern Agriculture. By 1860, the output of American factories, mills, shops, and mines exceeded in value that of agriculture. Almost eighty per cent of all such industry was concentrated in the North. An extraordinary growth of wheat and corn production had occurred on the Midwestern prairies. As the locus of breadstuff agriculture shifted westward, the farm implement industry swiftly developed, as the persistent labor shortage on Northern farms compelled the farmer to rely on machinery. Improved plows became commonplace; mechanical reapers replaced scythes; mowing machines cut the work of mowing hay by a third; and threshers, grain drills, rotary broadcast seeders, corn planters, cultivators, and corn shellers were all found on Western farms. Crop diversification increasingly characterized Northern agriculture. In the East, the swift growth of cities brought an increasing shift from grain culture to garden crop agriculture, orchards, and dairy farming.

Some Southerners expressed alarm at the growth of truck farming in Delaware and around Norfolk, Virginia, fearing that economic ties would soon disorient their allegiance to the South. Large-scale meat-packing enterprises grew up in Cincinnati, St. Louis, Jersey City, and Philadelphia. Swift freight trains carried perishable fruits, berries, and vegetables to urban markets in season, and a growing number of Northern farmers looked to the cities and towns for their profits. Without quite realizing it, the Northern farmer came to think of himself as a businessman rather than as a self-sustained agrarian.

Mercantile Capitalism. At the outset of the nineteenth century, most American businessmen were committed to commerce. The agricultural economy was dependent upon foreign consumers and the importation of manufactured goods. It was not unusual for the merchants to encompass every phase of commerce, building their own ships, serving as banker, insurance agent, commission agent or factor, and operating rope factories, distilleries, flour mills, or hardware shops. Only after 1815 did specialization of functions characterize commerce. The development of common carriers resulted in exporters using such ships rather than their own vessels. Numerous transient vessels prowled the seas seeking a cargo and following no particular route. In addition, there were numerous trading vessels that followed fixed routes and operated on regular schedules. A vast fleet of sloops transported huge quantities of goods in the coastwise trade. By the 1850s, magnificent clippers, often weighing over 1,500 tons, and achieving speeds unequaled by subsequent sailing ships of their size, carried the American flag over the globe. Large fortunes were accumulated by such traders as John Jacob Astor, Alexander Brown, and Stephen Girard—fortunes that found their way into urban real estate, banking, and manufacturing.

The Expansion of Industry. The growth of industry at this time was spectacular. Both woolen and cotton industries reached maturity in the decade before the Civil War. The introduction of the power loom at Waltham, Massachusetts, in 1814, by Francis Cabot Lowell, permitted the combination of spinning and carding in a single plant. Improvements in both looms and carding machines had added to the efficiency of the industry. By the 1850s Northern factories were consuming a quarter of all the raw cotton raised in the country. Similar advances occurred in the metal industry. The use of anthracite coal had improved the processing of iron ore in the 1830s; in the early 1850s, charcoal smelting was introduced to process pig iron. In 1851, William Kelly, a Kentucky ironmaster, independently discovered the Bessemer process for decarbonizing molten iron by forcing oxygen through it. As production exceeded 800,000 tons in 1860, machines processed finished iron into nails, bolts, files, screws, firearms, locomotives, and a wide range of other metal products.

An efficient machine tool industry had been established in the first decade of the nineteenth century under the guidance of Eli Whitney and Simeon North. Mass production through the use of interchangeable parts characterized such industries as watchmaking and firearms. The expansion of industry brought a rapid advance in the use of power resources. Water power had been almost fully exploited in New England by 1830. Elsewhere, steam power was generated to operate industries as varied as glass blowing and textile printing. Coal mining had been an insignificant activity in 1820; in 1860, well over 14,000,000 tons were produced.

The Rise in Patents. The traditional ingenuity of the Yankee expressed itself in a growing number of patented inventions. Between 1850 and 1860 alone, the average number of patents increased from 993 to 4,778 annually. Even as the war approached, Elias Howe's sewing machine, patented in 1846, promised to revolutionize clothes-making. Between 1840 and 1860 the value of manufactures quadrupled, reaching almost $2,000,000,000. Since the work force had not quite doubled within the same period, increasing from 791,000 to 1,311,000, the increase in manufactures indicated that worker productivity had more than doubled —largely as a result of the new inventions.

Northern and Southern Industry Compared. The disparity between North and South was sharply illustrated by the textile industry. Total Southern production barely exceeded $8,000,000, while that of New England exceeded $80,000,000. The city of Lowell, Massachusetts, alone produced more than the entire South. Although woolen textile production had almost tripled between 1840 and 1860 in the North, the wool industry was almost nonexistent in the South. Though Dixie might complain that the nation drew its wealth from Southern cotton, the North dismissed this as a pretense which ignored the obviously flourishing condition of Northern agriculture and industry. James Russell Lowell concluded that the origin of Southern complaints about the Union derived from jealousy of Northern prosperity:

> The fault of the Free States in the eyes of the South is not one that can be atoned for by any yielding of special points here and there. . . . Their crime is the census of 1860. Their increase in numbers, wealth and power is standing aggression. It would not be enough to please the

Southern States that we should stop asking them to abolish slavery,—what they demand of us is nothing less than that we should abolish the spirit of the age.

The New Society. The spirit of the age might well have been described as an enthusiastic pursuit of profit and a consequent amassing of wealth. In the North a wealthy industrial class had been created. The omnipresent factory had become the symbol of the North in much the same way that the plantation symbolized the Southern way of life. As the size of factories grew, legal innovation permitted the exploitation of joint-stock companies to disperse risk, and ownership was usually concentrated in the hands of a few well-to-do entrepreneurs. Until the 1850s, the labor force was drawn chiefly from native-born Americans. A good many were young farm boys and girls who took factory employment to supplement their families' inadequate incomes. An unusually large proportion of the workers was made up of women and children. In 1832, for example, the woolen factories of Massachusetts had a work force of which 58 per cent were women and children, while the cotton industry of Lowell, in 1836, employed more than 5,000 young women in a total work force of 6,000.

Factory Conditions. Hand-in-hand with the commercial success of the factories, however, went the deplorable conditions under which the factory employee labored. The average employee worked for twelve to fifteen hours a day to earn between one and six dollars a week. Factories were adversely compared by observers with prisons. Little provision was made for hygienic or sanitary conditions, and meals were as often as not eaten on the job. Efforts to improve his working conditions by organizing a union made the worker liable, under English common law, for prosecution on charges of conspiracy. The instability of the economy subjected the worker to sporadic employment. Only the existence of a farm homestead to which he could return protected him from the worst effects of recession or depression.

Nevertheless, life on the farm was often possible only with income earned in the factory, and employers interested in an ample supply of labor often resorted to the construction of large tenements in which to house their employees. It was not unusual for an employer to supervise the moral conduct of his workers and to provide Sunday school for his child employees. In Northern New England under the Waltham System, large numbers of young women were recruited to work in remote textile factories, and they were housed in adjacent boardinghouses. Strict supervision of the activities of these women, coupled with compulsory church service, was the hallmark of the system. Though the physical conditions of the dormitories were primitive by modern standards, they approximated standards experienced in the poorer sections of many towns and in virtually all farmhouses. The most striking aspect of the Waltham System was the efforts of its employees to achieve self-improvement. Though they worked a seventy-hour week, they made time to attend lectures, organize literary magazines, and to study foreign languages. And in several instances—the most spectacular being at Lowell, Massachusetts, in February 1834—they staged protest strikes against their living conditions; these strikes, though unsuccessful, attracted attention to the girls' long hours, and to their low wages of two cents an hour.

Laissez-Faire. Despite the extensive agitation for other types of reform during the ante-bellum period, little attention was directed toward improving working conditions. Ralph Waldo Emerson summed up the prevailing laissez-faire attitude of reformer sentiment on this subject when he announced that he resented having to give a dime to alleviate worker distress. One small reform measure was instituted in Massachusetts and Rhode Island when these states passed laws requiring the attendance of children under fifteen at school for at least three months of the year. And in 1848 Pennsylvania forbade the employment of children under the age of twelve. Usually, however, the dominant laissez-faire ideals of the American democracy determined the conditions of a workingman's life.

Worker Organization. The sporadic efforts made to improve working conditions before 1860 are most significant as a consequence of their failure. In Philadelphia, the failure of carpenter journeymen in 1828 to obtain a ten-hour day led to the organization of a workingman's party which seems to have played a role in mobilizing workingmen to vote for Andrew Jackson. The inflationary rise in the cost of living before 1837 spurred the efforts at organization. Most notable was the formation at New York, in 1834, by delegates from six manufacturing centers, of the National Trades' Union. It called at that time for public education, homestead legislation, restrictions on child labor, and minimum hours of employment. Strikes for higher wages and the ten-hour day were not uncommon, but the instability of the economy severely reduced labor's bargaining power. One major advance came in 1842, when the Massachusetts Supreme Court in the case of Commonwealth *v.* Hunt upheld the right of the worker peacefully to organize and to agitate for improvement of his conditions.

A good part of the agitation for improvement in working conditions, especially the campaign for improved educational facilities, originated with the middle class, who believed that a group of educated men was less apt to disturb the status quo than an ignorant mass. In addition, there was a strong demand for the lessening of the harsh laws governing indebtedness. It was estimated in 1829 that no less than 75,000 people were jailed annually for nonpayment of debt. Such agitation helped to alleviate the worst abuses, but usually worker organizations needed help to achieve their ends. Independent workingmen's parties were absorbed into the Jacksonian Democrats by 1832, where they provided a radical leavening. In New York they became the Loco Foco faction that often fought the conservative wing of the Democratic Party, and managed in 1834 to force Tammany to nominate a trades' union leader, Ely Moore, as Congressman. The Loco Foco emphasis upon the right of every man to pursue his self-interest unimpeded so long as he did not infringe on the "natural rights" of other men reveals an important aspect of trades' union organization that prevailed before the Civil War. The unions were often organizations of small independent producers (as opposed to factory workers) who were fearful that a state with strong regulatory powers would obstruct achievement of an equalitarian state in which all were accorded equal status and treatment.

The Ascendancy of the North. By mid-century the North had achieved the stature of an industrial power second only to Great Britain. Even the most simple of observers could deduce that the industrial might of the North would continue to grow by leaps and bounds. In one area—the growth and organization of railroads—the signs conclusively indicated that further massive changes impended.

RAILROADS

The key to the development of the American economy had become the railroad. Where scarcely a mile of track had existed in 1830, more than 30,000 miles crisscrossed the nation in 1860. To a considerable extent this leap in construction had resulted from the desire of various cities to secure to themselves the trade of the surrounding countryside. The unfortunate result was a variety of railroad gauges, ranging from the 4 feet 8½ inches that prevailed in New England to the 6 feet employed by the Erie Railroad. In the South a 5 foot gauge prevailed. In many instances the railroads proved mere extensions of already existing waterways. As farmers preferred the slower but cheaper water transportation to the high rates of rail transportation, trains were used most frequently to send goods to a port where they could be reloaded on barges. Even if a manufacturer or farmer had wished to use rail transportation only, he faced the difficulty and expense of frequent unloadings and reloadings as one line ended and another began.

The Trials of Railroad Travel. Railroad travel frequently presented as many problems as railroad shipping. Nor was travel exactly a pleasure. Fanny Kemble recalled her experiences while on a theater tour in America.

> The windows . . . form the walls on each side of the carriage, which looks like a long greenhouse upon wheels; the seats, which each contain two persons (a pretty tight fit, too), are placed down the whole length of the vehicle, one behind the other, leaving a species of aisle in the middle for the uneasy . . . to fidget up and down, for the tobacco-chewers to spit in, and for a whole tribe of itinerant fruit and cake sellers to rush through, distributing their wares at every place where the train stops.

Service was slow, often agonizingly so, and schedules, when they existed, were not observed. Since much of the system was single track, one train had to pull onto sidings for another to pass in the opposite direction. Any disruption of the schedule meant long waits while the trainmen determined whether it was safe to proceed. In winter the cars were frigid; in summer, torrid. Under the best of circumstances rail travel was a trial, and only by comparing it to stagecoach could one readily conclude that it was in fact an improvement over earlier conditions.

The Growth of Railroads. During the 1850s the investment in railroads increased from $300,000,000 to $1,150,000,000. The extraordinary dynamism of the American economy could be seen in the fact that the United States had almost half the world's rail mileage. Although the South had only a third of the nation's trackage, it had witnessed a spectacular rail growth, with its mileage increasing fourfold between 1850 and 1860. Only the Northwest, with an eightfold increase, exceeded Dixie's expansion. The extension of trackage in the South and West coincided with the establishment of trunk lines in the Northeast. By 1861 the Grand Trunk Railway of Canada connected Portland, Maine, with Detroit, Michigan, by way of Toronto and Montreal. Four trunk lines connected the Ohio River and Lake Erie with the eastern coast. The New York Central Railroad, under the guidance of Erastus Corning and Dean Richmond, linked Albany and Buffalo. To the south, the Erie, Pennsylvania, and Baltimore and Ohio provided passenger service across the Alleghenies; the trip took sixteen hours as compared to the week once needed to make the same journey by stagecoach.

Western Railroads. As railroads penetrated into the hinterland, Western towns boomed. Chicago, which had been a mere village in 1820, was a flourishing city of more than 100,000 by 1860. No less than eleven railroads entered the city. Built by funds provided by a congressional land grant, the Illinois Central ran the length of Illinois, offering, by 1856, seven hundred miles of continuous trackage. A sister railroad, the Mobile & Ohio, connected the South with the Chicago rail center. On the eve of Civil War a continuous road of more than one thousand miles paralleled the Mississippi River. By the late 1850s the major trunk lines from the East were energetically seeking access to Western terminals such as Chicago and St. Louis. Consolidation and standardization had become the goals of railroad management.

Economic Ties between East and West. The railroads substantially reoriented freight movement. Increasingly, bulk produce was transported eastward by rail to the Great Lakes ports, through the lake system to the Erie Canal, and then through it to the eastern seaboard, rather than southwest along the Ohio and Mississippi Rivers to New Orleans and thence by sea to the East. The railroad reoriented sectional alignments from West and South to West and East. The movement of wheat into Chicago increased ninefold between 1852 and 1856, while that of corn quadrupled in the same period. Cotton from the Upper South moved toward Savannah and Charleston rather than New Orleans. Water passenger service suffered a precipitous decline as rail transportation steadily improved. By 1860 the reduction of travel time between St. Louis and Boston to forty-eight hours, for instance, had dealt a death blow to the inordinately long trips by water and stagecoach. The railroad had revolutionized transportation by 1860.

The Transcontinental Railroads. American horizons had been expanded by the iron rails that now bound together the nation. Even before the Mexican War, plans for spanning the continent with a railroad had been considered with interest by both Congress and business. Chicago, St. Louis, Milwaukee, Memphis, New Orleans, and Vicksburg all labored to obtain the eastern terminus of the proposed western route. In March 1853 Congress appropriated $150,000 with which to chart surveys for four alternate routes. Secretary of War Jefferson Davis persuaded Franklin Pierce to request the purchase of the Gadsden territory (included in present-day Arizona and New Mexico) in 1853 in order to improve chances for the selection of the southern route. Stephen

Douglas pressed for the organization of the Kansas-Nebraska territories in order to improve the chances of the central route. Private entrepreneurs like former Secretary of the Treasury Robert J. Walker urged the development of a route that would cross Texas and then push on to California. Efforts to develop one or the other of these routes, however, ran afoul of conflicting sectional ambitions. Eventually all four transcontinental routes were constructed, but in the final years before the Civil War Congress failed to authorize any construction, since each section viewed the choice of the route as an index of its relative power. Once war came, the newly formed Republican Party redeemed a platform pledge and authorized construction of the central route. On July 1, 1862, in the midst of a rapidly expanding conflict, Abraham Lincoln signed the first Pacific Railway Bill. An excellent index of the North's power was its ability to prosecute a vast war effort while preparing to build a railroad to span a continent.

REORGANIZATION OF POLITICAL PARTIES

Immigration. All Americans, with the possible exception of Indians, have one thing in common: either they are immigrants or the descendents of immigrants. From its very beginnings, America has been the terminus of a long series of migrations; from all over the world, men have always looked to America as a haven in which to escape their problems—social, religious, economic, and political. Until the 1840s, the largest proportion of immigrants came from Britain. This was natural, as these early immigrants shared with the young Americans both a common language—English—and a common faith—Protestantism. After 1845, however, two new major streams of immigrants arrived in this country. One was drawn from the Catholic sections of Ireland, the other from western Germany. Between 1845 and 1855, no less than two million Irish poured into the country, and during the same period, at least a million Germans came. Their arrival created social problems that would substantially affect American life.

The Irish Immigrants. The migration of the Irish was an unplanned, terror-stricken flight from famine. The failure of the potato crops between 1845 and 1850 had brought death by starvation to more than a million Irishmen. A similar plight overtook the Germans, although most of them had a few small resources to protect themselves in their "flight from hunger." The systematic exploitation to which Ireland had been subjected by the British deprived the Irish peasantry of even the most elementary resources. "The emigrants of this year [1847]," reported one Irish newspaper, "are not like those of former ones; they are now actually *running away* from fever and disease and hunger, with money scarcely sufficient to pay passage for and find food for the voyage." A horde of destitute, often sick immigrants descended upon Boston, New York, Philadelphia, and New Orleans.

Immigration Laws. Faced with epidemics of typhus, cholera, and diphtheria, eastern ports established medical camps outside their confines. Since the welfare resources of these cities were never large, emergency legislation was rushed through to protect them from the cost of immigrant indigency. The Massachusetts state legislature passed a bill obliging shipmasters to deposit bonds of $1000 to protect Boston from the cost of maintaining destitute passengers. The New York immigration commissioners found their efforts to maintain quarantine and relief costly and difficult. When the annual cost of assisting immigrants in New York alone reached $380,000, anti-immigrant nativists protested loudly. Even so, as one commissioner noted, the funds barely scratched the surface of the need. "We are obliged," he wrote, "to keep supplies of provision in our office in the city to give those who come in famishing. . . . The women and children we cannot thrust aside."

Native Reaction to Immigrants. The paucity of their means caused most immigrants to settle in the port cities where they landed or in adjacent regions. They provided a dependable source of labor, the size of which depressed wages. That factor, along with their alien habits, created antipathy toward them among native Americans, and particularly offensive to many was the newcomers' Catholic faith. In the middle 1850s these antagonisms created an anti-immigrant political movement that, for a brief time, seemed on the verge of becoming a permanent political party.

The Rise of Anti-Catholicism. Outbreaks of violence against Catholics had not been unknown in America before the 1850s. A small minority in an overwhelmingly Protestant country, the Catholics had protected themselves from absorption by taking a strong stand against the use of any Bible other than the Douay version, by urging the establishment of parochial schools as a means of protecting the young from "perversion of their religious beliefs" in common schools, and by energetically proselytizing among non-Catholics. The exclusiveness of the Catholic Church convinced many Americans that it was an enemy to democratic institutions. A growing flood of anti-Catholic literature led Catholic authorities to protest:

Not only do they assail us and our institutions in a style of vitupera-
tion and offense, misrepresent our tenets, vilify our practices, repeat the
hundred-times-refuted calumnies of the days of angry and bitter contention in other lands, but they have even denounced . . . us as enemies to
the liberties of the republic, and have openly proclaimed the fancied
necessity of obstructing our progress, and of using their best efforts to
extirpate our religion.

During the 1830s anti-Catholic sentiment led to attacks upon Catholic
convents and churches. In Charlestown, Massachusetts, the Ursuline
convent was burned to the ground. Sordid descriptions of convent and
priestly life poured from the pens of such psychotics as Maria Monk,
whose *Awful Disclosures of the Hotel Dieu Nunnery of Montreal* titil-
lated the nation. It mattered little that Maria Monk was eventually revealed to be a woman of opportunist principles and loose morals; her
description confirmed the image of Catholicism that fitted Protestant
prejudices.

Against this background, the arrival of hundreds of thousands of
Catholic immigrants stimulated concerted political efforts to restrict the
inflow. The appearance of the American Republicans in 1843 marked
the inauguration of proposals that the period of naturalization be extended to twenty-one years, that only native-born Americans be elected
to political office, and that foreign interference in American institutions,
social, religious, and political, be rejected. Wide distribution of anti-
Catholic propaganda by the American Bible Society, the American Tract
Society, and the American Home Missionary Society added to the preparation of Americans for the political effort of 1854. Itinerant preachers
stirred crowds to attack churches in places as widely scattered as New
York City and Sidney, Ohio. Priests were waylaid and beaten; nunneries
in New Orleans and Charleston were threatened with destruction. The
year 1854 saw the fusion of anti-immigrant and anti-Catholic feeling in
a single political party.

The Immigrant as a Burden. "America has become the sewer into
which the pollutions of European jails are emptied." So proclaimed an
increasing number of agitators for immigration restriction. Plagued with
poverty, often driven into slums, and ignorant of American customs and
laws, the newly arrived immigrant frequently lapsed into criminality or
vice. More than half of the 27,000 persons convicted of violating the
law in 1850 were foreign-born, though the latter constituted less than
twenty per cent of the population. Furthermore, the immigrants gravely
dislocated political arrangements wherever they concentrated. In Boston,

between 1850 and 1855, the native-born voters increased by 14.72 per cent, while the foreign-born voters increased by 194.64 per cent. Fear grew that within less than a generation foreign-born voters would out-number the native-born. Even more disturbing was the immigrants' cus-tom of voting as a group, and usually in support of the party that opposed established authority.

The Order of the Star-Spangled Banner. Temperance reformers viewed with horror the conspicuous consumption of intoxicating bever-ages by both the Irish and the Germans. The tenacity which character-ized both groups as they clung to connections with the old country caused the doubters to raise questions about their loyalty. Committed to an alien church, they also seemed committed to alien nations. In 1849, Charles B. Allen of New York organized a secret patriotic society called the Order of the Star-Spangled Banner. It swiftly grew to nation-wide dimensions through the use of secret rituals which appealed to the Amer-ican propensity for lodge organizations. The explicit purpose of the movement was summed up in the question asked of a candidate for full membership: "Are you willing to use your influence and vote only for native-born American citizens for all offices of honor, trust or profit in the gift of the people, to the exclusion of all foreigners and Roman Cath-olics in particular, and without regard to party predilections?" Members were pledged to secrecy and their repeated reply to all questions—"I know nothing," gave them their nickname, the Know-Nothings.

The American Party. By 1854, the movement had entered into poli-tics as the American Party. It threatened to speed the disintegration of the two major parties. The American Party swept Massachusetts, where the entire state ticket and both houses of the General Court were over-whelmingly of their party. In Delaware and in Pennsylvania, where a combination of Whigs and American Party members prevailed, their in-fluence proved dominant. No less than 75 congressmen were identified with the movement. In 1855, Rhode Island, New Hampshire, Connecti-cut, Maryland, and Kentucky joined the new movement. In New York, California, Louisiana, Mississippi, Virginia, Georgia, Alabama, and Tennessee the Know-Nothings commanded unusual strength. In the South, the disintegration of the Whig Party had left former Whigs the alternative of joining the Democrats or the new American Party. Many chose the latter. So impressive was the strength of the new party that Catholic journals, along with such Democratic stalwarts as the New York *Herald,* concluded that election of a Know-Nothing as President in 1856 was a certainty.

The Republican Party. Out of the disintegration of the Whig Party and the free-soil split within the Democratic Party, there was erected a new Republican party. It was dedicated to the establishment of free soil, to the restriction of slavery to its existing confines, to the encouragement of industry with protective tariffs, to fiscal reform, and to the securing of transcontinental railroad routes terminating in the North. Since Republican commitment to free soil excluded any growth of strength in the South, the party accepted sectional rather than national dimensions. And as it grew in strength in the North, the South gave increasingly solid endorsement to Democratic candidates. Indirectly, at least, the emergence of the Republicans as a dominant party may be traced to Stephen A. Douglas; his Kansas-Nebraska bill united the discontented Whigs and Democrats for joint political action in 1854. Others, unwilling to join either of the old parties, settled for a new departure, assuming that in a new party an open organization would permit the ambitious a ready recognition normally denied in an established party. By the end of 1854, local groups at Ripon, Wisconsin, and Jackson, Michigan, had taken the label Republican. Elsewhere, the Anti-Nebraska label was used to describe those political malcontents who groped toward a new party. Unorganized, often incoherent in their program, frequently restricted to single states or regions of a state, Anti-Nebraska candidates swept New England local elections, elected a governor in Iowa, and carried all twenty-one house seats in Ohio. In Illinois, an Anti-Nebraska candidate, Lyman Trumbull, was elected to the Senate. When the Congress elected in 1854 convened, the Republicans fused with the Anti-Nebraska supporters to emerge as the second party in the land. It was an amazing development since there exists no evidence that the original movements had a central direction. Rather it had been the eruption throughout the North of political discontent, triggered largely by local leaders, acting independently, and only subsequently thinking of a national organization.

The Emergence of Two Major Parties. American politics had begun to polarize between the strident Republican demand for free soil and the insistent Democratic demand for a recognition of the rights of slavery. By 1857 Know-Nothingism, with its limited program, had faded; its members joined either the new Republican Party or the old Democratic Party. Either directly on the issues of slavery, or in some disguised expression of the same, Americans had come to a crisis of choice. The Democrats, seeking to compensate for losses from their ranks, appealed for immigrants' support, and declared in their platform against "the attempt to enforce civil and religious disabilities against the rights" of immigrants to acquire and enjoy citizenship. By so doing, the Democratic Party assumed an identification that has come to be called pluralistic democracy. Simultaneously it defended the Southern right to maintain slavery. It had suspended moral judgment and disregarded the American Protestant ethos. Its rival, the Republican Party, expressed the hopes and aspirations of a largely Northern, Protestant, primarily native-born, population. These two parties were destined to resolve the issue of slavery; and in the process, they would come to speak for the two Americas.

Chapter 16

On the Brink of Secession

The disintegration of the traditional parties during the 1850s signaled the final bankruptcy of sectional compromise. More than once the politicians had negotiated a settlement between the sections, but from 1854 they would struggle without success to resolve the slavery dispute. Everyone knew that the issue of slavery had to be removed from the realm of politics but no one knew how to do it. The search for resolution that had seemingly ended in success in 1850 actually ended in failure in 1861. By the time war came in April of that year, the country had accepted the succinct definition Lincoln had given the issue at Cooper Union (in New York City) in his speech of February 27, 1860:

> If slavery is right, all words, acts, laws, and constitutions against it, are themselves wrong, and should be silenced, and swept away. If it is right, we cannot justly object to its nationality—its universality; if it is wrong, they cannot justly insist upon its extension—its enlargement. All they ask, we could readily grant, if we thought slavery right; all we ask, they could as readily grant, if they thought it wrong. Their thinking it right, and our thinking it wrong, is the precise fact upon which depends the whole controversy.

But it had taken a seemingly innocent decision in 1854 to bring the controversy into sharp focus.

POPULAR SOVEREIGNTY

The Kansas-Nebraska Act. As part of the Compromise of 1850, the Utah and New Mexico Enabling Acts had left the future of slavery to the decision of residents in the territories. In leaving a final decision to those immediately affected, the question of slavery was removed from the national arena where it was apt to cause sectional discord. Since the Compromise aroused no immediate, perceptible criticism, it seemed that a sensible solution to the problem of free soil had been achieved. The Compromise also brought a lull in the agitation that had precipitated the crisis in 1850. The removal of this source of discord permitted the Democrats in 1852 to elect Franklin Pierce. The Whig candidate, Winfield Scott, carried only Vermont, Massachusetts, Kentucky, and Tennessee. The Democratic victory marked the end of the Whig Party as a national force (although the Democrats were not yet aware of it in the joy of their success) and laid the groundwork for the formation of a national anti-slavery party. Everything seemed to point toward a time of tranquillity and recuperation for the Democratic Party.

Pierce, a "dark-horse" candidate, soon revealed his indecisive character. He permitted William Marcy, his Secretary of State, and Jefferson Davis, his Secretary of War, to determine the course of national affairs. In Congress the young Senator from Illinois, Stephen A. Douglas, revealed a driving ambition that had already set its sights on the presidency. Then, on January 23, 1854, Douglas fractured the peace. He introduced into Congress an amendment to the bill organizing the territories of Kansas and Nebraska which provided that "all questions pertaining to slavery in the Territories, and in the new States to be formed therefrom [be] left to the decision of the people residing therein, through their appropriate representatives." Since the new territories were part of the Louisiana Purchase, the bill suspended operation of the Missouri Compromise on the ground that it had been superseded "by the principles of legislation of 1850, commonly called the compromise measures." Douglas had introduced the Democratic solution to Free-Soil: the doctrine of "Popular Sovereignty."

Precisely why Douglas chose to introduce his amendment remains obscure. There is little doubt that he was partly motivated by his wish to organize the territory in order to prepare for construction of the central route of the transcontinental railroad. His move was also a response to the determination of Senator Archibald Dixon of Kentucky to offer an amendment repealing the Missouri Compromise line. To avoid a sectional dispute that would divide the Democratic Party anew, Douglas chose to meet the offer, assuming that the earlier placid acceptance of the proposals incorporated in the Compromise of 1850 insured an easy solution. His comparative indifference to the extension or contraction of slavery made it difficult for him to understand the fears that his amendment would stir in antislavery and free-soil circles. It subverted the Wilmot Proviso by throwing open to the expansion of slavery not only the Mexican Cession but all federal territories. It made no difference that Douglas sincerely doubted that slavery would expand into any of the territories, or that he really believed that a sensible resolution of the slavery issue could be attained by leaving it to the local residents to decide its future.

Douglas' simple solution opened a veritable Pandora's box. Smith, Sumner, Chase, Giddings, and their antislavery allies seized upon the proposal as an opportunity to issue an *Appeal of the Independent Democrats in Congress to the People of the United States* in which they charged that the Kansas-Nebraska Act opened "all the unorganized territory to the ingress of slavery." The document pointedly described the bill as "a gross violation of a sacred pledge; as a criminal betrayal of precious rights; as part and parcel of an atrocious plot to exclude from a vast unoccupied region immigrants from the Old World, and free laborers from our own states, and to convert it into a dreary region of despotism, inhabited by masters and slaves." From that moment onward, the free-soil issue blotted out all other national problems.

The Ostend Manifesto. Fear of the seeming determination of the South to extend slavery was heightened by filibustering expeditions by adventurers into Central America and by efforts to annex Cuba. The sudden seizure by Spanish authorities of the cargo of the *Black Warrior,* an American steamer, provoked such sharp demands for retribution as the proposal by John A. Quitman (former governor of Mississippi) to organize a private invasion of Cuba for the purpose of making it into a slave state. On May 1, 1854, John Slidell of Louisiana proposed in the Senate a suspension of the neutrality laws. The proposal was sidetracked by the administration since it was unwilling to add to the blazing controversy precipitated by the Kansas-Nebraska Act.

Secretary Marcy, however, had secretly authorized Pierre Soulé, the American minister to Spain, to attempt purchase of Cuba for a sum not to exceed $130,000,000. If this proposal failed, Soulé was directed to use all his efforts "to detach that island from the Spanish dominion and from all dependence on any European power." To improve chances of success, Soulé was directed to meet with James Buchanan, Minister to Great Britain, and John Y. Mason, Minister to Paris, to "compare opinions as to what may be advisable, and . . . adopt measures for perfect concert of action in aid of negotiations at Madrid." At the conclusion of this consultation there appeared the Ostend Manifesto, an appeal compounded of explanations as to why the United States should purchase the island and why Spain should sell it. The Manifesto spelled out the consequences for the Pearl of the Antilles should they refuse to sell:

> Cuba, in the possession of Spain, seriously endangers our internal peace and the existence of our cherished Union . . . then, by every law, human and divine, we shall be justified in wresting it from Spain if we possess the power; and this upon the very same principle that would justify an individual in tearing down the burning house of his neighbor if there were no other means of preventing the flames from destroying his own home.

When enemies of the administration caused these proposals to be revealed on the floor of the House of Representatives, further weight was added to Northern charges that Southern expansionism was insatiable. The Pierce administration, eager to free itself from further embarrassment, dropped the proposal altogether.

Bleeding Kansas. Once the issue of Kansas had been raised, it quickly became the focal point in a tug-of-war between radical sentiments in the North and South. At first Southern opinion seemed unresponsive to charges that the Kansas-Nebraska Act was a deliberate conspiracy to expand slavery. In time, however, Southern newspapers and politicians began to answer Northern attacks in kind. Still, they seemed content to argue thus:

> The Nebraska bill contemplates only the recognition of a principle. All agree that slavery cannot exist in the territories of Kansas and Nebraska. . . . It is not, therefore, because of its effect in extending the sphere of slavery that the South advocates the repeal of the Missouri restriction, but solely for the reason that it would indicate the equality and sovereignty of the States. The single aim of the Nebraska bill is to establish the principle of *Federal non-intervention* in regard to slavery. . . .

In the years between 1854 and 1857, however, many Southerners came to believe that the authors of the Kansas-Nebraska Act had intended to make Kansas a "slave state."

Since the people of Kansas were to determine their own fate, both North and South recognized that the establishment there of a majority committed respectively to free soil or slavery principles was imperative for their cause. In the North, Eli Thayer, an abolitionist, organized the New England Emigrant-Aid Company to assist free-soil emigration into the Kansas Territory. Farmers began to enter the region from Missouri. Disputes over land titles and town sites soon confused the scene. Lawlessness and overt violence became an everyday characteristic of Kansas life. The Congressional decision on November 29, 1854, to call for the election of a territorial delegate, and a territorial legislature in March 1855 sent Missourians across the border to vote in the election. Often they combined voting with horse stealing, and both acts intensified an already explosive situation. Similar events in the Nebraska territory attracted little attention; it was in Kansas, and in Kansas alone, that the prelude to the national struggle over slavery had been inaugurated.

BUCHANAN AND THE URGENCY OF THE SLAVERY PROBLEM

The Election of 1856. By the time of the 1856 election, the political problems the republic faced had reached an impasse which seemed to bar any solution. The political flux of the decade had disrupted the normal party organizations as sectional ties came into conflict with political loyalties. The voter in 1856 was offered a choice among the Know-Nothings, the newly formed Republican Party, and the Democratic Party.

In the three-cornered race, former President Millard Fillmore, the candidate of the American Party, polled less than a million votes, while John C. Frémont, the Republican candidate, ran a strong second. James Buchanan, the Democratic candidate, was elected, but he received less than 46 per cent of the total vote.

James Buchanan. During the struggle over Kansas-Nebraska, Buchanan had had the good fortune to be away from the United States. He therefore escaped involvement in the disruptive issues raised by the Act. He had the additional virtue of having given yeoman service to the Democratic Party, providing diligent rather than brilliant leadership. Trained in the school of political compromise, he accepted his election in 1856 as a warrant for seeking out a new compromise which would eliminate the slave issue from politics. At his inaugural, he notified the nation that an impending decision of the Supreme Court would "speedily and finally" decide the future of the institution in the territories. He added as his own contribution the thought that the final determination of the question of slavery in a territory could be reached only when the size of the population justified the drawing up of a state constitution. By indirection, he seemed to commit himself to the idea that Congress could not exclude slavery from the territories. Within days of Buchanan's inaugural, the nation was rocked by a fateful Supreme Court decision.

The Dred Scott Case. Dred Scott, a Missouri slave, sued his ostensible owner, John F. A. Sanford, for his freedom on the ground that his previous residence in the Wisconsin Territory, which was closed to slavery under the Missouri Compromise, had freed him. At issue was not only the constitutionality of the Missouri Compromise, but also the question as to whether Congress or the territorial legislature was responsible for the regulation of slavery. Although they had originally intended to resolve the issue by upholding a Missouri decision which confirmed Scott's continued enslavement, two minority justices, John McLean and Benjamin Curtis, eventually announced their determination to issue dissents in support of the Republican contention that Congress had the power of regulation. To the announcement of this intention Justice James Wayne of Georgia replied that he would insist that the Court majority meet the challenge directly and find on the questions raised. He received support from Buchanan, who naively felt that the nation would "cheerfully submit" to the Court's decision. He ignored one thing: seven of the nine justices were Democrats, and five were Southerners; any decision favorable to the South would have a partisan and sectional flavor in the North.

On March 6, 1857, an aged and soft-spoken Chief Justice Roger Taney delivered the majority opinion which denied Scott's plea on the ground that as a slave he had no right to sue a citizen of one state, as a citizen of another, in a federal court. The Court decision then declared the Missouri Compromise unconstitutional: Congress had no power to interfere in the territories with property or other rights possessed in the states. To exclude a Southerner's slaves from the territories would be to deprive him of his property without due process of law as provided under the Fifth Amendment.

The Court had denied a major Republican premise—that Congress could regulate slavery in the territories—and had affirmed that the slave was not a human being but an item of property. The Court's decision, far from settling the fundamental issue, converted the question of slavery from a sectional to a national problem.

The North reacted quickly, loudly denouncing the decision. Northerners boggled at the implication contained in the decision that maintained, according to one critic, that ". . . slavery, instead of being what the people of the slave States have hitherto called it, their peculiar institution, is a Federal institution, the common patrimony and shame of all the States." The Northerners had been unwilling to support the Fugitive Slave Act; now they refused to accept Supreme Court decisions without question.

Robert J. Walker and Kansas. Violence in Kansas had proved the undoing of its first two governors, Reeder and Geary, neither of whom had been able to restore the peace. Buchanan, in an attempt to avoid sacrificing a third, appointed as governor Robert J. Walker, an old associate from the days of Polk and a man whose service as Secretary of Treasury had gained him considerable prestige. Walker accepted reluctantly and with the understanding that Buchanan and his cabinet concurred "in the opinion . . . that the actual bona fide residents of the territory of Kansas, by a fair and regular vote, unaffected by fraud or violence, must be permitted, in adopting their state constitution, to decide for themselves what shall be their social institutions." With this firm commitment to popular sovereignty, Walker journeyed to Kansas where he soon found himself challenged by the pro-slavery element. He labored, however, to obtain a final settlement which would both admit Kansas as a free state, and insure that the new state would send to Congress Democrats who would throw their weight behind efforts to protect slavery from radical Northern attacks. Since to achieve these goals he needed to persuade Free-Soilers to go to the polls, he assured them that the elections would be unhindered and that any state constitution finally composed would be submitted to a free vote.

The Lecompton Constitution. The state convention that was elected to draw up a constitution meeting at Lecompton was dominated by the pro-slavery element. Responsive to Southern demands, the members contemplated sending their finished work directly to Congress without first submitting it to the Kansans. (Rather than risk such a flagrant disregard for political form, the Lecompton convention, upon completion of its labor, had provided that the Kansans would be permitted to vote only on whether further admission of slaves into the new state was to be denied. Slave property already in the territory would be protected until 1864 when the Constitution could be amended. To this limitation Walker objected.) Complicating the already confused political situation, the October elections revealed that Kansas had elected a Republican as a territorial delegate to Congress and a Democratic territorial legislature. When Walker explored the returns, he realized that large-scale fraud had been perpetrated, and that the Democratic legislature had been elected by ballot stuffing.

Buchanan and Douglas. At stake in the subsequent national debate over submission of the Kansas Constitution to the electorate was the doctrine of popular sovereignty. The refusal to submit the entire constitution to the territorial electorate blatantly subverted Douglas' proposals. Since Douglas faced a strong challenge for his Senate seat in 1858, he could hardly accept such repudiation; his survival as a political leader was at stake. When Walker realized that the Buchanan administration planned to accept the Lecompton constitution, he allied himself with Douglas, and both men then broke with the President. When Buchanan threatened to discipline Douglas, the Little Giant declared: "I will show you that I will do what I promised. By God, sir, I made Mr. James Buchanan and by God, sir, I will unmake him."

Rift in the Democratic Party. The ensuing battle rocked the Democratic Party. In a nation beset with a financial crisis that was precipitated in the autumn of 1857 by overspeculation in land and railroads, and worsened by the inability of a chaotic fiscal system to meet a swift deflation, the political upheaval added to the general dismay. The 75 Southern Democrats in the House found many of their 53 Northern fellows openly allied with Douglas. Subjected to energetic challenges by Republicans, the Northern Democrats had to find a way to survive. For them popular sovereignty was the only answer to free soil; to renounce it was to destroy their major political selling point. When the Lecompton constitution (with slavery protected) was approved by Kansas in an election boycotted by Kansas Free-Soilers, renewed charges of fraud were heard. Douglas organized a vociferous Democratic minority pledged to popular sovereignty which soon made it obvious that they would disrupt the party rather than accept the Lecompton constitution. Despite Buchanan's efforts to have Kansas admitted under the Lecompton document, a stalemate developed in Congress. A compromise was finally hammered out in March and April of 1858, providing that the Lecompton constitution would be resubmitted to the Kansas electorate. The English Bill, as it was called, assured the Kansans that if they accepted the resubmitted constitution the federal government would grant the new state 3,988,868 acres plus five per cent of the sales price on 2,000,000 acres. If they rejected the constitution, Kansas would be denied admission until the census proved that she had the 90,000 inhabitants necessary for admission into the Union. As Walker predicted, Kansas voted down a constitution "baptized in forgery and perjury."

The façade of Democratic unity had been barely maintained. The circumstances were ripe for a final disintegration.

THE RISE OF ABRAHAM LINCOLN

Lincoln and Douglas. Douglas, aware that he had made mortal enemies among both Republicans and Buchanan Democrats, reluctantly accepted the English Bill. For a time, when the fight with Buchanan had been hottest, some Republicans had proposed that Douglas be made their candidate for re-election as Senator from Illinois. But he refused to make a final break with the Democratic Party, rejecting all efforts to lure him into a repudiation of the popular sovereignty doctrine. The administration, still smarting from his stubborn fight over Lecompton, determined to employ its full patronage power to remove him from the Senate. Once again Douglas plunged into the fray. He declared that the central issue of his campaign for re-election in 1858 was his intention to fight both Buchanan Democrats and Republicans.

To oppose him, the Republicans nominated Abraham Lincoln, a gangling lawyer whose acute reasoning had impressed all those who heard him speak. Lincoln had had only a brief national political career as a one-term Whig Congressman during the late 1840s. He had been born in a forest lean-to, had been raised in a log cabin, and was a self-educated lawyer. Possessed of both a wry sense of humor and an ability to define with precision the issues in any controversy, he presented a formidable challenge to Douglas. The Little Giant had one advantage: he was a national figure. To tap some of this support, Lincoln challenged Douglas to "divide time and address the same audiences." The incumbent reluctantly agreed to seven debates which would begin on August 21 at Ottawa, Illinois, and end on October 15 at Alton.

The Lincoln-Douglas Debates. The ensuing debates resulted in the re-election of Douglas to the Senate in 1858; but by establishing the national political reputation of Lincoln, they did much to insure his election to the presidency in 1860. Douglas, short and thickset, with a large head, dark complexion, and fierce bulldog look, offered a severe contrast to the tall, slender—many thought ugly—Lincoln. Both men were compelling speakers, but Lincoln, less well-known than Douglas, revealed himself as a man of commanding presence and forceful presentation. The ensuing debates, during September and October 1858, showed clearly that both men were capable of rapier-like thrusts and masterful exposition.

Douglas charged that Lincoln was unwilling to accept the nation that the founding fathers had created: a nation in which half of the states endorsed slavery. He charged him with advocating racial equality, which Douglas concluded was abhorrent to Northerners and Southerners alike. Lincoln denied that he advocated such a situation, arguing "I have no purpose, either directly or indirectly, to interfere with the institution of slavery where it exists." He added, "I have no purpose to introduce political and social equality between the white and black races." He did believe, however, that the Negro had "the right to eat the bread . . . which his own hand earns." And he believed that the territories had to be closed to slavery so as to put the peculiar institution on the road to extinction.

It was at Freeport that the debate illumined the essential disagreement between the two men. There Lincoln stated that, though he did not oppose the Fugitive Slave Act nor the right of a territory's inhabitants to choose slavery, and that he had never advocated the abolition of slavery in the District of Columbia nor the prohibition of the domestic slave trade, he did believe that Congress had the right to exclude slavery from the territories. He then asked Douglas a crucial question: how did he reconcile his doctrine of popular sovereignty with the Dred Scott decision? Could a territorial legislature close a territory to slavery? Douglas affirmed that it could. "If the people are opposed to slavery," he declared, "they will elect representatives to that body who will by unfriendly legislation effectually prevent the introduction of it into their midst." No Supreme Court decision could alter or prevent that result. Lincoln knew that this would inevitably be his opponent's position; although it might offend the South, Douglas would (in his own words) "let it offend them, as . . . he [meant] to hold on to his chances in Illinois."

When the Illinois votes were counted on November 2, 1858, the Republicans had polled 125,275 votes, as opposed to 121,090 for Douglas Democrats and 5,071 for Buchanan Democrats; but unequal apportionment of seats in the Illinois legislature assured Douglas' re-election. The Little Giant had nevertheless paid a heavy price for his victory, since the South viewed his Freeport stand as a denial of their full judicial rights. For the party as a whole the results of the 1858 elections meant disaster. Democrats were defeated throughout the North while Republican strength increased. The balance of power in the House of Representatives rested with the Douglas Democrats; by all rules, Stephen A. Douglas ought to have emerged as the dominant figure of the party. In the

North, Democrats, beleaguered by the growing Republican challenge, turned to the Illinoisan for guidance, but Southern Democrats resolved to prevent his nomination for President in 1860. Rule or ruin of the Democratic Party dominated its partisans' thoughts.

THE ELECTION OF 1860

The Charleston Convention. Rarely has a more inopportune place for a political convention been chosen than Charleston, South Carolina, in 1860. Here, in the citadel of disunion, the Democratic Party was fated to disintegrate. From the outset of the Democratic convention it was obvious that the Douglas men were a hard phalanx, and that the Deep South would press for federal protection of slavery as a platform plank. The decision of the Douglas supporters to accept the formulation of a platform *before* nomination of a candidate insured that a jarring fight would follow. The fight raged before a passionate audience of Charlestonians, who loudly supported the Southerners who insisted that neither Congress nor territorial legislatures had the right to exclude slavery from the territories. The Douglas men would only reaffirm the doctrine of popular sovereignty and willingness to allow the Supreme Court to settle disputes. It was evident that the Douglas men, even if they lacked votes to nominate their own man, had a sufficient balance of power to prevent the nomination of anyone they opposed. Confronted with defeat, the Southern radicals, taking their cue from William L. Yancey and the Alabama delegation, withdrew from the convention. The convention was adjourned shortly afterward, when it became obvious that Douglas' supporters were determined to nominate him. Plans were made to reassemble at Baltimore on June 18. There, amid scenes of intense bitterness, Stephen A. Douglas won the empty honor of running as the candidate of a hopelessly divided Democratic Party.

The Chicago Convention. On the shores of Lake Michigan in a great convention hall called the Wigwam, the Republicans opened their convention on May 16. The favored candidate was William Seward (of New York), whose long senatorial career had put him in the forefront of the new party. He had both the strengths and weaknesses of political prominence. He was admired by some and known by all; and yet he was deeply distrusted by those who feared that his previous radical stance against slavery would hasten the disruption of the Union. He had also made formidable enemies; Horace Greeley viewed his imminent nomination as a personal insult. When the convention gathered, efforts were afoot to nominate a candidate other than the New York Senator. David Davis, Lincoln's manager at the convention, made a series of promises to the Indiana, New Jersey, and Pennsylvania delegations. Wigwam galleries were shrewdly packed with Lincoln supporters who supplied vociferous enthusiasm in support of their candidate. On the third ballot, Lincoln won.

The Campaign. The confusion of the politics of the 1850s came to a climax in 1860. Four tickets bid for the American voter's support. After Douglas' nomination, the Southern Democrats nominated Vice-President John C. Breckinridge to run on a slave-code platform. A coalition of former Whigs, wishing only to preserve the Union, nominated John Bell of Tennessee. (Their opponents contemptuously dismissed them as the Old Gentlemen's Party.) Douglas carried his campaign throughout the nation, defending himself both in the North and in the Deep South. He fought, feeling certain that he would run second to Breckinridge in the Deep South, second to Bell in the Border States, and second to Lincoln in the North. His program was the preservation of the Union.

Lincoln viewed the torrent of hot threats pouring from the South without alarm. He dismissed the possibility that his election would result in "any very formidable effort to break up the Union." Persistent threats of secession were looked upon as bluffs. When Lincoln was urged to reassure the South that its institutions would not be challenged, he replied that the South needed only to read his previous statements to find the requested assurances.

When the votes were counted, Lincoln had won with 180 electoral and 1,866,452 popular votes. His combined opposition had 2,815,617 popular votes but only 123 electoral votes. Even if all the opposed votes had been cast for a single candidate, Lincoln still would have won by an electoral majority. As he himself would point out subsequently, he had won constitutionally; but one could hardly contend that a national consensus existed.

THE CRISIS OF SECESSION

Time and again Southern spokesmen had threatened to secede; in the course of the 1860 campaign they had singled out the election of a "black Republican" as a sufficient cause. If the South failed to act now, its threats in the future would be as wind among dry, fallen leaves.

The Confederacy. When the South Carolina legislature convened to elect a new governor, outgoing Governor Gist, bent upon secession, obtained authority from the legislature to order the election of a secession convention. On December 20, 1860, the Palmetto State severed its ties with the Union. Between January 9 and February 1, 1861, she was joined by Mississippi, Florida, Alabama, Georgia, Louisiana, and Texas. Though formidable Unionist sentiment existed in Georgia, Lincoln persisted in refusing to make any promises intended solely to enable this sentiment to prevail. On February 4, 1861, delegates from all the seceded states except Texas—the Lone Star delegation arrived later—met at Montgomery, Alabama, to form a confederacy.

Taking the name The Confederate States of America, the Confederacy was born in the excitement of a convention which knew that it was both creating a nation and disrupting a Union. The delegates occupied themselves with the thoroughly American task of writing a constitution, and the final document revealed the conservative inclinations of the Southerners: it often repeated word for word the Constitution of 1787. Only in its guarantees of state rights and slavery, and in its minor modifications of government machinery, did the new document differ from the original. Stringent restrictions were placed upon expenditures by the provision that all appropriation bills be approved by a two-thirds vote in both houses of Congress, and by giving the President the power to veto individual items in such bills. The President was restricted to one six-year term, "the right of property in Negro slaves" was confirmed, and Congress was forbidden to institute protective tariffs. To emphasize the confederate nature of the new nation, the preamble stated that the document derived its existence from "the people of the Confederate States, each State acting in its sovereign and independent character."

The convention finished its work by provisionally electing Jefferson Davis as the new nation's President and Alexander H. Stephens its Vice-President. Neither had been prominent in the agitation for secession. Davis had attempted during the 1860 campaign to have Douglas, Bell, and Breckinridge withdraw in favor of a single conservative candidate whom all opponents of Lincoln could support. But once Davis assumed the Presidency he supported the Confederate cause with singleminded devotion; it is unlikely that anyone could have performed more effectively in the post. Stephens, who had fought valiantly but unsuccessfully to prevent Georgia from seceding from the Union, followed his state. Yet he carried out his task dutifully rather than with any profound belief in the Confederate cause. Once Lincoln had issued his appeal to the North for troops after the bombardment of Fort Sumter, the task of mobilizing the South fell upon Davis.

With the beginning of war, Virginia, Arkansas, North Carolina, and Tennessee joined the original seven states of the Confederacy. None accepted secession with enthusiasm. When Virginia finally seceded (as did the others, despite strenuous Unionist opposition), the conflict of loyalties caused seventeen counties to detach themselves from Virginia during the summer of 1861, and to rejoin the Union as West Virginia. In the other border states—Delaware, Maryland, Kentucky, and Missouri—despite strong Southern sympathies, and the establishment in Kentucky and Missouri of secessionist governments, Unionist sentiment prevailed. But once any state had decided to secede, Southerners generally rallied to their new government.

Buchanan and the Secession Crisis. The "lame duck" President found himself trapped by the events following the election. On the one hand, he was sworn to uphold the Constitution; on the other, he found members of his official family actively aiding the seceding states. How was he to fulfill his constitutional oath? Buchanan's solution to the problem was to do nothing. With the guidance of Jeremiah Black, his Secretary of State, Buchanan decided that he would turn over to Lincoln a united nation. Since he denied that secession was possible, it logically followed that federal coercion could not be used; one cannot oppose what cannot happen. Instead, he left the final decision to the South. The federal government, he stated, would continue to perform its constitutional duties and would defend itself if attacked.

By early January, the Southern members of the cabinet had withdrawn. Buchanan's profound respect for the law now governed his behavior. Confronted with Southern threats of intervention to prevent Lincoln's inauguration, Buchanan promised, "If I live till the 4th of March, I will ride to the Capitol with Old Abe whether I am assassinated or not." At the same time, he urged all parties to explore the possibilities of compromise. His moderation kept the peace during the final weeks of his administration, even though both Republicans and Secessionists had gone beyond compromise.

No Compromise. The Senate organized a Committee of Thirteen on December 18 to seek ways out of the worsening crisis. At the very outset the Republicans followed instructions from Lincoln to entertain no compromise that involved surrender of the principle that the territories were closed to slavery. Of the several plans submitted, only that of Senator Crittenden of Kentucky had a chance of winning approval. He proposed six amendments to the Constitution, including one which extended the Missouri Compromise line to California, permitting and protecting slavery south of the line, and leaving it to the residents of each territory to decide upon their admission to the Union whether or not to continue slavery within their boundaries. The other amendments insured the continuance of slavery in the District of Columbia as long as its residents wished it and as long as Maryland or Virginia had slavery; forbade its abolition in federal territories within slave states; denied the federal right to regulate interstate slave trading; permitted Congress to compensate owners of fugitive slaves rescued by force; and finally denied the possibility of any future constitutional amendments aimed at disturbing the slavery settlement. The proposal foundered on Lincoln's determination to make no concession that would grant slavery room for expansion. Equally fruitless were the efforts of the House Committee of Thirty-three. Lincoln had determined that if the break were to come, it would have to be now.

THE INAUGURATION OF LINCOLN

On February 11, Lincoln started eastward from Springfield. As he traveled, he patiently constructed a cabinet which included all his major rivals for the Republican nomination in 1860. William Seward headed the State Department; Salmon P. Chase, the Treasury Department; Simon Cameron, the War Department; and Edward Bates received the Attorney Generalship. News of a plot to assassinate Lincoln as he passed through Baltimore brought a hasty revision of his traveling plans. On February 23, after an overnight journey from Harrisburg, Lincoln entered Washington. Nine days later he was inaugurated as the sixteenth President of the United States. Before a vast assemblage he delivered an inaugural address that combined plea and threat. He warned the South that the Constitution made it incumbent upon him "that the laws of the Union be faithfully executed in all the States" and notified the nation that "the power confided to me will be used to hold, occupy, and possess the property and places belonging to the government. . . ." He ended his address with the plea that "We must not be enemies." In a nation hovering on the brink of war, he eloquently invoked "the mystic chords of memory, stretching from every battlefield, and patriot grave, to every living heart and hearthstone, all over this broad land" which would "yet swell the chorus of the Union, when again touched, as surely they will be, by the better angels of our nature."

FORT SUMTER

The transfer of power from Buchanan to Lincoln had been effected quietly. For thirty-nine days Lincoln puzzled over which course to pursue. Then the question was resolved for him. Shortly after Lincoln's election, Buchanan had permitted the federal garrison at Fort Moultrie (which stood in an exposed position) to withdraw to Fort Sumter, far out in Charleston Harbor. The move had been allowed by federal authorities despite subsequent bitter protests from local residents. But a later move by Buchanan to send supplies had been repulsed. The garrison, commanded by Major Robert Anderson, was in danger of being starved into submission.

Lincoln's Stratagem. On April 4, 1861, Lincoln decided, over the protests of most of his cabinet and of General Winfield Scott, Chief of Staff of the United States Army, to send supplies to Fort Sumter and, at the same time, to send arms to Fort Pickens at Pensacola, Florida. He informed the secessionist government that the garrison was to be supplied, and assured it that the mission would be conducted peacefully. If there was to be a fight, the North was not going to fire the first shot. Lincoln had shrewdly placed the Confederate states in a position from which they could not readily extract themselves. If they allowed the North to supply the fort, they would have daily to stare at this bastion of federal authority in the center of one of the busiest harbors of the Confederacy; if they used force to compel its surrender, they would clearly label themselves rebels who defied the federal authority. Lincoln's maneuvering had focused the problem: if there was to be a war, the South would start it.

The War Begins. The South did not wait for the supply ship to arrive. At dawn on April 12, 1861, shore batteries under the command of General P. G. T. Beauregard sent the first shells over the harbor. On the following day, Major Anderson surrendered his command. The Stars and Stripes were lowered, not to be raised again for four years.

Lincoln responded to the attack by issuing a call for "the militia of the several States of the Union, to the . . . number of seventy-five thousand." The war was on.

As the first shell arched over Charleston harbor the agrarian republic perished. In the four years of war that were now to rack the nation, a torrent of blood would flow and mountains of treasure would be consumed. But the supremacy of the Union would be maintained. The old agrarian ideal of a confederate republic would be subjected to a test of arms and found wanting. On a hundred scattered battlefields a new republic would be forged. In the crucible of war a nationality would be confirmed.

Chapter 17

The Civil War

A civil war is, perhaps, the most tragic of wars. Within what has been a single nation, brother may fight brother, son may attack father, and friend may inflict wounds upon friend. The devastation, both physical and psychic, is borne by a single people. And when the war is ended, a single people know at the same time the triumph of victory and the despair of defeat.

Of all the wars America has fought, none has been more costly in terms of American lives than that fought between 1861 and 1865. Viewed at its outset as a chivalrous war in which the restraint of gentlemen would prevail, the War between the States had become, when it ended, a total war. A war of armies had become a war involving an entire people. The stakes were absolute, the targets both military and civilian. Cities were put to the torch; whole armies were wiped out. A social system founded in slavery was uprooted, and the government and nation that lost the war were utterly destroyed. The Confederacy established at Montgomery, Alabama, during February 1861, fought courageously for its existence; and, though it sacrificed without stint, it perished without a trace. It bequeathed to a reunited nation only its bitter memories and lost hopes. Its history is the story of the Civil War.

THE STRENGTH OF NORTH AND SOUTH

A simple comparison of the war-making potential of North and South would make it appear that in 1861 the North had an overwhelming superiority in every way. But a simple equation which treats both regions as units misses the complex divisions that plagued both Union and Confederacy.

Population. A comparison of white populations gives the North a preponderance of about four to one (the North having slightly more than 20,000,000 white inhabitants and the South slightly less than 5,500,000); but the addition to the Southern total of the more than 3,600,000 slaves, who provided a vast reservoir of agricultural and industrial labor, reduces the Northern advantage to slightly more than two to one. In fact, slave labor permitted the South to mobilize a higher percentage of its manpower than the North. A further bar to fine computation of the relative strength of the two sections is found in the divided loyalties which existed in the border states and among copperheads, those Northerners who opposed the war. Neither side could draw upon its total manpower, though the North, in terms of potential quantity, had a distinct advantage.

Industry. The North clearly had the advantage of industrial superiority. Against the 110,000 Northern industrial establishments and the 1,300,000 Northern industrial workers, the South had only 18,000 factories and 110,000 industrial workers. In an industry as basic to war as the iron industry, the leading iron-working state of the Confederacy, Virginia, had only 20 iron forges and rolling mills, whose produce in 1860 was valued at $1,667,000; while comparable figures for the leading Northern producer, Pennsylvania, showed 87 forges and rolling mills with an annual product of nearly $16,000,000. In the manufacture of firearms the Confederacy produced, in 1860, less than $73,000 of the national total of $2,342,700. Under the guidance of Josiah Gorgas, the Confederate Ordnance Bureau created a war industry almost from scratch. The Tredegar Iron Works at Richmond provided heavy guns. Farther south, at Salisbury, North Carolina; at Augusta, Atlanta, Athens, and Columbus, Georgia; and at Selma, Alabama, large Southern arsenals were developed. To supplement these internal sources of supply there were imports from abroad. Such imports continued almost to the end of the war, ending only with the fall of Wilmington, North Carolina, early in 1865.

Quality of Ordnance. Northern industrial superiority was also manifested in its superior equipment, though the War Department's decision to rely on muzzle-loader rifles rather than on breech-loaders deprived the Northern soldier of a large lead over his Southern opponent. It forced the Northern soldier to continue the laborious task of constant reloading. Even more serious was the failure to make quick use of the Spencer repeating rifle. When this rifle was introduced in 1864 it had a demoralizing effect upon Southern soldiers, who believed that their opponents had a gun which could be loaded on Sunday and fired for the rest of the week.

Railroads. Since the conduct of the war depended heavily on the utilization of railroads, the fact that of all the Southern states Virginia alone produced locomotives, and that her output made up only four per cent of the total American production, forced the South to fight with a steadily deteriorating supply of rolling stock. Furthermore, the total Southern railroad mileage was only slightly more than 9,000 miles, of a national total of 31,256; and more than a third was exposed to Northern attack and soon came under Union control.

Military Manpower. Figures on the size of the Northern and Southern armies are extremely unreliable. Somewhere between 1,500,000 and 1,900,000 men served in the Union Army, and about half that number in the Confederate Army. To achieve such mobilization, the Confederacy had to draft about twice the proportion of available manpower called up by the Union. To meet its needs, the Confederate government (which had moved from Montgomery, Alabama, to Richmond, Virginia, after the Upper South seceded) passed a conscription law on April 16, 1862, making white males between eighteen and thirty-five liable to the draft. Subsequent revision of the Southern conscription laws extended the limits until by February 17, 1864, males between seventeen and fifty were liable. At its peak in the spring of 1863, the Southern army numbered more than 300,000.

Scope of Mobilization. The need of the North to mobilize was not as imperative as that of the Confederacy. It did not emulate the Southern conscription law until March 3, 1863, when it passed a law which made males between twenty and forty-five liable to the draft (but only till thirty-five if they were married). A prospective draftee under this law could escape by hiring a substitute or paying three hundred dollars (the assumed cost of a substitute). The intention of this law seems to have been to meet military manpower needs by persuading volunteers to enlist. Probably less than 170,000 men were obtained under the draft law, less than ten per cent of the total manpower used by the North. By the end of the war, 800,000 men were serving in the Union Army.

An additional source of Northern strength grew out of the advance of its armies. Each Northern gain contracted the area from which the Confederacy could draw its strength. But in the first years of the struggle the more effective mobilization of the South enabled it to balance its opponent's over-all superiority. After the spring of 1863, when the North settled down to a war of attrition, the Confederacy fought from a steadily weakening position.

EARLY STRATEGY OF WAR

At the outbreak of the conflict neither side anticipated a drawn-out war. The initial willingness of the North to accept ninety-day enlistments gives some idea of the optimism that permeated the thinking of both sides. Each side thought that it would win, and that a single magnificent victory (such as the capture of the enemy capital) would suffice to cause its opponent to surrender. Each side also believed that it could not be vanquished in a single defeat. Each was determined to persist until total victory had been won. What neither side seemed to realize was that the combination of these beliefs would lead inevitably to a long struggle. But Robert E. Lee, who had reluctantly joined the Confederate cause, was sadly prophetic when he predicted a long and bloody conflict. His view, however, was an exception. Most Americans of both sides looked to a short conflict and early success for their cause.

Restoration vs. Independence. Northern strategic problems were more complicated than those of the South. Committed by Lincoln to the restoration of the Union, Northern armies had to carry the war into the South in order to force the Southerner to reaccept his renounced allegiance. To do this, the North would have to conquer an imperial domain on land and to blockade thousands of miles of coastline to prevent the South from receiving through commerce the supplies it needed.

The Confederacy was concerned from the outset with achieving its independence. It had, therefore, to preserve its borders intact until the North, having understood the price of a conquest of the South, came to terms. The Northern strategy of war was aimed at conquest, while that of the South was essentially one of defense. This gave the South the advantage of fighting from interior lines. Both sides anticipated a war fought in classic style, with great set battles, fought in the Napoleonic tradition; neither conceived that it would ultimately be a total war, sparing no one, and costing more than six hundred thousand lives.

Diplomatic Problems. Foreign intervention was a threat that the Union had to ward off, and an objective that the Confederacy struggled to bring about, since involvement of the European powers on the side of the South would probably have enabled the Confederacy to maintain its independence. To compel such intervention, the Southerners closed off cotton exports, assuming that the languishing cotton industry of Lancashire would force the British government to intervene. In this they gravely miscalculated. Not only were there substantial surpluses of cotton in English warehouses, but alternative English sources of supply developed in India and Egypt later as the war progressed. The English workingmen most severely affected by the cotton shortage also had a strong antipathy to the South and to slavery. Mill owners shared this attitude. The British government, much to the disappointment of the Confederacy, followed a strictly neutral policy. Britain threatened to intervene only when the British steamer *Trent* was stopped on November 8, 1861, by the Union warship *San Jacinto,* commanded by Captain Charles Wilkes, and the Confederate ministers to England and France, James M. Mason and John Slidell, were seized as contraband of war. Despite the popularity of the seizure among Northerners, and the efforts of Secretary of State William Seward to precipitate a foreign war in the hope that it would reunite the nation, Lincoln negotiated a peaceful settlement with the British. Mason and Slidell were released on January 1, 1862.

Although the Confederacy continued to strive for official British recognition as a sovereign independent power, and late in the war even went so far as to consider offering the abandonment of slavery in return for such recognition, the British never capitulated from their initial stand.

THE WAR DURING 1861 AND 1862

In the first year of the war, the South won a series of victories in the East, while the North steadily advanced its cause in the West.

The First Battle of Bull Run. The earliest sign that the North would not easily achieve its goal of restoration of the Union came in the First Battle of Bull Run. Lincoln, under great public pressure for an immediate victory, permitted an army under Brigadier General Irvin McDowell to advance against Richmond in July 1861. Some thirty miles from Washington, at a little stream named Bull Run, in Virginia, his army met the Southern forces under the command of General P. G. T. Beauregard on July 18. After a day of confused fighting (witnessed by residents of Washington, both men and women, who eagerly went forth to see the battle), the Northern army began to retreat. Retreat turned to flight. And the dusty roads to Washington were soon packed with rabble,

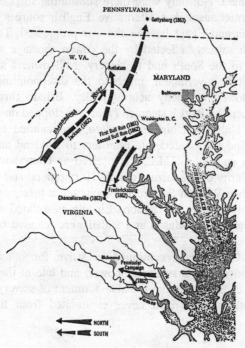

as soldiers and civilians sought safety within the fortifications around the capital. Only the disorganization and exhaustion of the Confederates prevented the South from entering Washington.

The defeat shocked the North into an awareness that a more disciplined effort was needed to defeat the South. Lincoln called George Brinton McClellan, who had stirred the North with some minor victories in West Virginia, to command the Army of the Potomac. Farther south, at Richmond, the Army of Northern Virginia was being fully organized by Joseph E. Johnston and Robert E. Lee. Each side had become aware that the other would fight. The ordeal of preparation had begun.

Victory in the West. By the spring of 1862, preparation gave way to battle. The Union forces had a double goal: to capture Richmond and to reopen the Mississippi. The first Northern moves came in the Mississippi Valley where, despite the defects of a command split between

General Henry W. Halleck in Saint Louis and General Don Carlos Buell at Louisville, an army under an obscure general, Ulysses S. Grant, attacked Fort Donelson, which guarded the entrance into middle Tennessee. Grant, approaching his fortieth birthday, was a phlegmatic West Pointer who had left the service in 1854 to avoid a court-martial for neglect of duty. By moving swiftly and coordinating his attack with a naval bombardment, Fort Henry fell on February 6, 1862. Ten days later Fort Donelson capitulated with some 14,000 prisoners. In less than two weeks Grant had opened the road to Nashville and had set the stage for the advance on Vicksburg.

THE WAR IN THE WEST 1861-1862

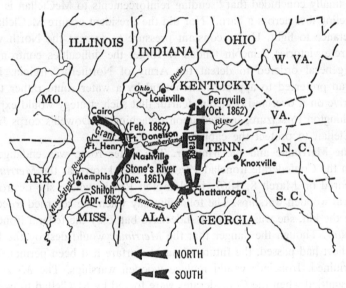

Shiloh. The reeling Confederates retreated across Tennessee and took up positions north of Corinth, Mississippi. By the end of March, Grant was encamped at Pittsburg Landing on the left bank of the Tennessee River. There, Confederate forces under Albert Sidney Johnston staged a sudden attack on April 6, 1862. Grant was caught unawares, but after an initial retreat, the North on the second day won a bloody battle. The Confederates, who had lost their brilliant commander, Johnston, in the battle, retreated into Mississippi. Total casualties for both sides numbered 23,741. The true meaning of the developing conflict began to come home to the combatants; it was a war of rule or ruin.

New Orleans and Memphis. The North won another major victory on April 26 when New Orleans fell to David Farragut, who was soon to become an admiral. On June 6, 1862, Memphis also fell to Northern gunboats. Meanwhile Grant, who was severely criticized for the heavy losses at Shiloh, slowly plotted a campaign against Vicksburg. The prelude to the final drive to open the Mississippi River had ended.

The Peninsular Campaign. George B. McClellan had made of the Army of the Potomac a magnificent weapon. Arrogant, stubborn, condescending to his military superiors, he was nevertheless a brilliant administrator and a considerable strategist. Prone to exaggerate his opponent's strength, he constantly demanded reinforcements from Lincoln, who finally concluded that "sending reinforcements to McClellan is like shoveling flies across a barn." Nor did the President admire McClellan's reluctance to fight. Under constant pressure to present the North with concrete victories, Lincoln tended to forget the difficulties confronting any general ordered to defeat the Army of Northern Virginia. McClellan preferred to approach Richmond by a water route rather than to drive on it overland. Lincoln, fearful that such strategy would expose Washington to seizure, insisted upon detaching McDowell's corps from McClellan to protect the capital.

The Merrimac and the Monitor. The water route was endangered when the Confederate ironclad *Virginia,* better known as the *Merrimac,* appeared on March 8, 1862, in Hampton Roads, where she destroyed several wooden warships. The following day when she returned to complete the kill, she was met in an indecisive battle by the federal ironclad *Monitor*. Though the danger that the *Merrimac* would destroy the federal fleet had passed, the future of naval warfare had been permanently determined. Ironclads would replace wooden warships. The *Merrimac* was scuttled when the Confederates were forced by McClellan to evacuate Norfolk (May 9, 1862).

"Stonewall" Jackson and the Shenandoah Valley. Moving with elegant slowness, McClellan, after departing from Washington on March 17, landed troops on the James Peninsula on April 4. Although he faced only minor opposition, he took more than six weeks to reach the vicinity of Richmond, scarcely seventy-five miles from his point of debarkation. While the Army of the Potomac dawdled, Robert E. Lee, who was serving as military adviser to President Jefferson Davis, directed Thomas "Stonewall" Jackson to open an attack up the Shenandoah Valley. Jackson, described by a contemporary as a man "of contrasts so complete that he appears one day a Presbyterian deacon who delights in theological discussion and, the next, a reincarnated Joshua," moved with incredible swiftness. At Winchester, he smashed Union forces under Nathaniel Banks (May 25, 1862); he handily dispatched forces under John C. Frémont at Port Republic and Shields at Cross Keys on June 9, 1862; he eluded pursuing forces under McDowell; and finally, after thoroughly panicking the North, he returned to join Lee before Richmond just as the Seven Days' Battle got under way.

The Seven Days' Battle. It was May 31 when McClellan stood on the threshold of Richmond, hardly seven miles from the city. To prevent a siege, Confederate General Joseph Johnston attacked at Fair Oaks (Seven Pines), where Johnston was wounded (May 31–June 1, 1862). Though Confederate casualties were heavier than those of the Union, McClellan's caution permitted Lee, Johnston's replacement, to entrench about the city and to accumulate reserves. On June 25, with a skirmish at Oak Grove, the Seven Days' Battle began. On the following day the Confederates were thrown back at Mechanicsville. After Lee had obtained a costly victory at Gaines's Mill on June 27, McClellan skillfully maneuvered his army in a retreat across the peninsula toward the James River. In the succeeding days bitter fighting raged at Garnett's and Golding's farms (June 28), Savage's Station (June 29), and at White Oak Swamp (June 30). On July 1, the Southern Army was sharply repulsed at Malvern Hill. McClellan had reached the safety of Harrison's Landing; but the two sides had sustained a total of more than 37,000 casualties, and Richmond had been saved by the South. The greatest of Southern generals had now emerged. Robert E. Lee, the epitome of Southern gentility, would add his strategic genius to the *esprit* of the Army of Northern Virginia. It would take a fully mobilized North almost three years to vanquish Lee and destroy his army. But for McClellan the end had almost arrived; General-in-Chief Halleck formed a single army under the command of General John Pope from the smashed remnants of the armies of McDowell, Banks, and Frémont. Lincoln ordered McClellan to withdraw from the peninsula to reinforce Pope.

Antietam. Utilizing swift movement, Lee sent Jackson to block Pope from moving deeper into northern Virginia. Lee then moved the remainder of his army to join Jackson. Together the united armies delivered a smashing defeat to Pope at the Second Battle of Bull Run on August 29. Once again the losses were staggering, approaching 25,000; Lincoln was compelled to remove Pope and to recall McClellan to command. Lee pushed forward into western Maryland, hoping that an invasion of Pennsylvania might draw off northern pressure upon Virginia. But the discovery of Lee's battle plans (found wrapped around three cigars that had fallen from a Confederate staff officer's pocket) enabled McClellan to maneuver his army into place at Antietam. After preliminary bloody skirmishing at South Mountain (September 14), the two armies met on September 17, 1862, in what proved the bloodiest single day of the war. When the fighting at Antietam was over, more than 26,000 men had been killed, wounded, or declared missing. Stunned by the savagery of the fighting, McClellan failed to press his advantage, and Lee escaped into Virginia. Lincoln, having lost all patience with the "slows" of McClellan, removed him from command of the Army of the Potomac on November 5. His replacement, General Ambrose E. Burnside, proved disastrously inept. On December 13, he sent his troops across the Rappahannock River to attack Lee's army entrenched on Marye's Heights outside Fredericksburg. The Northerners were slaughtered (casualties approached 13,000), while the losses of the Confederacy were scarcely 5,000. The grim war of attrition had been launched.

The Emancipation Proclamation. Lincoln used the victory at Antietam as an occasion for issuing a preliminary emancipation proclamation in which he flatly warned that if the Confederate States did not return to the Union by January 1, 1863, he would emancipate their slaves. The proclamation was preceded by the congressional decisions to abolish slavery in the District of Columbia (April 16, 1862) and in the territories (July 17, 1862). On the latter day Congress also passed the Second Confiscation Act, which provided for the immediate forfeiture of all property belonging to Confederate officials, and, when sixty days had elapsed, all property belonging to those who aided the rebellion. It also freed escaped slaves of rebel masters. Aware that emancipation would be favorably received in Europe, thereby making recognition of the Confederacy even less likely, and also aware of the growing Northern pressure, stimulated by radical Republicans, for drastic action, Lincoln issued his final Emancipation Proclamation on January 1, 1863. It declared that all slaves in territory under rebel authority were free. It held forth the promise that as the Union armies moved into the South they would come as liberators. The war had now taken on the aura both of a crusade for freedom and of a revolution. In the balance was the future liberty of more than 3,500,000 slaves.

THE TURN OF THE TIDE

Any chance for a final victory escaped the grasp of the Confederacy in 1863. The Union had resolved to press the fight no matter how long it took or how much it cost.

Vicksburg. Through the winter of 1863, Grant maneuvered to capture the Southern fortress at Vicksburg. After marching his army along the swampy west bank of the Mississippi to the south of the city in early May of 1863, Grant thrust swiftly inland to Jackson, Mississippi. He then countermarched to the west to Vicksburg, and settled down to a siege. After six weeks, the garrison and town's inhabitants, suffering from hunger, constant shelling, and disease, finally capitulated on July

THE WAR IN THE WEST 1863

4, 1863. Five days later, the last Confederate post on the Mississippi River, Port Hudson, surrendered. Grant had cleared the great river and split the Confederacy into two.

Gettysburg. In the East, Lee's army maneuvered the Army of the Potomac under General Joseph Hooker into a disastrous defeat at Chancellorsville. Taking cover in the dense woods around this hamlet, Lee opened his attack on May 1, 1863. Though the Northern army had a clear advantage (its manpower was double that of Lee), Hooker retreated into a strong defensive position. On May 2, Lee detached Jackson to push through the undergrowth where he could launch an attack upon Hooker's right flank. In the resulting confusion, the Army of the Potomac began to retreat along its entire front, not stopping until it had withdrawn north of the Rappahannock River. The victory was costly for Lee; Jackson, accidentally wounded by his own men, died eight days later. He was one of more than 30,000 casualties sustained by the two combatants.

Lee now carried the war into the North for the first time. General George Meade, who had replaced Hooker in command of the Army of the Potomac, cautiously followed as Lee advanced across Maryland into Pennsylvania. By late June, Southern cavalry under Ewell had ridden within sight of the Susquehanna River near Harrisburg. At the same time, Lee realized that Meade's forces, having marched along interior lines, were nearing his own army. He issued an order for a troop concentration at Gettysburg.

High Tide of the Confederacy. On July 1, the greatest battle of the war—the battle of Gettysburg—began. Ewell, returning with his cavalry from near Harrisburg, swept through Gettysburg but failed to seize immediately the fishhook-shaped row of hills known as Cemetery Ridge. Instead, Union forces, advancing from the south and east, secured Cemetery Ridge, from which they could command the Confederate forces encamped on Seminary Ridge to the west and north. For the next two days the Confederates launched vain attacks upon Little Round Top and Big Round Top at the south flank of the Northern position, and against Culp's Hill at the eastern end. Finally, on July 3, General George E. Pickett, with 15,000 Confederates under his command, made a frontal attack on Cemetery Ridge. In the assault, Confederate losses were enormous; though some Southern troops reached the crest of the ridge, they were soon compelled to retreat. As they fell away, the Southern tide began to ebb. Lee's army retreated southward into Virginia, never to return. The nation itself was appalled when it learned the cost of this, the greatest battle of the Civil War—51,112 casualties. But the South now knew that the North could not be destroyed. It remained for the North to discover whether the South could be conquered.

Chattanooga. In the West, federal troops under General William Rosecrans who had occupied Chattanooga prepared to invade northern Georgia. The Southern commander, Braxton Bragg, had been reinforced by James Longstreet's corps, detached from Lee in Virginia. On September 20, 1863, the combined Southern force inflicted a severe reverse on Rosecrans at Chickamauga; only the stubborn resistance of General George Thomas prevented complete disaster from enveloping the federal forces.

Lincoln moved swiftly to break the ensuing siege of Chattanooga, sending Grant and Sherman to the rescue. They broke the siege with the Battle of Chattanooga (November 24–25, 1863), and Bragg retreated into Georgia. The stage was set for the drive to the sea, some five hundred miles away.

THE PERIOD OF TOTAL WAR

Walt Whitman noted that by May of 1863 "the wounded are getting to be common and the people grow callous." Both sides had grown cold and indifferent to human suffering. The Confederate Partisan Raider John S. Mosby refused to refrain from bombardment of trains filled with women and children, commenting that he "did not understand that it hurts women and children to be killed any more than it hurts men." It revealed how far the South had lapsed from its professed ideals of chivalry. In camps like Andersonville and Libby Prison in the South, and Point Lookout and Elmira in the North, prisoners of war by the tens of thousands died from starvation, disease, and neglect.

The Strategy of Total War. By the end of the year, the North was prepared for a relentless drive to victory. In February 1864 Northern command was unified and Grant was promoted to the rank of lieutenant general. Union strategy called for a double drive, one against the Army of Northern Virginia and the other into the heart of Georgia. The attack upon Lee was based on simple mathematics: no matter how brilliant his defense, he could not afford the continuous losses that an unrelenting attack would cost. The North now meant to throw the full weight of its manpower into the scales; Lee and his army would be bled to death in a war of attrition. Under Sherman another army would tear out the heart of the Confederacy. The South would be taught the full agony of war. In the lurid flames of burning cities, towns, and plantations, and in the blood of thousands, the fate of the Confederacy would be sealed. The North had declared total war on the South. Before the year had ended a path of destruction was drawn for over a thousand miles from Atlanta to Goldsboro, North Carolina.

From the Wilderness to Petersburg. Grant smashed into Virginia at the head of an army of 100,000 on May 3, 1864. Lee blocked him with some 60,000 troops in the tangled underbrush known as the Wilderness.

FROM THE WILDERNESS TO APPOMATTOX

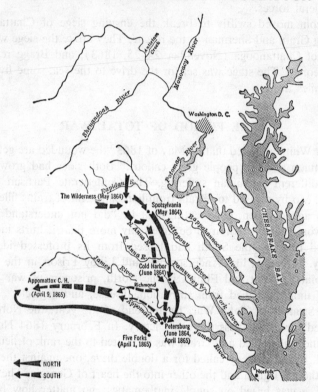

There, between May 5 and 6, the Army of the Potomac sustained losses in excess of 18,000, while Lee lost somewhat more than 8,000. Despite the bloody losses, Grant refused to slacken his advance. He plunged forward, only to be blocked at Spotsylvania Courthouse by Lee (May 7–20, 1864). There, on Confederate entrenchments, Grant lost more than 11,000 men. Still Grant pushed on. Once again Lee retreated in an effort to keep his army between Grant and Richmond. On June 3, Grant attacked Lee's entrenched men at Cold Harbor; eight minutes later, some 7,000 federal troops were casualties. The carnage shook even Grant. He subsequently confessed, "I have always regretted that the last assault at Cold Harbor was ever made." In a month of fighting, the two armies had lost more than 82,000 men. Grant was still outside Richmond, but he had dealt a mortal blow to Lee. Although replacements

SHERMAN'S CAMPAIGN IN THE SOUTH

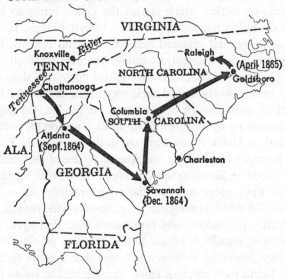

could be found for Northern losses, Southern losses were irreplaceable.

Sheridan and the Shenandoah. Unable to smash Lee's army, Grant, advancing always to the left, reached Petersburg, to the south of Richmond, where he settled down to a siege, and so immobilized Lee's army. Lee's efforts to lure Grant away by sending General Jubal A. Early to attack Washington failed; Early was repulsed. Grant then determined to clear the Shenandoah Valley of Confederate forces. He sent General Philip H. Sheridan with a force of 40,000 men to remove all ability of the region to furnish supplies to Confederate armies. The brilliant cavalry general swept up the valley, mercilessly destroying everything in his path. When, on October 19, Early suddenly attacked the Union force at Cedar Creek while Sheridan was absent, "Little Phil" returned to rally his men and destroy Early's force. From that moment the valley's threat was ended. The South could no longer obtain provisions in this fertile valley, nor could its armies use it as an avenue of approach to Washington. Bitterly, the valley's inhabitants complained that a crow flying over the devastated region would have to bring its own rations.

Atlanta to the Sea. As Grant was hammering Lee's army to death in Virginia, General William T. Sherman launched his drive on Atlanta.

In Joseph E. Johnston the Union Army faced a skillful antagonist. He forced Sherman to fight for every step he took in the direction of Atlanta, but his delaying tactics, which caused the Union forces to advance by flanking the Confederate force, provoked Jefferson Davis. In July, Davis removed Johnston and replaced him with General John B. Hood, who had a reputation for aggressive fighting. Sherman repulsed two thrusts by Hood on July 20 and 22, and then settled down to a siege of the city. As Union troops slowly inched their way to the south of Atlanta, they threatened to sever Hood's lines of communications. On September 1, the Confederate Army withdrew from the city, and on the next day Sherman entered. A Union Army was now in the heart of the Confederacy. Admiral Farragut had already, on August 5, closed the harbor of Mobile. In November, Sherman left Atlanta in flames and began his march to the sea. Four great columns moved relentlessly across an almost defenseless Georgia. Throughout a sixty-mile-wide swath, railroads, bridges, towns, plantations, and farmhouses were destroyed. Only desolate wilderness remained to mark the progress of Sherman's army. Hood's army, hastening westward in hopes that it could force Sherman to retreat, found itself ignored. Hood then decided to try to inflict commensurate damage on Union forces in Tennessee. Instead, he was first repulsed at Franklin on November 30, 1864, and finally overwhelmed by Thomas at Nashville on December 15–16, 1864. With his defeat, for all practical purposes, the only effective forces left in the Confederacy were concentrated in the east. On December 21, Sherman entered Savannah; and the South, initially split by Grant's conquest of the Mississippi, had now been quartered.

The Invasion of South Carolina. For six weeks, Sherman and his army rested. Then, on February 1, 1865, they marched into South Carolina. The destruction inflicted in Georgia paled in comparison with the fate meted out to the Palmetto State, where the seeds of secession had sprouted. The city of Charleston was already ruined by more than two years of siege. Destruction came to Columbia, capital of South Carolina, on February 17, when it was put to the torch. On March 23, Sherman entered Goldsboro, North Carolina. He no longer sought battle; enough blood had been shed.

The Collapse of the Confederacy. In Richmond, the beleaguered capital of the Confederacy, the Confederate Congress, on March 13, 1865, authorized the arming of slaves as a last desperate measure. Lee had recommended that those slaves who served for the Confederacy should be freed. Robert Toombs, one of the founders of the Confeder-acy, wondered why the South had been fighting if it now thought of emancipation. In a last desperate effort to prevent utter collapse, Lee ordered an attack on Fort Steadman (March 25); it was an unsuccessful diversion. For the next eight days federal troops mounted ever more emphatic attacks on the remnants of Lee's forces. On April 1, a federal attack was opened against Five Forks; it broke through the Southern lines the following day. On the same day Lee ordered the evacuation of Richmond. The Confederate government began a flight that ended with the capture of Jefferson Davis at Irwinsville, Georgia, on May 10, 1865. For Lee and the Army of Northern Virginia there remained a week of retreat that ended, after bitter fighting, at Appomattox Courthouse, on April 9, 1865. There, a remnant of Lee's magnificent army surrendered. All that remained was to effect the capitulation of the scattered remnants of Confederate strength, a task that was completed before the end of May 1865.

THE ASSASSINATION OF LINCOLN

Lincoln's Second Inaugural. At the very moment that the Civil War was ending, a new, overwhelming tragedy struck the nation. President Lincoln, haggard, heart-weary, had been inaugurated in March 1865 for his second term and had pledged the Union to fight until the end. Then there would be a just peace. In his Second Inaugural Address he promised that in a reunited nation there would be malice toward none and that the nation's wounds would be healed.

Lincoln's Death. Through the four years of bitter war, Lincoln had guided the country with a great and deepening wisdom. With the South's surrender early in April, he could begin to think of the needs of the peace ahead. Yet at the very moment when he could turn to the future with hope, he was stricken down by an assassin. On April 14, the Presi-dent and his wife had gone to Ford's Theatre in Washington to see Laura Keene in *Our American Cousin.* As he relaxed at the perform-ance, Lincoln was shot by John Wilkes Booth, an emotionally unbal-anced actor. The next day, Lincoln was dead. Booth believed he had vindicated a doomed South; yet his act brought only new hatred to the divided country. Simultaneous plots to assassinate William Seward, Andrew Johnson, and Ulysses S. Grant, though unsuccessful, accen-tuated the unresolved hostility.

THE REUNITED NATION

Although the war had ended and peace had returned, it was a peace of conquest. Conqueror and conquered, citizens of a single nation, had now to seek out a lasting peace. Yet for generations the sparks of four years of civil strife still remained to be extinguished; the search for reconciliation continued to be incomplete.

The political, economic, and social changes which evolved during and immediately after the Civil War were to affect profoundly the whole fabric of the reunited nation. The significance of Lincoln's leadership, and the full impact of the Civil War, can only be understood as the opening chapter of the next great phase in the history of the United States.

TABLES OF PARTIES AND PRESIDENTS

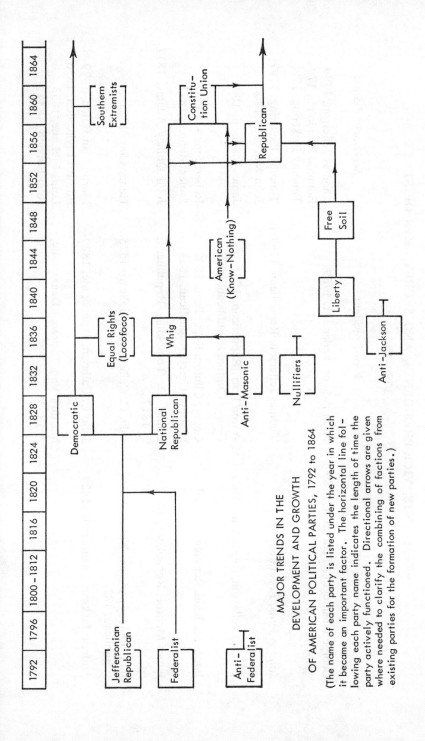

| 1792 | 1796 | 1800 - 1812 | 1816 | 1820 | 1824 | 1828 | 1832 | 1836 | 1840 | 1844 | 1848 | 1852 | 1856 | 1860 | 1864 |

Southern
Extremists

Democratic

Equal Rights
(Locofoco)

Constitu-
tion Union

Jeffersonian
Republican

National
Republican

Whig

Republican

Federalist

Anti-Masonic

American
(Know-Nothing)

Nullifiers

Free
Soil

Anti-
Federalist

Liberty

Anti-Jackson

MAJOR TRENDS IN THE

DEVELOPMENT AND GROWTH

OF AMERICAN POLITICAL PARTIES, 1792 to 1864

(The name of each party is listed under the year in which
it became an important factor. The horizontal line following each party name indicates the length of time the
party actively functioned. Directional arrows are given
where needed to clarify the combining of factions from
existing parties for the formation of new parties.)

PRESIDENTS, VICE-PRESIDENTS, AND SECRETARIES OF STATE
1789–1864

President	Vice-President	Secretary of State
George Washington, Federalist, 1789	John Adams, Federalist, 1789	Thomas Jefferson, 1789 Edmund Randolph, 1794 Timothy Pickering, 1795
John Adams, Federalist, 1797	Thomas Jefferson, Republican, 1797	Timothy Pickering, 1797 John Marshall, 1800
Thomas Jefferson, Republican, 1801	Aaron Burr, Republican, 1801 George Clinton, Republican, 1805	James Madison, 1801
James Madison, Republican, 1809	George Clinton, Republican, 1809 Elbridge Gerry, Republican, 1813	Robert Smith, 1809 James Monroe, 1811
James Monroe, Republican, 1817	Daniel D. Tompkins, Republican, 1817	John Quincy Adams, 1817
John Quincy Adams, National Republican, 1825	John C. Calhoun, Republican, 1825	Henry Clay, 1825
Andrew Jackson, Democratic, 1829	John C. Calhoun, Democratic, 1829 Martin Van Buren, Democratic, 1833	Martin Van Buren, 1829 Edward Livingston, 1836 Louis McLane, 1833 John Forsyth, 1834

President	Vice President	Secretary of State
Martin Van Buren, Democratic, 1837	Richard M. Johnson, Democratic, 1837	John Forsyth, 1837
William H. Harrison, Whig, 1841	John Tyler, Whig, 1841	Daniel Webster, 1841
John Tyler, Whig and Democratic, 1841		Daniel Webster, 1841 Hugh S. Legaré, 1843 Abel P. Upshur, 1843 John C. Calhoun, 1844
James K. Polk, Democratic, 1845	George M. Dallas, Democratic, 1845	James Buchanan, 1845
Zachary Taylor, Whig, 1850	Millard Fillmore, Whig, 1849	John M. Clayton, 1849
Millard Fillmore, Whig, 1850		Daniel Webster, 1850 Edward Everett, 1852
Franklin Pierce, Democratic, 1853	William R. D. King, Democratic, 1853	William L. Marcy, 1853
James Buchanan, Democratic, 1857	John C. Breckinridge, Democratic, 1857	Lewis Cass, 1857 Jeremiah S. Black, 1860
Abraham Lincoln, Republican, 1861	Hannibal Hamlin, Republican, 1861 Andrew Johnson, Unionist, 1865	William H. Seward, 1861

PRESIDENTIAL ELECTIONS
1789–1864

Year	Candidates	Parties	Popular Vote	Electoral Vote
1789	George Washington			69
	John Adams			34
	Others			35
1792	George Washington			132
	John Adams			77
	George Clinton			50
	Thomas Jefferson			4
	Aaron Burr			1
1796	John Adams	Federalist		71
	Thomas Jefferson	Democratic-Republican		68
	Thomas Pinckney	Federalist		59
	Aaron Burr	Anti-Federalist		30
	Samuel Adams	Democratic-Republican		15
	Oliver Ellsworth	Federalist		11
1800	Thomas Jefferson	Democratic-Republican		73
	Aaron Burr	Democratic-Republican		73
	John Adams	Federalist		65
	C. C. Pinckney	Federalist		64
	John Jay	Federalist		1
1804	Thomas Jefferson	Democratic-Republican		162
	C. C. Pinckney	Federalist		14
1808	James Madison	Democratic-Republican		122
	C. C. Pinckney	Federalist		47
	George Clinton	Independent Republican		6
1812	James Madison	Democratic-Republican		128
	DeWitt Clinton	Fusion		89
1816	James Monroe	Republican		183
	Rufus King	Federalist		34
1820	James Monroe	Republican		231
	John Quincy Adams	Independent Republican		1

1824	John Quincy Adams	Democratic-Republican	108,740	84
	Andrew Jackson	Democratic-Republican	153,544	99
	Henry Clay	Democratic-Republican	47,136	37
	William H. Crawford	Democratic-Republican	46,618	41
1828	Andrew Jackson	Democrat	647,286	178
	John Quincy Adams	National Republican	508,064	83
1832	Andrew Jackson	Democrat	687,502	219
	Henry Clay	National Republican	530,189	49
	John Floyd	Nullifiers		11
	William Wirt	Antimasonic		7
1836	Martin Van Buren	Democrat	762,678	170
	William H. Harrison	Whig ⎫		73
	Hugh L. White	Whig ⎬	735,651	26
	Daniel Webster	Whig ⎭		14
	W. P. Mangum	Anti-Jackson		11
1840	William H. Harrison	Whig	1,275,016	234
	Martin Van Buren	Democrat	1,129,102	60
	James G. Birney	Liberty	7,069	——
1844	James K. Polk	Democrat	1,337,243	170
	Henry Clay	Whig	1,299,062	105
	James G. Birney	Liberty	62,300	——
1848	Zachary Taylor	Whig	1,360,099	163
	Lewis Cass	Democrat	1,220,544	127
	Martin Van Buren	Free Soil	291,263	——
1852	Franklin Pierce	Democrat	1,601,274	254
	Winfield Scott	Whig	1,386,580	42
	John P. Hale	Free Soil	155,825	——
1856	James Buchanan	Democrat	1,838,169	174
	John C. Frémont	Republican	1,341,264	114
	Millard Fillmore	American	874,534	8
1860	Abraham Lincoln	Republican	1,866,452	180
	John C. Breckinridge	Democrat	847,953	72
	Stephen A. Douglas	Democrat	1,375,157	12
	John Bell	Constitutional-Union	590,631	39
1864	Abraham Lincoln	Republican	2,213,665	212
	George B. McClellan	Democrat	1,805,237	21

Index

Notes

DOUBLEDAY COLLEGE COURSE GUIDES

Analytic Geometry
        William L. Schaaf   U1 $1.95

The Calculus
        William L. Schaaf   U5 $1.95

Essentials of Zoology
        Leon Augustus Hausman   U3 $1.75

Fundamentals of Speech
        George W. Hibbitt   U8 $1.45

History of English Literature to 1660
        Martin S. Day   U10 $1.95

History of English Literature 1660 to 1837
        Martin S. Day   U12 $1.95

History of the United States to 1865
        James P. Shenton   U4 $1.75

Introduction to American Education
        S. E. Frost, Jr.   U2 $1.75

Introduction to American Government
        James Tracy Crown   U11 $1.75

An Introduction to Psychology
        John F. Hahn   U7 $1.45

An Outline of English Composition
        Alan B. Howes   U6 $1.45

Principles of Accounting
        R. Dean White and
        Floyd W. White   U9 $1.75